WOMEN AND THE POLITICS OF EMPOWERMENT

In the series WOMEN IN THE POLITICAL ECONOMY, edited by Ronnie J. Steinberg

OMEN AND THE POLITICS OF EMPOWERMENT

Edited by Ann Bookman and Sandra Morgen

Temple
University
Press |
Philadelphia

Women's Bldg

Temple University Press, Philadelphia 19122
Copyright © 1988 by Temple University. All rights reserved
Published 1988
Printed in the United States of America

The paper used in this publication meets the minimum
requirements of American National Standard for Information
Sciences—Permanence of Paper for Printed Library Materials,
ANSI Z39.48-1984

Library of Congress Cataloging-in-Publication Data
Women and the politics of empowerment.
(Women in the political economy)
Bibliography: p.
1. Women in politics—United States.
2. Working class women—United States.
3. Feminism—United States.
I. Bookman, Ann, 1948–   II. Morgen, Sandra.
III. Series.
HQ1236.5.U6W65   1988   320'.088042   87-6504
ISBN 0-87722-504-4 (alk. paper)

9/13/2000

Contents

Preface

This book, a thoroughly collaborative effort, represents the synthesis of our academic and political commitments. We, like many other women in this country, have worked toward two visions—a feminist movement that represents women of all races and class backgrounds *and* a progressive popular movement rooted in the working class that takes seriously the needs, the leadership, and the ideas of women. We have conceived and completed this book during a historical period which clearly tests these visions.

As we write, many unions are experiencing unprecedented contract concessions and decreases in membership. The restructuring of an economy in crisis is accompanied by the portent of a permanent "underclass" comprised mainly of female-headed families living in poverty. Meanwhile, working-class families are taking the brunt of the decline in the economy—the loss of many blue-collar union jobs and escalating costs for food, health care, day care, and other essential goods and services. Almost every day we see evidence of systematic attempts by the federal government to undermine civil rights, occupational health and safety, affirmative action, and other programs for the poor, for minorities, and for women. Local, regional, and national groups continue to fight for the programs and policies that will ensure their economic survival and expand their political clout. But the resilience and effectiveness of progressive movements, including the women's movement, have been affected by the shift to the right in the political climate of the 1980s. Futhermore, problems and contradictions internal to these movements have hampered a real coalition between the working-class, women's, and civil rights movements.

Given this historical context, we feel an urgency to document and understand the political struggles of the past period. We believe this book will be useful to a broad range of researchers and activists in assessing the current period and alternative courses for future political action. Although most of the studies in this book were conducted only a decade ago, the political distance between then and now seems somehow greater than the years might signal. We hope this distance will allow us to avoid the pitfalls of both romanticism and defeatism. We do not see working-class women as either "class-conscious militants" or downtrodden poor folk trapped in "worlds of pain." The cases of successful organizing in the book point to the potential of working-class women's activism. But in the process of documenting unsung heroines we do not intend to overestimate the current political consciousness of this group. Their consciousness and their actions contain elements of both consent and resistance, and embody contradictory ideas about their place as women, as minorities, and as members of the working class. Nevertheless, at a time when postmortems on the women's movement and the left are so common, this book reminds us how much collective action can achieve and how powerful groups can be when they organize on their own behalf.

As editors, we have utilized our respective strengths and experiences—Bookman in labor-based research and activism, Morgen in community-based research and activism—to examine the relationship between workplace and community organizing. Although we are both trained as anthropologists, we first met as political activists at a conference on "Childbearing Rights" in Worcester, Massachusetts. At the time Bookman was working as a machinist and union activist at the Lynn plant of the General Electric Company. Morgen was working at a feminist health collective and was involved in antiracist and community organizing in a northeastern city. Our relationship was renewed several years later after we had both taken administrative positions in women's research centers. With a return to the academy, our day-to-day activities had changed, but both of us were still looking for ways to continue the long process of bridge building between organized feminism and working-class women, between social theory and political practice. This book is part of that process.

The fifteen contributors to this book bring a vast amount of scholarly and political expertise to bear on the questions we are asking about working-class women's political consciousness and action. A number of the contributors have worked actively with and in the organizations and coalitions they describe. For example, Bookman worked in the factory she writes about and served as an organizer of the activities she describes. Morgen was a member of the coalition that fought health service cutbacks in the city where she did fieldwork. Chandler and Nicola-McLaughlin were activists as well as faculty members and administrators in the coalition that fought to improve Medgar Evers College.

Others related to the campaigns they described in a support capacity. For example, Costello provided strike support to the clerical workers at the Wisconsin Education Association Insurance Trust, and Luttrell worked with Edison High School parents by providing adult education programs and attending community meetings to support their campaign. Grenier originally went into the plant he studied to determine whether production teams could increase worker productivity. He came out an advocate of the union campaign and played an important role in exposing the company's strategy of union-busting. Spalter-Roth developed a policy paper (co-authored with Eileen Zeitz) on the street-vending regulations in Washington, D.C. while studying the lives of women street vendors. Susser supported the organizing of women in Greenpoint–Williamsburg through her participation at rallies and community meetings; and she served as a consultant for a movie, *Metropolitan Avenue,* based on their struggles.

For all of us, this research and its publication are part of ongoing efforts to support and further the struggles of working-class women—white women and women of color. This raises an important methodological issue concerning the relationship between political/ideological commitment and research. We believe a false equation has been fostered between distance, disengagement, and objectivity on the one hand, and quality scholarship on the other. We are convinced that the fine scholarship represented in this book was not only uncompromised but in fact sharpened by involvement on the part of the researchers in the movements that they studied.

The question of political commitment and its relationship to scholarly inquiry is complex. As researchers who have tried to understand how historical circumstance, ideology, and consciousness shape political action, we can scarcely ignore how our own consciousness and research praxis is historically and socially constituted. The contributors to this book are shaped by different racial, ethnic, and class experiences, political histories, and academic training. These differences among ourselves have affected how we have thought about and acted in our research situations, and taken together they become a collective strength of the book.

There is no one model of activist research in this book, nor even unanimity about the political meaning of the events we present. However, the researchers did make methodological decisions that brought them close to the experiences of the women they studied. Most of the contributors used both the tools of participant-observation and in-depth interviewing to study activism as it was happening. The very term "participant-observation" suggests the dual perspective particularly appropriate to many of these authors as both scholars and activists. We were trained in the social sciences *and* in the mass movements of the 1960s and 1970s. We are insiders and outsiders. The line between participation to *understand* and participation to *further* the efforts of women struggling for survival and justice often disappeared. We became involved because we shared the political goals of the women we studied and because we recognized that engagement was essential to our study of political action. The open-ended interviewing we did let working-class women speak in their own voices about their political experiences.

Like oral history, this methodology expresses a commitment to letting those who make history be directly involved in the creation of the historical record, an opportunity too often reserved for those with economic and political power.

Finally, this book has utilized the method of collective intellectual inquiry. This process began at a symposium, "U.S. Women and Resistance in the Workplace and the Community," Morgen organized under the sponsorship of the American Ethnological Society at the 1984 American Anthropological Association annual meeting. Following a positive response to this panel, Bookman and Morgen joined forces to co-edit this book, utilizing the papers from the symposium and soliciting other original articles. To facilitate collaboration, we brought together most of the contributors for a full-day meeting in the spring of 1985. At that meeting we discussed each of the articles and some of the overriding themes and concerns of the book. We wish to acknowledge the insightful contributions of Nina Shapiro-Perl, a participant in the American Ethnological Society Symposium, particularly as to the importance of understanding the sources of consent as well as resistance in defining women's political action. We hope that the excitement of intellectual and political exchange felt by all those who worked on this book is conveyed in its final form.

The development of this book parallels, at least in some respects, the political endeavors of the women portrayed in its pages. Both depend on the weaving together of support from different arenas of women's lives—our workplaces, our communities, and our families. This book was given initial support by both our workplaces—the Mary Ingraham Bunting Institute of Radcliffe College and the Duke–UNC Women's Studies Research Center. Margaret McKenna and Bill Chafe were particularly supportive, lending both encouragement and substantive ideas to our work. Both research centers helped to sponsor the day-long conference in April 1985 that brought contributors together to discuss the book's themes and the individual articles. We also want to thank the Women's Studies Program at George Washington University for their hospitality at the 1985 meeting. We owe special thanks to Aurelie Sheehan for her administrative support in helping prepare the articles for review by the publisher, and Paulla Ebron for her help with the notes. Within the last year, the final stages of the manuscript were completed with support from the Stone Center for Development Studies and Services of Wellesley College and the Women's Studies Program at the University of Massachusetts at Amherst. We have both been fortunate in being able to draw on the resources of workplaces with a commitment to scholarship on women's lives.

We also want to acknowledge the support and inspiration we have drawn from the communities outside our workplaces—communities of activists, scholars, and scholar–activists who have helped us to clarify our goals and methods in bringing this book to completion. There are many people with whom we have both worked in political movements over the past fifteen to twenty years. Countless study groups and coalitions will go unnamed here, but many of the ideas and experiences of their members have found expression in this book. Needless to say, we are deeply indebted to the thousands of women who were involved in the campaigns we describe herein. Their courageous actions and perseverance gave and continue to give us both a reason to write a book and a reason to continue the fight for justice.

Friends have helped us believe in this book when the work seemed endless, and have listened to and talked with us about our ideas. In particular we want to thank Polly Allen, Andrea Cousins, Christina Greene, Dale Melcher, Kathy Peiss, Arlene Pressman, Laurie Price, Paula Rayman, Carol Stack, and Meredith Tax.

Our thanks go also to Ruth Milkman for her insightful comments on the first draft of the manuscript. We are also grateful to our editors at Temple University Press, Ronnie J. Steinberg and Michael Ames, for their invaluable criticism, and to Mary Capouya for her support and technical assistance in making our manuscript into a book.

We owe special thanks to our families. Our parents raised us to believe in ourselves and to fight for what we believe in. For both of us the early years of our political involvement in the 1960s were characterized by a certain amount of political disagreement with our parents. But these disagreements produced an important dialogue with our parents that we value deeply. From our parents, Ruth Lowe Bookman and John Bookman, Mickey Block Morgen and Robert Morgen, we have both felt a deep love and respect that has been a strong foundation for our lives and our work.

We particularly want to thank our husbands Eric Buehrens and Robert Long. They have had to live with this book for more than two years and have given us both intellectual and emotional support over the long haul. We also want to thank Emily and Nicky Buehrens and Seth Morgen Long, not for cooperating (which they sometimes did and sometimes did not!) but for giving us a sense of the importance of understanding our political histories and building a just society in which we all can live.

WOMEN AND THE POLITICS OF EMPOWERMENT

Rethinking Women and Politics:

An Introductory Essay

Sandra Morgen

Ann Bookman

"EDISON SCHOOL MOTHERS FIGHT FOR NEW HIGH SCHOOL"
"CHICANAS 'CAN' UNION LEADERSHIP—DEMAND VOICE IN
  CANNERY LOCAL"
"FLEETPORT WOMEN WIN BACK HEALTH CLINIC"

Headlines like these rarely appear in the newspaper, yet news of working-class women's activism could be written every day. Women's grassroots political action does constitute the "news that's fit to print." This book examines the political activism of working-class women in the United States during the 1970s and early 1980s. These women defy the portrayal of working-class women so common in the popular press as passive, politically disinterested, unskilled, or ineffectual. Instead, they actively seek to change the places where they work, the neighborhoods where they live, and the schools, social services, and health facilities that serve them and their families.

The political worlds of working-class women have been obscured not only by the popular media but in much of academic literature as well. There have been studies of the political experience of women, but these have focused unduly on white and middle-class women.[1] Treatments of working-class political action are rarely differentiated by gender and usually focus on white men's organization in trade unions. Research on political movements among racial and ethnic minorities often fails to treat gender adequately. As a result, the political action of working-class women has remained largely undocumented. This neglect has contributed to the development of theories of political action and consciousness that fail to deal with gender as a salient analytic concept and do not recognize how race, ethnicity, and class specify women's modes of resistance. Feminist scholars have begun to challenge this neglect and change our thinking about women and politics.

The most powerful reason for the invisibility of women as political actors lies in the way politics is conceptualized in this culture. Politics is conventionally understood as the activities of elected officials and the workings of government, both out of the reach of ordinary people. Although in recent years middle-class women have made inroads into the arena of electoral politics, most of the substantive reforms benefiting working-class women have emerged from battles waged in extra-electoral terrains—the office, the factory, the hospital, the church, or the streets. And legislative reforms have emerged, for the most part, in response to pressure from grassroots activity.[2]

By making the political experiences of working-class women the central subject of their research, the scholars in this book are writing these women into the political history of the contemporary period and arguing for a new conception of politics. Twelve case studies document how working-class women's experience of multiple, interrelated oppressions, and their membership in diverse racial and ethnic communities, generate responses ranging from consent to resistance. Collectively, we tell the story of *empowerment,* and the conditions—material and ideological—that foster, constrain, and erode it.

We use the term *empowerment* to connote a spectrum of political activity ranging from acts of individual resistance to mass political mobilizations that challenge the basic power relations in our society. In this book we build on the insights and research of activists and scholars who view politics as activities that are carried on in the daily lives of ordinary people and are enmeshed in the social institutions and political–economic processes of their society. When there is an attempt to change the social and economic institutions that embody the basic power relations in our society—that is politics.

Empowerment is currently a fashionable term, particularly as it refers to individual self-assertion, upward mobility, or the psychological experience of "feeling powerful." Although these personal experiences may be a part of the processes we document in this book, our use of the concept of empowerment is different. For the women whose lives form the subject of this book, empowerment is rarely experienced as upward mobility or personal advancement. Rather, "feeling powerful" is constrained for them by the ways in which their gender, as well as their race and class, limit their access to economic resources and political power. For these women, empowerment begins when they change their ideas about the causes of their powerlessness, when they recognize the systemic forces that oppress them, and when they act to change the conditions of their lives.

Power is not only understood as something groups or individuals *have;* rather, it is a social relationship between groups that determines access to, use of, and control over the basic material and ideological resources in society.[3] Fundamentally, then, empowerment is a *process* aimed at consolidating, maintaining, or changing the nature and distribution of power in a particular cultural context. This process is rarely a linear one. It takes twists and turns, includes both resistance and consent, and ebbs and flows as groups with different relations to the structures and sources of power come into conflict.

HISTORICAL CONTEXT

From precolonial times to the present, working-class women have resisted their socially assigned positions. Slaves and indentured servants ran away from their masters, participated in revolts, and as individuals used daily acts of subversion in their quest for empowerment.[4] Free Black women fought for abolition and suffrage, and helped slaves to escape.[5] Women, mainly immigrants working in factories and sweatshops, not only won the earliest investigations of labor conditions in the Northeast; they also staged walkouts and strikes in their workplaces and organized auxiliaries to support work actions of husbands, fathers, and brothers.[6] Some of these women joined women's rights organizations or demonstrations and were involved in the various urban reforms struggles of the late nineteenth and early twentieth centuries.[7] They were very much involved in uprisings during the Depression and in the organizing of the Congress of Industrial Organizations (CIO) during its heyday in the 1930s and 1940s.[8] More recently Black working women provided a core of activists and an army of participants in the civil rights movement.[9] And working-class women from diverse backgrounds built powerful welfare rights and tenants movements in the 1960s.[10]

Although a full account of the history of working-class women's actions is well beyond the scope of this volume, several generalizations about this history are relevant. First, although their primary involvement has not been with organized feminism, working-class women have worked with mainly middle-class feminists for social reform. For example, the Women's Trade Union League and the settlement house movement constituted cross-class organizations that fought for improvements in community and workplace conditions. They have also joined with working-class men in the labor movement and with socialists and communists in radical movements for change. Second, though there is evidence of some multiracial organization, white women and women of color have often worked in separate (e.g., National Association of Colored Women) or parallel organizations (e.g., Young Women's Christian Association), for abolition and suffrage, against lynching, and for community reform. Finally, because we know that many instances of contemporary working-class women's grassroots organizing go unreported, we can speculate that this has also been true in the past. Though this does not tell us what women may have done, it warns against making judgments about their relative political quiescence.

Most of the case material in this book describes activities that took place in the 1970s.[11] The early years of the decade still resonated from the groundswell of activism that had characterized the 1960s. The courage and successes of the civil rights movement had paved the way for the rise of the feminist movement. Both of these movements won significant legislative and policy victories and were continuing to challenge racist and patriarchal ideas and practices. In addition to the growing antiwar movement, the 1970s saw other groups such as Chicanos, gays and lesbians, the elderly, and the poor organize. The fruits of these movements—some expansion of opportunities for women and minorities—

raised the expectations of many different groups for an increasing political voice in American society.

On the other hand, the 1970s was a period of economic decline and of changes in the international role of the United States. As the decade progressed, attention shifted from the building of a "Great Society"[12] to the "costs" of its programs. Public concern was focused by politicians and the media on problems of declining tax revenues and high tax assessments, declining productivity, and the expanding national debt. The changing international role of the United States was symbolized for the ordinary person by the defeat of the nation in Vietnam and the rising power of the Organization of Petroleum Exporting Countries (OPEC). During this decade institutions that claimed, at least nominally, to represent the working class—the Democratic Party and the trade union movement—were faltering. These forces combined to create confusion and political malaise.[13] Working-class women felt these conflicts and the uncertainties acutely, and these tensions are central to an understanding of their political responses.

It may seem paradoxical to talk about empowerment in the historical moment we have just described. But, as this book will demonstrate, the 1970s presented working-class women with both escalating problems and vivid evidence that collective action could achieve some (even if limited) change in their lives. Although we do not claim that these cases, even taken together, represent the full range of working-class women's political experiences, they do show women from diverse ethnic and racial backgrounds organizing in their workplaces and communities. The workplaces we describe include factories, offices, private homes, and hospitals, all of which have predominantly female work forces. In addition, an article on street vending adds a nontraditional worksite for women, one that has not received much scholarly attention. The articles on community organizing examine women's struggles to improve education, health care, neighborhood safety, and social services, issues that have mobilized women nationwide.

These studies reveal some of the important economic processes shaping the labor-force experiences of women across the country. The movement of traditional industries from the Northeast to the South and Southwest or the Third World has had different implications for women in different regions. In the Northeast women who used to work in the unionized textile and shoe industries now find employment in nonunion high-tech, service, and clerical occupations. In the South and Southwest, although new job opportunities have been created, women confront both traditional forms of employer antiunionism (*see Karen Brodkin Sacks, Chapter 3*) and new employer strategies to undermine different forms of employee organization (see *Louise Lamphere and Guillenmo J. Grenier, Chapter 10*).

Problems such as low pay and occupational segregation by race and sex are endemic to the workplaces we describe, cutting across the regional differences in job opportunity. Some of the worksites described are relatively homogenous in terms of race and ethnicity (*see Cynthia B. Costello on midwestern clerical work-*

ers, Chapter 5), whereas others are multiethnic or multiracial, with workers rigidly divided into different job categories by race and gender (*see Patricia Zavella on cannery workers, Chapter 9*), as well as by informal, ethnically based social groups (*see Ann Bookman on the electronics factory, Chapter 7*). The articles show that women's response to their exploitation as workers emerges from both the organization and the social relations inside the workplace and ideas and networks rooted in extra-workplace institutions.

The articles on community activism also suggest the large-scale political and economic trends that have galvanized women's grassroots struggles. Increasingly during the 1970s, social services, welfare, and health benefits were substantially cut back as the need for these services intensified with rising unemployment and economic dislocation. In each of the cases, local community action was waged in the context of economic and political retrenchment—the undoing or undermining of social programs in the name of fiscal responsibility, and the decreed "failure" of these programs.

The decision of a local hospital to close outpatient clinics for low-income women discussed by Sandra Morgen in Chapter 4 was not an isolated instance; rather, health service cutbacks were among the earliest of the social service cuts.[14] And although the Greenpoint–Williamsburg struggles discussed by Ida Susser in Chapter 11 took place in the context of New York City's fiscal crisis, this instance foreshadowed the response of other urban centers to "taxpayers' revolts" and the loss of federal dollars. The two chapters on education also represent more general national trends. Declining support for public education and the racist response to desegregation marked many of the educational struggles of the 1970s. Wendy Luttrell's study of a Philadelphia high school (*Chapter 6*) and Andrée Nicola-McLaughlin's and Zala Chandler's article on Medgar Evers College (*Chapter 8*) exemplify how women became prime movers in organizing community support for educational reform. Although most of the case studies of community organization show women basically defending their communities from the loss of services, Cheryl Townsend Gilkes' study of Black women community workers (*Chapter 2*) focuses on strategies for building "Black-oriented" social service and community agencies. Her case represents community organizations' potential to transform, not just defend, community services and interests.

THE ORGANIZATION OF THE BOOK

The articles in this book are organized into five parts, each of which focuses on one aspect of our approach to the analysis of women's political experience. The five components of this approach are:

1. To challenge conventional definitions of politics;
2. To analyze the ways gender structures women's political experience and the ways race, ethnicity, and class intersect with gender in shaping political action and consciousness;

3. To demonstrate how the interconnections between women's social relationships in the family, the workplace, and the community generate particular forms of resistance and consent;
4. To situate grassroots activism in the context of larger political and economic processes; and
5. To analyze the relationship between women's political practice and political theory.

Each of these sections contains material on both community and workplace activism. Our decision to group together articles on these different kinds of organizing breaks with convention. Scholars and activists alike tend to specialize in either labor or community-based political activities. Moreover, labor historians and social scientists who study working-class political behavior have tended to neglect community organization and have assumed that workplace activism is the most important and characteristic political activity of the working class (*see Sandra Morgen's article, Chapter 4, for elaboration of this point*). By examining the book's central themes with material from workplaces and communities, we underscore the importance of redefining and highlighting the interconnections between different forms of political action.

EXPANDING AND REDEFINING THE POLITICAL TERRAIN

In reaction to the rise of the second feminist movement, many mainstream political scientists and journalists have attempted to "feminize" conventional definitions of politics. They have done so with increased attention to women candidates who run for local, state, and national office and an analysis of women as a constituent force, that is, the "gender gap." It is our view that although it is important to examine the roles of women and the values they express in the electoral arena, it will not allow us to comprehend fully working-class women's political worlds. The structure of our political and economic system is such that working-class women and men cannot rely on the culturally legitimated realm of electoral politics to work in their best interest. The narrow distribution of political power in this country reflects the concentration of economic resources and power in the hands of wealthy individuals and corporations. More than anything, the low rates of voter registration and use of the franchise, particularly by the poor, are evidence not of apathy but of realism. Until we broaden our definition of politics to include the everyday struggle to survive and to change power relations in our society, working-class women's political action will remain obscured.

From the earliest days of the contemporary women's movement, a redefinition of politics was central to feminism. The slogan "the personal is political" embodied a deep critique of American politics. In asserting a direct relationship between politics and everyday life, and between the individual's everyday needs and social change, feminists broadened the political agenda dramatically.[15] Issues formerly regarded as women's individual or private problems—abortion and reproductive rights, violence against women, sexual harassment, child care, and housework, for example—became hotly contested in national political discourse. The claim that the personal was political subverted the distinction between the public and private worlds. It also challenged the ideological restriction of politics to the narrow realm of elections, candidates, and lobbying. Politics came to mean, at least for some people, efforts to challenge entrenched power relations—whether between individual men and women or between groups with and without economic and political power.

Despite the radical implications of this redefinition of politics, feminist political practice all too often emerged from the personal issues of white and middle-class women, coalescing in political organizations and alliances that did not represent all women.[16] In this way, the feminist movement also defined politics too narrowly and failed to attract the broadest possible base of women. The definition of *political* must be understood as more than an issue of theory. How one conceives of politics ultimately delimits who is regarded as ally and who as enemy, which issues are important, and which means are used to achieve political ends.

Feminists are not, of course, the first to have challenged the popularly understood definition of politics. Marxist theory and practice are based on the assumption that political struggle is essentially structured by class relations and that the transformation of class-based social relations is necessary for the political empowerment of the working class. Nevertheless, Marxist conceptions of politics are limited in two important respects. The classical Marxist conception of politics centers on the actions of workers fighting the capitalist class at the point of production, particularly at large socialized workplaces from which, so the theory goes, organized workers can potentially cripple the economy with their actions. The focus on the "point of production" ignores and devalues community-based political struggles in which working-class women have historically played major roles. It also tends to give top priority to the kinds of workplaces—large industrial production facilities—from which women have traditionally been excluded both by owners and by organized labor.[17]

The articles in this book seek to redress these shortcomings on the part of both feminist and Marxist conceptions of politics. All of the articles focus on how the class position and the racial and ethnic backgrounds of women specify their personal and political concerns and shape the types of political involvement they choose to participate in. The articles on hospital, office, and domestic work focus attention on organizing in workplaces that have a predominantly female labor force. It is interesting to note that when union membership was declining in the 1970s and 1980s, clerical and service unions, representing primarily women, were growing rapidly.[18] The article on street vending, a nontraditional workplace for women (*see Roberta M. Spalter-Roth, Chaper 12*), further challenges the myopic view of classical Marxism regarding point-of-production organizing.

The articles on community organizing document the political meaning and breadth of women's efforts to transform urban space and public policy. In contrast to the popular view that sees these activities as "voluntary associations" or "mutual aid societies," these cases show women challenging the power of the state and the interests of landlords, developers, and other private institutions. These are certainly political activities, and women come to understand and confront political and economic power as much in community struggles as in workplace or feminist campaigns.[19]

The three articles that compose Part I particularly elucidate the importance of broadening our definitions of political terrain. Bonnie Thornton Dill's article on household workers (*Chapter 1*) demonstrates that everyday acts that assert personal dignity and "stand up to the missus" are empowering. A domestic worker's interaction with her boss challenges and can alter important power relationships in her place of work. Dill argues that, in the particular conditions of domestic service, individual actions can be essentially "political." Furthermore, if we understand empowerment as a process, individual strategies of resistance employed by domestic workers can be linked to collective forms of action. Dill's data lead one to imagine how the action of a woman like Rosa Parks—a domestic worker who refused to give up her seat on a segregated bus in Montgomery, Alabama—was shaped not only by her association with the civil rights movement, but also by her experiences in confronting individual white women employers.

The multiple ways that Black women community workers build "Black spaces" in social service agencies and fight to make these organizations accountable to the needs of the poor are portrayed by Cheryl Townsend Gilkes (*Chapter 2*). She reveals the potentially political nature of such social service work. Social service has been regarded by many political observers and activists as distinct from *real* political activity.[20] The community workers Gilkes describes not only try to change their workplaces (agencies) so that they can better serve the Black community, but also negotiate the complex world of interagency relationships to the same end. Their struggles against racism encompass confrontations with individual white social workers and insensitive social service bureaucracies. When successful, social service work becomes a challenge to those racist public policies that threaten the survival and undermine the political power of the Black community.

Finally, Sacks's article (*Chapter 3*) poses a significant challenge to male definitions and models of political leadership. By studying women's involvement in a hospital union drive, Sacks discovers that important leadership roles are played by what she calls *centerpeople*. Though not publicly recognized as leaders, "centerpeople" have the ability to connect people who have mutual concerns and to understand and utilize existing networks both inside and outside the workplace for social change. Acknowledging "centerpeople" as leaders not only brings women to the fore, it also demonstrates how the particular skills women learn in their families and communities are translated into effective political leadership. Sacks also counters the stereotype of the southern worker as antiunion by showing the long-term commitment made by a diverse group of workers to the cause of organizing their workplace.

It is worth noting that the studies by Dill and Gilkes are based on the lives and struggles of Black women. African-American women also predominate among the "centerpeople" whom Sacks studied. It is no accident that the articles best illustrating the value of reconceptualizing politics focus on women of color. Given the pervasiveness of racism in the everyday lives of women of color, it is not surprising that their attempts to fight the system should explode traditional political boundaries. The structure of domestic work, which is done in isolated private homes, has contributed to the difficulty of achieving collective forms of organization,[21] so these women have had to rely on more individual strategies. Nevertheless, there is a social dimension to these strategies. Domestic workers share their work experiences with friends and other domestic workers in community-based social clubs and receive other forms of support from their communities. Additionally, Black professional and lay community workers take the victories derived from direct action on the streets and extend these victories to their work in transforming the policies and personnel of social service agencies. They also break down limited views of the sites of political action, serving their communities from their kitchen tables as well as from their agency offices. The triple oppression suffered by many women of color has fostered innovative methods and approaches to political organizing.

GENDER AND THE SHAPING OF WOMEN'S POLITICAL CONSCIOUSNESS

Part II explores the changes in women's consciousness that flow from their participation in political struggle. What makes women aware of their individual powerlessness and oppression? What feeds women's ability to change their ideas and their material circumstances to realize their collective power? Though "consciousness-raising" groups were a powerful vehicle for the politicization of white, middle-class women in the feminist movement, "consciousness raising" for many working-class women came about through their involvement in workplace and community organizing.

The case studies in Part II pay particular attention to the *process* of politicization. Women's consciousness of their oppression as women—and the motivation to work to change the system in which they live—is shaped by a complex set of social relations. These are structured by class, ethnic, and racially specific experiences. The studies in this book show that working-class women, while often rejecting the label "feminist," may develop ideas and political concerns that fall within the repertoire of feminism. These women can also come to understand and reject patriarchal domination as they organize around issues that are not solely "women's issues."

As Sarah Eisenstein has argued in a study of working-class women in early twentieth-century New York, the gender consciousness that emerges in working-class women's lives involves an active "negotiation" between the prevailing and the oppositional ideologies available to them. They make sense of these contending ideas, including feminism, in *terms* of the material conditions of their lives.[22] In the studies in Part II we examine this active negotiation as women organize a clerical union, fight to preserve vital health services, and organize to demand quality education for their children. In each instance, a distinctive political consciousness emerges in which gender becomes politically meaningful, but this does not always happen in the same way. By focusing on the dynamics of politicization rather than on its outcome, we can see that the development of political consciousness is neither a linear process nor an automatic response to oppression.

In examining the nine-month struggle of women in Fleetport (a pseudonym) to get a local hospital to reopen prenatal and gynecology clinics, Morgen (*Chapter 4*) examines the development of political consciousness in coalition members. She argues that the process of politicization is shaped by the particular events of a campaign as these are interpreted and given political meaning by those involved. Her first extensive example involves the process of the coalition's undermining of the hegemonic ideology that health care professionals should monopolize health care decision making. She goes on to illustrate how the meanings of gender and class changed over the course of the campaign as group members developed increasingly sophisticated understanding of the constitution of social relations of power. Morgen uses this case study to challenge a prevailing view among scholars that women's involvement in community organizing stems from their roles as wives and mothers. Without denying the way women's domestic responsibilities shape their political consciousness and action, Morgen advocates an approach that recognizes how race and class specify women's community-based needs and their involvements in grassroots politics.

Among women clerical workers in a Wisconsin insurance office, a militant consciousness rooted in gender-based grievances emerged from a work culture that opposed management policies. In response to a series of new "sexist" work rules, these women became active members of their union and ultimately organized a two-month strike. Costello (*Chapter 5*) arugues that women's experiences in a sex-segregated workplace and their family commitments and responsibilities together fostered a "female-centered consciousness." This consciousness combined aspects of women's traditional culture (for example, playing on the name of a soap opera for their strike newsletter) and their militant work culture. But Costello warns that the "radical work-based consciousness" was not without limits. The women's demands encompassed only a few changes in work rules formulated during favorable economic times and in a workplace with a cooperative ideology. In this case the ebb and flow of women's militant consciousness was closely linked to management strategies to control the workers.

The final article in Part II depicts a community campaign for quality education in Philadelphia. White working-class women in a coalition with Black and

Hispanic women successfully challenged white, middle-class, male-dominated institutions, winning for their children a new, integrated high school. Luttrell (*Chapter 6*) shows how the Edison High School mothers held many contradictory ideas about themselves as women and their experiences as students. These contributed both to a wavering sense of self-esteem *and* a resolve to provide quality education for their children. The process of confrontation with educational and political leaders deepened the women's awareness of their own class and gender positions in society. The experience of working in a multiracial coalition helped to erode racist preconceptions that the white women had held about their Black and Hispanic neighbors. Analyzing rich interview material, Luttrell shows the ways in which political consciousness both reflects the day-to-day frustrations and confusion in people's lives and helps clarify the sources of these frustrations and confusions. In resolving these contradictions, Edison High School mothers overcame self-doubts and became both community leaders and more assertive family members.

REVERBERATIONS AMONG THE SPHERES: FAMILY, WORKPLACE, AND COMMUNITY NETWORKS

In the mid-1970s feminist theory tended to analyze women's oppression as a universal feature of human societies. Rejecting biological explanations, feminists developed theories that looked for structural causes of universal "gender asymmetry." One of the most influential of these theories held that social structures were differentiated into public and private or political and domestic spheres of life; women's subordination was attributed to her association with or restriction to the private or domestic sphere.[23]

Despite the current disaffection of many feminist scholars with the "separate spheres" model, the ideological assumptions on which it is based have been resilient. An oppositional view of work and family, public and private, personal and political still predominates in the culture as a whole, and in some feminist thinking. Rosalind Petchesky and other feminist theorists have argued that instead of seeing these spheres as opposed, feminists should examine the interconnections between them: " 'Production' and 'reproduction,' work and the family, far from separate territories . . . are really intimately related modes that *reverberate* upon one another and frequently occur in the same social, physical and even psychic spaces [emphasis added]."[24]

The studies in Part III, and others throughout the book, illustrate our attempt to understand these interconnections or "reverberations." Although we do not deny that a powerful cultural ideology perpetuates the ideas that work and family, personal and political, community and workplace constitute separate spheres, we emphasize the fact that a common set of macroeconomic, political, and social forces determines the social institutions in which women live their lives. For example, the home, the workplace, and the community have all been affected by such phenomena as the recent dramatic rise in the numbers of working women and working mothers, the recession, and the growing influence of the neoconservative movement.

A common consequence of the separate-spheres model is the tendency to see women's concerns for their children and their social caretaking roles as determinant of all their activities outside the home. By looking for interconnections we can see that women's experiences as community members and workers may affect their family roles and responsibilities as much as the reverse. More important, by recognizing women's day-to-day experience of shifting back and forth between these spheres, we can understand how, as Martha A. Ackelsberg argues (*Chapter 13*), their particular social locations and multiple responsibilities across these realms create distinctive forms of political consciousness and activism. Working-class women (especially women of color) have never been simply consigned to the private or domestic realm,[25] and their history of political action has been shaped not by their role(s) in any one sphere but by their multiple responsibilities between and across spheres.

The articles in Part III build on important breakthroughs in the ways feminists look at the relationship between the family and the workplace, as well as the relationship between the family and the community. The articles break relatively new ground in exploring workplace–community interconnections and networks as these undermine or facilitate effective political action. Zavella's study of two approaches to organizing Chicana cannery workers—one based on gender, one on ethicity—detail how Chicano nationalism and community organizations played different roles in different rank-and-file formations (*Chapter 9*). She argues that the success of efforts to democratize the union depended in part on extra-workplace factors, such as the use of the Spanish language in caucus literature, the participation of caucus members in friendship networks, and common churches, schools, and neighborhoods. In an all-women's caucus, these kinds of workplace–community networks supported the women cannery workers' attempts to change their workplace. Additionally, gender-based commonalities experienced by the women both within the factory and in their homes and communities contributed to the strength of the group. Zavella argues that both the United Farm Workers' movement and the feminist movement were important components of the political context in which the cannery workers fought ethnic- and gender-based occupational segregation in the work force and the undemocratic practices of their (Teamsters) union.

Similarly, Bookman's study of union organizing in an electronics factory (*Chapter 7*) highlights how the union utilized key Portuguese social and religious organizations to generate support for the union drive among recent immigrant workers. The union's decision to conduct bilingual union meetings and distribute bilingual leaflets encouraged their participation. The union also solicited the endorsement of Portuguese religious and community leaders for the union drive. Like the role of César Chavez and the United Farm Workers, the growth of the

Armed Forces movement in Portugal created a cultural and political backdrop that directly supported unionization.[26]

Workplace and community are further connected in the cannery and electronics factories by the work cultures[27] women have constructed. Both Zavella and Bookman paint a picture of the intense bonds that are built among women workers growing out of the ethnic communities from which they come. In the more ethnically homogeneous cannery example, the bond of a common cultural heritage was the foundation from which they were able to fight both the company and their undemocratic union. In the electronics factory where there was a multiethnic work force, the sharing of foods, photographs, and holidays among women of different ethnic groups enabled women workers better to resist the "divide and conquer" strategies of the company and build a union organizing committee of workers from diverse cultural backgrounds.

Workplace–community connections are also evident in the cases of community organization. Many community activists are deeply influenced by either their own experiences as workers or those of family and friends. Whether or not the women have themselves been part of a union or other workplace struggle, labor activism is often a part of the history of their families and communities. Many community campaigns utilize tactics and strategies developed in workplace struggles. It is common to hear about rent strikes, tenant unions, school boycotts, and other tactics taken directly from the history of the trade union movement in this country. For example, the long-term campaign for educational equality at Medgar Evers College in 1982 was initiated by a two-week student strike (*see Nicola-McLaughlin and Chandler, Chapter 8*).

The connections between workplace and community are manifested in several aspects of the Medgar Evers case. The initial coalition of students and faculty reached out to nonprofessional clerical and service workers at the university as well as to community residents and organizations. The demands put forward by the coalition encompassed the needs of Central Brooklyn residents for access to higher education as well as the concerns of university faculty for reduced teaching loads and greater job security. The fact that African-American women constituted the majority of coalition members generated an additional set of demands related to their multiple roles as students, mothers, community members, and workers. The demands for an on-campus child-care center and a center for women's development mobilized women during the campaign and created a base for ongoing activism afterward. Like the United Farm Workers' movement and the Armed Forces movement described by other articles in Part III, the Black liberation movement created a political climate conducive to militant local struggles. Thus, in all three cases, the connections between workplace and community movements served to strengthen the level of political organization and consciousness in each campaign.

CONDITIONS AND CONSTRAINTS: POLITICAL ECONOMY AND WOMEN'S GRASSROOTS ACTIVISM

Working-class women's struggles for empowerment are best understood in a framework that situates local struggles in the context of developments in the political economy of the United States. Grasping the political economy of a nation as large and diverse as the United States is no easy matter—either in our attempt to briefly capture it here,[28] or as working-class women try to understand how it structures the forces they are up against in a particular campaign. Whatever the local character of grassroots campaigns in the 1970s, they were profoundly conditioned by the concentration of political and economic power in the hands of the few, the internationalization of capital,[29] and the dramatic growth of the state apparatus in the last forty years. Each of these interrelated features of advanced capitalism had tremendous implications for working-class political action in this period.

After World War II, the U.S. economy fluctuated dramatically, ranging from a period of unprecedented affluence and economic growth in the 1950s and 1960s to falling productivity and recession in the 1970s. Working-class families did not experience these changes uniformly. Many white working-class men in the traditional manufacturing sector faced massive layoffs, and, when unionized, saw major wage and job security concessions in their contracts. Minority men continued to experience high rates of unemployment and restricted access to higher-paying and higher-status jobs, although some were the beneficiaries of expanded opportunities created by affirmative action and job-training programs.

Working-class women experienced ever greater financial pressure. Those in dual-income families increasingly found even two paychecks insufficient, and those who were single heads of households found themselves closer to or entrapped by poverty. These women continued to be channeled into the low-paying clerical and service sector, which was growing but maintained its overall character as highly segregated by gender and race. Or, they found themselves dependent on the state and social programs that shrank at precisely the moment they were most needed, with dramatic economic dislocation in the mid-1970s.

This was a period of economic crisis in this country. More and more jobs moved overseas to low-waged, nonunion workforces, and U.S. industry became less competitive in critical sectors such as steel and car production, shipbuilding, and electronics-related manufacturing. The labor movement was forced to settle for concessions on the traditional issues of wages and benefits. Furthermore, the unions were unable to generate new demands and programs to fight layoffs, plant closings, and other issues related to the declining productivity and competitivess of U.S. companies. This loss of ground by American labor came just as women and minorities saw legislative and legal changes designed to promote greater equality of opportunity. Zavella's case is a poignant example of how the mobility of capital and the international division of labor undercut the realization of substantial gains by women and Chicanas even after they won a legal victory concerning discriminatory labor practices.

As the economic pendulum swung from a high in the 1960s to the lows of the 1970s, so the era of social reform to build "the Great Society" was effaced. Some argued that the programs which minorities and women had fought so hard to win constituted "government interference" in family matters or had failed to alleviate the social ills they were designed to address. Others believed that the programs were too costly and could not be continued without increasing taxes and the budget deficit. Nevertheless, women as a group continued to support social programs in much greater numbers than men. Frances Fox Piven argues that this is because women's relationship to the state has undergone dramatic change since World War II as they became both the primary clients and the primary workers in the social service bureacracy.[30] Women have come to expect at least the minimum of financial security offered by state-sponsored social services, and they have organized in tenants, welfare rights, and antipoverty organizations to protect these programs.

The case presented by Louise Lamphere and Guillermo J. Grenier on a union drive in a high-tech plant (*Chapter 10*) exemplifies some important shifts in the management style, type of production, and location of U.S. industry. The high-tech plant they studied had been recently opened in the Southwest because of the availability of a nonunion, low-wage, female work force. The company employed a new type of "participative management." This was a strategy tied directly to the attempt by U.S. industry to become more competitive in the world market through the fostering of work environments designed to push workers to new heights of productivity by giving them a say in production decisions. The drive was ultimately unsuccessful, partly because of the negative impact of these new management strategies, which maximized company control in the guise of worker participation. We are given a shop-floor view of how "team structures" operated to blur lines of authority and control and functioned to undermine union activity. Both the white women and the Hispanic women employed at HealthTech found themselves caught between their individual economic vulnerability and the macroeconomic forces shaping the political economy of the Southwest.

The article on women street vendors in Washington, D.C. (*Spalter-Roth, Chapter 12*), examines the response of vendors to new city regulations designed to force them off the streets. These regulations were imposed as part of an overall strategy on the part of the downtown business community to transform and more firmly control urban space through gentrification and "mallification." When the state intervened in support of this plan, street vendors organized a union to defend themselves from the disastrous effects of the new regulations. This union was not dealing with traditional union issues like wages and job security. Rather it had to confront the city government and its plans to transform the economy of downtown Washington, D.C. Spalter-Roth shows how the state's active support of organized business was partially forestalled by the union and individual acts of noncompliance by the street vendors. The combination of collective and individual action was particularly important for women whose day-to-day problems included not only the new regulations but the gender-specific concern of sexual harassment. This harassment came from consumers, the police, and also from the women's "allies" in collective action, male street vendors.

Ida Susser's article on community organizing in Brooklyn (*Chapter 11*) reveals how both major shifts in the economy and changing state policy play a critical role in the development of a campaign for better neighborhood services. Susser traces the history of a working-class neighborhood plagued by rising unemployment and deteriorating social services. These trends, she argues, produce a situation where residents reconceptualize the responsibilities of the state to a growing sector of nonworking or low-paid workers. Women's political activity develops, focusing on maintaining and expanding state-supported services that the community needs for survival. In Susser's case the economic recession acts as a catalyst for community organization, and neighborhood women (and men) in Greenpoint–Williamsburg participate in a successful fight for the preservation of a firehouse in their neighborhood and for a summer lunch program. Susser concludes by suggesting that in communities such as the one she studied in Brooklyn, women's community activism constitutes an increasingly important form of working-class activism. Members of this community are unable to rely on their unions because the jobs and the unions are gone. They are less able to rely on elected officials with whom they have less clout because their economic base has disappeared. As a result, the extraction of resources directly from the state becomes a matter of survival.

The material conditions of working-class women's lives are greatly affected by the changing fortunes of regional economies and the relative strength of U.S. capital in the global marketplace. As women experience layoffs, social service cutbacks, and union busting, these may often be perceived as the cruel and unusual punishment of a particular company or social service agency. In fact, these events are usually the reflection of forces well beyond one particular workplace or neighborhood. It is the ability of working-class women to understand and analyze these often invisible economic and political forces that makes the difference between victimization and political action. Of course, overall structural change cannot be achieved simply through local political organization, but the cases presented in this section underscore the importance of creating regional and national coalitions to "think globally, act locally."

GRASSROOTS ORGANIZING AND POLITICAL THEORY: TOWARD A SYNTHESIS

The final section of the book, Part V, reflects on the case material from the preceding parts to explore the relationship between women's political practice and political theory. In the nascent days of the women's movement, the vitality of feminist research and teaching stemmed, in large part, from its direct relationship to the struggles women were waging in the larger society. Today, the relationship between feminist scholarship and women's everyday struggles for empowerment is more attenuated. Women's Studies have become more institutionalized. While this guarantees many students and faculty an opportunity to make women's experiences central to their learning, it has also allowed an increasing distance to grow between feminist theory and women's lives and activism. The essays in this section suggest that feminist scholarship can remain vital if it reflects an active engagement with both the diverse realities of women's lives and movements for social change. One of the ways this can be fostered is through more dialogue between researchers and activists. The final two essays of the book are intended to promote that dialogue as they explore a number of issues that have implications for feminist political theory and activism.

Martha A. Ackelsberg (*Chapter 13*) focuses on the implications of the case material for the development of political theory that takes women seriously. She brings us back to the major themes of the book, particularly the theoretical implications of redefining the political and the relationship between the "public" and "private" in women's lives. She challenges us to construct a new model of democracy, arguing that by understanding women's grassroots political action we can develop a different perspective about what constitutes and motivates participation in the political process. While Ackelsberg argues that the study of women's activism leads her to question conventional ideas about politics as an expression of individual interests, she avoids the trap of dichotomizing men's and women's political experience. Rather, she offers the idea that traditional political theory distorts both men's and women's political consciousness, particularly in its neglect of how human "connectedness"—in communities and networks—is essential to politics.

In the final chapter, "Carry It On": Continuing the Discussion and the Struggle," the editors draw out some of the important implications of the case material in the book for organizing strategy. Some of the issues we consider have long and contentious histories of debate within the women's movement and the left, for example, the value of autonomous political organization by women and the politics of coalition building. Other issues have not received enough attention from feminists, such as how to build on the multiplicity of women's roles in families, communities, and workplaces and how to develop and strengthen workplace-community networks. In examining some of the lessons the case material suggests for organizing, we attempt to understand both the conditions that facilitate successful campaigns and those that impede working-class women's political mobilization. Finally, we argue that the success or failure of particular campaigns must be viewed as only part of the story of empowerment. The changes that the women depicted in this book experienced in the process of individual resistance and collective action are equally important. Their empowerment is visible in the transformations of their views of themselves as women and in their capacity to understand and change the world they live in.

GENDER AND POLITICS: CONTENDING VIEWS

The case studies in this book, indeed the history of women's political activism, pose fundamental challenges to Western political theory. The material presented here belies the proposition, central to the canon of this theory, that women *are* or *ought to be* peripheral to politics.

The dominant tradition in Western political theory regards men and women as fundamentally different beings with consequently divergent social roles and spheres of interest and influence. The "political" sphere has been regarded as a male domain that has excluded women because of women's particularistic, affiliative, or familial concerns and roles. Okin, who has written an impressive study of women in Western political theory, argues that philosophers' views about women and politics derive from their understanding of the "necessity of the family."

> The most important factor influencing philosphers' conceptions of, and arguments about, women has been the view that each of them held concerning the family. Those [the majority] who have regarded the family as a natural and necessary institution have defined women by their sexual, procreative, and childrearing functions within it. . . . The assumption of the necessity of the family leads the theorist to then regard the biological differences between the sexes as entailing all other, conventional and institutional differences in sex role which the family, especially in its most patriarchal forms, has required.[31]

Jean Bethke Elshtain traces the influence of an Aristotelian conception of politics on the Western tradition. This conception posits an "essential difference" between free males and both females and unfree males. Whereas the former are regarded as "integral parts of the state," the latter do not participate in public/political life but rather "provide the basis or precondition on which that public life rests."[32] In classical political theory, women's relationship to politics has been regarded as the relationship of wives, daughters, or mothers to the state; women's definition by and within the family has been construed as natural, evolving from innate sex differences.

Essentialist themes have also been prominent in feminist political theory and practice, although feminists have drawn different implications from essentialist propositions. Ruth Bloch coined the term *moral mother* to refer to a changing ideology of gender around the turn of the nineteenth century[33] that was institutionalized by the "cult of true womanhood" and finally appropriated by late-nineteenth-century feminists. For example, Jane Addams argued that women's family values and roles made women particularly suited for the "housekeeping" necessary to reform the political arena.[34] During the heyday of women's suffrage and social reform activism in the late nineteenth and early twentieth century, women were presumed to possess a superior morality that could allow them to apply the nurturance, care, and order they practiced as wives and mothers to the public and political world as voters, reform activists, and public persons.

Essentialist theory has once again taken root today and has found receptive audiences among many feminists.[35] Unlike traditional or nineteenth-century feminist theories, current perspectives rarely explicitly endorse a biological essentialism. "Difference" is often conceived in more psychosocial terms, with the link to biology implicit, and sometimes denied. Nevertheless, essential male and female natures are posited; what is assumed is "the existence of an essence of gender, so that the differences between men and women are seen to establish and define each gender as a unique and absolute category."[36]

Discussions of women and politics—whether in the larger society or in some feminist theories—often turn on essentialist assumptions and themes. For example, the widely discussed "gender gap" in attitudes toward militarism and defense spending is frequently explained in terms of women's "peaceful" or "cooperative" nature. In a similar vein, the "caring" or "maternal" aspect of women's nature is said to explain women's greater support for social welfare programs. In both feminist and nonfeminist versions of these explanations women are presumed to be essentially nurturant, peaceful, and cooperative; their political consciousness is described in a moral language with constant reference to woman's maternal role, or her reproductive or psychosexual constitution.[37]

One of the popular versions of the new feminist essentialism posits that women's particular relationship to reproduction and nurturance predisposes them to gynocentric ways of thinking and acting. For example, Carol Gilligan's work has been interpreted as evidence that women's conception of morality differs from men's, specifically because of the primacy of social relationships to women and their orientation to responsibility to others. Drawing on the work of Nancy Chodorow, Jean Baker Miller and others, Gilligan argues that women have a "different [moral] voice" based on a distinctly female ethic, *a* womanly way of thinking.[38]

One feminist theorist who has given careful thought to the question of gendered political thought is Sara Ruddick. She argues that the social practice (she is careful not to reduce this to biology) of mothering fosters an attitude that she calls *holding,* which is "governed by the priority of keeping over acquiring, of conserving the fragile, or maintaining whatever is at hand and necessary to preserve the child's life."[39] Ruddick contends that maternal thinking (which is neither restricted to mothers nor found in all mothers) includes a preservative form of love that is "incompatible with military strategy but consonant with pacifist commitment to nonviolence."[40] She reasons that the social practice of mothering is incompatible with both the "abstraction" necessary to justify human destruction and the goal of destruction.

Ruddick has attempted to develop a theory that avoids some of the worst faults of essentialism, and she is careful to premise her argument on the *social practice* of mothering. Nevertheless, there are a number of thorny problems with her theory that should alert us to the dangers of the new essentialism. The most significant problem is her failure to analyze how women's presumably distinctive consciousness is highly conditioned by history, culture, race, and class. Although she admits that not all women exhibit "maternal thinking" or draw pacifist conclusions from their maternal practice, she does not explore how different groups of women, differentiated by race, class, or culture, may construct different relationships between the social practice of mothering and pacifism/nonviolence from those she has elucidated. For example, varieties of "maternal thinking" could be implicated in the selective neglect of sick or weak children[41]; in the practice of infanticide by female slaves or their participation in violent revolts[42]; or in the participation of women in armed revolutionary movements.[43] The relationships between women's reproductive capacities and their familial obligations are not invariant across time and place nor have these led to a uniform perspective on peace, nonviolence, and social justice. Women's political consciousness may certainly be influenced by their concerns as mothers, but it is also deeply affected by aspects of their gender which are not rooted in childbearing or family relations.[44]

While none of the articles in this book deals explicitly with pacifism, they do shed some light on the difference between essentialist and historical–social constructionist theories of women's political consciousness. The conditions of working-class women's lives in contemporary American culture powerfully shape their experiences of motherhood and their social practice of mothering.[45] The articles here show that most working-class mothers are highly vulnerable workers who are often consigned to low-paying, unskilled jobs and frequently subject to seasonal or permanent layoffs. These conditions create real obstacles to active political involvement. Working-class mothers who are outside the paid labor force are often without accessible and affordable social and health care services that they need in order to care for their families. These conditions present further issues that affect their political involvement.

Many of the articles show working-class mothers responding to these structural conditions with both collective and individual acts of resistance. The authors argue that the range of political responses stems from the social relations and responsibilities these women face as workers, family members, and members of their larger communities. Like Ruddick, these contributors are concerned about how the responsibility for children and families fosters particular kinds of activism or a "female consciousness," but in no case is maternalism abstracted from the particular race and class of the mothers involved.

For example, Luttrell (*Chapter 6*) examines how women's roles as mothers affect their involvement in educational issues. But she argues that this is only one aspect of their political consciousness. Their political understanding is also conditioned by their experiences as working-class students and by their participation in a multiracial coalition (that "refocused and reshaped" their political views.) Susser attributes women's involvement in neighborhood organizations not only to their "daily rounds of domestic responsibilities" as mothers, but also to their rejection of certain aspects of these traditional domestic responsibilities. Women demand that the state take over some aspects of "caretaking" because of poverty created by unemployment and industrial decline. Morgen argues that when women extend their familial concerns to collective political action, they do so not as generic mothers but as women from historically constituted race and class groups.

These articles show that although gender is a powerful tool for understanding women's political experiences, it is not a sufficient tool. Gender does not have a simple effect that can be deduced from an analysis of women's embeddedness in family or gender socialization. While the activists we present were motivated and constrained by aspects of "being a woman," their views of themselves as women were also changed by their political experiences. Each of these women is living at a time when women's lives and the meaning of gender are being transformed by the women's movement, by changes in the economy, marriage, and family, and by changing state policy. To suggest that their political natures are fundamentally determined by an *essential* female experience neglects both the changes in that "female experience" over the past several decades *and* the ways that race and class differentiate gender experience.

To return briefly to the "gender gap," available evidence on voting patterns suggests that gender alone is not responsible for differences that show up between men and women in the electoral arena. The gap is largest among women between twenty-five and fifty-four (that is, women of working age); among women who are clerical or blue-collar workers (working-class women); and among women who are separated or divorced (women who are economically vulnerable).[46] In other words, particular subgroups of women are responsible for a pattern that is widely explained solely in terms of gender. Problems such as this are further evidence of the need to examine how particular conditions of women's lives foster different kinds of political consciousness and action.

The essentialist perspective conceals the all-important fact of differences among women. This perspective also runs the risk of exaggerating, or understanding out of context, certain features of women's experiences, particularly motherhood. To obscure differences among women in pursuit of a theory of male–female difference is certainly problematic, but it is especially so when analyzing women's political experiences. Social relations of power are so fundamentally structured in contemporary American society by the intersection of gender, race, ethnicity, and class that women's struggles for empowerment cannot be understood without making these factors central to the analysis.

Feminist theory is currently at a crossroads. The two major paradigms underlying current feminist praxis—essentialism and historical–social constructionism—are both being elaborated in increasingly sophisticated ways. We believe that the continued vitality of feminist scholarship depends on more dialogue between theoreticians and activists whose work is influenced by feminist essentialism and those whose work falls within the framework of historical–social constructionism. On the one hand, we need to acknowledge the strengths of both of these perspectives and explore the possible points of intersection and overall complementarity between these diverging explanatory models. On the other hand, the debate needs to be sharpened to clarify the implications of the different persectives for understanding and guiding women's political action.

We see this book as a contribution to the development of the historical–social constructionist perspective. Taking the significance of race, class and cultural differences among women seriously, we have articulated analytical frameworks that attempt to encompass and understand both the "lines that divide [and] the ties that bind"[47] women in their struggle for empowerment. Ultimately, we believe the value of different approaches to the analysis of gender depends on the extent to which they help women meet the very real political challenges they face in their communities, their workplaces, and their families.

NOTES

1. Although there has been, within the last decade, increasing scholarship on women's political experience, much of it has focused on women and electoral politics or on middle-class women's political involvements. For general discussions of women and politics, particularly electoral politics in the contemporary United States, see Sandra Baxter and Marjorie Lansing, *Women and Politics: The Invisible Majority* (Ann Arbor: University of Michigan Press, 1980); Janet A. Flammang, ed., *Political Women: Current Roles in State and Local Government* (Beverly Hills, Calif.: Sage, 1984); Marianne Githens and Jewel L. Prestage, eds., *A Portrait of Marginality: The Political Behavior of the American Woman* (New York: Longman, 1977); Ethel Klein, *Gender Politics: From Consciousness to Mass Politics* (Cambridge: Harvard University Press, 1984); Ruth Mandel, *In the Running: The New Woman Candidate* (New Haven: Tichnor and Fields, 1981); Virginia Sapiro, *The Political Integration of Women: Roles, Socialization and Politics* (Urbana: University of Illinois Press, 1983).

2. Frances Fox Piven and Richard A. Cloward, *Poor People's Movements: Why They Succeed, How They Fail* (New York: Vintage, 1979).

3. For an expanded discussion of power as social relations, see, for example, Michel Foucault, "Two Features," in Colin Gordon, ed., *Power/Knowledge* (New York: Pantheon Books, 1980); or Antonio Gramsci, *Selections from the Prison Notebooks* (New York: International Publishers, 1971). For a theoretical discussion of women and social relations of power in contemporary capitalist society, see Zillah Eisenstein, *Feminism and Sexual Equality* (New York: Monthly Review Press, 1984), esp. 87–110.

4. Angela Davis, *Women, Race, and Class* (New York: Random House, 1981); Paula Giddings, *When and Where I Enter: The Impact of Black Women on Race and Sex in America* (New York: Morrow, 1984); Jacqueline Jones, *Labor of Love, Labor of Sorrow* (New York: Basic Books, 1985); Dorothy Sterling, *We Are Your Sisters: Black Women in the Nineteenth Century* (New York: Norton, 1984).

5. Giddings, *When and Where I Enter;* Suzanne Lebsock, *The Free Women of Petersburg: Status and Culture in a Southern Town, 1784–1860* (New York: Norton, 1984); Sterling, *We Are Your Sisters.*

6. Of all the categories of working-class women's political action, this is probably the best studied. Here we note only some of the best-known book-length studies. Other

references abound in the notes to individual articles throughout this book. Sarah Eisenstein, *Give Us Bread but Give Us Roses* (London: Routledge & Kegan Paul, 1983); Dolores Janiewski, *Sisterhood Denied: Race, Gender and Class in a New South Community* (Philadelphia: Temple University Press, 1985; Alice Kessler-Harris, *Out to Work: A History of Wage-Earning Women in the U.S.* (New York: Oxford University Press, 1982); Ruth Milkman, ed., *Women, Work and Protest: A Century of U.S. Women's Labor History* (Boston: Routledge & Kegan Paul, 1985); Karen Sacks and Dorothy Remy, eds., *My Troubles Are Going to Have Trouble With Me* (New Brunswick: Rutgers University Press, 1984); Meredith Tax, *The Rising of the Women: Feminist Solidarity and Class Conflicts, 1880–1917* (New York: Monthly Review Press, 1980).

7. For example, Ellen DuBois, *Feminism and Suffrage: The Emergence of an Independent Women's Movement in America, 1848–1869* (Ithaca, N.Y.: Cornell University Press, 1978); Barbara Sicherman, *Alice Hamilton* (Cambridge: Harvard University Press, 1985); Tax, *The Rising of the Women*.

8. Staughton and Alice Lynd, eds., *Rank and File: Personal Histories by Working-class Organizers.* (Boston: Beacon Press, 1973); Sharon Stromm, "Challenging 'Woman's Place': Feminism, the Left and Industrial Unionism in the 1930's," *Feminist Studies* 9(1983): 359–387.

9. Bettina Apthecker, *Women's Legacy: Essays in Race, Sex and Class in American History* Amherst: University of Massachusetts Press, 1982). Ellen Canterow and Sharon O'Malley, "Ella Baker: Organizing for Civil Rights," in Ellen Canterow, ed., *Moving the Mountain: Women Working for Social Change.* (Old Westbury, N.Y.: Feminist Press, 1980); Sara Evans, *Personal Politics* (New York: Random House, 1979); Giddings, *When and Where I Enter;* Sharon Harley and Rosalyn Terborg-Penn, eds., *The Afro-American Woman: Struggles and Images* (Port Washington, N.Y.: Kennikat, 1978); Jones, *Labor of Love,* 275–321; Gerda Lerner, *Black Women in White America: A Documentary History* (New York: Random House, 1972); Anne Moody, *Coming of Age in Mississippi* (New York: Dell, 1968).

10. Cheryl Gilkes, "Holding Back the Ocean with a Broom," in LaFrances Rodgers-Rose, ed., *The Black Woman* (Beverly Hills, Calif.: Sage, 1980), 217–231; Susan Hertz, "The Politics of the Welfare Mother's Movement: A Case Study," *Signs* 2 (Spring, 1977): 601–611; Ronald Lawson, ed., *The Tenant Movement in New York City, 1904–1984* (New Brunswick, N.J.: Rutgers University Press, 1986). Kathleen McCourt, *Working Class Women and Grassroots Politics* (Bloomington: Indiana University Press, 1977); Nancy Seifer, *Nobody Speaks for Me* (New York: Simon & Schuster, 1976); Ida Susser, *Norman Street: Poverty and Politics in an Urban Neighborhood* (New York: Oxford University Press, 1982); Guida West, *The National Welfare Rights Movement: The Social Protest of Poor Women* (New York: Praeger, 1981).

11. Obviously in this brief discussion of the 1970s we can only highlight certain of the important aspects of the decade. For a more extensive social and economic history, see, for example, William Chafe, *The Unfinished Journey: America Since World War II* (New York: Oxford University Press, 1986). More focused discussions of changes in the political economy during this period can be found in Samuel Bowles, David Gordon, and Thomas Weiskopf, *Beyond the Wasteland* (Garden City, N.Y.: Anchor Press, Doubleday, 1983); Walter Burnham, *The Current Crisis in American Politics* (New York: Oxford University Press, 1982); and William Wilson, *The Declining Significance of Race* (Philadelphia: University of Pennsylvania Press, 1979).

12. Although we refer to the general trend of "building the Great Society" in the 1960s, we are quite aware that, despite the national rhetoric, the social reforms of the 1960s were never a coherent national policy but rather a series of programs intended to deal with the most pressing needs articulated by the protest movements.

13. See Chafe, *The Unfinished Journey,* chap. 14.

14. Ronda Kotelchuck and Howard Levy, "Federal Health Cutbacks: Health Policy at the Crossroads," in David Kotelchuck, ed., *Prognosis Negative: Crisis in the Health Care System* (New York: Random House, 1976), 389–404.

15. For a discussion of the meanings of the slogan in the movement's early days, see Ann Popkin, "The Personal Is Political: The Women's Liberation Movement," in Dick Cluster, ed., *They Should Have Served That Cup of Coffee: Seven Radicals Remember the Sixties* (Boston: South End Press, 1979).

16. There are a great many critiques of the feminist movement by women of color that make this point. Here we note just a few of them. Angela Davis, *Women, Race, and Class;* Bonnie Dill, "On the Hem of Life: Race, Class and the Prospects for an All-Inclusive Sisterhood," in Amy Swerdlow and Hannah Lessinger, eds., *Class, Race, and Sex: The Dynamics of Control* (Boston: G. K. Hall, 1981); bell hooks, *Feminist Theory: From the Margin to the Center* (Boston: South End Press, 1984); Gloria Hull, Patricia Bell Scott and Barbara Smith, *All the Women Are White, and All the Blacks Are Men, but Some of Us Are Brave* (Old Westbury, N.Y.: Feminist Press, 1982).

It is important to realize that these critiques formed one of the most important foundations on which feminist theory of the late 1970s and early 1980s was based. Our perspective in this book is indebted to the insights of women of color as they articulated the necessity of understanding how race, class, and gender must be understood together in developing feminist theory.

17. We are indebted to socialist–feminist theory for our general critique of traditional Marxism. For book-length treatments, see especially Lydia Sargent *Women and Revolution* (Boston: South End Press, 1981); Zillah Eisenstein, *Capitalist Patriarchy and the Case for Socialist Feminism* (New York: Monthly Review Press, 1979); and Michelle Barrett, *Women's Oppression Today* (London: Verso Press, 1980). For a discussion of the current challenges socialist–feminism poses for developing Marxist theory, see Sandra Morgen, "Making Connections: The Socialist-Feminist Challenge to Marxist Theory," in Jean O'Barr, ed., *The Politics of Knowledge: Feminist Reconstructions for a New Academy* (Madison: University of Wisconsin, forthcoming).

18. In Milkman, *Women, Work, and Protest.*

19. Others who argue that class consciousness emerges in community organization include Manuel Castells, *The City and the Grass Roots* (Berkeley: University of California Press, 1984); Norman Fainstein and Susan Fainstein, *Urban Policy Under Capitalism* (Beverly Hills, Calif.: Sage, 1982); and Ira Katznelson, *City Trenches, Urban Politics and the Patterning of Class in the U.S.* (New York: Random House, 1981). Works that examine both gender and class consciousness as they are shaped in community organization include Martha A. Ackelsberg, "Women's Collaborative Activities and City Life," in Flammang, ed., *Political Woman;* and Cynthia Cockburn, *The Local State* (London: Pluto Press, 1977).

20. The dichotomy between "activism" and "service work" was particularly strong among members of the left in the 1970s.

21. Attempts to organize domestic workers began in the 1930s; see, for example, Lerner, *Black Women in White America,* 231–234. For more recent discussions of domes-

tic workers and collective action, see Phyllis Palmer, "Housework and Domestic Labor: Racial and Technological Change," in Sacks and Remy, *My Troubles Are Going to Have Trouble with Me.*

22. Eisenstein, *Give Us Bread but Give Us Roses,* 37–54, particularly 47.

23. This theory was developed by Michele Rosaldo, in Michele Rosaldo and Louise Lamphere, *Woman, Culture, and Society* (Stanford: Stanford University Press, 1974). Rosaldo provides a succinct discussion of some of the problems with her own theoretical paradigm in "The Use and Abuse of Anthropology: Reflections on Feminism and Cross Cultural Understanding," *Signs* 5, No. 3(1980):389–417. For a more recent critique of the public–private model, see Linda Nicholson, *Gender and History: The Limits of Social Theory in the Age of the Family* (New York: Columbia University Press, 1986.)

24. Rosalind Petchesky, "Dissolving the Hyphen: A Report on Marxist-Feminist Groups 1–5," in Zillah Eisenstein, ed., *Capitalist Patriarchy and the Case For Socialist-Feminism* (New York: Monthly Review Press, 1979), 373–389, 376.

25. See especially Jones, *Labor of Love,* and Kessler-Harris, *Out to Work.*

26. The Armed Services Movement overthrew the undemocratic Caetano regime in Portugal in 1975, and replaced Caetano with a more liberal leader, Spinola.

27. A number of contributors to this volume were pioneers in the identification and study of women's work culture. See especially Ann Bookman, "The Process of Political Socialization Among Women and Immigrant Workers: A Case Study of Unionization in the Electronics Industry" (doctoral dissertation, Harvard University, 1977) esp. 147–156; the articles by Cynthia Costello, Louise Lamphere, and Patricia Zavella in a special section of *Feminist Studies* 11, No. 3 (Fall 1985) on Women's Work Culture. See also Susan Porter Benson, " 'The Customers Ain't God': The Work Culture of Department Store Saleswomen, 1890–1940," in Michael Frisch and Daniel Walkowitz, eds., *Working-Class America: Essays on Labor, Community, and American Society* (Urbana: University of Illinois Press, 1983); Barbara Melosh, *"The Physician's Hand": Work Culture and Conflict in American Nursing* (Philadelphia: Temple University Press, 1982); and Nina Shapiro-Perl, "Labor Process and Class Relations in the Costume Jewelry Industry: A Study in Women's Work" (doctoral dissertation, University of Connecticut, 1983).

28. We have tried to condense an admittedly complex and fast-changing political economy to contextualize the articles in the book. Obviously the intricacies of the decade of the 1970s are much more complex than we can hope to reveal in this brief discussion. For a more in-depth discussion of the changing place of women in the political economy of the 1970s, see, for example, the special issue on "Women and Poverty," *Signs* 10, No. 2 (1984), and Julie Matthaei, *An Economic History of Women in America: Women's Work, the Sexual Division of Labor and the Development of Capitalism* (New York: Schocken Books, 1982).

29. For an extended discussion, see June Nash and Maria Patricia Fernandez-Kelly, *Women, Men and the International Division of Labor* (Albany: State University of New York Press, 1983).

30. Frances Fox Piven, "Women and the State: Ideology, Power and the Welfare State," in Alice Rossi, ed., *Gender and the Life Course* (New York: Aldine, 1985), 265–287.

31. Susan Okin, *Women in Western Political Thought* (Princeton: Princeton University Press, 1979), 9.

32. Jean Bethke Elshtain, "Aristotle, The Public-Private Split, and the Case of the

Suffragists," in *The Family in Political Thought* (Amherst: University of Massachusetts Press, 1982), 53.

33. Ruth Bloch, "American Feminine Ideals in Transition: The Rise of the Moral Mother," *Feminist Studies* 4 (June 1972): 108–126.

34. Jane Addams, *Newer Ideals of Peace* (Chautauqua, N.Y.: Chautauqua Press, 1907), 180–207.

35. Hester Eisenstein, *Contemporary Feminist Thought* (Boston: G. K. Hall, 1983), xvii–xix.

36. Nancy Chodorow, "Gender, Relation, and Difference in Psychoanalytic Perspective," in Hester Eisenstein and Alice Jardine, eds., *The Future of Difference* (Boston: G. K. Hall, 1980), 3–11, 4.

37. Feminist essentialist perspectives on peace, for example, can be found in many of the pieces in Pam McAllister, ed., *Reweaving the Web of Life: Feminism and Non-Violence* (Philadelphia: New Society, 1982). For a critical assessment, see Micaela di Leonardo, "Morals, Mothers and Militarism: Antimilitarism and Feminist Theory," *Feminist Studies* 11 No. 3 (1985): 599–617.

Although we discuss feminist essentialism in rather monolithic terms, there are in fact quite different versions of it that the careful reader must acknowledge. Our goal here is to look at general themes in essentialist thought, rather than to examine its intellectual variants.

38. Carol Gilligan, *In A Different Voice: Psychological Theory and Women's Development* (Cambridge: Harvard University Press, 1982); Nancy Chodorow, *The Reproduction of Mothering* (Berkeley: University of California Press, 1978); Jean Baker Miller, *Toward a New Psychology of Women* (Boston: Beacon Press, 1976).

39. Sara Ruddick, "Maternal Thinking," *Feminist Studies* 6, No. 2 (1980), and reprinted (in a shorter version) in Joyce Trebilocot, ed., *Mothering: Essays in Feminist Theory* (Totowa, N.J.: Rowman & Allanheld, 1983), 213–230, 217.

40. Sara Ruddick, "Preservative Love and Military Destruction," in Treblicot, *Mothering,* 231–262.

41. Nancy Scheper-Hughes, "Infant Mortality and Infant Care: Cultural and Economic Constraints on Nurturing in Northeast Brazil," *Social Science and Medicine* 19, No. 5 (1984): 535–546.

42. Paula Giddings, *When and Where I Enter.*

43. See, for example, some of the portraits in Margaret Randall, ed., *Sandino's Daughter: Testimonies of Nicaraguan Women in Struggle* (Toronto: New Star Books, 1981).

44. We have chosen to discuss Ruddick's ideas because we believe they are among the best of those making the argument for a women's consciousness with deep roots in maternalism. Ruddick is cognizant of some of the problems we have found with the concept "maternal thinking." Moreover, her essay "Preservative Love and Military Destruction" was written in 1982, two years after "Maternal Thinking," and represents an attempt to depart more clearly from an essentialist perspective. Nevertheless, it is not enough to recognize (as she says she does) that differences among women might lead to varieties of maternal thinking. That approach takes the concept and examines its variant applications among different groups of women. Rather, we advocate beginning with the experiences of different groups of women, particularly those structured by race, class, and culture, and developing from these experiences theories that comprehend maternalism as it is constructed from women's real-life circumstances.

For a longer discussion of problems with the concept of maternal thinking, which shares much with our analysis here, see Jean Grimshaw, *Philosophy and Feminist Thinking* (Minneapolis: University of Minnesota Press, 1986), 227–253.

45. Zillah Eisenstein, *The Radical Future of Liberal Feminism* (New York: Longman, 1981), esp. 14–30 and 201–219; Gloria Joseph, "Black Mothers and Daughters: Traditional and New Perspectives," *Sage* 1, No. 2 (Fall 1984): 17–24.

46. Zillah Eisenstein, *Feminism and Sexual Equality* (New York: Monthly Review Press, 1984), 139–159, esp. 142.

47. Johnnetta Cole, ed., *All American Women: Lines That Divide, Ties That Bind* (New York: Free Press, 1986).

EXPANDING AND REDEFINING

THE POLITICAL TERRAIN

1

"Making Your Job Good Yourself":

Domestic Service and the

Construction of Personal Dignity

Bonnie Thornton Dill

This article explores the ways Black women household workers negotiated the employer–employee relationship to gain the respect of their employers and construct their own sense of self-worth and personal dignity. It describes their strategies for gaining mastery over work that was socially defined as demeaning and demonstrates how they actively resisted the depersonalization of household work. It also conveys their efforts to assert the values of a rationalized work setting within a workplace with rules and norms based primarily on personal relationships and family life. Finally, the study demonstrates the ways in which individual acts of resistance, even within the work setting of a private family, can have collective consequences for the overall organization of domestic labor as an occupation.

THE STUDY

The data on which this paper is based are drawn from a larger study exploring the relationship between work and family among African–American women who were employed as private household workers for a major portion of their working lives.[1]

Data were collected through life-history interviews with twenty-six American-born Black women between the ages of sixty and eighty-one.[2] These women had worked in New York and Philadelphia for most of their working lives and had raised children during their years of employment. The overwhelming majority of them had migrated from the South to the North between 1922 and 1955 and had completed about eight years of schooling. Approximately half had mothers who had done some kind of domestic work and most had fathers who were farmers or laborers. On the whole, they had had limited opportunities for education, and many had begun working when quite young.

Most of the women agreed to be interviewed, in part, because they wanted to help me. Many expressed a sense of pride and satisfaction that young Black women now had opportunities that had been closed to them. I became, in their eyes, part of the generation of "daughters" and "granddaughters" for whom they had sacrificed, worked hard, and prayed so that we would have a better life.

THE OCCUPATION

Private household work has always been, and remains, women's work. It has low social status, low pay, and few guaranteed fringe benefits. The private household worker's low status and pay, like that of the housewife who employs her, is tied to the work itself, to her class, gender, race, ethnicity, and the complex interaction of these within the family. In other words, housework, both paid and unpaid, is structured around the particular place of women in the family. It is considered unskilled labor because it requires no training, degrees, or licenses and because it has traditionally been assumed that any woman could do it.

Black women in the United States were concentrated in household work until as late as 1960.[3] This was a direct carry-over from slavery and a result of racial discrimination. By the time most of the women who participated in this study entered the occupation, in the early 1900s, a racial caste pattern was firmly established. The occupation was dominated by foreign-born white women in the North and Black freedwomen in the South, a pattern which was modified somewhat as southern Blacks migrated North. Nevertheless, most research indicates that Black women fared worse than white immigrant women, even in the North.

> In 1930, when one can separate white servants by nativity, about twice as large a percentage of foreign as of native women were domestics. . . . As against this 2:1 ratio between immigrants and natives, the ratio of Negro to White servants ranged upward from 10:1 to 50:1. The immigrant was not the northerner's Negro.[4]

Black women had far fewer employment options than did white women and as a group they were older and more likely to be married. Thus, whereas private household work for white women of diverse nationalities was often an entry point into urban settings, a stepping-stone to other jobs, or a way station before marriage, it was none of these for Black women. Instead it was an essential means of support for them and their families.

Nevertheless, the preferences of individual Black women had an impact on the overall structure of the occupation. Responding to the needs of their own families, they changed it from a primarily live-in system of employment to one in which most workers "lived-out," in their own homes, and worked during the day for their employers.[5] This was referred to as doing "days' work." According to historian David Katzman, this shift occurred between 1870 and 1920. Before that time, most household workers "lived-in" and were virtually on call twenty-four hours a day.

The shift to live-out work did provide the worker with greater personal freedom, less isolation from friends and family, and more limited working hours, yet many of the factors that had contributed to the occupation's low social status did not change substantially. The work continued to center around the performance of personal services, making it virtually impossible to make a clear distinction between work-related duties and those necessitated by the eccentricities of particular employers. As a result, the domestic worker faced a situation in which the duties of and expectations for performance were unstandardized and varied from one job to the next. Additionally, the occupation offered little opportunity for advancement. Once a worker had perfected her skills as cook, housemaid, laundress, or whatever, there was no place for her to go except to another house. If she was lucky, her next job might bring higher pay, but she would perform essentially the same tasks. Legal protections and benefits available in other work settings, such as minimum wage, social security coverage, and unemployment compensation, were not extended to include private household work until the 1970s; and they have been slow to take effect and remain difficult to enforce.

Finally, the norms of this workplace were shaped by a social ideology based on the values and practices associated with family life. The modern American family was socially constructed as an arena for personal and affective relationships, and its economic activity was generally described as consumption rather than production. These concepts hindered the growth of rational bureaucratic and universalistic principles of labor relations and retarded change in the occupation of household work. Thus, these workers faced a peculiar dilemma. They sought the rights, privileges, and protections associated with the workplace in a sphere governed by personal and familial values. An article written around 1913 conveys the ideology that has continued to influence the organization of this occupation even until today: "No fixed contract can be drawn up. For the home is a place where things cannot be regulated by rule and schedule. It is a place of adjustment, like the joint in a suspension bridge. . . . In short, the house is maintained for the advantage of the family."[6]

The result was that both employers and employees ultimately focused their attention on personal traits: the employee's manner of speech or dress, her attitude and appearance, or the employer's kindness and generosity. In reality, personal traits assumed importance because the occupation was shaped by an ideology that excluded consideration of basic principles of labor and management. The employer was more mystified by this ideology than the worker who knew that she was entitled to a fair wage for a day's work. Yet the worker also understood the nature of the occupation and developed her human relations skills, because she learned quickly that they would become important tools for survival.

CONSTRUCTING PERSONAL DIGNITY IN A LOW-STATUS OCCUPATION

Most of the women who participated in this study were keenly aware of the low social status of their occupation, yet they rarely presented themselves as defeated by it. Instead, they portrayed themselves as having been actively engaged in a struggle to assert their individual worth. Their stories about work depict them as attempting to gain personal mastery over a situation in which they were socially defined as object. They sought to gain autonomy and control over their tasks and dignity in the mistress–servant relationship.

Contrary to popular conceptions, the overriding attitude domestic workers expressed toward their work was not disdain or loathing but ambivalence.

Zenobia King, a household worker for thirty years said:

> I don't think domestic work is demeaning work. It's what people make it—like you have to use the back elevators, and can't eat the same food. . . . It's not demeaning work to do.

Corrine Raines, who had attended a normal school in the South and done domestic work for thirty years in New York, said:

> So many people have gotten their education by it, and it isn't any disgrace. . . . I wasn't embarrassed that I'd done that because I knew I was prepared for something else. I did it because it was something I could do to help my husband out. . . . I think I should be proud and want to work. Domestic work is nothing to be ashamed of, but it's an art, just like anything else. You just have to learn how to do it.

Opallou Tucker, a forty-year veteran of the occupation and a migrant from South Carolina, said:

> I mean, people don't advertise it, but at the same time if they have a good job, they are not particularly ashamed of it, it's nothing to be ashamed of. You see, I think a lot of times we go into this business of talking about a menial task, and that's what put a lot of us on welfare.

Queenie Watkins, who worked for one family for more than thirty years and had received some normal school training, said:

> First you got to make your job good yourself. You work at it every day. . . . The only thing about it is that we have to learn how to live with our job. Your job is your livin' and you learn how to do it good. Nothin' is perfect.

In these comments, the women talk about not being embarrassed, disgraced, demeaned, or made to feel ashamed of being household workers. Though all four women seek to provide a strong case for the worthiness of their life's work, it should be noted that their statements are defensive ones, reading more like disclaimers than affirmations. Corrine Raines says that she wasn't embarrassed about her work because she knew she could do something else, while Opallou Tucker argues that doing household work is a lot better than being on welfare. These essentially negative arguments in support of domestic service reflect a feeling on the part of the women that they must defend or justify the dignity and merit of their work to others. This defensive posture is largely a response to the social stigma attached to domestic service and domestic service workers.

These statements also have a positive side, however, one that conveys the worker's determination to make her occupational role personally meaningful and socially acceptable. These women make positive characterizations of the work, such as its being "an art" or a source of pride and satisfaction. They exhort other workers to work hard and *make* their jobs rewarding. When Zenobia King states that domestic service is "what people make it," she is asserting that the work is not inherently menial but that the negative associations are socially created and can therefore be changed. Queenie Watkins suggests that the worker herself has more power and influence over the job than even she, perhaps, realizes.

These statements were made, for the most part, near the end of lifelong careers in domestic service. Through the years, the women had encountered a variety of work settings—some that were painful and humiliating, others that were challenging and rewarding. As they reflected on their lives in household work, they were able to identify the ways in which society had limited their options because they were Black women, confining them to the least desirable sectors of the economy. They could also elaborate upon the ways they had asserted their worth as individuals and gained pride and self-satisfaction for the work that they had done.

Their life histories demonstrate that the three most important means by which they gained mastery over their work were managing the employer–employee relationship, building a career, and utilizing supports within the Black community. In each of these arenas they found the materials that they used to construct and enhance their own sense of personal dignity. Their resistance to oppression was based on both the creation and the defense of their sense of self-worth.

MANAGING THE EMPLOYER–EMPLOYEE RELATIONSHIP: STORIES OF RESISTANCE

One of the most striking aspects of the life histories was the portrayals of the employer–employee relationship. I have labeled these descriptions "stories of resistance" because, almost without exception, the women related incidents in which they had used confrontation, chicanery, or cajolery to establish their own limits within a particular household. They used these techniques to define what they would and would not give to their employers in the way of time, commitment, and personal involvement. The basic message that these stories communicate is that the employee did not permit the employer to push her around.

Oneida Harris took her first job when she was sixteen years old, as a live-in nanny. She had migrated from Georgia to Philadelphia under the guidance of her aunt, who had found her the job.

> At the time I was very young and I didn't know how to cope. It was my first job. Maybe the children would come in from school and the floor might be a little damp. . . . She'd say, "Oh, you didn't scrub the kitchen floor today." I said, "Sure, I scrubbed it." She said, "Look at all the dirt." I said, "Well, one of the children came in." She said, "That dirt was there when I left—you just a liar and that's all!" That was unpleasant.
>
> The thing I had to learn was not to let it get to me, and to call her a liar back. My aunt says, "Listen, you've got to learn, when you work for people, to treat them as they treat you. If they're nice and sweet, you can be that, too. But if they use bad words to you, you gotta use 'em back. . . ." That's what I had to learn to do. I had to learn not to cry 'bout it, but to find some kind of way to get back at her. And that way I survived.

Her description of these early work years demonstrates that learning to set limits was critical to the worker's maintenance of self-respect and increased her ability to survive in the occupation.

Fighting back as a key to survival in the occupation was a recurrent theme in the women's life histories. While Oneida Harris provides some insight into her personal struggle to acquire these skills, Bea Rivers's story focuses upon the utilization of these skills to protect her rights as she saw them.

> One weekend her [the employer's] boyfriend was having a party and so she said, "You'll have to cook the turkey because it's Paul's birthday." I said all right. But this weekend, I think my sister was sick, and I decided I would not go back to work. So I called her [the employer] and she got real nasty. Well, I hung up and then she called me back. She apologized and said she was sorry, she had just got upset. I told her it was all right. When I came back, she said to me, "Well, one thing about you, Bea, nobody could ever say anybody took advantage of you."
>
> I said, "Well, maybe they can't say it, but you certainly have tried. The only difference is you didn't succeed, because this job here is *your job*. This job is not the type of job that I have to live with the rest of my life. I lived before I ever came here and I could leave here and go back to the city and find another job. Don't ever feel that

this is the only job. When I came here I didn't sign any contract. I work here and I do enjoy it, but if there comes a time when things can be so unpleasant that I no longer enjoy it. . . . Now when you call me when I'm on leave and I'm home for a weekend and do a thing like that and I'm staying home on account of my sister's sick, it makes me feel very bad towards you. It means that you only live for yourself."

The determination to fight back was tied to the worker's perception of herself in relation to her job. Beatrice Rivers's comments to her employer suggest that she had established clear boundaries between her own life and her work. Her statement may be read as an assertion of her independence, independence that is epitomized in the phrase "this job here is your job." With these words she indicates her refusal to "own" the job or to be owned by it. It follows, therefore, that she would be unwilling to suppress her needs in favor of those of her employer, in spite of the fact that she needed and enjoyed the job. Instead, she characterizes her employer's behavior as an infringement on her rights, an attempt to "take advantage" of her. This kind of detachment from the job provides a buffer against the employer's insensitivity to the worker's personal needs. In essence, the employer rejected Bea Rivers's sense of her own humanity by refusing to give her the personal consideration Bea felt she so often gave to the employer. A degree of detachment from the job, even if expressed only in anger, was an important defense in managing the relationship.

Direct confrontation with an employer and threats to quit were two of several strategies the women developed to resist what they considered to be unreasonable treatment. However, their stories indicate that these techniques were not employed capriciously. Most of the women needed their jobs; otherwise they would not have taken them. Like Bea Rivers, however, they describe themselves as making clear to their employers that they were not in such desperate need that they would jeopardize their sense of self-worth. Thus, they often used more indirect strategies of assertion in relating to their employers.

> I went to the employment agency, and I'd have to take what she'd give me and try 'cause I needed to work and I needed to make ends meet. But, I always used to interview them [employers]. In fact, I used to make a lot of them very mad because I'd ask them all those questions about why their girl had quit and what did her duties entail, and what kind of work did they want done and what I would do and what I wouldn't do. And I made some of them very angry. [Helen Satterwhite]

Through these "interviews," Mrs. Satterwhite, who began work at the age of sixteen, and was still working part-time when she was interviewed at seventy-six, not only gathered useful information about the work itself but gained insight into the employer. Her approach was an attempt to establish a degree of respect and dignity for herself at the outset of the relationship. It was an approach she had developed through experience.

Chicanery was another strategy that the women used to establish their position with an employer. Zenobia King migrated to Baltimore at twenty and began working there as a live-in housekeeper. She worked at several domestic jobs, including one that had been her sister's job. In 1944 she moved to New York, where she continued to do household work.

> This other family was very prejudiced. She'd always show me things in the paper about colored people. One day she asked me, "Where did all the bad colored people come from?" I said, "I really wouldn't know, any more than you would know where all the bad white people come from." To put a stop to this, one day I showed her a clipping in the paper where some white [men] had robbed a bank. I said, "Oh, look at this, isn't this terrible. They robbed a bank. And they're white, too!" After that she never showed me those clippings anymore.

Helen Satterwhite related the following incident:

> She [the employer] told me what she wanted done and then she said, "My girl always scrubs the floor." Well, I noticed down in the basement that she had a mop, and she had taken the mop and hid it. So I cleaned the whole house and everything, but I didn't mop the floors. And when I got ready to go, I took the bucket, the brush, and the knee-pad and set them in the corner. When she came in she was very pleased. She said, "The house looks beautiful, you've done a lovely job." She went into the kitchen and she looked and she said, "But you didn't scrub the floor." She had a daughter who was ten years old, and I know I'm not her girl, I'm just the lady who came to do the days' work. So I said, "Well, you said your girl cleans the floor, and I'm not your girl . . . and I don't scrub floors on my hands and knees." "Well," she said, "tomorrow I'll go out and buy a mop." So, I got my coat on and I said, "Why don't you just let me go down in the basement and bring the mop up?"

These stories are reminiscent of the tales of Br'er Rabbit, which have the same message of the allegedly weaker character—the rabbit in the folktales and the maid in the above stories—cleverly outwitting a more powerful adversary.[7] It is not surprising that this type of story should appear among the life histories of a group of household workers. As an oppressed group whose working conditions carried many remnants of slavery, these domestic workers convey in their stories their struggle to assert their human rights in the face of seemingly overwhelming obstacles. The strategies that are used in the above stories represent the workers' attempt to achieve some kind of parity within the confines of a relationship of domination.

Ultimately, of course, the worker could walk out of the relationship, and many women did. Quitting was a major item in the women's histories and in some ways the ultimate form of resistance. David Katzman has suggested that "quitting a position [was] the only way to improve conditions that [was] available to a servant."[8] However, for most of the participants in this study it was the ultimate weapon and was preceded by other defensive strategies. Helen Satterwhite said:

> When I went out to work . . . my mother told me, "Don't let anybody take advantage of you. Speak up for your rights, but do the work right. If they don't give you your rights, you demand that they treat you right. And if they don't, then you quit."

Without exception, these women characterized themselves as leaving jobs when *they* tired of them. Only one woman admitted to having ever been fired from a job, and she was quick to insist that this was the *only* such instance in her entire working career. Queenie Watkins told the following story about quitting:

> I worked there with them until she made me angry one morning. I had a bad toe, and the doctor had told me to stay off my feet. Her mother wanted to have a Seder dinner there. I had entertained Christmas and Thanksgiving, and I said, "This is too much. You know the doctor told me to stay off o' my foot, and I just can't take care of fifteen people." She said, "Well I'll just tell my mother you can't."
>
> That Thursday morning I went to take her breakfast on the tray—she had a friend that spent the night with her. When I went in I heard this woman say to her, "You do what I do, tell her if she can't do it you'll hire somebody else who will. Nothing wrong with her. What's a drain in her toe?" I got so angry. I heard what she said. When I set the tray down, she [the employer] said, "Queenie, I just got through talking to my mother and she wants the Seder dinner here. If you can't serve it, I'll hire somebody who will." I said, "Mrs. Jonas, this is your job, you do what you want to it." And I never said another word. I just walked right out and started to pack my clothes.

Queenie Watkins's irate pronouncement to her employer that "this is your job" is reminiscent of Bea Rivers's statement above. Again, the work situation was described as enjoyable and rewarding, carrying with it some degree of responsibility and autonomy and affording recognition for work well done. Also, both women considered their pay to be adequate. Nevertheless, at the point of confrontation, they indicated considerable readiness to dissociate themselves from the job, symbolically throwing it back in the employer's face. All of this suggests that the employer–employee relationship represents a fragile peace. The basic opposition of interest of the two parties, and the resulting self-protective behavior of the employees are two possible reasons for the instability of the relationship. Albert Memmi, the French philosopher, however, offers a related but slightly different explanation in his discussion of domestic servants. He says:

> Domestic alienation is one in which the desire to identify with the master is at the same time the strongest and the most thwarted. . . . Their lives are . . . so interwoven, by the very practice of the daily job, that they are in a way part of each other, so that it would be impossible for the servant to withdraw himself. . . . However, this forced identification is condemned, by definition, to remain an illusion. There will never be a complete identification for there is a kind of denaturation of all the servant's acts, no matter how hard he applies himself. . . . This thwarted hope, this feeling of coming as close as possible and yet remaining infinitely far away, creates a state of unbearable tension.[9]

Most of the women recognized and openly acknowledged the unbridgeable nature of this gulf between employer and employee. As Jewell Prieleau said, when asked if her employers of thirty-one years saw her as a member of the family:

> Well, they tell you that. But of course you have the feeling, because you know that if something goes wrong, something they didn't like, how fast they would let you go. . . . There is just a feeling between you that you can cover up for years and years, but that feeling in both parties is there. They nice and they treat me nice like a person would treat a maid. But you know they wouldn't go out of their way so much.

Like the women studied by Judith Rollins in her recent book on household workers and their employers, these women did not identify with their employers.[10] Nevertheless, it is the tension of the master–servant relationship that explodes in Mrs. Rivers's and Mrs. Watkins's statements. They react angrily to their employers because they feel betrayed—betrayed not because they cannot completely identify with the employer but because the employer's actions are a denial of their humanity.

In both cases the employers are depicted as crude and unfeeling people riding roughshod over the worker's human feelings, the very things that, in the worker's opinion, make her the same as everyone else. To ignore those things is to treat her like a machine and to negate the last, yet most important shred of identity between them. The statement "this is your job" can thus be understood on two levels: It is the worker's reminder of the boundaries between herself and her job, and it is her angry rejection of the employing family because they refuse to acknowledge her humanness and give her the kind of empathy and concern that she gives to them. At either level, it is a statement of her alienation.

It is apparent that the stories of resistance crystallize around the workers' feeling that their rights were always subject to violation, that they must be prepared to defend and assert their humanity to make the work situation tolerable or to terminate it with a sense of self-respect. As Bea Rivers points out, it was not that her employer did not try to take advantage of her, but that she did not succeed because of Mrs. Rivers' resistance.

The stories of resistance are therefore assertions of self-respect. They seek to dispel the notion that anyone doing domestic work must be so downtrodden that she would do anything an employer asked of her in order to keep her job. While the need to retell these stories derives in part from the defensive position of an oppressed group, it indicates that the women perceived a certain degree of autonomy within their situation. The data indicate that the women recognized a variety of types of jobs and employers within the field of private household work. They felt further they had some choice in the matter of whom they worked for and some control over the work relationship. Knowledge of the occupation and experience in a variety of jobs were key elements in the women's ability to resist and negotiate the employer–employee relationship to their own advantage. This knowledge was developed through the process of building a career.

GETTING WITH ONE GOOD PERSON: BUILDING A CAREER

According to the sociologist Everett C. Hughes, a career includes "not only the processes and sequences of learning the techniques of the occupation, but also the progressive perception of the whole system of possible places in it and the accompanying changes in conceptions of the work and one's self in relation to it."[11] The life stories of these twenty-six women reveal their perceptions of the "whole system of possible places" within the occupation of household work based on their increasing knowledge of the types of jobs, types of employers, and range of pay available to them. The women learned these things early in their work lives and sought to settle into jobs that offered increased security, comfort, and satisfaction. Jewell Prieleau told the following story about her first job in service in the North:

> When I first came [to New York], I was sent here by a minister. He was like an agency down there, and these people would send the money to him and he'd put you on a ship and send you here—come second class, of course. That was in about 1936. So the people would meet you right to the boat, take you off the boat, and they'd put you right on the floor to scrub or to mop. When he send you to that family it was like you was bought. . . . And you had to work until you pay the money back no matter what happened.

Mrs. Prieleau's language clearly conveys her sense of being treated like a slave. She describes herself as being moved around like a piece of cargo, "put on" and "taken off" the ship, "put on the floor to scrub or mop." The transition from feeling like a piece of cargo to having a job that she actively owned and identified with took forty years. In order to reach that point, like many of the other women, she had to endure some harsh times.

Among the harshest were the Depression years. During the 1930s, when many of the women were driven out of the rural South and migrated to the North in search of greater opportunities, street-corner labor markets grew up in several cities. They were referred to as "slave markets" because every day twenty to thirty low-income Black women could be found standing on street corners in middle-class neighborhoods in the Bronx, Brooklyn, Philadelphia, and other cities, waiting for a white housewife to come along and offer a day's work cleaning her home. The wages were well below subsistence. Two descriptions, one of Philadelphia by Helen Satterwhite and a second of the Bronx by Jewell Prieleau, follow:

> It wasn't easy to get jobs. You would go and stand on the corner, and people would come out and pick you up. Everybody in North Philly was standing on corners to get work. And I was mostly the smallest one there. And they said, "Well, you look like you're the only one here so I'm gonna have to take you, but you certainly don't look like you can do the work. . . ." It was very hard housework. They wanted you to scrub floors and windows and all kinds of stuff. Those were the first jobs I had when I came up here.

> You would go to the Bronx, and there was certain corners that you would sit on. So some people had a box they would sit on, some would lean up against a store or wall. . . . And they would come and just pick out a nice clean girl they thought they could trust. And you worked, thirty-five cents an hour or a quarter, or when you finished they give you what they thought—which was good in times like that [ca. 1937].

One of the most striking aspects of these descriptions is that while the women present themselves as selling their labor on street corners, they also make it clear that their entire person was evaluated as part of the sale. They had to look trustworthy, strong, and clean in order to be selected for a day of heavy housework. They had to be willing to subject their very being to the scrutiny of women who were shopping for a person to clean their houses.

These descriptions of early experiences in household employment demonstrate a kind of objectification of the woman as worker. The women describe themselves as being made synonymous with the work itself, mere instruments by which the tasks of housework were to be carried out. A major part of the worker's ongoing struggle to attain mastery over the work was directed against this kind of objectification. In their life histories the women describe themselves as seeking and finding satisfaction in job situations where they received personal recognition. It has already been pointed out that the confrontations that were related in many stories of resistance were reactions to the employer's failure to recognize the employee's personal needs and concerns or to give recognition for a job well done.

While not every woman in the study shared these early negative experiences of being shipped to New York or looking for work in the "slave market," all of them had had experiences that served to remind them of their subservient position. Within this context, the struggle for respect and mastery over the occupation takes on even greater meaning.

The data indicate a common pattern among women who spent a lifetime working as household workers. Helen Satterwhite described it thus:

> I started off going to the employment agency. The lady would send me out on a job, and some of them were real rugged and nasty. I'd work that one day, but I would never go back. Then, once you got with one good person, you didn't need to worry about anything else.

These sentiments were elaborated upon by Lena Hudson, who spent forty-three years as a household worker.

> When you first started out, you had to start out in the Bronx, and then on, as I say, one job always got me another. I was working for a lady once, and she said to me, "I hope to see you get into a family of people that would be really able to pay you for what you was worth." So you see, one job just got me to another.

The critical element in the process referred to above was accumulating good references by gaining entree to a circle of people who were likely to treat the employee with relative decency and pay her well. Lena Hudson contrasted the employers on her later jobs with those she had encountered while working in the Bronx.

> Those [later] jobs paid more. Well, that was a better class of people. . . . What I mean, they were more able to pay and quite natural, some of the jobs [in the Bronx] would take advantage of you because they know you had to work. . . . Well you know there is different in classes of people, how they handle you for what they are. If you work for a nice class of people, they recommend you to another, somebody in that category.

The importance of finding a "good" employer could not be overestimated, and the women who participated in this study tended to equate an employer's social status with the quality of the job. In general, high-status employers were thought to be better ones. Discussions of household work have often implied that workers acquired status in direct relationship to the power, prestige, and wealth of their employers. Katzman, however, argues that "there is nothing to support the assumption that within their own community, Black domestics attained high prestige by virtue of the social standing of their employing family."[12]

Although prestige by association was a concern for some of the women, the employer's social position was important for other, more pragmatic reasons. In some cases, personal recognition and interaction with people of wealth and power increased a worker's feelings of self-worth and her sense of the value of her own work. More important, however, was the belief that high-status employers were better able to pay high salaries and provide fringe benefits such as social security, sick leave, vacation pay, and holiday bonuses. Workers felt that they were more likely to have a good working relationship in high-status families because these people were likely to have had prior experience in managing household help and would therefore be both fair and generous. Additionally, wealthier households were likely to have more staff, and a worker could benefit from more clearly defined job responsibilities as well as camaraderie with other workers. Thus, the desire to work for wealthy and powerful employers was a reasonable aspiration, and these jobs came to represent the top rung of the occupational ladder.

Working for wealthy employers also offered the worker a chance to interface with the social elite. According to Corrine Raines:

My most pleasant experience, in the later years, is doing catering for parties and preparing and decorating beautiful dishes. Very well-dressed people, very cultured people, come in and give me compliments on what I've done. I get some money or something. That's been some of my pleasure.

Opallou Tucker, who had worked as a laundress, general housecleaner, and then caterer's helper, said the following about one of her jobs:

You have the opportunity, if you worked in the right environment, of meeting and coming into contact with some of the world's biggest people, men and women. In my work, I've come in contact with people, and I mean not only just see them once. They visit these different places, different friends of theirs at different times. They remember you, they ask for you, they come and talk to you. They talk to you about things in their countries and things that are here. And it shows you that you are not just a piece of furniture there.

As both women indicate, working for a "good" family was a means to increased self-respect. The rewards of the situations described above were important not only in overcoming objectification but also because the people who gave this recognition were among the elite.

Nevertheless, committing oneself to a job with a good family could still have negative repercussions for some workers. The story of Mattie Washington, who had worked for one family for thirty-three years, provides an example. She said: "I say I gave them all my youth life." In fact, that is exactly what Mrs. Washington had done. She had left the South when her daughter was quite young and had moved to New York so that she could earn more money to support herself and the child after she and her husband separated. She was a young woman when she went to New York and eventually found a job as a live-in worker. She helped raise the family's child and served them devotedly, moving into her own apartment only after the employer's child was grown. She never remarried, though she had the opportunity to do so, and was able to visit her own daughter, who remained in the South throughout her childhood, only once a year.

The idea that a household employee could give any portion of her life to an employer's family is very poignant. It implies a relationship that reaches out beyond the bounds of any job description and into the very depths of the employee's daily life and personal aspirations. As such, it suggests the possibility of commitment to the work relationship at the expense of personal commitments outside of work. Mattie Washington's statement, therefore, is also a mournful one, made even more somber by the recognition that the relationship is one of inequality. She did not relinquish her youth to an equal partnership, but to employers who had the economic and social resources she came to rely upon. Because she was far away from her daughter and did not remarry, she became even more dependent on her employer's beneficence and on an affectionate relationship with their child.

Mattie Washington's story is unusual among household workers in her era, because most moved out of their employers' homes and into their own apartments or into boarding houses. This transition also brought about important changes in the worker's definition of self and of her relationship to the employer.[13] Only one other woman who participated in this study had lived in her employers' home for a long time, and that was Jewell Prieleau. Mrs. Prieleau, however, had married, moved out, and moved back in again when that marriage failed. She was also active in some social clubs, and these helped her achieve some emotional distance from her job. The life histories of the women who participated in this study reveal a strong relationship between physical and emotional separation from the employer and the construction of personal dignity. "Living out," in their own homes, combined with participation in clubs, churches, and other aspects of Black community life, provided workers with a buffer between themselves and their jobs and helped sustain their efforts to assert their sense of self-worth.

WE'RE ALL IN THIS TOGETHER: DRAWING STRENGTH FROM THE BLACK COMMUNITY

The Black community was one of the most important resources for household workers in their efforts to maintain a positive sense of themselves in the face of the social stigma attached to domestic work. Specifically, the attitudes of friends, family, neighbors, and community leaders toward domestic service provided additional support and information.

Between 1890 and 1960 the majority of employed Black women were classified as domestic workers. The high concentration of Blacks in the occupation had a major influence on community attitudes. In addition, these women provided a network of support and reinforcement for one another in a variety of ways. Mothers, aunts, and female family friends taught young women how to survive in the occupation, often referring them to jobs or "passing on" their own jobs to the next generation. One-half of the women who participated in this study reported that their mothers had done some kind of domestic work. Johnetta Freeman, one of the interviewees, described how she was taken to work with her mother when she was seven years old and taught both how to do the work and how to interact with the employers. Other women described being given general advice about the kinds of tasks and behavior that would help them survive in the occupation. One example was the advice given to Oneida Harris by her aunt: "Learn to treat them as they treat you."

A second kind of informal support came from the camaraderie that developed among women who rode the bus together daily or stood on street corners waiting for work. In her fictional account of days and conversations in the lives of domestic workers entitled *Like One of the Family,* Alice Childress vividly recreates conversations about employers and strategies for handling problems that occurred on long bus rides from middle-class white neighborhoods to the communities in which Blacks lived.[14] Though fiction, her account is revealing and dramatizes everyday occurrences in the lives of these women. Her writing, like that of Verta Mae and historian Elizabeth Clark-Lewis, emphasizes the importance that the sharing of experiences and information had among domestic workers. In fact, Clark-Lewis documents the kinds of support networks that developed among household workers who were living in boarding houses in Washington, D.C., during the early 1900s. Several of the women whom she interviewed talked about the kinds of help and advice that they received from other workers about how to handle various situations at their jobs.[15]

A third kind of support was found in social clubs of domestic workers, such as the one in which Jewell Prieleau had participated.

> In the late forties and fifties domestic girls used to get together and have clubs—social clubs. We would put money away all year, and then at the end of the year we would have a big dance someplace. At the time, the girls work in bars and girls work in restaurants, they always look down at domestic workers. So the girls working domestic had their [own clubs]. We would meet every Thursday night. Sometime girls would be looking for a job and you discuss why they want to leave and things like that. At that time a girl that get a job on Park Avenue or on the East Side [New York City] were supposed to be a big shot.

This statement conveys both the supportive and pejorative elements in Black community attitudes toward domestic work. The notion that it was low-status work and looked down upon is reflected in this description of the attitudes of other groups of working women in the Black community. Nevertheless, it is also apparent that clubs such as the one described and communities of boarders counteracted these negative views.

Although in my own research I did not come across additional information about the social clubs, their existence, along with the support of family and coworkers, offers some insight into the ways in which household workers fought the isolation of their work and found support for their efforts to resist depersonalization in the job. The clubs, even though they were ostensibly social ones, provided the formal structure for the development of a shared consciousness about the conditions and nature of domestic work. This formal structure was buttressed by a wide range of informal alliances that also provided support. All of these become an important link between the individual worker and the labor force as a whole. Thus, the clubs were one of the primary means through which individual acts of resistance became more widely known among workers, and a climate for negotiation and resistance was reinforced. Although these groups cannot be compared to some of the unions of domestic workers that were formed to bring about changes in wages and working conditions, they must be acknowledged as an important element in the domestic worker's struggle to gain mastery over her occupation.[16]

Although domestic servants as a group were not likely to have been classified among the middle and upper classes in the Black community, they were likely to have been viewed with respect and accorded prestige in the community.[17] The concentration of Black women in the occupation is only one reason for this. Sociologist James Blackwell has pointed out in his book *The Black Community* that analyses of stratification within the Black community tend to indicate that "secondary variables" such as family background, place of residence, status symbols, membership in formal and informal associations, voluntary groups, friendship cliques, church membership, and lifestyles were all important indicators of social status.[18] The low status accorded household workers in the society as a whole was ameliorated for Black domestic workers somewhat by their status in their own community. Their participation in various social groupings, particularly in the church, and their reputations as decent, law-abiding, hard-working citizens offset the low status of domestic work. Thus, within the Black community the women found both support and sympathy for the decency of their labor, accompanied by a distaste for the work itself and criticism of the social inequities that severely limited their options.

THE PARAMETERS OF RESISTANCE

Judith Rollins, in the conclusion of her book, introduces the concept of *ressentiment,* a French term for the "long-term, seething, deep-rooted negative feeling toward those whom one feels unjustly have power or an advantage over one's life."[19] She argues that domestics feel *ressentiment* and have little choice but to play out their role as the dominated party in the relationship. The discussion here, however, suggests a modification in this concept, one that does not deny the worker's knowledge of her subordinate position or her recognition that this position places limits upon her actions. What it does suggest, however, is that the workers played their parts with a skill and acumen that often redefined the employers' notion of the relationship. In other words, these women did not see their options as being limited to the employers' definition of the situation. They walked, instead, a very thin line between the knowledge that if they did not "pretend to be unintelligent, subservient, and content with their positions, . . . the position could be lost"[20] and their own determination to "make the job good yourself."

For the women in this study, making the job good meant managing the employer–employee relationship so as to maintain their self-respect. They insisted upon some level of acknowledgement of their humanity from the employer. They actively fought against the employer's efforts to demean, control, or objectify them, and in this struggle used such strategies as chicanery, cajolery, and negotiation. When those strategies failed, they quit. The pattern of quitting was characteristic of their early years in the occupation when they experienced the harshest working conditions. Also, most acknowledged swallowing some indignities in those early years because they needed the jobs desperately and had not yet learned how to handle the work situation to their best advantage. The workers' sense of self-worth and the fighting spirit that many of them conveyed were nurtured and supported by family members, friends, and other household workers who shared the same boarding houses, were members of the same clubs, or rode the same public transportation. The Black community also supported them by valuing quality of character over position in the economic order. The organizations of the Black community, especially the church, provided a place in which domestic workers could achieve status based upon their participation, making their occupational performance relatively unimportant.

The effort to maintain dignity in a low-status occupation was a continuous struggle, and household workers utilized a variety of resources in this process. The women were often willing to lose jobs or leave them if they could not establish limits and assert their self-worth in some way. Rollins explains this "remarkable sense of self-worth" as deriving from

> their [the workers'] intimate knowledge of the realities of employers' lives, their understanding of the meaning of class and race in this country, and their value system, which measures an individual's worth less by material success than by "the kind of person you are," by the quality of one's interpersonal relationships and by one's standing in the community.[21]

Like the women in Rollin's study, the women whom I interviewed had an intimate view of their employers' lives and did not wish to be like them. Jewell Prieleau's words profoundly express the sentiments felt by many others:

I've never seen anything like it. They like flocks of birds. They all flock down to Florida now and from March they come back to New York. And they see each other every day on the beach. They come back to New York and they want to sit and eat every day . . . . Oh, I wouldn't like switching place with her because I have noticed that although people are very, very rich and they have everything, they very unhappy underneath and it sometimes shows on them. I don't want to be unhappy. I don't know, I just don't admire them because I've noticed they come to dinner and they complain about hangnails and little things like that. And they just get to themselves and cry. And do you know that half these rich people around here they wind up on all sorts of things. I don't think I would want to change, but I would like to live differently. . . . But if I was to change life with them, I would like to have just a little bit of they money, that's all.

It is my contention that these sentiments were nurtured and developed through years of observation and negotiation. They are both the source of the ability to resist oppression and the product of years of resistance. In addition, they are the result of a collective consciousness that was developed and passed from one generation to the next, shared among workers as they rode the buses or talked in their boarding houses at the end of the day, and reaffirmed by the knowledge of social inequities that unjustly consigned Black women and their daughters to this low-status, low-paid, and dirtiest of women's jobs.

ACKNOWLEDGMENTS

The author gratefully acknowledges the comments and suggestions of Cheryl Townsend Gilkes and the editors, Ann Bookman and Sandra Morgen, on an earlier version of this manuscript.

NOTES

1. Bonnie Thornton Dill, "Across the Boundaries of Race and Class: An Exploration of the Relationship between Work and Family among Black Female Domestic Servants " (doctoral dissertation, New York University, 1979). The study focused upon the perceptions and symbolic structures through which the women presented the strategies they used in managing work, family, and the interpersonal relationships involved in each. It also examined the ways the women conceptualized and experienced social structural factors such as race, class, poverty, and a low-status occupation.

2. Interviews for this research were conducted between January and October of 1976. The names used here are pseudonyms. This sample of twenty-six women was located by three methods: referrals by individuals, visits to senior citizen centers in New York City, and contacting organizations of household workers and employment agencies.

3. Between 1890 and 1960 a higher percentage of Black women were employed in private household (domestic) service than in any other single (broad) occupational category. By 1960, 60 percent of Black women were employed in service occupations, but only

37 percent were in private household work, with 23 percent in other service work. By 1970, only 18 percent were in private household work and 27 percent were in other service.

4. George J. Stigler, "Domestic Servants in the United States: 1900–1940," Occasional Paper No. 24 (New York: National Bureau of Economic Research, 1946), 220. Also see discussion in Judith Rollins, *Between Women: Domestics and Their Employers* (Philadelphia: Temple University Press, 1985), 55, of the two functions of domestic service in twentieth-century United States, which identifies the distinctive pattern of ghettoization of racially subordinate groups in the occupation.

5. David Katzman, *Seven Days a Week: Women and Domestic Service in Industrializing America* (New York: Oxford University Press, 1978).

6. Annie Winsor Allen, "Both Sides of the Servant Question," Social Services Series Bulletin No. 29 (Boston: American Unitarian Association, ca. 1913), 8.

7. J. Mason Brewer, *American Negro Folklore* (Chicago: Quadrangle Books, 1968), 3–4.

8. Katzman, *Seven Days a Week*, 222.

9. Albert Memmi, *Dominated Man* (Boston: Beacon Press, 1968), 174–175.

10. Rollins, *Between Women*, 222–225.

11. Everett C. Hughes, "The Study of Occupations," in Robert Merton, L. Broom and L. S. Cottrell, Jr., eds., *Sociology Today: Problems and Prospects* (New York: Harper Torchbooks, 1956), 456.

12. Katzman, *Seven Days a Week*, 247.

13. Elizabeth Clark-Lewis, "This Day Had A' End: The Transition from Live-In to Day Work," Working Paper No. 2 (Memphis, Tenn.: Center for Research on Women, Memphis State University, 1985).

14. Alice Childress, *Like One of the Family* (Brooklyn, N.Y.: Independence, 1956).

15. Verta Mae, *Thursdays and Every Other Sunday Off* (Garden City, N.Y.: Doubleday, 1972).

16. For a discussion of efforts to organize domestic workers, see Dorothy Bolden, "Organizing Domestic Workers in Atlanta, Georgia," in G. Lerner, ed., *Black Women in White America* (New York: Pantheon, 1972).

17. Katzman, *Seven Days a Week*, 246. For a discussion of the differences between prestige and class in the Black community, see Reeve Vanneman and Lynn Weber Cannon, *The American Perception of Class* (Philadelphia: Temple University Press, 1987).

18. J. Blackwell, *The Black Community* (New York: Dodd, Mead, 1975), 73.

19. Rollins, *Between Women*, 225–232, 227.

20. Ibid., 227.

21. Ibid., 212–213.

2

Building in Many Places: Multiple Commitments and Ideologies in Black Women's Community Work

Cheryl Townsend Gilkes

Popular perspectives on Black communities and their problems often fail to comprehend the tremendous efforts at internal transformation that exist alongside persistent efforts to combat racism. Historical struggles against diverse expressions of institutional racism such as slavery, Jim Crow, ghetto poverty, and political disenfranchisement, for example, have also addressed internal problems and conflicts that would impede participation, autonomy, self-reliance, and dignity. For instance, many Black abolitionists were also involved in educational and benevolent organizations that were working for the survival of Black communities. The legal and direct actions of the civil rights movement existed side by side with activities designed to educate and empower Black communities. The Urban League worked to transform external economic structures that peculiarly oppressed, exploited, and excluded Black people at the same time as it developed a corps of Black social workers whose efforts would enhance the success of Black women and men in the labor force. Historically, a struggle for social justice and institutional transformation never developed without a struggle for group survival. The struggle to transform white racist attitudes and intergroup antipathies was inextricably linked to concerted efforts to foster social uplift and self-esteem.

Women have been central to this work for social change in the wider society as well as for survival and uplift within the Black community. Their consciousness highlights the strategic importance of women to the emergence and mobilization of what Nina Caulfield called "cultures of resistance."[1] Black women see the consequences of racism not only in their own lives as Black women but in the lives of their husbands and other male relatives, of their friends, and of their children. Even those community workers who had no children of their own were deeply involved in children's and young people's issues. Thus, these experiences provide three sources of anger to fuel the political consciousness of Black women. Their historical role as agents of social transformation and community uplift emerged during slavery, the rise of Jim Crow, and urban migration. In each period, this multifaceted perspective on racism has been evident in Black women's public activities.[2]

Within the historical traditions associated with a distinctive Black experience, working for "the Race" emerged as a central historical role and a highly esteemed social status. Formerly called "Race men" and "Race women," the men and women who do such work are often called community workers now. That term, arising during the late 1960s and early 1970s, focused emphasis on community control, group solidarity, and cultural pride. There was also a shift that included occupational settings (especially in the human services) as arenas in which to shape social change. Community workers are found in a wide variety of occupations and professions—they are nurses, teachers, lawyers, ministers, social workers—and are prominent within the Black community as people who have "worked hard for a long time for change in the Black community" and, less often, are prominent outside the Black community as "Black leaders." Although those men identified as community workers are usually, but not exclusively, clergy, the women are spread across a broad range of human service professions.

Black women's community work, with its duality of external and internal efforts, is a complex phenomenon. Certain aspects of community work demonstrate the manner in which these women define and execute their historical role in contemporary human service settings. As contemporary representatives of a historical tradition of Black women making social change, they decide for themselves and their community the appropriate objects of their efforts and the new goals to be achieved. The civil rights and Black power movements removed the more overt symbols of racial oppression and nurtured a militance that opened new pathways into predominantly white settings for "qualified" Black people. Such changes made it possible for community workers to discover the more subtle and complex realities of institutional racism and its pervasive consequences for their everyday lives and their futures. No longer did the healing of the wounds of racial oppression require simply an internal effort based in voluntary associations, nor could the elimination of oppressive domination be effected simply by concerted public and collective action. This newer era brought a need for complex, dynamic organizational approaches both to transform white institutions and to nurture and strengthen Black ones.

This study focuses on the activities, ideologies, and perspectives of prominent Black women community workers in a Northeast urban setting called Hamptonville.[3] The women see their social role as "building 'Black-oriented' institutions" in the many places they work. A Black-oriented institution is an organization or agency that responds to and cooperates with the needs and aspirations of individuals and groups in the Black community. For community workers, the "Black community" encompasses not only the people in their ghetto in Hamptonville but also a national community, formerly called "the Race" and sometimes called "Black America"; there is also an international identification, "wherever Black people are." Not only do the Black-oriented institutions evince cooperation and responsiveness; these places also depict and advocate a "Black perspective" within the organizational setting. In order to produce these institutions, community workers utilize a wide variety of friendships, associations, and ideologies, and they maintain numerous memberships in organizations and on boards of directors. This strategy of diverse but pragmatic affiliations produces a connectedness and cohesion within a pluralistic Black community. It also provides a limited degree of empowerment and visibility beyond the ghetto walls, and an acceptance of ideological diversity. The honors community workers receive symbolize not only the admiration of their community and of their professional colleagues but also the importance of the women's networks.

THE STUDY
During 1976 and 1977, I interviewed twenty-five women who had been identified as women "who have worked hard for a long time for change in the Black community" by individuals and newspapers in Hamptonville. Twenty-three of the women were between thirty and sixty years old, and the two oldest women were in their eighties. The younger women were employed in human service settings and were members and directors of local and national agencies and organizations. The older women had long, distinguished careers in racial uplift and religious organizations and, although retired from the labor market, served on the boards of directors of human service organizations, some of which employed the twenty-three younger women. These younger women were human service professionals who managed agencies, projects, or programs that were in some way related to the social, educational, economic, or political life of Hamptonville's Black population. Their past and present positions—in employment training, teaching, child welfare, social welfare, civil rights enforcement, health care, electoral politics, and the ministry, to name a few—touched upon every conceivable area where the private troubles and public issues of surviving in a racist society merged and surfaced.

Although some observation was conducted at public events and meetings, the study relied primarily on interviews. The sampling procedure was reputational and emphasized the community's perception that these women performed a public, political role central to its collective needs—in spite of the women's occupational and political diversity. In crises, these women were the ones upon whom Hamptonville residents called in order to seek advice and to shape responses. Community workers were women who saw their own problems as public issues shared by their friends, neighbors, and relatives—other Black people.

Beyond that, they also observed and understood the problems of others. Their attempts to engineer collective, rather than individual responses brought them into the social world and historical tradition of community work.

BUILDING IN MANY PLACES

Nikki Giovanni's poetic insistence, "I mean it's my house . . . 'cause I run the kitchen and I *can* stand the heat . . . ," aptly describes the determination of community workers to strive for social change regardless of the "heat" in the places where they are employed.[4] They perceive that institutional racism takes the form of bureaucratic indifference and abuse, and this perspective shapes their strategies to promote change in their everyday lifestyles. Through their own daily confrontations with a variety of problems, they eventually learn that the institutions of the dominant society are not organized to "be responsive" to Black community needs. The older women had created pathways into these institutions, and the younger women perceived their task as the making of these institutions into "Black-oriented" ones.

The places these women manage and administer reflect their attitudes toward the organizational practices of the dominant society. In order to fashion new organizational structures and practices and to transform old ones, the women become involved in two kinds of conflict. First, they rebel against traditional human service practices that appear to perpetuate institutional racism. Second, they restructure their own organizational settings to make them "Black-oriented."

By virtue of their positions, the women are members of the "helping professions" and they have "clients." Although they are not (with two exceptions) members of such established professions as law and medicine, they participate in occupational groups whose members espouse professional ideologies, exercise administrative and public authority, and hold more power than the people they ostensibly serve. Community workers judge certain of these professional ideologies and practices to be inimical to the interests of their community by reinforcing patterns of racist domination. Consequently, they rebel against aspects of this professionalism and seek to redefine the client–professional relationship. Since community workers are primarily political actors who view their client constituencies as peers, they do not see professional expertise and occupational status as legitimate bases for sociopolitical differentiation. Instead, professional expertise and training are aspects of their commitment to the community.

The women are also in a position where they are able to make demands upon white institutions to accommodate the needs of Black people. They use their positions to create a "Black orientation" or "Black presence" in these white institutions as a means for Black community empowerment. They work to force white institutions to "do right" by demanding that white officials and professionals do their jobs properly, by blocking opportunities for white institutional abuses, and by setting alternative examples for other white and Black professionals. This involves both teaching and confrontation. Although the women enunciate the need for total systemic change, they act on whatever level they happen to find themselves through employment, appointment, election, or simply membership.

Thus, the administrations of these women are consciously Black administrations. The alternatives they create reflect their critique of certain social relations that they perceive as contributing to the problem of institutional racism in the United States. Their strategy is to attack aspects of a multifaceted problem and to make a conscientious attempt to translate their images of community into the practices and procedures of dominant institutional settings. Wherever, whenever, and by almost any means community workers carefully build their alternative styles of administration in order to eliminate racism.

"DOING WITH": RESPONSIVENESS RATHER THAN PROFESSIONAL DISTANCE

Since the women live and work in the Black community, there is already a lack of physical distance between themselves and the people they serve. The early-morning and late-night phone calls, a permanent feature of their "typical day," are symptoms of their distaste for professional distance. Their places of employment represent one activity among a consistent line of activities. Their *work* extends beyond the boundaries of *a job,* eliminating the compartmentalization between professional, political, and social activities. Their specific jobs represent one place among the many political structures that govern Black people's lives. In the face of accusations that "you are being unprofessional," these women act to replace professional styles that reinforce dominance with something more responsive and humane.

Being "unprofessional" means a "laying on of hands." The women, thoroughly schooled in the textbook definitions of appropriate professional distance, physically reach out to do things *with* (not *to* or *for*) the people they serve. One woman worked as an administrative assistant under a stream of social workers before being hired as the director of an occupational and family service program. While discussing the meaning of the term "qualified," she mentioned that her job normally required a Master of Social Work (M.S.W.) degree, which she did not have. She reflected:

> Somebody will say to me, "You have to have an M.S.W." If I tried to get this job today, I would have to have an M.S.W. I don't have that, yet I've been doing this job and no one's complaining. . . . We had one lady who came here who was technical about everybody that walked in that door. . . . I was the [assistant] then. I'd be sitting there and laughing and talking with someone . . . waiting to be interviewed by her, and she said that it was *"naht professionalll"* behavior [doing an exaggerated imitation of the social worker's proper behavior] because you don't do that unless . . . you know how to have a discussion with that person.

She described her own style of giving services as reflective of the wishes of a board of directors who were themselves Black women community workers. She said:

> One thing I think the [agency] can do, they can give you a personal service, not sit down and you come for a service. "I'm going to call you next week; a year from now I might look through my lists and say, 'I'll call you and see if you're still doing all right.' " And, you see, that's the kind of personal service we give. And so when we find out they have children, you say, "How are your children doing in school? Can we get them a tutor?" "Do you want . . . ?" We try to think of the person as a whole human being with all their various needs.

She then went on to describe the various kinds of survival needs that could be linked to other problems and needs. The critical perspective she developed while observing the proper social worker also led her to ignore the rules of social distance. She described doing things *with* the people who came to her for help. She said:

> He may need legal assistance. People don't know all the services available. One thing about Hamptonville, it has every kind of service for a price. . . . But you've got to know where; you get tired of being sent from here, here, there, there. . . . Then a person gives up! So that's why we try to see it through. We have workers that will go out with you and see if that's the place you belong. If it isn't, then she'll go to the next place with you, wherever that is. So we try to make our services very personal, so that we can't say that we do this, that, and the other. We can say that we do what the person needs.

Like other community workers, this woman sees individual helping as one facet of the agency's role. The clients' political activism was also a necessary ingredient for meaningful social change and community survival. She described her agency's attempts to change laws and legislate programs concerning unskilled women and household domestics. Her open identification with the women seeking help penetrated her description. She exclaimed:

> When things began to deteriorate in this inflation that they refuse to call a depression, then all low-income women were in the same boat. And we'd like to have them all feel the same about it [referring to a previous discussion of attempts to reduce the stigma felt by household domestics]. We've all got to get together and say, "We're not going to let you shaft us any longer. We do the work; we want the money, and we also want the jobs opened up!"

Through her actions, the internal work of providing services to people in trouble was linked to concrete political action to change the laws related to the problem.

A mental health program director minimized totally the distance between herself and her troubled clients. Her husband's reaction, when she approached him with her idea for starting an innovative outpatient program, was very supportive. She said, "He was worried but said, 'If you want to work with them all day, eat with them all day, and sleep with them all night, it's all right with me.' " However, he "put his foot down" in the area of arrests and insisted that she not go to police stations alone in the middle of the night. Another mental health worker also gave her phone number freely to patients and other community people.

Most women discussed the troubled people who came to their homes. For some problems, home meetings were better than office meetings. One woman said:

> I had a person call me this morning, at six this morning, wanted me to give her a decision as to whether she should have an abortion . . . and I talked to her at length. [After a long, detailed recounting of the conversation] I told her I would meet with her tomorrow morning [at home].

Since the women viewed their work as part of a total lifestyle, they rarely regarded their homes as inviolate sanctuaries from the troubles of the Black community. When they discussed the troubled neighbors who came to their doorsteps, it was not to complain. Instead, their descriptions of the home visits served to show how important their visitors' problems truly were. One woman took her role for young Black women so seriously that she "dressed for business" when she was at home in order to be a good role model when she answered the door.

This lack of social distance between the women and other members of the community paralleled their insistence that they and their organizations be accessible and flexible. One director of an educational services agency commented at length on the importance of this organizational style. She said:

> We try to present an informal approach because most Black people . . . are kind of timid because of the way they have been dealt with by bureaucratic institutions. . . . We have a very good rapport with parents and the students; they walk in and out any time they feel like it. . . . I've had mothers come in here very excited and crying, and if she's got to stand there and explain her story to a receptionist first and then a secretary before she gets to see someone to talk to, by that time she feels as though "What's the use!" I know myself, as much as I've been through and as knowledgeable as I am about the system, that after three or four phone calls, and I have to keep repeating myself, I attempt to find some sort of alternative . . . because by then I'm totally disgusted.

Sometimes the women were criticized by agency employees and board members committed to a more elitist and traditional style of professional helping.

Such board members and employees had to be taught patiently but firmly that things should, to the minds of the community workers, be different. Some women were effective agents of change precisely because they had been trained in elite institutions of social work and had developed long and distinguished careers in traditional agencies as well as in national associations, both Black and white. One such professional, who managed a large agency, talked at length about her enforcement of her philosophy of service delivery. She said:

> They [people from traditional agencies] had to learn to work with minority peoples, which many of them had not had that experience before, and particularly minority people who were calling the shots. They had to learn to use their agencies in a positive way because we were making demands on them. . . . It gave them a different view of how to treat a client. We firmly believed that human beings had a certain dignity. And we didn't care whether they came in dirty, whether they came in drunk, whether they came in high—and, by the way, there wasn't too much drug use in our community at *that* time—whether they tried to manipulate us or not. We were there to provide on-site services and we did it.

Still another woman with a similar background, whose agency was large and contained several quite different programs, underscored the importance of accessibility and flexibility to her own professional effectiveness as well as to that of the organization. She said:

> If I remove myself entirely, then they've lost the benefit of what I know, and I've lost the opportunity to stay in touch. . . . Which is also the reason why here we try very hard, and it may not be good administration, and we've been criticized for it, "Are you going to be administration or are you going to be the people who run out?" We really try to remain accessible to people. . . . If somebody comes in off the street without an appointment, we have to do a little screening on that because that can take up all your time. But you're never that big that you can't talk to somebody about something that concerns them either on the phone or in person.

The importance of accessibility and flexibility as expressions of responsiveness is illustrated by the manner in which community workers use their agencies when a community crisis arises. Sometimes it is a crisis involving the total community. At other times it is something involving only those having a direct relationship with the agency, its program, or the related public politics. An agency director who is also a community worker will open her agency at night or keep it open past closing time in order to accommodate meetings. Several times I arrived for interviews and observed offices showing the telltale signs of late-night meetings—coffee cups, chairs, and full ashtrays. My observations were always confirmed.

Such responsiveness means that these women never expect to leave their offices on time. Those who do not control their own buildings must usually close their offices at five o'clock. Those who do not have to leave their offices make use of the public time for people in need of services and use time after their agencies close to complete paperwork, answer mail, and return phone calls. Because one women's program depended upon other agencies' being open for services, her efforts to be flexible placed additional burdens upon her. She said:

> We've even had to take somebody home with us. Other agencies, they work with a client until it gets to be four o'clock, and then, "Oh my goodness, I haven't got a place for you; go to the [agency]." Five o'clock, here comes somebody—no home, no money, no anything, no references, no job experience. So you take them home!—until you find a place for them. That is not required of the job, but, on the other hand, *what do you do with a sister?!* Do you say [in a sweetly sarcastic and exaggeratedly professional tone], "Sorry about that. It's five o'clock."

Not shutting their doors in the faces of "sisters" and "brothers" is part of the personal commitment that makes community workers' agencies and programs responsive, "unprofessional," and, therefore, different.

OUR HOUSE: ENFORCING A BLACK PERSPECTIVE

Besides transforming abusive organizations, professional practices, and ideologies, community workers want to create and maintain organizations that depict and advocate a Black perspective on social problems and their solutions. In addition to representing the Black community's perspective in white institutions, they enforce it in their own agencies. Essentially, that perspective centers on the sharing of power in organizations and social institutions.

When community workers have the power, they want to build "Black-oriented" organizations. A Black-oriented organization, according to these women, is one that starts from the premise that competent Black people can be found to manage and provide services flexibly and accessibly, without compromising legitimate professional standards. Over and over again community workers said, "The word *qualified* has racist connotations." Some said, "I don't use that word [*qualified*]." One woman said, "Qualifications don't mean a thing. Can the person actually *do* the job?" Their experiences in predominantly white institutions of higher education cause them to question the realistic meaning of credentials. One program director, who was still working on her graduate management degree said:

> The schools . . . can't give you the feeling for people. I don't think there's a course in it. . . . There could be. There could be just a little old playing thing on the days you don't feel too well; have somebody

come who's blowing alcohol in your face, and see how you feel
about it, and how you overcome that without giving the person a bad
feeling.

For some women, the experience of succeeding at a job without the traditional
credentials gives them a realistic basis for criticizing the obsession with credentials. A veteran social worker highlighted the contrast between credentials and
experience that contributed to her critical stance. She declared:

That's a sore point in terms of overestimating what an earned degree
means. And yet I'm not saying people shouldn't have them. All I'm
saying is don't make this a hard, fast criterion that opts out the value
[of] somebody's life experience, which in the long run, . . . if that
person is a capable person, will enable that person to move much
faster into whatever the job than a person who is fresh out of school
with a degree.

If these views were expressed by unsuccessful people, it would be easy to
dismiss them as rationales for failure. Instead, these community workers have
performed well enough to maintain their own organizations. They have received
awards not only from members of their community but, oddly enough, from their
professional peers. The women write well enough to obtain funding for their
programs, and they negotiate the bureaucracies of government and foundations
to acquire funds in difficult circumstances. Several women had conducted demonstration projects and programs that were later cited by their funding agencies
as models for both Black *and white* communities. One woman's project had
become part of a national funding policy package from which other cities could
obtain funds to start an agency like the one she had founded.

Ideally, Black-oriented organizations should be full of people, both Black
and white, who understand the legacy of institutional racism in the United States,
the ways by which the dominant society historically has excluded Black people
from decision making and economic opportunity, and how such powerlessness
has shaped troublesome conditions in the lives of Black people. If service agencies hired only community workers who shared the women's sense of mission
and identity, there would be fewer problems for the women who manage them.
Rather, the size and complexity of their agencies and programs require that they
hire both Black and white professionals who subscribe to the dominant societal
values and who protest and complain about an alternative professional style.
Consequently, the women are accused of nationalism, particularism, and reverse
racism. It is then that community workers must carefully articulate and enforce
their ideals. Sometimes they must attempt to enforce their values in white organizations serving predominantly but not exclusively Black people. Besides other
people of color, there are white clients living in or near Black neighborhoods
who confront similar economic and political problems and come seeking help.

The women are sympathetic to the disorientation of their employees, but they continue to advocate the importance of Black empowerment. One director of a large, racially mixed agency expressed her feelings quite plainly. She stated:

> I think that I am bent on self-government, meaning that Black people are able to govern themselves, are able to efficiently handle the various programs, and so forth. I am not sympathetic to those white people who work in the community and feel that forever and a day they will be in charge of things. I am more inclined to let them know in one way or another that they will be moving over as we move in. And I don't find that a problem because I still hold to a human relations approach as far as people are concerned, so I tend not to challenge them. For example, I don't ever use the word *racist*. I don't find it necessary to call a white person a racist. I consider that a cultural "given"—that in the United States it is a fact that this particular group does see itself as the group that consciously or unconsciously feels it is due certain things, that they as a people are due certain things. . . . I work around the offensive approaches, but I think I do it in such a way that people feel it. I let them know that it is my intention to move people up; that job mobility is important and that what I would do within programming is look for those opportunities for Black people, Hispanic people, et cetera.

Another agency director, who employed quite a few white professionals, insisted upon educating her staff to new attitudes and organizational order. As part of her administrative tasks, she said, "I see myself as an educator." She explained her administrative style:

> The way I like to function around here with my staff is that this whole thing is a learning process and that the only way we can have a good running operation is for us to learn from each other and to recognize that we all have something to offer the goals of the organization.

She then described an incident in which conflict among her staff members had erupted around a newly hired Black professional who was perceived as "militant." "I mean, said the director, "she's got 'UJIMA' on her license plate."[5] When the white staff members labeled this woman a racist, the director called a meeting. She said:

> This was just a couple of weeks ago, and if I closed my eyes I would have thought I was in a white middle-class establishment. I mean that's how upset I really then became—very concerned! And I said to the people who were sitting there, "This is a Black health center,

it serves predominantly Black patients, and it's got a Black administration, and that's what we're going to be about. Now we're going
to have to learn what that means."

She then spent time talking with white staff members about the traditional expectations of Black people by white people and how changing Black attitudes would
no longer allow an accommodating response to those expectations. She gave an
example of one of her discussions with individual staff members so that they
would realize that what Everett C. Hughes called the "cooperative representative" of a subordinate ethnic group was not the only type of leader in the community.[6] She said to one man:

> I said, "Duncan, you didn't even understand what was going on
> here. The fact that Edith doesn't have any time to teach white people
> anything anymore doesn't mean that she's a racist; it just means that
> she doesn't want to waste any more time." I said, "There are de-
> grees of integration. . . . I consider myself a totally integrated per-
> son, in the sense that if I put you on a continuum, you're a liberal
> over here, and Edith is over there [using her hands to indicate two
> extremes], and I think my position [using her hands to indicate the
> middle], given the nature of this center, has to be able to understand
> the environment that we're operating in. . . . You're using your own
> self-reference criteria to decide that what she's doing is offending
> you. . . . My job is to help you become a little more integrated so
> you can get out of that." When I used the term *self-reference criteria*
> and whatnot, he finally understood what I was saying in terms of his
> not being able to deal with what Edith was saying and where Edith
> was coming from.

Not wishing always to work around the offensive approaches to organizational
change, this director eventually hired a human relations consultant to "take care
of all the 'fallout' and anxieties caused by change."

Several women had worked in child welfare. The issue of adopting across
racial lines was quite explosive at the time of my research. One woman felt the
need to reeducate her central agency. She said, "I call it the 'Big House.'" The
agency, she claimed, perpetuated the distortion that Black families would not
take in Black foster children. She described her own professional priorities as a
child welfare worker in a predominantly white agency.

> Now I do have a problem when it comes to a choice as to who will I
> service first; it's going to be the Black girl; it's going to be the Black
> community . . . because it's harder to place our Black kids. And I
> show them. They said you couldn't place Black kids in Black homes,
> because you couldn't get Black homes. I've shown them just the
> opposite. I have a lot more Black homes than I have white homes.

Her ability to recruit Black foster parents created an unusual situation where during several emergencies she was forced to place white children in Black homes.

> That's the reason we have to place some of our white girls in Black homes for the same reason that we didn't have enough white homes. [Visiting professionals] asked whether I was placing them across racial lines. I said, "Well, I try not to because [the teenagers] are under stress as it is, and I don't want to add another problem to their situation. But I haven't had as many white homes as I've had Black homes, and I have placed white girls in Black homes as long as they can get along with it." And they reacted [imitating the visitors' shocked surprise]: "How has that worked out?!" I said, "Extremely well. Black folks have been taking care of white folks' children since we've been here!"

Another child welfare worker explained that her coworkers could not understand her opposition to the placement of Black children with white families. She exclaimed:

> *I had to give them a little history lesson!* They were placing "mixed racial" kids. . . . I said, "We've got to stop this stuff because they're not 'mixed racial'—they're Black." And they said, "They're half white and half Black." I said, "Look, according to you-all—you-all are the ones who made a fine science out of defining how much Black blood we had!, and how much white blood we had." So we went through all the quadroons and the octoroons and mulattoes. They had never even heard the terminology. I said, "You know these were Black folks who had some white in them, but they never got to be white. So how can these Black babies get to be white? They can't be half white because there's no such thing as half white. If you have one drop of Black blood, you're Black. That is the criterion white people have set, so, therefore, these are Black kids and they need to be brought up by a Black family." . . . We've gotten some mixed-up little kids back; they're so sad to see.

I expressed shock: "They actually brought the kids back?" She replied, "We'd get the kids when they were really messed up; they had been through adoptions . . . and then been placed in several foster homes." Although intense debates raged in the area of child welfare over the adoption of Black children by white families, this welfare worker's own perspective developed over a period of time after her observation of the psychologically damaged children with whom she worked.[7] She discussed the course of her reaction to adoptive parents who returned their children, saying:

> The ultimate rejection . . . the first time I saw that, I didn't know that it could happen. I mean it should have been a natural progression

of thought that if natural parents can give up their kids, certainly adoptive parents could. But the concept just blew me away!

As she talked further, she mentioned the "need to have an identity base," her concern for "the defense mechanisms that need to be ingrained," and her personal and professional feeling that "love is not enough in that situation because the total society is not going to accept this kid as white."

Other women discussed the change in their attitudes that occurred over time. They also talked of the lectures that they felt called upon to deliver to white workers when the need arose for socialization to the more assertive Black attitudes and the more vocal community demands for power. Even people who were the most outstanding examples of interracial cooperation could become unexpectedly rebellious and insistent in their demands for power and simple justice. One elderly community worker was considered just such an example of interracial cooperation. She described an episode that illustrated the type of teaching confrontation often necessary in community work, when federal officials discovered her successful program for household domestics and requested that she share the program. She said:

A [Cabinet] secretary down in Washington wrote me a letter and said that she'd like to know the format . . . for this program. So I told her that we weren't willing to give it to them; that we felt it was our own program; we didn't want anybody copying it and then saying that it was their program. I wrote such a letter! She said she never got such a letter and so she wanted to meet me.

The agency then invited her to Washington and provided transportation. When she arrived in Washington, they sent her to talk with a Black department head. She said:

I said to him, "They're siccing you on me, aren't they?" He said [in a mocking high-pitched voice], "Oh, no, no, no; this is my job." I said, "Well listen, dear, you can just tell the Secretary we're not releasing any of our information to anybody. The Black folks have gotten tired of people taking away all their copyrights and everything they've got and giving it a new name and starting it off under their own aegis. And we're not doing it." I said, "I'm not going to do it while I'm living. We started it; we're in the North; these are Southerners coming to us; we originally all came from there and we've had something in common. And we're going to stick together with this and make it pay. And any money the government's got in this direction, we're determined to get our share."

In her early eighties at the time, this woman also said much the same to the Secretary and insisted that her own organization should administer the program and teach others about it. She returned home and wrote a proposal. One of the organizations on whose board of directors she served administered the grant that she received to set up similar projects in other cities.

The opportunity for successful confrontation is not always available. Community workers in large, white-controlled and predominatly white organizations are limited to more modest goals. A Black perspective may be advocated, but it cannot be enforced. One woman occupied an appointive position whose tenure was limited. There were limits to the impact she was able to have through direct confrontation. While maintaining her desire to build a Black-oriented institution, she used other strategies and maintained her idealism. She said:

> I still do some of the things that slaves did. I don't always say to them what I'm thinking. I've learned at points to keep a blank face. There are times when I feel great anger, but I have learned to control it *if* the controlling of that anger means that I can advance, whatever I'm about doing, better by controlling it. There are other times when I don't bother to control it. . . . I'm determined by the time I leave the [agency] . . . that there will be a salt-and-pepper kind of combination of workers here as opposed to what there was when I came a few years back. I'm determined that Hispanic and Black [clients] will be better understood and better treated. And I hope that the quality of [service] for all people, Black, white, green, purple—any color—will be improved by the time I leave.

Teaching the politically unaware is a task that extends for these women beyond the boundaries of their own organizations or "houses." The heat generated within their administrations prepares them for the problems that stem from political confrontations in other settings such as the boards of directors, boards of trustees, and membership meetings of the interracial, political, economic, educational, cultural, and health organizations in which they participate. These positions are also part of the role of community worker. They are what one woman called the "small pieces" that make up, along with their full-time jobs, the total lifestyle and role set of the contemporary community worker.

"LOTS OF SMALL PIECES": THE DYNAMICS OF MULTIPLE COMMITMENTS

Community workers assumed that if the agencies were responsive to the most oppressed and deprived, they were by definition responsive to everyone. Simply changing professional ideologies and practices and reshaping white attitudes toward Black professionals and clients was only one part of the struggle. The women also found ways to confront the larger power structure of which their "Black-oriented institutions" were a part. Beyond their full-time human-service positions, the twenty-three younger women participated in a wide variety of organizations aimed at interracial cooperation, political empowerment, economic advancement, education, cultural enhancement, and community endurance— "lots of small pieces." While attempting to summarize her style of life in community work, the woman who had coined this phrase captured the complexity and multiplicity of all the women's activities and the diversity of the community and its problems. She said, "You see, there are lots of small pieces that I'm involved in, and [they] take very specific actions at very specific times. . . . It's hard to explain!"

Black community politics revolve around the web of intragroup and intergroup affiliations of community workers. As they build Black-oriented institutions in many places, their web of affiliations expands, and they are recruited to join a variety of boards and organizations. As new problems and crises arise, these diverse activities contribute to the duality of community work—overall social transformation along side everyday community survival. From the outside, an urban Black community can appear divided as debates between competing ideologies and organizations proceed. The organizational ties among community workers act as a cohesive force in spite of this diversity. These pragmatic affiliations of individual community workers provide the social basis of unity in spite of diversity, something that James Blackwell identified as characteristic of the Black community.[8]

It is through these pragmatic affiliations that the women contribute to the full range of tasks comprised by community work. The network of community workers extends a web of support through various boards of directors. The women sit on one anothers' boards and provide the kind of support they have in the past received. Besides administration, they perform the tasks of advocacy, community organizing, planning policy, political strategizing, raising funds, and managing confrontations. Through participation in "lots of small pieces," they attempt to change what one woman called "the big picture"—the social, economic, and political position of the total Black community and the systemic context in which this position is embedded.

"BY ANY MEANS NECESSARY": PRAGMATIC AFFILIATIONS

The variety of these affiliations often makes no ideological sense. Rather, the affiliations are reflections of the locations and types of problems in the community. Although a community worker may have a well-articulated political ideology, her affiliations are not always a reflection of her choice between sides of an ideological debate such as integration versus separatism or radical political strategies versus traditional party politics. The women's affiliations with white-controlled institutions are a reflection of where they feel Black folks need to be in order to exert some control over their lives and futures. They may find certain organizations objectionable, but if the quality of life for Black people is affected by one of these organizations, they will accept a position.

A community worker involved with the Red Cross commented on such an incongruous affiliation. She said, "I know, to Blacks, when they hear the words 'Red Cross,' I know a lot of people had bad experiences with the Red Cross." She then referred to its history of racism and to the differences among local chapters. She talked about other organizations that seemed antithetical to the Black experience, finally saying, "You know, it's all good and well to sit back and criticize these organizations, but if you don't sit in with them and become part of them, how are you ever going to bring about a change?"

Another woman discussed her "deviant" affiliations more bluntly; "It's like being properly dressed. You do something you don't want to do [like emphasizing that she is Catholic by birth], so you can come back and fight." I replied to her statement with my own analysis: "So you can manage to get your weapons to the line of battle?" She responded eagerly, "Right!"

Several of the women were Republicans. They had long histories of working for Republican candidates and had occasionally run for local office on the Republican Party ticket. One woman discussed her political affiliation in contrast to her other affiliations, which were "responses to community needs, the needs of Black people." She said, "Certainly being a Black Republican would not be considered a response by the Black community to a need. . . . But, yet and still, I am able to do some things *because* I am a Black Republican." Another woman recalled her recruitment as a lobbyist by the national office of the NAACP during the debates on the Civil Rights Act. Because of her position in the state party, senators and representatives welcomed her to their offices. Other women's affiliations created ties between white conservative religious organizations and radical protest groups and between traditional interracial service organizations and Black nationalist ones.

Often affiliations with cultural institutions, such as museums, fine arts organizations, scientific associations, and zoological societies, serve two purposes: Black children from various agencies administered by these women or other community workers gain free admission to public programs, *and* the women develop talking relationships with powerful representatives of white economic, political, and educational institutions. Though they often learn that their potential impact on the social structure is more limited than they had hoped, community workers use these talking relationships to chip away at some of the attitudes and assumptions related to the maintenance of the status quo. Since these community workers are often the *the* Black trustee or *the* Black board member, they try to represent sincerely a Black perspective on policies.

These affiliations with white organizations are never isolated from women's more numerous affiliations within the Black community; these are the Black interests that they represent elsewhere. Their affiliations with boards governing a variety of Black community activities are broadly pragmatic, placing them in direct relationships with particular social problems and needs and with diverse ideological perspectives. The woman whom whites may consider to be the most cooperative interracial worker may be intimately linked with some other community worker whom whites consider to be "too radical" and "hard to get along with."

The full range of the women's diverse gifts and talents are also utilized in these various organizations. The elderly community worker teaches the younger community workers. The woman who is a "native" of Hamptonville is able to sponsor the woman who has migrated from the South. The "bourgeois" community worker is the one who lectures other status-conscious members of the Black middle class concerning their responsibilities and relationships with Hamptonville's ghetto problems. She is the one who is able to shame and to recruit the more privileged members to more visible forms of support. The interracially cooperative community elder has the moral authority to chair a meeting between frightened white liberals and Black activists perceived as "militants."

The women are familiar with each other's "gifts," so that differences of opinion, style, and ideology may be coordinated to the best advantage of the community. The cooperative representative in interracial affairs may recruit the uncooperative radical to serve on a board. This not only guarantees the expression of the Black community's most extreme feelings on a matter but also allows the cooperative representative enough freedom to negotiate. One woman, often cast in the radical role, said, "People like Mrs. Lawson [a community elder] used to sit beside me [at board meetings] saying, 'Tell 'em! Tell 'em!' [whispering and jabbing her elbows to demonstrate Mrs. Lawson's manner]; and when I'd 'tell 'em', then [whispering like Mrs. Lawson] she'd say, 'You talk too much; you've said too much, now you've got me in trouble.' "

Many women mentioned that their first year on a board was spent silently observing the variety of performances necessary in order to set policy and to guide administrators. Once they have had experience, community workers are valuable to a network. The number of board positions offered to them can be overwhelming. After experience is gained, they learn to choose their board positions according to their perception of both long-range goals and immediate needs. They learn to distinguish between "honorific" and "working" boards and become more selective in their acceptance of appointments.

Selectivity, however, does not prevent overload. Community workers will quickly join a board to "help a sister." One woman could not even remember the name of an organization to whose board meetings she went religiously. She said to me, "What's Harriet's organization? Well, I'm on that board." An elderly community worker, referring to one of her board memberships said, "That's Audrey's. I'll always help her out."

One worker outlined the dynamics of one of her board memberships, highlighting the strategic support provided by fellow community workers.

> I'm on the board of trustees of [agency]. The director of the program and I used to work together. So she was having trouble with that [agency board], and she trusted me so she asked me to come on. I've had a lot of problems working with people in the community [on boards]. They don't know what their role or their function is. [Talk at length about her socialization of unsophisticated neighborhood board members during the poverty program.] She knew that I had raised a lot of hell over here, so she figured she needed some raised

over there. They [the board] just take it over. . . . I challenged them on everything they did. . . . "You do have a role and function, but let's delegate some of the responsibility to the director. It's an insult to her integrity that you feel as though she can't do it. Do you think for everything she's going to come to you? That's how white folks do it; they can't trust you so you have to come to them to check out every dollar. Either you hire someone you can trust, or give it up."

An agency head on the other side of a similar relationship said:

I wish that you could meet this member of our board. She does a lot, and she has been the one that has made the board leave me alone. And she knows what's going on here. She hears all the gossip, and she lets me know, maybe a year later after the problem has passed, that she knew what was happening. She's into so many things like the V.F.W. and labor unions, things you don't normally associate with Black people. But she's been key and instrumental in helping me get this work done with no interference from the board.

The cumulative experience of working on various boards allows the women, as they move through their public careers, to evaluate carefully what they are able to do and the kind of role that they will play on a particular board. Token and honorary positions that have no strategic political value are rejected.

One woman's career in public life blossomed faster than she was able to evaluate it. She reached a point when she became so overwhelmed by meetings that she sat down and carefully reflected on her affiliations in terms of their practical value. She reported that she said to herself, "Winnie, you've had the opportunity to serve on a wide variety of boards, so let's cut some things out." She then described what she did. She said, "So I wrote and I felt good about those. It was like I had done something that I wanted to do, 'Regretting having to resign, boom boom boom!' But I stated my reasons and I did it." I then asked her, "How many boards were you on?" She replied:

Oh, Lord, a lot! And the thing about it was that people accepted that. . . . What it meant to me was that if you're going to contribute to something that you can believe in, that's going to advance a change or that's going to be an engine for social change in the community, [then] you must be able to transmit or transfer that change. And I just couldn't do that, so I said, "The heck with it. I've done what I can and I'll have to move on and make room for some younger person and someone who might have more time. . . ." I have become a lot more, at this age, selective about the things that I do. I think that that [selectiveness] is much more positive and practical . . . than to say, "Yeah" because they say they need you. They'll still be saying they need me when I'm dead. . . . I'm able to ask certain questions which then help me to decide whether or not, for them and for me, it is worthwhile.

The women's descriptions of their processes of self-criticism and evaluation imply that an element of community work is the constant fitting together of talents and actions in order to develop appropriate and effective political strategies. The ethic "by any means necessary," although associated with the radical revolutionary style of the late 1960s, adequately describes the women's multiple commitments and pragmatic affiliations. These diverse activities are the collective action through which community workers exert pressure against the broadest possible variety of dominating institutions and bind together the widest possible array of constituencies within the Black community. Rather than perceiving their differences in style and opinion as impediments, community workers utilize the differences among themselves as resources to be used in the most strategically productive manner. Community workers evaluate each other in terms of their contribution to all of the "small pieces" that could possibly change "the big picture."

HONORS AND AWARDS: SYMBOLS OF CONNECTEDNESS AND MISSION

Members of the Black community recruit the community workers because they trust these women to act in their interests. The community then reinforces and rewards with honors their activities on its behalf. These honors symbolize the importance of community work and increase the public exposure and visibility of the community worker. Consequently, she is more vulnerable to recruitment to higher positions and more intense commitment to service. The awards also highlight her role in unifying the community by publicizing her pragmatic affiliations. Her determination "to set my people free" is acknowledged and honored by members of the community.

Awards are an expression of the mandate that Black people have given to these community workers to represent the community. As spokeswomen, administrators, trustees, and directors, they are, through these awards, reminded of the faith and trust being offered to them.

The relationship between community workers and the community expands in complexity over their life course. The number of people affected by their work expands, becoming an awesome responsibility. The fatalism expressed in one worker's comment, "What people mandate, I've got to do!" emphasizes a sense of shared fate with very real people having very real needs. The work, and the expansion of opportunities for more community work, increases each woman's individual expertise and political resources. Additionally, the women move in different directions as historical circumstances and crisis intervene in their lives. Particular public issues provide different perspectives on how and by what means the system of racial oppression can be "jacked up." The sharing of their acquired resources and divergent perspectives within their network of community workers and community organizations reminds them that, despite their diverse tasks and locations, they are still involved in the same struggle—the advancement of the interests of the Black community. It becomes community workers' responsibility, by virtue of these symbols of trust and connectedness that they receive, to continue in the struggle. When they describe this aspect of their work, community workers often borrow from the spirituals and hymns of their religious experience, using such phrases as "run on and see what the end will be," "run the race," and "move on up a little higher." The constant motion of their careers and their everyday lives is reflected in these themes.

The awards and honors are important at another level as well. The women experience a community-sponsored upward mobility precisely because of their reasoned and pragmatic dedication to the cause and the struggle. Since their professional experiences are augmented by their trustee positions, board memberships, and organizational participation, their human capital, in orthodox economic terms, increases. Paradoxically, the women become upwardly mobile in the very same occupational structure and political economy they are trying to change. Awards and honors, and the public ceremonies associated with them, serve to remind the women of their purpose in increasingly difficult circumstances. Whatever opportunities they seek or are offered they evaluate with reference to their role as a community worker.

Over the years, organizations have seen some women and men acquire skills and, according to one worker, "let go of us as a community, as a people." Another worker vividly described the attempt of a white institution to lure her away from community work and her highly vocal, visible, and effective activism. The community culture recognizes—"everybody knows"—that the potential for co-optation exists. The community counters this with its only weapon and resource—public admiration, honor, and awards. Through these awards the community openly encourages the building process that transforms institutions, represents the Black perspective, creates a presence beyond the ghetto walls, and maintains unity in the context of the community's diversity.

CONCLUSION: THE POWER OF POWERLESSNESS

This study focused singularly on women. In spite of the overwhelming visibility of male leaders in the civil rights and Black power movements, women outnumber men in the local world of community work. The women are aware of the fact that they do the bulk of the community work. Many men openly acknowledge this fact as well. The most visible male community workers are usually ministers, and their sudden moves to new congregations can disrupt coalitions and projects. Moreover, their primary allegiance is to their congregation, and occasionally they must represent that constituency in conflicts and disputes. The fact that white politicians invariably approach the minister before they approach the women produces occasional hostility. Thus, men may at times be a problem in the world of community work.

The position of Black women at the bottom of both the status and income hierarchies produces an interesting paradox in their politics of liberation. They have a better and more comprehensive view of the dynamics of oppression. As the mothers who, like many Black women workers, depend upon older friends and relatives for child care, Black women community workers participate in the intergenerational network of women simply to survive. As mothers and friends of mothers, they apprehend more sharply the consequences of racism for the total life course and for both boys and girls. They also suffer the consequences of Black men's oppression as their limited work lives, criminal justice encounters, and other humiliations place additional burdens upon the women. From such a deprived position, Black women have advanced some of the most powerful critiques of the racist society in which they live.

Historically, the Black community has recognized the power of Black women's powerlessness. Such collective wisdom emerges in both folklore and historical practice. Zora Neale Hurston depicted this wisdom in dramatic terms when she utilized "mulés and men" as the central metaphor for the Black experience. The "mules" were the Black women who bore a disproportionate share of the weight of racial oppression.[9] In *Their Eyes Were Watching God*, Hurston inserts this wisdom into the mouth of a wise Black grandmother as she schools her granddaughter in the realities of race and gender. It is the peculiar intersection of race and gender that undergirds the grandmother's desperate strategies to "protect" Janey through an arranged marriage. She says:

> Honey, de white man is de ruler of everything as fur as Ah been able tuh find out. Maybe it's some place way off in de ocean where de black man is in power, but we don't know nothin' but what we see. So de white man throw down de load and tell de nigger man tuh pick it up. He pick it up because he have to, but he don't tote it. He hand it to his womenfolks. De nigger woman is de mule uh de world so fur as Ah can see. Ah been prayin' fuh it tuh be different wid you. Lawd, Lawd, Lawd![10]

Beyond the folkore, the collective recognition of this power of the powerless women emerged in the "larger share" of public power Black women were granted within their communities in organizations and movements.[11] Drake and Cayton observed that "Bronzeville" residents—both men and women—were able to name prominent women as local and national heroines who represented their interests. Furthermore, they suggested that Bronzeville *trusted* its "Race women" more than it trusted its "Race men." Perceiving the limits of women's opportunities, the community noted that the women could not capitalize on their activities in the same way as men could.[12] Thus, while men—ministers moving to new congregations and politicians seeking public office—were a suspicious source of instability, women were perceived as more committed to the everyday life, troubles, and interests of the community.

This trust can be an important constraint and a source of anguish for the women. The less skilled and more deprived members of the community see the middle-class trappings of their work and lifestyle and assume the women have more power than they actually possess. The women, on the other hand, because of their upward mobility, perceive more clearly the depths of the crisis confronting the community and the all-too-real limits of power. Excessive trust in the women's ability to get things done may sometimes undercut their ability to organize massive community participation before a problem reaches crisis proportions. Among the most powerless in the larger society, Black women community workers have moral power and prestige because they are women who represent the total community's interests and who build carefully a culture of resistance through community work in many critical places.

Katie G. Cannon has described four basic struggles that shape the consciousness of Black women—the struggle for human dignity, the struggle against white hypocrisy, the struggle for justice, and the struggle for survival. As a result of the historical constancy of those struggles, she argues, black women "articulate possibilities for decisions and actions which address forthrightly the circumstances that inescapably color and shape black life."[13] The historical tradition and contemporary practice of community work is a predominantly female social institution[14] that demonstrates the powerful way in which consciousness is shaped and an alternative history is forged. No matter how high they rise, and no matter how diverse and many the places they go to build, Black women community workers are the ones who will come home to the community.

ACKNOWLEDGMENTS
An earlier version of this study was presented in 1982 at the Kirsch Center for Marxist Studies of the University of Massachusetts–Boston. Support for various stages of the research and writing was provided by the National Fellowships Fund, the Minority Fellowship Program of the American Sociological Association, and the Center for Research on Women at Memphis State University, Memphis.

NOTES
1. M. Caulfield, "Imperialism, the Family, and Cultures of Resistance," *Socialist Revolution* 4, No. 2 (1974): 67–85.

2. Several old and new works describe this complexity and historical depth: Angela Davis, *Women, Race, and Class* (New York: Random House, 1981); Elizabeth Lindsey Davis, *Lifting As They Climb: A History of the National Association of Colored Women* (Washington, D.C.: Moorland Spingarn Research Center, 1933); St. Clare Drake and Horace Cayton, *Black Metropolis: A Study of Negro Life in a Northern City* (Chicago: University of Chicago Press, 1970); Sharon Harley and Rosalyn Terborg-Penn, *The Afro-*

American Woman: Struggles and Images (Port Washington, N.Y.: Kennikat Press, 1978); Paula Giddings, *When and Where I Enter: The Impact of Black Women on Race and Sex in America* (New York: Morrow, 1984); Alfreda Duster, ed., *The Autobiography of Ida B. Wells* (Chicago: University of Chicago Press, 1970).

3. All of the names of persons and places in this study are pseudonyms. Unattributed and uncited quotations are from the interviews and field notes.

4. Nikki Giovanni, *My House* (New York: Morrow, 1972).

5. *Ujima,* meaning collective work and responsibility, is one of the seven principles of *Kwanza* outlined in Ron Karenga's doctrine of *Kawaida.* The other six are *Umoja* (unity, *Kujichagalia* (self-determination), *Ujamaa* (cooperative economics), *Nia* (purpose), *Kuumba* (creativity), and *Imani* (faith). These are described in detail in Alphonso Pinckney, *Red, Black and Green: Black Nationalism in the United States* (New York: Cambridge University Press, 1976), esp. 129 and 140–143.

6. Everett C. Hughes, *The Sociological Eye: The Collected Papers of Everett Hughes* (Chicago: Aldine, 1971).

7. Joyce Ladner, *Mixed Families: Adopting Across Racial Boundaries* (Garden City, N.Y.: Anchor, 1976).

8. James E. Blackwell, *The Black Community: Diversity and Unity* (New York: Harper & Row, 1985).

9. Zora Neale Hurston, *Of Mules and Men* (Bloomington: Indiana University Press, 1963, 1978), 80–81.

10. Zora Neale Hurston, *Their Eyes Were Watching God* (Urbana: University of Illinois Press, 1978), 29–32.

11. Drake and Cayton, *Black Metropolis.*

12. *Ibid.*

13. Katie G. Cannon, "The Emergence of Black Feminist Consciousness," in Letty M. Russell, ed., *Feminist Interpretation of the Bible* (Philadelphia: Westminster, 1985), 30–40, esp. 40.

14. Deborah Grey White, in the most comprehensive and scholarly analysis of women's experience during slavery, argues persuasively that "the female slave network" stood with the slave family and slave religion as a social institution that facilitated survival and selfhood. See Deborah Gray White, *Ar'n't I a Woman?: Female Slaves in the Plantation South* (New York: Norton, 1985), 119–141.

3

Gender and Grassroots Leadership

Karen Brodkin Sacks

This article is about the different ways that men and women exercised leadership in a hospital union organizing drive. At one level the research stems from an effort to apply anthropological methods and concepts to the larger feminist scholarly enterprise of building theory from the observed and lived experiences of women. Like women's studies, ethnography is an experience in seeing with new eyes and trying to understand concepts and categories that are often at loggerheads with those conventionally applied. In some ways, too, interpretive anthropology joins radical, Black, and feminist scholarship in the wider critical discussion of objectivity and agency.[1] Both the anthropological and the feminist enterprises necessarily involve confrontation and dialogue between actors' and observers' systems of meaning and interpretation.

In what follows I look at political activism through women's eyes, more specifically, through the eyes of mostly Black working-class women. I ask what politics and leadership look like when these women's vision and voices are placed at the center of analysis. The results of this enterprise suggest a significant revision of our concepts of political process and leadership, at least when we are dealing with transformative politics at the grassroots level. Examining leadership in a grassroots movement through working-class Black women's eyes and actions shows leadership to be a collective and dynamic process, a complex set of relationships and negotiations rather than a mobilization of parallel but individual actors.

In this union drive, most of the workers were women, and most of the militancy, movement, and leadership came from Black workers. It was a situation in which workers were mobilized simultaneously on the basis of race, gender, and class. Analyzing this mobilization requires engagement in the current feminist discussion of the ways in which gender, race, and class consciousnesses are interrelated.[2] The issues of race and gender here become entry points—they force the question of how class is constituted: What are its kin structures (entailing gender and generational structures and relationships) as well as its racial and ethnic structures? Here my anthropological concerns merge with feminist ones to urge a revision of "class" as an analytic category. It is not a relationship of individuals to education or income nor, in Marxist usage, is it individual relations to the means of production.

One of the findings that is beginning to emerge from feminist scholarship is that kinship and race are key ways by which class is internally structured and important bases of working-class organizing.[3] Family relations and kin networks and obligations, along with the cultures and values that people learn in families, are important elements of class structure and consciousness. Likewise, neighborhoods and communities structure class relations as well as being structured by them. Working-class communities have been separated from one another racially and ethnically, and that segregation reflects long-standing patterns of racism in American society. The domestic code and occupational segregation have also separated male and female workers. These patterns in turn have stimulated different gender, racial, and ethnic/cultural patterns of expression and resistance.

These are the genealogies and interests that have shaped the particular way I approach working-class women's political activism. I explore the notion that women's workplace activism and investment are retarded by their family investment and responsibilities. I want to know whether and how families and family values foster women's activism in the waged workplace. My working hypothesis is that they do.

BACKGROUND AND METHODOLOGY

This article is about the different ways women and men exercised leadership in a union organizing drive at Duke University Medical Center. The events recounted here took place between 1974 and 1979. I was a participant observer in 1978–79, the last years of more than a decade of intense efforts by hospital workers, led by Black service workers, to form a union. This drive involved some two thousand clerical, service, and technical workers; they were about 80 percent women, approximately half Black and half white. Although the workers did not win the election, their long struggle, including several walkouts and job actions, did bear fruit. It led to the creation of two smaller unions and to significant improvements in both wages and working conditions throughout the medical center.

I had twin purposes in the union drive. One was to work on the organizing committee in whatever capacity might be useful. The other was to learn about and describe the ways in which women were activists and leaders. When I raised the issue of leadership among a group of Black and white women activists on the organizing committee, one woman expressed her belief that "women are organizers; men are leaders." Her view was acknowledged by other women in the room. They suggested that women created the organization, made people feel part of it, and did the routine work upon which most things depended, whereas men made public pronouncements and confronted and negotiated with management. A 1974 walkout by data terminal operators (DTOs), and the secretaries who staffed the desks in hospital wards seemed also to reinforce this notion. Although those involved in that walkout were overwhelmingly Black women, they chose the walkout's "lone Black male" to present their petition to hospital management (though they were right behind him). These views did not sit well with me as a feminist activist, and I did my best to promote women's leadership.

The result was a methodology I can best describe as "leading with my chin." I shared with women on the organizing committee the prevalent notion of leadership and acted upon it. This notion implicitly equated public speakers and negotiators with leaders and accepted the distinction between "organizing" and "leading," though these things became clear to me only in retrospect. The incident that forced me to rethink this notion of leadership was a situation in which I was one of three middle-class feminists (two white and one Black) who set up a public forum for hospital workers on the organizing committee to address a sympathetic audience and build community support for their unionizing efforts. We engineered a situation in which all five speakers were women workers (two white, three Black) and where none of the usual male public leaders spoke. The women did beautifully, and I felt I had furthered women's leadership role until the women themselves called me into a meeting where they expressed fairly sharp criticism. After talking among themselves, they had discovered that they were all quite angry at being manipulated and pressured into doing something they did not want to do, even though they too thought they had done well. Although I agreed with their criticisms about manipulation and pressure, I could not understand why they were afraid of "saying something wrong," and why they did not want to be public speakers.

As I reexamined the data from my research to try to answer that question, I came to believe that the notion of leadership I had inadvertently promoted was a class-, gender-, and perhaps race-biased one. It implicitly equated political leadership with the movement's public spokespersons. In so doing, it obscured an equally crucial aspect of leadership, that of *network centers,* who were almost all Black women. At Duke, though women and men both took leadership, they did so in different ways. Men were public speakers, representatives, and confrontational negotiators (I will merge these activities and refer to those who do them as *spokespersons* or *spokesmen*). Conventional equations of leading with speaking recognized only spokesmen and missed Black women's key leadership role as what I call *centerwomen.* At Duke, leadership involved mobilizing already existing workplace social networks, as opposed to individuals, around class-conscious or at least job-conscious behavior and values. *Centerpeople,* who were almost all Black women, were key actors in network formation and consciousness shaping, and leadership of the union drive resided in the interaction of *centerwomen* and *spokesmen.* It is the relationship between these two roles that constituted the structure of movement leadership.

Participants often recognized this relationship even when conventional language did not make it easy to express. "Women don't lead . . . but they *do* lead!" was how an official of an already existing service workers' union tried to answer my question. He described a typical union meeting that he had chaired; he had been able to speak freely and make any suggestions he chose, but "nobody had anything to say." It was not until one or more of five or six well-respected women (whom I would call *centerpeople*) commented up or down on something he said that people moved. If these women were silent, so was everyone else, and nothing happened. These were women who had been active in organizing the local from its beginnings and who were as much leaders as was the official. It was the *interaction* of centers and the official that made things happen.

This situation is different from the idea that while men have formal authority, women exercise power informally, or behind the scenes. That formulation tends to focus on the goals, strategies, and impacts of *individuals* and implicitly sees women as having less power than men.[4] My analysis deals with the process of creating collective goals and strategies where speakers and network centers are the leadership that structures an oppositional movement. In such a movement, the usual distinctions between power and authority, or formal and informal power, are not really meaningful. Both power and authority are very limited in any oppositional movement, almost by definition.

WORKPLACE SOCIAL NETWORKS

In the following pages I discuss how workplace networks at Duke Medical Center were created and politicized around unionization and the role centerwomen played in transforming social networks into a political force. These women built and sustained informal social networks among their coworkers at the hospital. The people in these networks shared a family idiom: they celebrated family and life-cycle events and often referred to themselves as "like family." Sometimes individuals referred to particular coworkers as mothers or sisters, indicating a relationship with more widespread mutual obligations. The existence of dense social networks also facilitated sharing a somewhat different kind of family idiom—namely, notions of work, adulthood, responsibility, and conflict mediation that many women had learned in their families. Embedded in the multiple meanings of these concepts were positive values about hospital workers, their work, and their rights. All of these values were in opposition to the messages workers received about themselves from the hospital administration, and these values became a shared language by which workers expressed their union politics. Centerwomen were also important in directly politicizing social networks. Not only did they hold these networks together as social forces, but they also embodied and publicly articulated the oppositional and job-conscious meanings of family values. Furthermore, the centerwomen mediated internal conflicts as part of developing and expressing a movement consensus.

The roots of unionization in particular, and of resistance in general, lie in Duke Hospital workers' everyday social ties and networks and in the efforts of these networks' centerwomen to maintain and mobilize them. In workplace networks there is a tension between accepting working conditions and medical center relations as they are and making organized efforts to improve them. Most workers probably spend most of their time using social ties to make the best of a bad (or less than ideal) situation. Although much of hospital social life is informal, there is also an institutionalized aspect to it involving rituals that stress family and life-cycle events and make use of a familylike set of symbols that cross racial and class lines. Events that are associated with family and "nonwork" are brought into the workplace to join workers in an attempt to overcome (or deny) the things that divide them and to establish a "family" language or framework for workplace unity.

What seems to move workers to keep their jobs, for the most part, is each other. Because the hospital is the largest employer in a fairly small city, many families have several members working there. Predictably, many workers I came to know had several immediate and not-so-immediate kin and in-laws scattered throughout the medical center. For some, the hospital was the place where they had met their closest friends, and it was the center of much of their social lives. Many workers, both Black and white, were born and raised in the town and have ties of kinship, marriage, school, community, and church that are all interwoven. As a result, there are many other workers in the hospital with whom they share at least one set of ties, and often more.

Workplace socializing, social networks, and family ties are complex. People refer to the hospital as a hotbed of gossip, "a little Peyton Place," where everybody knows one anothers' business, and most workers are related. This is not entirely true, since race and class are dividing lines for socializing outside work, but the union drive was certainly an important place where Black and white workers socialized together.

Social ties operate in varied and sometimes contradictory ways. On the one hand, they are sometimes so important that workers seem almost willing to endure miserable working conditions for them. On the other hand, they are sometimes a sort of worker telegraph system, carrying a collective message of protest against unfairness.

The institutionalized aspect of social life lies in the covered-dish lunches, breakfasts, and dinners that are organized for holidays, wedding and baby showers, and farewells. Everybody in a unit is invited and expected to make some contribution in food. Some of these events, especially those around holidays, are initiated—or sponsored—"from above" by the head nurse or the attending physician in charge of the unit. A birthday, shower, or goodbye party is usually set in motion by a close coworker, but these celebrations also involve the unit authorities in planning and permission for time to arrange things, and they become all-unit events. The size and elaborateness of a luncheon—how many people come and what they bring—are indications of other workers' closeness to the person and the closeness of the unit.

In-hospital parties were usually successful in overcoming the racial divisions that were embedded in and exacerbated by systematic job segregation. Because they were located in a shared work space, centered around shared experiences in a unit, such parties used family events and symbols to reinforce commonalities. As a result, they usually joined Black and white, professional, clerical, and service workers, and technicians reasonably comfortably.

When parties, even quasi-official unit Christmas parties, were held in someone's home, class and race lines were not always so easy to cross. Most people felt able to cross one line—either one—but crossing both class and race lines at once was considerably harder. On one hospital ward, all the DTOs (data terminal operators) were Black and all the RNs (registered nurses) were white. The nurses tended to be the organizers of parties and dinners for the ward, in the hospital or in people's homes. DTOs praised the good relations between Black and white workers on their ward. But they also said that the Black workers—DTOs, messengers, housekeeping staff—did not go to the parties outside the hospital even though "they [doctors and nurses] all get after us the next day for not coming." The Christmas party posed a special problem. Every year the Black workers talked among themselves and resolved, "If you go, I'll go," but they never did.

When I asked why, one woman said they were all afraid that they would not fit in outside the hospital and that discovering that they were not welcome would jeopardize the good work relations they had. Another woman contrasted house parties with parties and showers held in the hospital to which everyone went and brought gifts. "Because everyone's here," they belong and do not have to explain themselves. Both these women also indicated that the root of the uneasiness Black workers felt about going to the homes of the nurses lay in the hospital's segregated hiring patterns. One said that if there were more Black nurses, Black workers would be more comfortable in going. They would not have to jump both barriers at once.

As to doctors, the general feeling was that they socialized separately. Most workers indicated that they did not attend events that doctors organized outside the hospital except, one woman said, "Maybe the female ones but not the males." The unspoken consensus was: "We don't go to their parties; they know each other and we don't know them. They get together with their families and wives." In some places, the gulf was between doctors and RNs on one side and everyone else on the other. The doctors people generally spoke about were house staff. They were very much a part of most ward and clinic working communities—but not as equals. Several clinics and wards would have parties when the house staff rotated out. "We bring food for the doctors to show we miss them; we don't eat it; it's for them." But when coworkers bring food for one another, everyone eats.

Although there is variation in the actual amount of in- and out-of-hospital socializing, there are certain forms recognized by all workers at Duke. The potluck for everybody who works in a particular place seems to be a standard event in American workplaces wherever women are concentrated, on standard occasions. Events that are associated with family and "nonwork" are brought into the workplace to establish a familistic language or framework for workplace unity.

This language was of limited help, however, in building bridges across racial lines at Duke. To a great extent this was because of the particular spatial patterns of job segregation. Workers included in the bargaining unit were often in all-Black or all-white departments. The kitchen had a large concentration of Black workers; office secretaries were almost all white and were scattered in tiny offices throughout the medical center. In many racially integrated units the jobs held by white workers were often not part of the bargaining unit. This was the case on wards where mostly Black DTOs and messengers were eligible for the union, but the mainly white RNs (and the mainly Black LPNs, or licensed practical nurses) were not. The union itself was a place where Black and white workers could come together and where many did. But to a great extent it seemed that Black and white workers organized in parallel efforts, even though they shared many of the same symbols and values.

FAMILISTIC LANGUAGE, JOB-CONSCIOUSNESS, AND WORKER MILITANCY

At this point I want to use the notion of *familistic values* in a somewhat new way. I think my usage represents an emerging concept in feminist scholarship that differs from the association of family values with submissive domesticity for women. I want to focus on notions of work, adulthood, and responsibility. Duke women workers first learned these notions in a family context and later used them to form the basis for an oppositional working-class-conscious culture. Social networks became politicized when they mobilized around these oppositional values, and centerwomen were key in forming and politicizing them. These networks provided the structure for several successful walkouts, one of which is described below and all of which helped catalyze the union drive.

Women workers at Duke discussed being a good worker in the hospital in many of the same ways that they discussed becoming a good adult in their family. The links were particularly clear with regard to work, responsibility, respect, and conflict mediation. Underlying particular values was an awareness of the importance of interpersonal skills—a key part of the "invisible skills" that hospital workers are required to exercise but for which they are not compensated. Centerwomen embody and exemplify these skills; this is part of what makes them so good at forming and sustaining work-based networks and in linking them to union organizing.

Familistic symbols and values seem to be the antithesis of confrontation politics or radicalism. Part of the strength of these values lies in their multiple meanings and their ability to bridge racial, gender, and occupational divisions.

Thus, contradictory meanings can be embedded in work-time potlucks and baby showers without causing any conflict. They can reinforce deference or patronage in the workplace hierarchy, but they can also steal back a little social time and invert (at least for the event) the hierarchy of decision making.

Widely shared familistic values and concepts contain oppositional meanings and political potential. For example, the concept *work* carries such varied meanings. Women whom I interviewed discussed their *work*—hospital and household work, child care, and the part-time waged jobs they performed while still in school—in qualitatively similar terms. Neither housework nor hospital work was described as lists of tasks, although that is how job descriptions most often read. Instead, the women workers focused on the responsibility and initiative they took for knowing what needed to be done. In their descriptions, the mental and organizational aspects of work were central. In discussing childhood household responsibilities, several women indicated that the mental and organizational skills involved were rewarded by praise and by additional responsibility. One woman's father told her that she released him from having to worry about whether the house was clean: "If you're around, I know everything's taken care of." She described how she arranged her part-time job, school, and housework and how she threw her brothers and sisters out of the house on Saturday mornings so she could get the cleaning done when she had time. The women focused on the way they arranged their lives so they could do all they had to do and wanted to do.

Thus work, especially the responsibility and decision making involved in its mental organization, is an important part of adulthood. At the hospital, women workers—housekeepers, lab technicians, secretaries, and clerks—stressed the importance of "setting your priorities," of arranging how you were going to accomplish all the goals you had set (within the constraints of the job). They indicated that they had been taught in their families that housework and work for wages shared a key similarity in the mental organization (coordinating things, setting priorities of time and effort) required, and that this was a significant source of pride and a sign of adulthood.

Workers used the term *adult* to mean someone who could take responsibility for meeting commitments and obligations, for making decisions, and for arranging her own life so that she could do what she had to do. The job was a means to, but not a definition of, adulthood. As one woman put it, holding a paid job is a necessary part of being a mother and an independent person. "I have six kids and I'm thirty-six years old. I'm a mom. I'm a housekeeper . . . I'm everything. I just do the things that's natural for my children. And working is one of them . . . working is a part of my job."

In families, however, the relationships among work, responsibility, and adulthood were not always smooth, especially when parents tried to retain responsibility for their children's non-housework decisions. Several women had begun to fear as teenagers that their parents were coming to depend on them too much in terms of work responsibilities but were not willing to allow them to make decisions about their lives that they felt they had demonstrated the capacity to make. Several women had felt that if they remained at home they were going to be given the major responsibility for running the house, but that their parents would continue to make decisions for them about their hours, social time, and friends. Both Black and white women gave these reasons for moving out of the house as soon as they could get a job to support themselves.

As I see it, these women learned in their families that work in the house and work for wages are not qualitatively different, and that the mental organization of both is a most significant source of pride and of adulthood. The rub came when parents were reluctant to yield autonomy in nonwork aspects of their children's lives and when they tried to retain responsibility for their children's decisions.

All the women who spoke of this conflict had resolved it by moving out. Significantly, they all said that there was no bitterness about the move, no break in the relationship; rather that the move made for a positive change. Interviews with mothers of two of these women confirmed the daughters' perceptions. The mothers noted that children were grown when they were able to take responsibility for living on their own. Parents then recognized and reinforced the children's claims to increased adult autonomy. Daughters then went to their mothers for advice—adult to adult—instead of having their minds made up for them. Adulthood was gained as a process rather than as a single event.

Whereas women were able to command adult treatment from their parents by moving out and demonstrating their capacity, the hospital's bureaucratic hierarchy did not allow analogous movement to more responsible jobs. Moreover, workers felt that management's view of their jobs, and by extension of themselves as the people who performed them, was that they were childlike, requiring constant supervision and direction. The hospital's rigid job ranking and minimal opportunities for mobility through the ranks combined to doom most clerical, service, and technical workers to permanent "child" status at work. In the absence of individual opportunities for "adult" recognition, the only alternative was one of collective protest and unionization.

Adulthood and respect are concepts that are closely interrelated and even used interchangeably in many conversations among workers. One becomes an adult by an active process of learning a variety of things ranging from basic skills to how to make a decision and how to create and sustain a variety of interpersonal relations. Women stressed the experiential process more than they did major events (parenthood, jobs). Being an adult means achieving competence in making decisions for oneself and being accorded the right to make such decisions. Those rights need to be respected. Indeed, that seems to be the central meaning of respect: to be accorded the right to make up one's own mind, to plan one's own activities, and to have and express one's own feelings—and not to have feelings, decisions, or beliefs denied, appropriated, or subsumed by a dominant other. In this sense, respect is symmetrical or reciprocal in all adult relationships in that all adults are to be accorded it regardless of their social position.

Black and white women alike said that respect in their families was based simultaneously on *reciprocity* and *hierarchy*. "I never talked back to my father. I did disagree and brought my point up, but not to the point of impudence." "part of Black family teaching is to give respect to elders in your behavior." "I would never walk into my mother's house with so much as a beer." Because of their social relationship, parents and elders have certain rights to establish ground rules and to command services, and some deference, from their children. All adults are to be accorded respect by all other adults (as well as by children) regardless of their social position. Children are also to be accorded respect in particular areas of their lives as they grow toward being able to take responsibilities and fulfill commitments. "Children are expected to make decisions, rather than parents imposing them." One woman explained how yelling at a child was not good. She pointed out that her son had said this was part of child abuse. He was "disappointed more than scared. It makes him mad—maybe the same way as being yelled at on the job—it's demeaning."

At work DTOs, secretaries, clerks, lab technicians, and housekeepers were prepared to work for and to grant people prerogatives they felt were due to their place in the job hierarchy, but they were equally insistent on their rights as adults. These included the right and expectation that they would organize their work on their own, would "assign their own priorities" (a phrase that cropped up often), and would not be watched and directed. In this reciprocal sense, respect was a recognition of adulthood and the competence it connoted.[5]

Data terminal operators were particularly eloquent about their need to teach doctors and nurses to treat them as adults: "I'm an adult; I'm grown. If you can't speak to me without yelling, don't speak to me at all." One DTO described difficulties she had had with a nurse who had spoken to her as if she were "dirt" when she had first arrived. The DTO had responded to this public criticism by insisting on discussing it with the nurse in the back room together with another DTO. She emphasized that a public fight or criticism was both embarrassing and demeaning. This type of approach cuts through barriers of hierarchy and authority. Holding fast to status prerogatives can make it almost impossible to solve problems and resolve conflicts so that people can continue working together. Almost all DTOs, as well as many other clerical and service workers, told some version of the following story: "When I first came I really had trouble with doctors [or supervisors, administrators, or nurses], and I had to set them straight. Now they know their limits and we get along fine."

When workers (male and female) complained that they were not being treated with respect on the job, they were insisting on their right to make decisions about how they would work and about the part that their work would play in their lives—basic adult perogatives. As we will see below, in both a 1974 walkout by DTOs and in the union drive, workers placed this familistic and reciprocal demand for "respect" high on their list. One DTO, in summing up the victories of the walkout, noted, "We got respect. You know how doctors throw charts? Now they can't."

Another familistic practice transported to and transformed in the work place is *conflict mediation*. Many clerical workers have a particularly difficult job in that they need to coordinate the activities of people who are above them in the hospital's pecking order. Some of the latter—notably doctors—seem to operate by an informal code that it is acceptable for a superior to criticize a subordinate publicly but not vice versa. This contradicts the reciprocal notion of respect shared among the workers.

One clerical worker described how she learned the difference between the right and wrong ways to deal with interpersonal conflict. When she was new at the hospital, there was a doctor with whom she could not get along. Their daily arguments upset her and resolved nothing. Looking back, she realized that the doctor was wrong to pick a fight in public but that instead of responding in kind she should have taught him how to behave. To do that, you "take them in the back room and argue it out one on one." She stressed how important it was to insist, calmly, on correct and considerate behavior even in small things and to have a sense of humor. She illustrated her meaning by describing one doctor who was in the habit of dumping a mixture of charts, with and without written orders, into her in-box. This created extra work for her because she had to search all the charts for orders. She told him this, and he grudgingly separated them, saying, "You want anything else?" She answered, "Yes, I'd like a cup of coffee." In this case she had explained the consequences of the doctor's actions for her workload and had done so without anger. The doctor's response was ambivalent: he accepted the correction but resisted being criticized by someone below him. The DTO then used humor to upset the status relationship and to reinforce the positive, coworker aspect of the doctor's response. That gave him both reason and reinforcement to act as a coworker. He got her the coffee.

All these familistic understandings are at loggerheads with job classifications and descriptions that distinguish mental from manual labor and almost deny that service and clerical workers need to use their heads. Women's familistic interpretations have the potential to counter management notions of work with a sophisticated understanding of the planning and coordinating needed to carry out waged work and housework alike. Not surprisingly, many workers consider close supervision and assemblyline pacing demeaning as well as exploitative in that they are thereby robbed of adult decision-making prerogatives. Here, too, familistic values challenge management notions of economic rationality, and in that respect operate as a language used by women for creating an oppositional worker consciousness. Centerwomen are structurally important for sustaining perspectives and values that are simultaneously working-class-conscious and familistic. These values affirm the worth of women workers and the work they do, provide an oppositional language to hospital management, and lend support for militant activities.

NETWORKS AND PROTEST

Efforts to unionize Duke Hospital workers began in 1974, stimulated by a very strong walkout of DTOs in the spring of that year. Their job action showed the importance of workplace networks mobilized around oppositional familistic values. Many of the DTOs involved in the walkout had come to Duke as part of a high school cohort who were active in and beneficiaries of struggles by Durham's freedom movement in this politically active city. Many of the DTOs from Durham's Black community shared ties of school, church, neighborhood, and kinship with other hospital workers.

The hospital's system of work organization determined which of the many potential ties were developed and deepened, and which were not. Many DTOs made their closest friends at the hospital, from among the DTOs and LPNs with whom they worked. People at the hospital tend to tell friends and relatives about job openings and to recommend them, so that ties of kinship, work, and friendship reinforce one another. Most workers agree that friendships come from or are deepened at work. In short, one brings family and family values to work, and one creates family and re-creates family values at work.

In 1974, the hospital's lines of work organization established close contact between DTOs within a unit or between paired wards, so that those on all shifts within a unit were in daily communication. Informal social networks reinforced these lines of communication, with DTOs and nurses (mainly LPNs, but also RNs) getting together for holiday parties, informal cookouts, picnics, and dinners throughout the year. In fostering friendships unit lines seemed more important than physical proximity in the hospital. Indeed, DTOs on a ward of one service, such as medicine or surgery, could not think of any DTOs they knew on a ward of another service. Likewise, adjacent wards of the same service under different unit supervison had little day-to-day contact.

Until about 1979 most training of new DTOs was done on the wards and was the direct responsibility of senior DTOs. As these women taught new workers their definition of the job and its worth, they also created new ties between trainer and trainee. Along with these ties a consciousness of themselves as responsible adults was also transmitted to the trainees and of their right to insist on decent pay and adult treatment and to stress cooperation over domination and subordination.

Organization "from below" among DTOs who knew each other from non-hospital contexts brought together different units and services. The core network in 1974 seemed to be the cohort hired between 1968 and 1971. They were concentrated in the two largest services, medicine and surgery. This network included almost weekly out-of-hospital socializing among mainly single DTOs and nurses on several wards of both services.

Each of these data terminal operators was also part of some kind of network on her unit. Thus, two surgery DTOs from this core group, together with several others on their unit, acted as centerwomen for holding meetings and informing those on their wards of events. Those who missed meetings checked in with the two "core network" DTOs. Another DTO from the core network who worked nights tried to bring the news to people on that shift.

Services other than the two largest were less involved in the walkout. To the extent that people from these services joined it, they seem to have been connected to people in the core by ties of kinship, friendship, or neighborhood. Some from one small service stayed out not only because of the general issues but also because their friends from the core group expected them to. On the services where friendship and social networks were most dense and the bases of trust and communication most secure, participation in the walkout was highest and fear of retribution was lowest.

CENTERWOMEN AND NETWORKS

In the early 1970s, Beverly Jones became active in the Black liberation movement, spent some three years working at a hospital job up North, and spoke on East Coast college campuses. She moved to Durham specifically to work on the Duke Medical Center union drive. She applied for a job as a DTO at Duke several months after the walkout to help organize the union. As soon as she finished her probationary period, she publicly identified herself to management as well as to her coworkers as a union organizer. She became a member of the organizing committee and a centerwoman, the latter in part from personal and political predilections and in part because the male political leadership of the drive did not give her public speaking assignments.

As Jones analyzed it, being a political activist and an organizer encouraged her to think in group terms. Her assignment, to sign people up for the union, meant "I talked to everybody. That was fun work!" As an activist, she gravitated toward the group of militant DTOs from Durham who had been at the center of the walkout. Even today, some members of this group list Jones as a member of their high school cohort.

Beverly Jones utilized traditional hospital activities as part of her network building and union organizing. For example, she gave a goodbye party at her house for a DTO who was leaving Duke. From that point on, DTOs began getting together for dinner every two weeks, and Jones was instrumental in keeping them going. Dinners and other social events have kept the group together for some five years. This particular network joins DTOs on all four wards of a unit and has expanded from time to time to cover larger numbers of DTOs and nurses. It has managed to remain intact through factionalizing and years of political inactivity.

Most DTOs who were also active in the union drive described the political cohesiveness, pro-union strength, and intense social networks that sustained them as having their roots in the walkout. As networks in the kitchen, in outpatient areas, and in other areas mobilized politically in the course of the drive, the social density and political intensity of each increased, particularly where key people were members of the organizing committee. Centerwomen in such work-based networks exemplified family values and reinforced them by their actions. Their initiatives in setting up social groups and activities were important parts of the process by which coworkers "become family" and were able to teach and enforce familistic values in the workplace.

For centerwomen especially, among the most important family-rooted values are these interpersonal skills of mediating, resolving conflicts by reconciliation, and providing emotional support and advice. These are required but uncompensated skills in many clerical and nursing jobs and in creating and sustaining good relations and solidarity among coworkers. Some women are more highly skilled than others. Some seem to have developed these skills in their families; others learned a great deal from their coworkers and from the informal work culture that affirms and teaches them.

Centerwomen also embody these familistic skills and values of work, adulthood, and respect, and reinforce them by their behavior and actions. Most of centerpeople in the workplace networks I observed seemed also to be centerpeople (or to have been trained for such a role) in their family networks. The role involves keeping people together, ensuring that obligations are fulfilled, and acting to express the group consensus. From family interviews and participation in DTO and union activist families, it appears that hospital centerwomen were also trained to be centers in their families but often practiced the role first at work. Most described particularly close relationships in their childhoods with the family center—usually a grandmother, aunt, or mother.[6]

Centerwomen, however, act in ways that are not commonly perceived as leadership methods. They have a great deal of responsibility but little authority. One centerwomen put it succinctly: "I'm usually the one to initiate anything. People say, 'Jones, why don't we do this?' And they wait for me to do it." But it is a dialectical relationship. If you take initiatives, people check in with you to find out what you and others think, to find out what is happening. Part of checking in then involves suggestions and expectations that are placed on centerpeople but also given by them. Because they are at the center, they are at once repositories of others' opinions and keepers and shapers of the consensus. Although this gives them a certain latitude, they are also constrained by the limits of consensus.

The ability to mediate and resolve conflicts by reconciliation and to provide emotional support and advice are skills that the women I interviewed brought up frequently and valued highly. To be able to do these things was a reflection of being able to demand and give respect. This was something that was learned in families and in informal on-the-job training. Centerpeople were particularly adept and were called upon to mediate either directly or indirectly; the skill involved the ability to resolve a conflict in a way that did not demean either party.

GENDER-LINKING AND ROLE-COMPATIBILITY

The way hospital jobs were allocated by gender and race reinforced the gender differences in how men and women exercised leadership in the union drive. Women made up almost all of the "invisible administrators"—the office secretaries and DTOs, receptionists and nurses—whose work, like that of centerwomen, depended heavily on their skills in smoothing conflicts, coordinating, and compromising, and whose jobs fixed them firmly in one locale. Black men tended to have jobs that took them all over the medical center, transporting patients and supplies; there were very few white men in jobs that would be in the union. Two leading spokesmen chose such mobile jobs precisely for their organizing potential. Their mobility not only put them in contact with many workers but also embedded them less in a fixed, face-to-face work group. Still, gender-linking of leadership roles also seemed to arise partly from an unchallenged sexism. In any event, sexist attitudes and occupational segregation seem to have reinforced each other.

Both as invisible administrators and as network centers, women were encouraged to develop skills and strategies for conflict resolution that were incompatible with the goals and tactics of confrontation. Both strategies are needed in different contexts. Centerwomen do negotiate with supervisors and administrators with and on behalf of coworkers, but if they do not prevail by forceful persuasion, confrontational negotiation may be necessary, and they tend to seek out spokesmen. Though the particular headset and values embodied in persuasion and sustaining cordial relations conflict with the demands of confrontation, it is important to stress that this did not hold workers back from confronting Duke Medical Center management. Quite the reverse, but centerwomen were at their best in a group; it was solo performances that seemed to be risky. Solidarity underlay worker militance and the workers' ability to confront hospital administrators directly. It made possible petitions and walkouts by dietary workers over work schedules and job duties, by housekeepers over the addition of new duties, and by DTOs over pay, scheduling, and supervision, as well as strong union rallies and well-attended social events.

When conflicts among workers led to confrontations within the ranks of prounion workers, the consensus upon which their militant solidarity rested was severely threatened. This is what seems to have happened when two leftwing groups involved in the movement began to attack each other publicly in the midst of the union drive. Several centerwomen and union activists I interviewed described the fighting as something they did not want to deal with, either at the time or in retrospect. Faction lines cut across networks and affected both men and women. These antagonisms confronted centerwomen with conflicting expectations and demands from friends on different sides of the fence, all of whom wanted harmony—on their own terms. Because their role stressed finding and expressing a consensus, some of the most activist women found themselves immobilized—and furious at the situation. One ex-centerwoman, in explaining why she had opted out, noted, "This way I don't need to entertain, to see that no one's feathers get ruffled, to keep the relationship going." Her complaint about the role was: "I find myself always in the middle of ten thousand different people who don't like one another pulling at me."

To be a center is to be empowered by resistance efforts embedded in a shared work culture and values. Thus, when one DTO analyzed whether or when DTOs as a group might mobilize around a particular grievance, she named several centerwomen and said, "If they complained, others would follow suit." On the other hand, centerwomen seem also to be constrained to stay within hearing distance of network opinions and within limits of a manageable consensus because their authority lies in expressing that consensus.

The role of spokesperson actually has several aspects that I have merged in the process of highlighting centerpeople. In the company of workers, spokespeople express workers' views and demands in large meetings designed as public confrontations with management. Here they act as confrontational negotiators representing the workers. With a change in setting, the negotiator is replaced by the workers' advocate—someone who is for the workers but not of them. When spokespeople negotiate without the company of workers, in small meetings with management, the pressure increases for them to bargain and to mediate. No one is there to give them strength and leverage. Likewise, when they deal with the media or outsiders, the context encourages their role of speaking for workers rather than of being part of a leadership process involving interaction with networks and network centers. To the extent that centerpeople are detached from this structure, they are vulnerable to becoming mediators among groups rather than part of the group of workers. By speaking out publicly one becomes visible to management, and Duke regularly offered visible activists promotions to supervisory positions. Workers were aware that this was a divide-and-rule strategy on management's part, just as they were aware that job qualifications were structured so that becoming management was often the only avenue for promotion. More common were situations where visible people were persuaded to act as brokers, to become intermediaries between management and workers, ostensibly on behalf of the workers. Several women were particularly consistent in their opposition to workers' agreeing to "straddle the fence," as one of them put it.

These concomitants of the spokesperson role appeared to be particularly threatening to centerwomen. Women activists seemed less fearful of punishment than of becoming conspicuous to other workers and perhaps vulnerable to management bribes—perhaps becoming a broker between groups rather than a representative of their own. People who are firmly embedded in workplace networks face considerable peer constraint. Centerwomen's fear of "saying something wrong" may have been a fear of contextual pressure to speak like a broker, which derived in part from a sense that they did not have the experience in walking the tightrope of confrontational negotiation that was part of being an effective spokesperson.

CONCLUSION

The leadership of the union drive at Duke Medical Center was based on a mutually reinforcing dynamic between centerwomen and spokesmen. Centerwomen created and sustained social networks and mobilized them around a militant work culture. That culture validated their view of their work and its worth through a consensus language based on "familistic values"—namely, a notion of adulthood and responsibility conceptualized in family terms and contexts. These values capture concretely the unity or continuity between family and work that feminist scholarship is seeking. To recognize this structure of leadership, and to expand the term *leadership* to encompass it is to make the invisible visible. It valorizes some of the important ways in which women have exerted leadership and moves beyond equating oratory with leadership.

I have tried to show here that looking at grassroots leadership through women's eyes leads us to a fairly fundamental re-vision of political conduct, one that redefines both the categories for studying political structures and the dynamics of activism. This is central for feminists and anyone else who would understand and further grassroots and transformative politics.

Analytically, it is important to recognize that centers and speakers are *functions* or *dimensions* of leadership, and hence separate issues from *who carries them out*. Experience at Duke University Medical Center raises, but does not answer the question, can one person be both a spokesperson and a centerperson? Do these functions necessarily pull an individual in opposite directions? Also—a thornier issue—are these roles necessarily gender-linked as *spokesman* and *centerwoman?* One ought not assume that either role must be gender-specific or that these roles require different people. After all, neither organizers nor analysts know very much about the structure and dynamics of informal work organization or about the dynamics of grassroots political activism. I would suggest that part of the remedy lies in applying feminist perspectives to the analysis of male shop-floor culture and grassroots leadership. Such an endeavor, or even a re-analysis of the literature on male work culture, might reveal center*men* and a form of resistance similar to that found among Duke Hospital women. A feminist perspective that looks at links between work, family, and political action, may be valuable for understanding the dynamics of men's activism as well as that of women.

ACKNOWLEDGMENTS
Research for this paper was supported by a National Sciences Foundation grant and a National Institutes of Mental Health postdoctoral fellowship at the Center for the Study of the Family and the State at Duke University. For a more extended discussion of hospital worker organizing, see my book *Caring by the Hour: Women, Work and Organizing at Duke Medical Center* (Urbana: University of Illinois Press, 1987).

NOTES
1. P. Giddings, *When and Where I Enter* (New York: Bantam, 1985); bell hooks, *Ain't I a Woman* (Boston: South End Press, 1981); B. Neugarten, "Interpretive Social Science and Research on Aging," in A. S. Rossi, ed., *Gender and the Life Course* (Chicago: Aldine), 291–300; P. Rabinow and M. Sullivan, eds., *Interpretive Social Science: A Reader* (Berkeley: University of California Press, 1979); T. Roszak, *The Making of a Counter Culture* (New York: Doubleday, 1969); J. Ladner, ed., *The Death of White*

Sociology (New York: Vintage, 1973); H. Eisenstein, *Contemporary Feminist Thought* (Boston: G. K. Hall, 1983).

2. A. Cameron, "Bread and Roses Revisited: Women's Culture and Working-Class Activism in the Lawrence Strike of 1912," in R. Milkman, ed., *Women, Work and Protest* (Boston: Routledge & Kegan Paul, 1985), 42–61; Mina D. Caulfield, "Imperialism, Family and Cultures of Resistance," *Socialist Revolution* 20 (1974): 67–85; Cynthia B. Costello, "WEA're Worth It: Women's Work Culture and Conflict at the Wisconsin Education Association Insurance Trust," *Feminist Studies* 11, No. 3 (1985): 497–518, which appears as Chapter 5 here; K. Day, "Kinship in a Changing Economy: A View from the Sea Islands," in C. Stack and R. Hall, eds., *Holding onto the Land and the Lord* (Athens: University of Georgia Press, 1982); R. Goldberg, *Organizing Women Office Workers: Dissatisfaction, Consciousness, and Action* (New York: Praeger, 1983); T. Kaplan, "Female Consciousness and Collective Action," *Signs* 7 (1982): 545–566; Ladner, *The Death of White Sociology;* L. Lamphere, "On the Shop Floor: Multi-Ethnic Unity Against the Conglomerate," in K. Sacks and D. Remy, eds., *My Troubles Are Going to Have Trouble with Me* (New Brunswick, N.J.: Rutgers University Press, 1984), 247–263; B. Melosh, *"The Physician's Hand": Work Culture and Conflict in American Nursing* (Temple University Press, 1982); R. Rapp, "Family and Class in Contemporary America," *Science and Society* 42 (1978): 278–300; S. Rowbotham, *Women, Resistance and Revolution* (New York: Pantheon, 1973); C. Stack, *All Our Kin* (New York: Harper Colophon, 1974); M. Tax, *The Rising of the Women: Feminist Solidarity and Class Conflict, 1880–1917* (New York: Monthly Review Press, 1981); L. Tilly, "Paths of Proletarianization: Organization of Production, Sexual Division of Labor, and Women's Collective Action," *Signs* 7 (1981): 400–417; S. Westwood, *All Day Every Day: Factory and Family in the Making of Women's Lives* (Urbana: University of Illinois Press, 1985).

3. See Sacks, "Computers, Ward Secretaries and a Walkout in a Southern Hospital," in Sacks and Remy, eds., *My Troubles,* 173–192, for a discussion of these issues.

4. See J. Collier, "Women in Politics," in M. Rosaldo and L. Lamphere, eds., *Woman, Culture and Society* (Stanford: Stanford University Press, 1974), 89–96; and L. Lamphere, "Strategies, Cooperation, and Conflict Among Women in Domestic Groups," ibid., 97–112; for analysis of women's tactics and strategies for exercising informal political power.

5. See C. Barrow, "Reputation and Ranking in a Barbadian Locality," *Social and Economic Studies* 25 (1976): 106–121, for a similar discussion of respect in Barbados.

6. See Sacks, *Caring by the Hour,* passim, for a fuller discussion.

GENDER AND THE SHAPING OF

WOMEN'S POLITICAL

CONSCIOUSNESS

4

"It's the Whole Power of the City Against Us!": The Development of Political Consciousness in a Women's Health Care Coalition

Sandra Morgen

The literature on working-class resistance in the United States has focused primarily on the labor activism of working-class men. A focal theoretical concern of this literature had been the explanation of the relative quiescence of the American working class. In the past decade feminist scholars, as well as social and labor historians, have unearthed a rich history of working-class political activism by looking beyond white male trade unionism to explore a wider range of political activities, including women's community activism. Nevertheless, political activity outside the workplace or the electoral arena, particularly women's political activism, still remains peripheral to the historical record and to theories of working-class political life.

The tendency to privilege male political activity and labor activism together contribute to the relative neglect of women's community-based collective action. Similar assumptions mask the importance of women's and community-based activism. Community organization is often seen primarily in terms of its *local* character and women's collective action is viewed as a political extension of *family* rather than, for example, class concerns. I argue that both of these conceptualizations are narrow and obscure the ways that the political economy of capitalism engenders and shapes resistance outside the workplace. Neither community organizing as a form of collective political action nor women's activism fit neatly into either Marxist or traditional frameworks for the analysis of political mobilization. Taking women and community organization seriously involves challenging the presumed theoretical primacy of the social relations of production (over the social relations of reproduction and consumption) and of class (over gender, race, and ethnicity).

97

Here I examine a nine-month campaign waged by a cross-class, multiracial coalition of women in response to a local hospital's closing of outpatient gynecological and prenatal clinics for low-income women. I explore the development of women's political consciousness over the course of the campaign. On the basis of that analysis, I suggest that working-class women's community-based political activism calls into question fundamental assumptions about the importance of different forms of political action and the nature of women's political experience.

OVERVIEW

In the summer of 1977 the major local hospital in a city of one hundred thousand in New England closed its outpatient prenatal and gynecology clinics. These clinics, like the eight or so other clinics that were not closed, featured a sliding-scale fee schedule (based on ability to pay), making health care accessible to low-income women. The decision to close the clinics was a joint decision of the hospital and the ten white male obstetrician–gynecologists (ob/gyns) in the city who had staffed the clinics on a rotating basis for many years. Alternative options for prenatal or gynecological care were limited in this community. In the absence of the clinics women could receive care from private doctors—general practitioners, or these ten ob/gyns, who were organized into two group practices located in the same building. Or they could use a local feminist health clinic (services limited to family planning and the most routine gynecology, with a physician on staff only three to eight hours a week), or, obtain contraception from the family planning clinic at the hospital.

"Fleetport," as I call it here, is distinguished by higher than average state and national rates of unemployment and poverty, large minority and elderly populations, considerable ethnic diversity, and a half-century of economic decline with the erosion of the city's industrial base.[1] The 1980 census reported that 49 percent of women over sixteen years of age were in the labor force, 20 percent of families were female-headed, and the mean household income for a female-headed household was about $9,500, one-third less than for a male-headed household. The socioeconomic characteristics of the community[2] suggest a compelling need for low-cost health care, and the pattern of attendance at the prenatal and gynecology clinics before the decision to terminate clinic services confirmed that the services were needed and widely used.

Soon after the clinics were closed, several members of the feminist health clinic, myself included, met with concerned representatives from a number of social service agencies in the town for the purpose of planning a community meeting to mobilize clinic users and supporters to pressure the hospital into keeping the clinics open. Almost fifty people attended that meeting, most of whom had been clinic users. They formed an organization I'll call here "Citizen Action for Health" (CAFH) and delineated the following goals: the reopening and improvement of the prenatal and gynecology clinics and representation of low-income people on the hospital board of trustees.

I was the only person from the group that had planned the original meeting to continue to be actively involved in CAFH. At the time of my involvement I was a participant–observer in the local feminist health clinic,[3] pursuing research on the women's health movement. I became an active member of CAFH, participating as both an activist and a researcher, functioning like any other member of the organization in terms of decision making, group actions, and public visibility.

Over the next eight months the group pursued a wide variety of tactics designed to win the reopening of the clinics. These included public meetings, pickets and demonstrations at the hospital, a petition campaign, meeting with the hospital board of trustees, taking their concerns to the local council of the Health Systems Agency (HSA),[4] conducting a survey of patients utilizing the private practices of the obstetrician–gynecologists, and filing a "Ten Taxpayers" suit[5] against the hospital. In the end, the hospital reopened the prenatal clinic, and the HSA convened a task force to develop a proposal for a neighborhood health center to provide affordable, comprehensive community-based health care in Fleetport. This neighborhood health center was established within two years. The campaign represents an example of successful community organizing by a coalition of working- and middle-class women from diverse racial and ethnic backgrounds.

CAFH AND ITS MEMBERSHIP

CAFH was a cross-class, multiracial women's community organization with a fluid membership that fluctuated over ten months from a low of seven to a high of thirty women attending its (generally biweekly) meetings. The women who formed the core of CAFH ranged in age from the early twenties through the late fifties. Although the group was predominantly white, Black women, particularly Cape Verdean women, participated actively in the coalition as both members and leaders. More than half of the white women were of Portuguese descent, including several first-generation immigrants from Portugal or the Azores. Working-class women—employed and unemployed factory workers and service workers, and students—constituted the core of the group throughout most of the campaign. The professional women in CAFH were a lawyer, a nurse, a social worker, and I. A substantial portion of the group was made up of single parents.

CAFH membership reflected in broad terms the population of women who had used the hospital clinics. The two largest groups of clinic users were Medicaid recipients (60 percent of the clinic users) and low-income women with no health insurance.[6] The dependence on clinic services of the working poor and unemployed women on welfare was conditioned by low wages, high unemployment, and underemployment for the city's women and minorities. In particular, Black, Hispanic, and immigrant women faced the bleakest of economic options as they experienced the combined effects of gender, ethnic, and racial discrimination.[7]

Joining CAFH was for most participants their first engagement in community-based political activism. During much of the campaign a mother and daughter played leading roles in the organization. Jean Alves (all names are pseudonyms), a working-class woman of Portuguese descent, was a widow in her early forties. For years she had been employed as a stitcher, but she had been laid off several months before the clinics were closed. At some of her jobs she had been a union member, but she said that she had never been actively involved in any other political organization. She once mentioned having been contacted by a neighbor who was organizing a block association and said she had felt "suspicious" and had refused to join.

Her daughter Pam Alves was twenty-two and had been a clinic user before and since the birth of her three-year-old daughter. Pam was receiving Aid to Families with Dependent Children (AFDC) at the time of the campaign and planned to be married within several months. She joined CAFH and became a public spokesperson because of her own experience of the consequences of the clinic closings:

> With the clinic closed, I won't go to a doctor if I can't afford it. At the clinic I didn't have to get and pay a babysitter. The best thing was having them willing to babysit there. You could get everything done in one place—x rays, prescriptions too. There was a social worker and a nutritionist [from the Women, Infant and Children (WIC) program] there. They treated you like people. You were a person there.

Among the other women who formed the core of CAFH were Carol Barros, a young, recently married Cape Verdean woman who had not found a job since graduating from a nearby regional state university; Joanne Conway, a white nursing student; Rose Olivera, a recently divorced Portuguese immigrant raising her young son on AFDC; Joy Neto, a young Portuguese woman raising her two-year-old son and attending the regional university on a Pell grant; Chris Rosa, a Cape Verdean college student; and Fay Stein, currently employed at an electronics factory as part of the organizing committee for a union.

THE CAMPAIGN TO REOPEN THE CLINICS

At the founding meeting of CAFH, the group developed plans for a public meeting with the doctors and the hospital administrators responsible for the decision to close the clinics. They planned to present their demands for reopening and improving the prenatal and gynecology clinics and an additional demand that low-income people be appointed to the hospital board of trustees to represent the needs and perspectives of poor and working people in the community. Leaflets were distributed across the city depicting a woman driven to her knees by a burden of health-care costs, deploring the clinic closings "without input from the community" and charging the hospital with forgetting "its responsibility to the working women of the city."

At the public meeting one month after the initial meeting, more than 150 angry people (mostly women) confronted four of the doctors and a hospital representative with their demands. Women who had been clinic users explained their reasons for supporting the reopening of the clinics. The sliding-scale fees made health care "affordable and dignified," according to one supporter. Others spoke of the importance they attached to having all the necessary services in one location (doctors, laboratory, pharmacy, x rays, social workers), reducing the time, transportation, and inconvenience involved in getting health care. The "relaxed atmosphere" of the clinics was counterposed to treatment in the physicians' private offices. Clinic users testified to looking after each other's children during appointments at the clinic so that patients felt comfortable bringing children with them, obviating the need for child care. Over and over, clinic users reported that they felt that the non-physician clinic staff—all women—"treated us like real people." In the words of one woman, "We aren't second-class citizens at the clinics like we are for private doctors."

At the meeting the doctors and the hospital representative refused to grant CAFH's demands and angered the assembled crowd with their opinions about the "inability of consumers to judge what is quality health care." One doctor promised that they would "never respond to demands," and the doctors refused to set up a sliding-fee schedule for their private practices, promising instead to arrange payment plans for individuals who needed extra time to pay their bills. The hospital representative echoed the doctors' views that the closing of the clinics would result in higher-quality care through the doctors' private practices and rationalized the decision as a "cost-containment strategy" aimed at ending the "duplication of services" between the clinics and private medical care.

After asking the health professionals to leave the meeting, the group decided to stage a demonstration at the hospital and initiate a communitywide petition campaign. Fifteen new women joined CAFH and helped organize these activities. Two days later 125 people staged a demonstration at the hospital, and CAFH demanded a meeting with the hospital board of trustees. The chairman of the board responded that this issue should be taken up with the local council of the Health Systems Agency (HSA, a federally mandated mechanism for joint consumer and professional planning of health care) and refused to meet with CAFH until the HSA had considered the matter.

CAFH members went to the next meeting of the HSA and, after pleading their case, won the formation of a six-member HSA task force to investigate the impact of the clinic closings. A wealthy female attorney from a prominent Fleetport family was named as its chair. Several weeks later the HSA held a fact-finding meeting, inviting representatives from the community, social services, the doctors, and the hospital to speak. After the meeting they promised to issue a report "soon."

CAFH members were dissatisfied with the fact-finding hearing and once again demanded to speak to the hospital board. They were granted a twenty-minute appearance and instructed to send no more than four representatives.

CAFH organized a demonstration outside the hospital during this meeting, which drew almost a hundred supporters. The four CAFH representatives spoke briefly to the board and were immediately shuffled out of the room. The board refused to respond to any of their demands. Once outside the women spoke to the crowd. Angry that the local press had declined to cover the demonstration or attend a press conference, the group decided to go to the newspaper office; they staged a rally inside the newsroom demanding (and receiving) press coverage of CAFH's actions and concerns.

Over the next month CAFH members circulated petitions in the community, gathering more than two thousand names in support of their demands; organized fundraising events and the writing of letters to hospital board members; visited other community organizations and local radio shows to solicit support; and completed research on the backgrounds of members of the hospital board.

In early January, four months after the formation of CAFH and two months after the HSA fact-finding hearing, the head of the HSA task force informed CAFH that the HSA report was ready. She said, however, that the report would not be made public because she had given "her personal word" to the doctors and the hospital that they could have one month to consider the findings first. CAFH members were infuriated. At the next HSA meeting they protested "closed door decision making." Several days later they staged a small demonstration to protest the action of the task force.

In the course of what they saw as protracted inaction, CAFH began to plan a public hearing to mark the six-month anniversary of the clinic closings. They initiated a survey outside the office of the ten ob/gyns to elicit patient attitudes toward the closing of the clinics and opinions whether adequate arrangements were being made for patients unable to pay for private services. More than three hundred women were surveyed over the next month. In the meantime, a lawyer in CAFH advised the group to file a "Ten Taxpayers" suit to prevent the hospital's inaugurating a major capital improvements campaign on the grounds that the hospital was refusing to act in the best interests of the community. CAFH did file this procedural suit as a means of pressuring the hospital to accede to its demands and also as a means of gaining information about the clinics that the hospital had consistently refused to release throughout the campaign.

The "Ten Taxpayers" suit became more time-consuming than anticipated and entangled CAFH in legalistic, bureaucratic tasks to the increasing exclusion of grassroots activity. CAFH members, particularly working-class members, complained that meetings had become "alienating" and "boring," more like "classes with all the big words and abbreviations," as a result of the legal strategy. In the context of group demoralization over the suit and the lengthy campaign, a decision was made to postpone the six-month hearing and to await the release of the HSA report scheduled for late February.

Three days before the HSA meeting at which the task force report was to be publicly released, an article appeared in the local newspaper announcing the reopening of the prenatal clinic because, "The hospital and the physicians, despite great harassment, have on their own felt the needs of the indigent patients. . . ." CAFH members were furious that their role in the campaign was not acknowledged and they were concerned about a number of provisions of the clinic's reopening, including the plan to restrict clinic use to women without any form of third-party payments. This would mean that Medicaid recipients, who had been active in the campaign to reopen the clinics and who had made up more than half of the clinic population before the closings, would be refused admittance to the clinic. Other improvements the group had sought, such as the hiring of Portuguese and Spanish translators and multilingual outreach for the clinics, were not addressed. Nor did the hospital agree to place a representative of low-income families on its board.

Over the next two months CAFH continued to organize around these issues. The group discussed plans to become an ongoing women's health advocacy group. However, in the last several months of the campaign many of the active working-class members of the group, demoralized and dissatisfied with the direction CAFH had taken (in the "Ten Taxpayers" suit), had left. The undermining of CAFH's victory by the hospital, the doctors, and the HSA served so to demoralize most of CAFH's present and past members that, despite their successful political mobilization, they disbanded the group.

DEVELOPMENT OF POLITICAL CONSCIOUSNESS IN THE CAMPAIGN
Accounts of resistance often focus on how particular historical and material conditions shape the contours of resistance by conditioning the constitution of groups that experience particular forms of oppression, fostering a political consciousness that leads to activism. All too often, however, these analyses fail to examine how the events and conditions of the struggle itself, and the social construction of political meaning by the participants, affect the development of political consciousness and the choices of political action. I begin from the premise, common to both Marxist and feminist scholarship, that consciousness is dialectically related to social being. It is an approach grounded in history that begins from an appreciation of the relationship between material conditions and ideas, situating consciousness in the "confluence of ideology, social reality, and feeling."[8] My focus is on the development of political consciousness as it is shaped by and expressed within political struggle. In the following pages, I explore how the meaning of specific events for members of CAFH reveals the group's evolving understanding of the social relations of power, particularly of class and gender, as the group confronted the physicians, the hospital administration and board, the HSA, and the local media.

In analyzing the construction of political meaning in a campaign, it is important to understand how ideology informs the active interpretation of experience. Drawing on the work of Sarah Eisenstein, I examine the *process* by which ideologies, history, and material circumstances are interpreted and actively "negotiated" by women in their efforts to comprehend and change the conditions of their lives.[9] In my view, this process entails both the recognition of dominant and oppositional ideologies as they structure consciousness and the explication of the process by which hegemonic ideas are challenged, eroded, or reinforced in a particular historical context. The Fleetport case affords the opportunity to examine the processes of contestation and hegemony.[10]

A distinguishing characteristic of community organization is the relative difficulty (compared to labor organization) of disentangling the social relations of power as these shape and affect a particular campaign. An important feature of the campaign in Fleetport as it evolved over time was the ideological clash over the definition of the very social relations that defined the issues of power and responsibility for health care decision making.

From the first statement they made at the public meeting, the doctors and the hospital administrator cast the issue as one between "providers" and "consumers" of health care. In addition, the doctors set the terms of the relationship between these two groups with the assertion of professional dominance. The first response by a physician to CAFH's stated demands was, "I will not respond to demands, arguments, sneering, or being told what to do." Another doctor reiterated this position tersely: "I, as a provider, will never respond to a demand." The doctors responded to the women's expressed preference for clinic over private care with statements such as, "You are not a judge of quality care. You don't know what quality care is." When women pointed out that the closing of the clinics meant their loss of sliding-scale fees and ancillary services, one doctor's response was, "That's a sacrifice you ladies are just going to have to make." This statement underscored the denial of both the legitimacy and the power of consumers in health care decision making.

After making these statements, the health professionals were asked to leave the meeting, and the large gathering of women expressed its outrage about the "callous," "disrespectful," and "insensitive" treatment. One woman claimed they had all been "slapped in the face." What had begun as a feeling of being denied access to the decision to close the clinics was transformed through direct contact with the doctors and the hospital into a recognition, in the words of Jean Alves, who chaired the meeting, that "they think we are stupid and unworthy of having our views taken seriously." The doctors were presumed to be motivated by greed (they could make more money doing private care during the hours they had staffed the clinics), and both the doctors and the hospital were perceived as "insensitive" to women's concerns.

Over the next few months of the campaign the group began to understand how the strategy of defining the issues as *medical* (as opposed to political) and asserting the legitimacy of professional dominance of health care decisions masked the real social relations of gender, race, ethnicity, and class that in fact constituted the dynamics of power in the campaign. This process began with a conflict within CAFH over the use of the term "demands" to define their goals in the campaign. After the physicians' refusal to respond to "demands," some members of CAFH suggested dropping the term since it was "alienating" the doctors. Others defended the use of the term precisely because it reflected their right to be involved in what they saw as a political rather than a medical issue. Two events ultimately influenced the group to retain the concept of demands. The first was a statement made by one of the doctors during a radio interview that CAFH had changed the term on the petition from "demand" to "urge," indicating its understanding that consumers could not make demands of private physicians.[11] The second incident occurred during the HSA fact-finding hearing when a nurse rebuked CAFH with the comment, "You don't 'demand' of doctors. You wouldn't make demands of your husbands." These incidents consolidated CAFH's position that the retention of the term "demands" on petitions and in public statements was politically important. Moreover, the nurse's statement made explicit what had been only implicit to that point in the campaign—that women were overstepping their bounds not only as consumers but as *women*. This statement catalyzed considerable discussion within CAFH about women's right to make demands of both doctors and husbands.

When the chairman of the hospital board realized that CAFH was not going to give up, he informed CAFH that the hospital would take no further action until CAFH had "gone through appropriate channels." He explained that the HSA was the appropriate channel for consumer input to public health policy. It was in their experiences with the HSA that CAFH members began to develop an increasingly sophisticated understanding of the social relations that made some consumers more legitimate than others in health care decision making. Over the next weeks, CAFH began to deconstruct the categories of "provider" and "consumer," unmasking the gender, race, ethnic, and class relations that were reinforced ideologically by these particular definitions of social groups and the assumption of professional dominance of health care. The process of analyzing the category of "consumer" involved CAFH's increasing understanding that the HSA was ultimately little more open to their input than the doctors and the hospital and that certain "consumers" (that is, economically and politically powerful ones) did profoundly influence health policy.

This became clear to members of the group during the fact-finding hearing sponsored by the HSA. CAFH members noted that the doctors did not express any "anticonsumer" comments in this forum. Furthermore, they understood that the micropolitics of interaction at the fact-finding hearing indicated differential treatment of "consumers." For example, the testimony of the doctors, hospital staff, and social service representatives was not interrupted, nor was it challenged. When CAFH members spoke, however, they were repeatedly interrupted by the meeting chairman. They were questioned about their sources of information and were asked on numerous occasions to refrain from telling "anecdotes" or "personal stories." These so-called anecdotes and personal stories were reports by women in CAFH about their own experiences or the experiences of other women that supported CAFH's claims that the termination of clinic services had imposed financial and other hardships on ex-clinic users and that some women were not receiving prenatal care.

At one point in the meeting, the chair of the HSA task force expressed her disbelief that any woman who "really wanted a baby" would be deterred by the cost of prenatal care and suggested that there must be a "cultural gap at work here." Almost immediately CAFH members left the room to caucus about a response to their treatment during the meeting. After several minutes they returned, and Jean Alves made a statement that reflected the group's position. She identified the interruptions and the challenges to CAFH's testimony as an "effort to intimidate us, to keep us from using what we know best, the experiences of real women whose lives prove that the clinics must be reopened if women are to get necessary health care." She continued with an analysis of the role of class in the meeting: "This meeting is middle- and upper-income people making decisions about low-income people without understanding our needs at all."

In this statement CAFH countered the position of the health care establishment that the relevant social relations in this campaign were those of "provider" and "consumer." Instead, Jean Alves proposed that class and gender dynamics and relations were at work. Pam Alves reasserted the primacy of class in her statement that what the chair of the HSA task force saw as a "cultural gap . . . operating" was "really an income gap." These statements reflected the group's discussion during their caucus. One point that surfaced during that discussion, which was not raised publicly, was a belief that the HSA's intolerance for what it called "personal stories" stemmed from a sexist association of women with gossip rather than "facts." One CAFH member argued, "That's what they think of women, and because people believe it [that their stories were gossip rather than fact] they don't believe us."

An increasingly sophisticated consciousness of the social relations of domination emerged within CAFH as the women confronted and struggled to understand the class alliances they saw operating in the campaign. Once they forced the chairman of the hospital board of trustees to grant them permission to address a trustee meeting, they began to research the backgrounds of the twenty-four individuals on that board. When the results were presented at the next CAFH meeting, it became clear that the group's understanding of the constitution of power in the campaign encompassed a broadening understanding of the political economy of health care.

It was reported that of the board's twenty-four members, three were white male bankers, five white male attorneys, four white male health professionals, six white male corporate executives, one minority male retired school teacher, one white male retired union official, and four were white female "housewives" (these were the occupations as listed by the hospital). It was emphasized that each housewife was identified only as "Mrs." followed by her husband's first and last names and that each resided in the most affluent neighborhood in Fleetport. A Portuguese immigrant member of CAFH responded to this report with the statement, "This isn't just a struggle with the doctors and the hospital; *it's the whole power of the city* against us [emphasis mine]." Jean Alves added that it was "no wonder" the doctors hadn't talked against consumer input at the HSA meeting since members of the HSA and the hospital board were also consumers.

She concluded that it was not *consumer* input that bothered the doctors but rather "consumer input" from "those of us who aren't bankers, lawyers, executives, or married to them."

By this point in the campaign, the hegemonic discourse had been rejected by members of CAFH who had evolved an alternative understanding of the role of gender, race, ethnicity, and class in defining those groups with and without legitimacy and power in health care decision making. The ideological mystification, which had obscured the nature of class relations and class alliances at work in the campaign, had finally worn thin.

These understandings were amplified several weeks later when the head of the HSA task force informed CAFH that she would not, as promised, release the recommendations of the task force at the next HSA meeting, having given the doctors and the hospital her word that they would first have time to consider the findings. When charged with betrayal, she urged CAFH members to "calm down," implying that the recommendations were favorable to CAFH's demand for the clinic's reopening. At an emergency meeting of CAFH members expressed frustration, anger, and, once again, their understanding of the class alliances being used against them. Jean Alves remarked, "The more I think about it, the madder I get. The *whole upper echelon* has those recommendations, and they are discussing them behind closed doors [emphasis mine]."

By this point the events of the campaign had provided the forum for CAFH members to understand the constitution of what they had come to see as an *upper echelon*. In the first public meeting they saw the doctors and the hospital close ranks in opposition to community demands. The hospital board of trustees demonstrated the collusion between financial and corporate power and the power of the doctors and hospital administrators. When the local newspaper refused to cover the group's demonstrations, the links between the newspaper publisher and those holding economic and political power in the community knitted more tightly in CAFH members' minds the constitution of the upper echelon.

The end of the campaign was a final lesson for CAFH about the operation of hegemony by the upper echelon. In giving the doctors and the hospital a month to consider the recommendations of the HSA before they became public, the chair of the task force had opened the door to what she called "face-saving" for the doctors and what CAFH experienced, in the words of one of its members, as a "theft" of their victory. Because the report was not released before the announcement of the reopening of the prenatal clinic, it was easier for the doctors to claim, as they did in the newspaper report of the decision:

> The hospital and the physicians, despite great harassment, have *on their own* felt the needs of the indigent patients who have difficulties paying their medical bills, and have therefore decided to re-open the [prenatal] clinic. (emphasis mine)

Despite the fact that CAFH wrote a letter to the newspaper editor (which was published) claiming its role in this victory, the women recognized how limited a victory it was. Not only had the doctors and the hospital, in one CAFH member's phrase, "come off clean" in the eyes of the larger community because of their humanitarian impulse to respond to the needs of indigent patients, but no lasting changes in the balance of power occurred as a result of the campaign. No low-income consumers were placed on the hospital board, and the fiction of physician responsibility replaced the reality of successful grassroots organization as the mechanism of change for both the historical record (the newspaper account) and in the minds of residents of Fleetport.

GENDER AND CLASS IN CAFH'S POLITICAL VOCABULARY

The events of the campaign to reopen the clinics afforded members of CAFH an opportunity to develop an understanding of the social relations of power and domination as these were directly experienced and interpreted in the context of political struggle. I want now to turn to an examination of how the development of political consciousness is revealed in the group's own evolving consciousness of collective identity and the dynamics of power in the campaign. I have shown how gender, race, ethnicity, and class have shaped the dynamics of power and domination in the campaign. However, political consciousness is not an automatic reflex of political economy. The group's self-conception or collective identity shifted during the campaign, and gender, race, ethnicity, and class were not equally accented.[12] This section focuses on the ways CAFH members came to understand the relationship between gender and class *in particular* as interrelated dimensions of their collective identity and their relationship to power.

In the first public document of CAFH's campaign, a leaflet produced by women (including myself) at the feminist health collective that helped to organize the first meeting of CAFH, a woman is pictured as pushed to her knees by the burdens of health care costs, which are drawn as little boxes on her back labeled with the costs of routine gynecological and prenatal procedures. A call is made to the "working women of Fleetport" to discuss the closing of the clinics, and the hospital is charged with "forgetting its responsibility to the working women of the city."

The next leaflet retains the graphics but calls on "community women" and "low-income women" and refers to the "particular needs of "low-wage women." By November, two months later, the language of outreach materials (for example, for the demonstration outside the hospital during the meeting of the board of trustees) and public statements used class and family idioms (for example, "low-income families" and "low-income people)." Moreover, this change in emphasis continued throughout much of the rest of the campaign. I suggest that this shift in political vocabulary is evidence of the evolving class consciousness of CAFH, a class consciousness, however, that is far from gender-blind.

One could argue that this shift is evidence that gender was never a salient category for CAFH members and that the references to working, low-income, and community *women* in the original materials resulted from the role of feminists in the production of the early leaflets. Once working-class women took over the leadership of CAFH, their language was a language of class. Such an argument would support the contention of scholars such as Marilyn Gittell and Nancy Naples[13] that middle-class (read "feminist") and working-class women gravitate to different sorts of issues, the former to gender-specific issues and the latter to community issues.

Although I would agree that the gender emphasis in the early materials may have come from the influence of feminist ideology on the producers of the leaflets, I would argue that the language in the later leaflets reflects the salience of class rather than the neglect of gender. In fact, gender remained a compelling political category for CAFH members. But for the women in CAFH the question was not the academic primacy of gender versus class but rather an evolving understanding of the intersection of gender, race, ethnicity, and class in the constitution of the social relations of power. For example, as we have seen, they were rebuked with the statements, "You don't make 'demands' of doctors. You wouldn't make demands of your husbands." They understood from these statements the relationship being drawn between their roles and powerlessness as women and their roles and powerlessness as a class.

In an early discussion of why the prenatal and gynecology clinics were singled out for termination, CAFH members expressed their understanding that gender discrimination was involved. As one member phrased it, "First they closed the clinic for kids a few years ago and now its the clinics for women. Its like sending people overboard—women and kids first." Sexist treatment by hospital administrators, trustees, doctors, and HSA members was discussed within CAFH. CAFH members bristled when the chairman of the hospital board called them "girls" *and* when the head of professional services at the hospital referred to them as "ladies."

More subtle forms of gender oppression were also noted. In an initial meeting Jean Alves was accused by the chairman of the hospital board of being "overly emotional." After the HSA hearing she explained that she had felt so afraid of reinforcing the stereotype of the emotional female that she felt she had been dispassionate and therefore less effective in her testimony: "The other night I was so afraid of losing my temper and seeming emotional that I went too far in the opposite direction." Moreover, Pam Alves implicitly understood how gender stereotypes were being used against CAFH when she noted that the HSA discounted their evidence of women's inability to get private obstetrical care because of financial considerations as "personal stories" or "gossip."

During the campaign the political meaning of gender was highly contextualized by class. For example, despite their contempt for the (female) receptionists and nursing staff in the doctors' private practice (who were repeatedly indicted by CAFH for insensitivity to poor women), CAFH members refused to accept a physician's claim that "the biggest problem I have in the office is what my girls say to patients on the phone." He was responding to a complaint by a CAFH member that a friend had been told she could not see the doctor until she had paid an outstanding bill for twenty-three dollars. The CAFH member who reported the story noted the attempt to make a scapegoat of the receptionist and replied, "I'm sure *your girls* are following orders."

Perhaps the clearest evidence of the importance of gender in the campaign is revealed in the perceptions of CAFH members of gender solidarity. Gender bonds were reinforced in a variety of ways in the campaign—asking a man not to attend any more meetings of CAFH, telling "sexism stories" (references to sexist incidents), the recognition that some middle-class women actively supported the campaign (as members of CAFH) despite the fact that they did not personally use the clinics. However, CAFH members did not extend the feeling of gender solidarity to the wealthy women on the hospital board or the HSA. These women were not presumed to be allies and were never contacted to elicit their support *as women* for other women. Nor was there any value placed on the appointment of a woman as chair of the HSA task force; it was known that she came from an affluent and politically powerful family in Fleetport. Although there is evidence throughout the campaign that CAFH members understood that the closing of the clinics affected them as women, their experience of gender was class-specific.

In like manner, although the developing political consciousness of CAFH members involved an increasingly sophisticated understanding of class, the experience of class was textured by gender, ethnicity, and race. CAFH members understood that the upper echelon was economically privileged and male, overwhelmingly white and native born. On the other hand, they understood that those who were being denied access first to health care and then to health care decision making were not only low-income and female but were overwhelmingly immigrant women and women of color. The exceptions—women on the hospital board and HSA, middle-class supporters of CAFH, the one minority member of the hospital board, and the several on the HSA—did not obscure the clarity of the analysis CAFH evolved regarding the constitution and dynamics of the social relations of power.

Ultimately, what I am trying to say here is that the categories of both "class" and "gender" became politically meaningful in the context of a very real struggle over community resources. Although race and ethnicity were not so primary as class and gender in the political vocabulary of the campaign, they colored, if you will, the meaning of class as it came to mean something very concrete about who were allies in the campaign and which groups had access to power. Moreover, class and gender were inextricably linked for the women in CAFH as these simultaneously, if in different ways, conditioned their relationship to economic and political resources.

"WIVES AND MOTHERS"? WOMEN AND COMMUNITY ORGANIZING
The foregoing analysis has implications for the final argument I want to make here: that women's involvement in community organizing cannot be simply explained by or reduced to their roles and responsibilities as wives, mothers, or

daughters. The literature on women and community organizing tends to do just that—account for women's involvement as an extension of their roles in the family. For example, Lawson and Barton explain the composition and nature of the tenants' movement in New York city as follows:

> An awareness of the division between home and community on the one hand and workplace on the other is vital to understanding the participation patterns we found. The home is regarded as primarily the sphere of women rather than of the man. Consequently, when a rent increase or a deterioration in services impinges on the home, it is usually the woman's task to deal with it since it lies within her sphere. This pattern holds true more frequently in working-class than in middle-class households because of the greater separation of roles typically found there.[14]

Lawson and Barton essentially construct an argument that presumes a sexual division of political response (responsibility) based on the acceptance of gender-divided public and private worlds and family and work spheres.

Although Lawson and Barton are more explicit than many others who have explained women's grassroots community activism in terms of women's greater interest and responsibility for domestic issues, the theme is commonplace. Wekerle, for example, suggests that

> Women's concern with the home has led them to become more active in community issues and self-help movements to improve living conditions related to housing, childcare, food cooperatives, and neighborhood planning.[15]

Though this explanation does make clear an important connection between forms of resistance and the concrete conditions of women's lives, it tends to flatten out women's political consciousness by rooting it in domestic roles or particularistic or familistic attitudes. I do not mean to deny the profound ways that women's roles in and responsibilities for their families influence their definitions of political priorities and shape their political involvements. Nor would I minimize the importance of the evidence that scholars such as Gilkes,[16] McCourt,[17] Seifer,[18] and Mayo[19] provide for working-class women's own explanations of their political involvement in terms of the problems they face and responsibilities they shoulder as wives and mothers.

However, my case material suggests that women's community-based political activism is a conscious and collective way of expressing and acting on their interests as *women,* as *wives and mothers,* as *members of neighborhoods and communities,* and as *members of particular race, ethnic, and class groups.* To collapse a complex political consciousness into the more narrow confines of domestic values, interests, and roles is to distort both the motivation and the political implications of this mode of resistance. I argue instead that working-class women's community activism must be understood in terms of their relationship to the state and to the larger political economy.[20] The women who were involved in the campaign to reopen the clinics were not generic wives and mothers. It is true that many of the women who joined CAFH did so as potential (and actual) mothers seeking prenatal care or were the relatives (mothers, sisters, cousins, daughters) of women who needed gynecological care. More precisely, however, these were women whose dependence on the sliding-scale hospital clinics was conditioned by their class position and whose power to influence the political economy of health care was effectively limited to political activities such as grassroots collective action. Because of their gender, their class, and, in some cases, their race and ethnicity, they are firmly anchored at the bottom of a political economy in which they are trying to survive and which they are struggling to change.

The argument that women become involved in community organization as an extension of their roles as wives and mothers presumes rather than explains the particular nature of the relationship between historical circumstances, ideology, consciousness, and action. It is an explanation rooted in essentialist assumptions about women and politics (see the editors' discussion of the problems of essentialism in the final section of the Introductory Essay).[21] In addition, the argument that women *as* wives and mothers participate in neighborhood and community activism exemplifies a more general problem with current theories of political action and consciousness. Much of our social theory rigidly separates gender, race, ethnicity, and class and tends to account for the generative (mobilizing) power of each in a different sphere of social life. Ira Katznelson's work on urban political action suggests that the North American working class is plagued by a fragmented consciousness that sees class as important primarily in defining social relationships in the workplace, whereas other collective identities such as race and ethnicity (he ignores gender) are more important in defining social relationships outside the workplace.[22]

I think this same sort of fragmentation has plagued social scientists, including feminist scholars, as we have analyzed social life and resistance. We tend to associate particular modes of resistance with specific kinds of consciousness— for example, class consciousness with labor activism; feminist consciousness with gender-specific political issues and organizations; and race and ethnic collective identity with community-based struggles. The conceptual error is to investigate the relationship between material conditions and consciousness in a way that fails to see the interconnections between gender, race, and class in different "spheres" of social life and in the constitution of social relations of power.

We need to develop approaches that do not rigidly differentiate these arenas of social life and struggle, that examine resistance wherever it appears, and that search for the variety of political, economic, and social forces that are implicated in the appearance and dynamics of collective action. Essentially I am arguing against the splintering of human agency into radically separate channels of experienced oppression or resistance. The study of the development of politi-

cal consciousness in working-class women can guide us in developing conceptual frameworks that capture the complex ways that gender, race, ethnicity, and
class become politically meaningful in their interrelatedness in daily life and
political involvement.

ACKNOWLEDGMENTS

I want to gratefully acknowledge the many conversations I had during the course
of this campaign with activists directly involved in the struggle and others active
politically in the community. That they go unnamed (to preserve anonymity) in
no way belies the value of their insights and contributions.

NOTES

1. "Fleetport" is a pseudonym for a community of approximately one hundred
thousand people in the northeastern United States. For a more detailed discussion of the
community and its health care, see Sandra Morgen, "The Dynamics of Cooptation in a
Feminist Health Clinic," *Social Science and Medicine* 23, No. 2 (1986): 201–210.

2. During my fieldwork I conducted a study of the health needs and attitudes of
low-income women in Fleetport. The results of the survey of more than 250 low-income
women showed very real problems of cost, accessibility, and atmosphere facing women
seeking health care from the available sources. Clinic care was perceived to be problematic in terms of concerns ranging from length of waits for appointments to crowding.
Nevertheless, clinic care rated much higher than private care on such items as affor-
dability and the perceived treatment of patients. At the time of the termination of clinic
services, in the autumn of 1977, attendance at the prenatal and gynecology clinics was
high.

3. I was a participant–observer in the feminist health clinic from April 1977
through late 1979. During my involvement with CAFH I was regarded as a representative
of the feminist clinic to CAFH by both CAFH and feminist collective members.

4. The Health Systems Agency (HSA) discussed in this paper was a local subarea
council. HSAs, established nationwide with the 1974 passage of the National Health
Planning and Resource Development Act, are mechanisms for joint planning of health
care by professionals and consumers. HSAs exist on the state, regional, and (in some
cases) local level. There are complicated formulas for mandating representatives from
different sexual, racial, age, and occupational groups. For a discussion of HSAs and their
limitations in fostering consumer/community-controlled health care, see articles in Victor
and Ruth Sidel, eds., *Reforming Medicine: Lessons of the Last Quarter Century* (New
York: Pantheon, 1984).

5. The "Ten Taxpayers" suit is a procedural suit that can be filed by any ten
"taxpaying citizens" in a community. The suit made these ten taxpayers (and CAFH)
party to a petition filed with the state department of Public Health concerning a proposed
capital improvement campaign by the hospital. Although I do not discuss in detail the
impact of the filing of the suit on the coalition, let me note here that the suit did ultimately
create considerable tension between working-class and middle-class women in the group.
Although everyone had agreed that CAFH should file the suit as a means of securing the
information it needed for its continued successful organizing, legal intricacies became all-

too-frequent topics of discussion at meetings. The working-class women found meetings dominated by discussions of the suit "alienating." They felt at a considerable disadvantage relative to middle-class, better-educated women during these discussions. Moreover, they felt that the legal strategy was undermining the grassroots, activist character of the group. A complex analysis of the class conflicts within CAFH is beyond the scope of this article. However, I think that the class-based tensions within the group were both affected by and served to highlight the growing awareness of the ways in which class alliances were being used against CAFH by the "power of the city." Furthermore, the growing class consciousness of the working-class members of CAFH bred distrust, resentment, and anger within the group. The final decision to disband the group even in the face of a campaign victory was probably in part attributable to the rarely expressed but still very real problems arising from cross-class community organization.

6. The survey referred to above (*note 2*) indicated that 11 percent of the respondents had no form of third-party payment—meaning either individual or group health insurance or coverage by Medicaid, Medicare, or other federal health benefits.

7. The pattern of occupational segregation in Fleetport is such that Black, Hispanic, and immigrant women have the highest rates of unemployment, poverty, and underemployment in the city. These women form the labor pool for low-paying services jobs and seasonal, nonunionized, dead-end jobs in textiles, fish processing, and other unskilled factory work.

8. Rosalind Petchesky, *Abortion and Woman's Choice: The State, Sexuality, and Reproductive Freedom* (Boston: Northeastern University Press, 1984), 366.

9. Sarah Eisenstein, *Give Us Bread but Give Us Roses* (London: Routledge & Kegan Paul, 1983).

10. My analysis of hegemony draws heavily on the work of Antonio Gramsci—for example, *Selections from the Prison Notebooks* (New York: International Publishers, 1971).

11. For a discussion of the implications of the ideological split between "public" and "private" as that can affect and constrain effective political mobilization, see Martha A. Ackelsberg's article (*Chapter 13*).

12. Although not emphasized either in the evolving campaign or in my analysis of it, there were aspects of the campaign that had a great deal to do with race and ethnicity. One of the things that angered the women involved in community meetings was the widespread understanding that the doctors referred to Wednesday, the day on which they saw Medicaid recipients in their offices, as "Pig Day." Black women in particular decried this slur; they believed that it came from a mistaken racist association between women of color and welfare, and from a desire to segregate private patients from Medicaid patients, particularly women of color.

13. Marilyn Gittell and Nancy Naples, "Activist Women: Conflicting Ideologies," *Social Policy* 12 (1982): 25–27.

14. Ronald Lawson and Stephen Barton, "Sex Roles in Social Movements: A Case Study of the Tenant Movement in New York City," *Signs* 6, No. 2 (1981): 230–247.

15. Gerda Werkerle, "Women in the Urban Environment: Review Essay," *Signs* 5, No. 3 (1980 supplement): S209.

16. Cheryl T. Gilkes, "Holding Back the Ocean with a Broom: Black Women and Community Work," in LaFrances Rogers-Rose, ed., *The Black Woman* (Beverly Hills, Calif.: Sage, 1980), 218.

17. Kathleen McCourt, *Working Class Women and Grassroots Politics* (Bloomington: Indiana University Press, 1977).

18. Nancy Seifer, *Nobody Speaks for Me* (New York: Simon & Schuster, 1976).

19. Marjorie Mayo, *Women in the Community* (London: Routledge & Kegan Paul, 1977).

20. Cynthia Cockburn, *The Local State* (London: Pluto Press, 1977).

21. For a related discussion of the explanation of women's antimilitarism consciousness and action, see Micaela di Leonardo, "Morals, Mothers, and Militarism: Antimilitarism and Feminist Theory," *Feminist Studies* 11, No. 3 (Fall 1985): 599–617.

22. Ira Katznelson, *City Trenches, Urban Politics and the Patterning of Class in the U.S.* (New York: Random House, 1981).

5

Women Workers and Collective Action: A Case Study from the Insurance Industry

Cynthia B. Costello

> We decided to tally out loud how many "yeses" and how many
> "nos" as far as the strike vote was concerned. It kept going yes, yes,
> YES! I get goosebumps just thinking about it now. And after it was
> all counted, everybody just cheered and hugged each other. There
> was a mixture of happiness and "I'm scared to death" in the room.
> —Bargaining team member, the United Staff Union

In the fall of 1979, fifty-three office workers at a small Wisconsin insurance firm,
the Wisconsin Education Association Insurance Trust (the Trust), initiated a
strike. Faced with low wages, sex-discriminatory work rules, and patronizing
managerial attitudes, the unionized clerical workers at this workplace developed
a consciousness of their right to working conditions that respected them as working women. In the process, the women transformed their work culture and their
labor union, the United Staff Union, into vehicles for collective organizing.
When contract negotiations further polarized management and union employees,
the women voted to strike.

The documentation of this strike began with an initiative by Catherine
Loeb, a feminist editor, who attended a support rally for the striking women.
After learning that the strikers required greater media coverage, Loeb arranged
an interview with several strike leaders at a local alternative radio station and
enlisted Joanne Whelden, a feminist therapist, to coauthor an article for a small
Madison newspaper. Impressed with the transformative impact of the strike on

Editors' Note: This chapter is based, in large part, on a previously published article, " 'WEA're
Worth It!': Work Culture and Conflict at the Wisconsin Education Insurance Trust," *Feminist Studies*
11, No. 3 (1985): 497–515. We gratefully acknowledge the permission of *Feminist Studies*, Inc., c/o
Women's Studies Program, University of Maryland, College Park, MD 20742, to reprint Costello's
work in this collection.

the lives of the Trust women, Loeb and Whelden joined with Susan McGovern, Barbara Melosh, Ruth Powers, and me in the spring of 1980 to form the Women's Oral History Project. Fifteen of the oral histories that provide the basis for the analysis of this strike were conducted by the Women's Oral History Project. After deciding to utilize the oral histories for my dissertation research, I conducted an additional thirteen interviews with managers and clerical workers at the Trust.[1] Because of the unique conditions under which this research was initiated, I gained access to information and personal accounts that might otherwise have been unavailable. Although not all of the Trust women will agree with my conclusions, I have tried to retain the integrity of their experience. What follows is a discussion of the factors that have shaped resistance among working women in the past and an analysis of the formation and diffusion of a militant work culture at the Wisconsin Education Association Insurance Trust.

WOMEN'S WORK CULTURE, CONSCIOUSNESS, AND COLLECTIVE ACTION

In the traditional literature in industrial sociology and labor history, working women are viewed as unlikely candidates for collective action. Many researchers have assumed that women's gender identity—their primary identification with family rather than work roles—blocks the development of class consciousness. Others have maintained that the patriarchal characteristics of women's wage work discourages women's activism.[2]

Recent feminist scholarship has challenged this view of working women's passivity, uncovering a rich history of women's activism both inside and outside the labor movement. We now know that women were among the first wage-workers to protest collectively the cost-cutting initiatives of mill owners in the first half of the nineteenth century and that they provided crucial leadership in the movement for the ten-hour day. The extensive organizing among late-nineteenth-century working women in the garment, textile, and cigar-making industries has been amply documented. And feminist scholarship has also revealed the extension of women's organizing initiatives into the mass-production industries of auto and steel manufacture in the twentieth century, as well as their organizing efforts in the service industries of insurance, retailing, and hospitals.[3] What much of this research documents is that, faced with sexual hierarchy in the workplace, the family, and the labor unions, working women demonstrated a significant capacity to mobilize for collective action.

Other feminist scholars have focused on working women's informal strategies designed to establish control on the job. Challenging traditional assumptions regarding the conservative character of women's consciousness, commitments, and networks, researchers have documented that women's gender identity has often underwritten a woman-centered consciousness and strategy at work and in the community. At the center of this new scholarship is the concept of women's work culture: the ideologies, rituals, and practices through which women forge a relatively autonomous space for action on the job. Examples include women's own definition of "respectful treatment"; their participation in showers and parties at work to commemorate engagements, marriages, and births; and women's utilization of gossip to share information about problematic male managers. Emphasizing the radical possibilities in women's work-based networks, Barbara Melosh has argued that women's work culture can provide a "powerful wedge for claiming and extending [their] control on the job."[4]

The recent feminist scholarship offers an invaluable corrective to the traditional and stereotypical assumptions about the commitments and activities of working women. But as Ruth Milkman has argued, if we are not careful we run the risk of replacing the old assumptions with new ones which are equally one-sided.[5] Where the old orthodoxy saw in working women an essential passivity, the new one sees an inexhaustable reservoir of female militancy. As the mirror image of the old, this new perspective fails to specify the structural opportunities for protest or to acknowledge any constraints on working women's organizing efforts. Without abandoning the feminist focus on gender, we need to develop a more complex approach to working women's culture and activism. In most work situations, women's work culture combines behaviors and attitudes that both reinforce and challenge managerial prerogatives and control.[6] Whether women's work-based networks generate consent or resistance is dependent on a number of factors: the available resources, a supportive ideology, and the characteristics of the work setting.

Feminist scholars have demonstrated that the combination of resources and ideological support has been crucial to the success (and failure) of women's organizing initiatives in the past. Roslyn L. Feldberg's research shows how the resources of the Women's Trade Union League (WTUL) were essential to the increase in clerical unionization between 1900 and 1920. Had the support and leadership of the WTUL been supplemented by the resources of the labor movement, clerical workers' organizing efforts would no doubt have been more successful. But the perception that clerical workers were "unorganizable" shaped the decision of labor leaders to allocate scarce resources to other workers.[7]

Sharon Hartman Strom's research similarly shows the mixed legacy of the Congress of Industrial Organizations' (CIO) relationship to female office workers during the 1930s. The financial resources, the institutional support, and the power to impose a closed shop provided by the CIO unions made it possible for thousands of clerical workers to organize during the thirties and for many to initiate strikes. But at the same time the sexual hierarchy of the CIO—exhibited in patronizing attitudes, male control over union locals, and the exclusion of women from bargaining units—limited what might otherwise have become a major movement among clerical workers. Moreover, the decline of the WTUL during this period left female office workers without alternative resources or a supportive ideology to underwrite their organizing efforts.[8]

The capacity of women to challenge managerial policies is enhanced by organizations that provide women with opportunities to participate democratically and define their collective goals. It is weakened by bureaucratic and male-dominated organizations that reinforce the sexual hierarchy women experience at work and in their family lives. But while support from labor unions or feminist organizations extends women's ability to challenge managerial authority, the impulse for such initiatives comes from working women's own experience on the job. Without strong work-based dissatisfactions, working women are unlikely to mobilize for collective action.

Women's grievances may arise from either the class hierarchy or the gender hierarchy they confront at work. Marxist theorists of the labor process have provided rich descriptions of the authoritarian class strategies such as reprimands, firings, and wage cuts that catalyze resistance.[9] Feminist theorists have argued that the gender-specific strategies utilized by male managers can also generate opposition. Sexual harassment provides the most explicit example of the manipulation of the gender hierarchy by men in order to assert their prerogatives over women. But sexual harassment is only the extreme example of a whole category of behaviors that Dair Gillespie and her colleagues label "gender-baiting," "the constant reminder in an organizational setting that women are being judged, responded to, and evaluated by virtue of gender rather than of job performance." Requests that women perform "domestic services," as well as attitudes such as "a woman's place is in the home" qualify as gender-baiting. Communicated in an organizational setting, such behaviors reinforce the gender hierarchy at work.[10]

Coercive class or gender policies can provoke clerical workers to initiate collective action. But more than a clear target for their grievances is required for women to forge a militant work culture. Also necessary is a strong sense of solidarity. In some work settings, the organization of work promotes clerical interaction, fostering the development of cohesive social networks on the job. The contradiction facing many clerical workers, however, is that precisely those working conditions creating dissatisfaction—such as authoritarian supervision, sexual harassment, or tight productivity standards—also produce a vulnerable and fragmented work force.[11]

This article attempts to specify the circumstances under which contemporary clerical workers are more likely to engage in collective action. Through a case study analysis of a small strike among Wisconsin clerical workers, I argue that the formation and diffusion of militance in this workplace diverged from the patterns associated with the models of women's passivity and women's activism. In order to mobilize for a strike, these women faced significant obstacles based in their gender positions at home and at work. They also demonstrated the power in women's work-based networks as they transformed their work culture into a vehicle for collectively challenging managerial prerogatives and control. I will demonstrate, however, that the ebb and flow of women's militance in this case was most closely linked to changes in managerial strategies of control.

Though my evidence for this argument is drawn from the analysis of a single workplace, the implications are of broader significance. One out of three working women works in an office job. And within the office sector the finance industries of insurance, banking, and real estate employ one in four clerical workers. Only about 20 percent of public and private sector clerical workers are unionized. In the finance industries, less than 3 percent of the office work force belong to unions. Still, the examination of a unionized insurance firm can shed light on the factors that constrain and facilitate collective action for unorganized as well as organized clerical workers. There is little question that unionized clericals have access to resources unavailable to most working women. Nevertheless, in order to mobilize for collective action, working women must often confront a sexual hierarchy in their unions as well as in their workplaces (and their families). An analysis of a unionized insurance company can therefore shed light on the circumstances that push working women to challenge male-dominated institutions to respond to their demands for respect and equal treatment in the workplace.

THE EMERGENCE OF A MILITANT WORK CULTURE AT THE TRUST

The Trust was founded in 1970 by the Wisconsin Education Association (WEA) to provide insurance coverage to school system employees. As the arm of the largest union in the state, the Trust was an unusual insurance company. The fact that the Trust management reported to a union-appointed board of directors prevented the implementation of blatantly antiunion policies. At the same time, however, the Trust's status as the arm of a union did not protect the company from competitive pressures. Constrained to function competitively according to insurance industry standards (or else WEA would switch to a major insurance carrier), the Trust management organized the work process according to a traditional, patriarchal hierarchy and managerial mentality.

During the early 1970s, two male managers set policies and directed the work of the five female claims adjustors who performed the entire range of manual tasks required in claims adjusting: opening the mail, setting up the file for the insured, deciding on the claims payment, and typing the insurance checks. In 1975, two female supervisors were hired to solve what one manager described as the "communication problems" that had surfaced between management and clerical employees. But this strategy did not eliminate conflict between the two groups. The location of the Trust offices in the same building as the union offices of WEA brought the Trust clericals into contact with two groups of unionized employees: the professional staff of WEA (the lawyers and contract negotiators) and the associate staff of WEA (the clerical support staff for the professionals). Both groups were members of the United Staff Union (USU), the state local of the National Staff Organization, an independent union representing employees of teachers' unions.

In the summer of 1975, the professional wing of the USU initiated negotiations with the Trust management to bring the five Trust clericals into the union. The institutional relationship between WEA and the Trust constrained the latter from actively opposing the unionization initiative. Nevertheless, the Trust management's reluctance to recognize the union was revealed in the first contract negotiation in the fall of 1975. One of the union negotiators recalled that "every word in the first contract had to be pulled from the Trust management."[12]

Over the next two years, the addition of several insurance benefit plans significantly increased the Trust's business. Management responded to growth by hiring twenty additional employees, expanding the managerial hierarchy, rationalizing the claims process, and moving its employees to two separate locations. The geographical separation between the two buildings posed a barrier to communication among the Trust women, causing problems as the union entered its second negotiations in the fall of 1977. The union bargaining team was very much dissatisfied with the management proposal for a reduction in leave time and wages. Resentment also surfaced over the attitude of the management negotiator who, as bargaining team members recalled, justified the low wage proposal as "sufficient for secondary wage-earners working for pin money."[13] The union bargaining team recommended that its membership reject the contract and consider a strike. But in the absence of strong interdepartmental ties and a shared assessment that working conditions were unacceptable, the Trust women could not reach a consensus. They voted against a strike.

Six months later, the Trust management moved its forty union employees to a new location. With the move came new sex-discriminatory work rules that clearly demarcated the rights of managers from the rights of union employees. Management installed a time clock and followed this action with individual and group reprimands of union employees for as little as one-minute tardiness; directed the union employees to use the side door and the stairway, reserving the front door and the elevator for themselves; and instituted a rigid schedule requiring the women to take staggered breaks and lunches by department. To separate the women within departments, management erected carrels. The new work rules contributed to extensive dissatisfaction among union employees at the Trust. One woman emphasized that managerial priorities were reversed: "It seemed that the new rules were set up to fit the women into the building rather than vice versa." In the claims and clerical departments, supervisory surveillance solidified the union women's dissatisfaction with the new work rules. Supervisors monitored their subordinates' phone calls, issued written reprimands for talking, and followed employees to the bathroom. One woman commented that the scene in Jane Fonda's film *Nine to Five,* where the supervisor followed the employee to the bathroom, must have been modeled on managerial behavior at the Trust. Both were equally ridiculous.

In the year leading up to the strike, several incidents heightened the women's frustration with managerial policies at the Trust. Management denied leave time to a union steward who asked to visit her dying father; suspended a second woman with two children for leaving work in the middle of a snowstorm; and denied leave without pay to a third woman who needed to visit her asthmatic daughter in the hospital. One woman recalled that these managerial decisions were accompanied by the rationale that "women who have responsibilities for their children should stay out of the work force." These incidents struck the Trust women as particularly ironic. When management needed to legitimate their low wages or limited promotional opportunities, they defined the union women as "secondary wage-earners." But when the women requested leave time to fulfill their family responsibilities, management denied their requests. As one woman explained, "These men had no sympathy for working women and wives."

The union women came from diverse family backgrounds: 51 percent were married, 16 percent were divorced, and 27 percent were single parents. A few of the married women whose husbands earned comfortable incomes did view their jobs as temporary. But the majority of the married women and all of the single women—particularly the single mothers—considered their incomes essential for the support of themselves and their families. It was not that their family responsibilities were subordinated to their wage-earning responsibilities. Many of the women spent a major portion of their "off hours" maintaining their households and caring for their children. For the women at the Trust, both jobs were primary.

By imposing sex-discriminatory work rules, intensifying supervisory monitoring, and denying leave time to women with family responsibilities, the Trust management created a common target for the union women's grievances. But it was not until preparations began for the 1979 bargaining that the Trust women began to translate those grievances into a coherent oppositional culture and strategy. In anticipation of bargaining, the union formed committees and selected eight women—six of them claims adjustors—for the bargaining team. They came up with the motto "WEA'RE WORTH IT!" (a reference to their employer) and ordered T-shirts and buttons that all the women wore on bargaining days. And they requested that a woman lawyer from the professional wing of the USU act as legal advisor during the negotiations. Because she was a strong feminist and union activist, this lawyer's support was crucial. "She made us believe in ourselves and feel we had a right to stand up to management!" one woman explained.

With the commencement of negotiations on August 1, 1979, the bargaining team started a newsletter, "As the Trust Turns." The newsletter became a central vehicle for communicating the developing polarization at the bargaining table. Management's original contract offer included an elimination of the salary schedule (which guaranteed semiannual raises), a reduction in leave time, and an elimination of seniority rights for layoffs. The union's proposal called for expanded fringe benefits, language clarification, and strong union input into work rules. Bargaining disputes arose over many issues. One was management's insensitivity to the needs of working women. "[Management has] no empathy or even insight into the problems that we, as women, face when combining jobs and homemaking," the newsletter reported.

> And they seem to tie in this lack of empathy with the fact that we are all "clerical" workers. If ignorance is bliss, they are damn tranquil!!

> Regardless of the job title—be it teacher or clerical worker—women
> do have distinct problems which need attention and addressing in a
> contract!!

Additional conflicts developed over the salary schedule. According to one newsletter report, the management representative stated during negotiations, "We
have to get to a point where we get a day's work for a day's pay." The newsletter
retorted, "If we worked according to our pay—little would get done!!!" And
finally, the issue of union input into work rules provoked extensive controversy
at the bargaining table. The newsletter outlined the differences between management and union over work rules:

> In addition to much needed (and deserved) monetary gains, we have
> other proposals in the area of employee rights. Management takes
> the position that such things should not be included, "cluttering up
> the contract." We, however, are unwavering; our concept of contract
> language is of equal importance to that of management.

When the Trust management remained firm in its opposition to employee input
into work rules, the newsletter reasserted, "Management seems reluctant to include certain employee rights as part of the contract. WE disagree. Second only
to monetary gain, human rights and principles are sacred issues!!!"

In mid-August, management and union reached a stalemate at the bargaining table. According to one member of the union bargaining team, management
representatives refused to sit across from the union women, negotiating instead
with the male union representatives. "It was startling how management acted,"
she explained.

> Usually, the two teams sit across from each other but the Trust man-
> agement wouldn't do that. They wanted to sit clear down on the
> other side of the table. . . . They didn't want to deal with the wom-
> en. The usually problematic conditions were heightened during
> bargaining.

In the assessment of the union women, management was unwilling to take their
demands seriously. The women therefore began to prepare for the possibility of a
strike.

Union meetings became a central vehicle through which clerical strategies
were forged. Before the bargaining began, few of the Trust women identified as
active union members. Ironically, a significant number of the Trust women came
from union backgrounds. Sixteen percent had belonged to labor unions before
they came to the Trust. An additional 43 percent had experienced indirect contact
with labor unions through family members. For bargaining team members, the
contact with labor unions was even more significant: Six of the eight women had
previously belonged to unions or had come from backgrounds where either their
parents or their husbands were union members. But before the strike mobilization, many of the Trust women had defined unions as "male organizations."

"My dad had always been in a union and so was my husband," one woman explained, "but I never thought that unions were for women."

In addition, the domination by the male professionals over the USU had dissuaded the Trust women from identifying with the union. In principle, the union was structured to represent the interests of all three bargaining units of the USU: the twenty-five-member mostly male professional staff, the twenty-five-member female associate staff, and the fifty-three Trust women. But in practice the priorities of the professionals often took precedence. The Trust women reported that the formal and legalistic procedures utilized by the professionals prevented the office workers from participating in general membership meetings. "The professionals had a technique for talking above the union women's heads," one woman emphasized. "It gives you the impression that they know more than you do. They dominated." Because the USU contained three separate bargaining units, each unit had the option of calling its own meetings. This provided the Trust women with the opportunity to imprint their own work culture on their bargaining unit—to replace the exclusionary policies, language, and rules of the general membership meetings with the informal ties and language of the women's own work culture. Describing *their* union meetings as spirited and democratic, the Trust women underscored that their bargaining unit encouraged participation and contributed to Trustwide discussions of working conditions and feelings of solidarity.

As the contract expiration date approached, the confrontational relationship between management and union intensified. Management issued production standards for the claims adjustors, warning that a failure to meet them would result in discharge. "As the Trust Turns" reported that with this latest development management had joined the "ranks of the Ayatollah Khomeni." Some of the claims adjustors responded to the production standards by slowing down their work. Management, in turn, reacted by instructing the claims managers to increase their monitoring of their subordinates. "It appeared that there was a work slowdown compared to work at other times," one manager recalled. "It might have been due to a slowdown or a decrease in employee morale. There was a lot of concern that union people would try to mess things up. We were supposed to watch to make sure things weren't taken out of the building."

In carpools on the way to work and by phone at night, the Trust women anticipated how a strike might affect their work and family lives. Some felt excited about the challenges of a strike. Others worried what a picket line might require. "I had no idea what a strike would be like," one woman remembered. "I disliked the idea of a strike immensely. I didn't feel I wanted to quit though. I felt I could go along with a strike." Some felt confident that their families could accommodate a strike. But for others, their family situations provoked anxiety. "The anticipation of the strike made me nervous," one woman explained, "because we were expecting a baby and I was trying to get the bills out of the way." At work, the union women communicated their strategies through an underground communication system. The carrels prevented supervisors from observing that women were using the phones not to discuss insurance policies with subscribers but rather to develop strike plans. In addition, the women responsible for mail delivery carried news between departments. As stories of management "mistreatment" and refusals to bargain traveled across departments, the women grew more determined. "When one woman was upset, everyone became upset," one woman emphasized. "This feeding off each other was what started the strike." A second woman recalled, "We felt we weren't going to be pushed around anymore. Management was not acting respectful toward our bargaining team. So we decided to stand up for our rights!" And, in the words of a third woman, "We felt, 'We'll show you, we've taken your garbage long enough!' "

During the last week of September, the union women grew more bold. The newsletter encouraged the women to prepare for the strike:

> It's hard to think strike—but we must. It's scary to think strike—but we must. It's hard to rock the boat and take a risk—but we must. Our livelihoods now and for years to come depend on it. WE'LL MAKE IT TOGETHER!!!!!

In full view of their supervisors, the office workers openly discussed plans for a strike. And on the Friday afternoon before the strike vote, the union women packed up and removed all their personal and work-related materials from the office. This gesture communicated to management the seriousness of their intentions. Two nights later all fifty-three women gathered at the Sheraton Hotel in Madison, Wisconsin. The two male negotiators for the union agreed that evening to accept management's outstanding bargaining proposal. When the news reached the Trust women, they were furious. It was not their understanding that the male negotiators had the power to accept a contract without their approval. The union women decided to proceed with the strike vote. The result: unanimous support for the strike.

THE STRIKE

The two-month strike further consolidated the clericals' militant work culture. Freed from the constraints of the workplace hierarchy, the women found opportunities to assert themselves and act in new (and sometimes unexpected) ways. On the picket line, well-liked supervisors were given preferential treatment. But managers and supervisors who had harassed union women found themselves the object of insults and ridicule. The strikers wrote songs and chants, many of which poked fun at management. Having endured insults to their "womanhood," they seized this opportunity to insult upper management's "manhood." "There were women who came up with fantastic ideas," one woman reported.

> From the youngest, single woman to the oldest, all got crazy occasionally. . . . All the women got loud and rowdy, held up nasty

signs, and said things they wouldn't usually say. I myself said something really nasty to the top manager when he bumped me with his car. I was shocked as were the other strikers. The managers' eyes bugged out when I insulted him. But all the other strikers laughed.

The strike required that the union women confront conventional norms about "proper feminine behavior." For some, this provoked ambivalence. "The strike was quite traumatic for many of the women," remembered one woman in her late fifties. "Several were not happy with picketing and did not want to picket but they did. I myself felt in very alien territory. I couldn't act as vociferously as the others." For other women, it was their husbands' reactions to the strike that caused the greatest conflict. Some of the married women reported supportive spouses who totally endorsed the strike, increasing their household and child-care contributions to fill in where necessary. But others emphasized that the strike provoked significant strain in their marriages. Having just supported her husband through a two-month strike of his own, one woman described the unexpected and unsettling impact of the strike on her family life:

> My husband was fed up. I lived strike twenty-four hours a day and was gone a lot at meetings. My husband did much of the child care, housework, and cooking. I was worried about my marriage but felt I couldn't give up the strike. I've never gone through anything so stressful in my life.

In some cases women responded to their husbands with assertive claims about their right to participate in the strike. When her husband demanded that she quit the strike, one woman replied, "I don't care if you like it or not. I'm in this strike and will be until the end. And there isn't much you can do about it!"

Whatever their family situations, the strike provided an opportunity for the union women to share their personal lives and develop close ties with coworkers. On warm days women brought their children to the picket line, an act that, according to one woman, "management resented because it made them look bad." No longer segregated by department, the women formed strong friendships and commitments on the picket line. "As the strike progressed," one woman recalled, "the issue became not only gaining a good contract but also protecting my friends." While the picket line helped to solidify the ties among the union women, management's strike behavior contributed to a heightened sense of "us" versus "them." During the first few weeks of the strike the management bargaining team refused to bargain altogether. "They had the attitude," reported one woman, "that they would punish us bad little girls for striking." When management did agree to bargain, its representatives responded to the union's demand for female representation at all bargaining sessions by calling in an outside mediator. For many of the Trust women, management's actions reflected an attitude that, as one woman put it, "We were just a bunch of dumb little women who didn't know what we were doing."

The union women faced other challenges as well. The strike received little newspaper or television coverage.[14] Though a few other labor unions—a local nurses' union, AFSCME, and a teachers' union (Madison Teachers' Incorporated)—helped out on the picket line, extensive support from the community was not forthcoming. The union women felt that their own inexperience was partly responsible for the low level of support. But some of their initatives revealed a sophisticated approach to strike strategy and politics. The most unique tactic involved Jane Fonda in a ploy to inform the members of WEA about the situation at the Trust. A month into the strike, the union women discovered that WEA had invited Fonda to be the keynote speaker for its yearly convention in Milwaukee. The trust women contacted Fonda, who agreed to incorporate into her speech a statement prepared by the strikers. Before five thousand teachers, Fonda concluded her speech by stating,

> And what if I told you that there are fifty-three women who work for an insurance company who, like Blacks in the days when they had to sit at the back of the buses, aren't allowed to walk in the front of the building and take an elevator to their offices? They have to come in a back door and walk up the back stairs. So little respect is given them by management that there is one supervisor assigned to every five clerical workers; that the supervisors follow them and time them even when they are in the restrooms . . . that these skilled workers, some of whom have worked for a long time as clericals, get as a starting pay $3.08 an hour . . . when half of these women support families by themselves? And what if I told you that they're *your* employees?

According to the union women, the president of WEA and the management of the Trust were furious. Fonda's comments were both unexpected and embarrassing. But for the Trust women, the Fonda speech was a high point of the strike: It resulted in more publicity, increased support from WEA members, and perhaps most important, confirmation that the strike was a legitimate action.

Eight weeks into the strike, the impasse in bargaining eroded the union women's morale. Having anticipated a strike of several weeks' duration, several women were forced to take part-time jobs.[15] The majority of the women continued to picket, but the bargaining team recognized that if the strike persisted into December some of the union women might abandon the strike effort. They therefore recommended to the membership on November 23 that the union accept the contract proposed by the mediator. The contract included improved grievance language and strong union input into work rules but no schedule. The Trust women agreed to the contract and returned to work on November 28.

THE DIFFUSION OF MILITANCE AT THE TRUST

The process of participating in the strike led to the solidification of the women's relationships and a growth in their critical consciousness. Shared sensibilities about rights and goals, only partially formed until the collective action promoted further understanding, were forged on the picket line.[16] The central element of this "shared sensibility" was a consciousness of working women's rights. "Before the strike, I would have done whatever I was told, not thinking I had the right to say otherwise," one striker explained.

> Now, I do realize that . . . if you are not getting treated equally and fairly, you do have the right to say otherwise. . . . I learned not to be afraid . . . [Before] I felt like I was stepping on pins and needles all the time. . . . I learned I didn't have to take that anymore.

A second woman echoed: "We proved that we wouldn't take harassment, that we would take action if pushed around."

The strike brought real reforms to the Trust. Within several months, WEA had established a task force to investigate the problems there. As a result, three managers were fired, many of the outstanding grievances were resolved, job openings were posted, and the union women gained access to the front door and the elevator. In addition, changes were instituted in the managerial hierarchy. From the perspective of the union women, the most important change was a shift in responsibility for personnel from one particular male manager—the target of many of the women's prestrike grievances—to a female manager. Crediting these changes to the strike and its aftereffects, most of the union women noted a significant improvement in working conditions six months after the strike. What they failed to anticipate were the more challenging managerial strategies that would follow.

In the two years following the strike, the Trust management promoted several of the strike leaders to higher grade-level union positions (including the union position of unit supervisor) and first-line supervisory positions.[17] Though these jobs carried little decision-making power, they did establish a hierarchy among the union women. This created an uncomfortable situation for the Trust women. Some were jealous of their friends' new jobs. Others felt that the women promoted into supervisory positions had "defected to the other side." The strongest criticism was expressed by one of the strike leaders: "I feel very strongly about principles, and one of those is you don't go from union to management. That is defection!"

If the promotion of strike leaders fragmented the women's work culture, the programs initiated by management to "open up communication" with union employees removed much of the basis for the union's prestrike grievances.[18] Shortly after the strike, management brought in a psychologist to interview managers and union women about the problems at the Trust. Management then instituted a monthly luncheon at which union employees could air their grievances, initiated training workshops to facilitate greater communication between management and union, and formed discussion groups for supervisors to explore more "open ways" to deal with their subordinates. These changes led many Trust women to conclude that management had taken their strike demands seriously. It was for this reason that the automation of the claims process caught the union women off guard.

The deployment of computerized office technologies was not new at the Trust, but it did accelerate in the Dental Claims Department during the three years following the strike. Before the strike, keypunch machines were used by data-entry operators to enter information from the billing, accounting, and claims departments. In the clerical department, video display terminals (VDTs) were utilized to access files and to generate worksheets for the claims adjustors. After receiving a VDT-generated worksheet (which included the relevant information on the insured), the skilled claims adjustor determined whether the medical procedure was warranted, decided the appropriate payment, entered the payment on a code sheet, and sent the code sheet to the data-entry operator to be keypunched.

By the summer of 1982, responsibility for adjusting the simple claims in the Dental Claims Department had shifted from the claims adjustors to the less skilled VDT operators, who typed into the terminal the name of the insured, the dental procedure code, and the charge for the service. After determining whether the charge matched the service, the computer either paid or rejected the claim. The more complex claims—the claims that required "human judgment"—were still manually adjusted by the claims adjustor. Left with the more complicated claims, the one remaining dental adjustor now had, in one sense, a job that had been "upgraded." But viewed from the perspective of the Trust clerical work force as a whole, the automation of the dental claims process resulted in a deskilling and downgrading of jobs.[19]

From the perspective of management, automation increased the productivity of the dental claims process while shifting responsibility for monitoring employee performance from the supervisor to the "machine." In a work situation where conflict between supervisors and union employees (particularly in the Dental Claims Department) had been partially responsible for the strike, the shift to "on-line" claims adjusting provided the Trust management with another advantage. As one manager explained, automation promised to eliminate an important source of conflict:[20]

> Before when the supervisor monitored productivity, there was a lot of room for subjectivity. . . . The supervisor–employee relationship got in the way and got personalized. Now, the computer becomes the expert. It monitors keystrokes per hour, the time away from the desk, the number of hours at the machine. It is really wonderful and THE WOMEN DON'T QUARREL WITH THE MACHINE! [my emphasis]!

The fall 1982 contract negotiations revealed the complex consequences of the shifts in managerial policies at the Trust. With four of the six bargaining team members veterans of the previous bargaining, the Trust women entered the negotiating sessions with greater knowledge and confidence than had been the case before the strike. But what was missing this time around was a strong oppositional work culture at the Trust. The economic recession and the conservative political climate partially accounted for the lower level of militance among the

Trust women in 1982. In an economic recession, working women are less likely to take actions that might jeopardize their jobs. And in the context of a corporate assault on the large labor unions, a small union like the USU would have difficulty maintaining an aggressive bargaining stance. The turnover at the Trust in the three years following the strike provided an additional reason for the reduced militance. Between 1979 and 1982 fifteen to twenty new employees had been hired to replace the women who had left the Trust. Not having shared the experience of prestrike working conditions or the strike itself, many of the new employees were reluctant to involve themselves in union activities. For long-term employees, intimate knowledge of the "costs of a strike" partially contributed to a cautious attitude. Though the union women reaffirmed their commitment to "take action in the face of harrassment," they also saw a strike as a strategy of last resort.

Most important, the shifts in managerial policies at the Trust removed the basis for the acute and pervasive dissatisfaction that had catalyzed the strike. In 1979, the explicit forms of management harassment and discrimination had provided a common, personalized target for the women's grievances. By contrast, management's poststrike strategies did not provoke this same type of dissatisfaction. The promotions were controversial; but for the most part the women directed their resentment, not toward management, but rather toward their coworkers. The institution of a more humanistic managerial approach led to cynicism among some women; but it generated "consent" to their working conditions among others. The automation of the claims process caused concern among some women; but most failed to perceive the negative consequences and potential hazards in office automation. In short, compared to the prestrike managerial policies that had polarized management and union, the poststrike managerial policies failed to provoke the shared sense of dissatisfaction necessary for the development of a strong oppositional work culture.

The union women entered the 1982 contract negotiations with a proposal that protected union input into work rules, reinstated the salary schedule, extended union benefits, and increased union wages. In the end, the union accepted the advice of its legal adviser and gave up both contract language that required management to negotiate any new work rules with the union (one of the central gains in the 1979 strike) and the reinstatement of the salary schedule in exchange for retaining leave time and gaining a raise. Defined by management as lying outside the purview of management–union negotiations, technological changes were not addressed. Bargaining team members stressed that many of the union women were unhappy with the new contract, particularly with the loss of control over work rules and with the inequities in the salary system. One strike leader projected the possible negative consequences of the union's loss of control over work rules: "Ultimately, management could implement work rules around production standards. . . . That would kill us. . . . With the previous language, management couldn't have done this."

CONCLUSION

The strike at the WEA Trust offers powerful testimony to the capacity of clerical workers to respond to authoritarian and patriarchal management policies with militant collective action. The focus on conflict reveals the ways in which these women were actors attempting to gain control and self-respect, rather than passive objects of managerial strategies and familial constraints. Confronted with sex-discriminatory practices and attitudes, as well as a hierarchy of surveillance and control, these women initiated a strike. For many of the women, the strike provoked ambivalence. It required that they risk financial hardship, challenge traditional power relationships with management and husbands, and confront conventional expectations about proper feminine behavior. Though these pressures caused a significant level of discomfort for many of the women, for all but a few misgivings were overridden by a commitment to "see the strike through."

Still, the working conditions at the Trust were not unusual. Particularly in the finance industries of insurance and banking, sexist and coercive managerial policies are typical.[21] Collective actions, however, are not. At the Trust, the capacity of these women to translate gender-based grievances into an oppositional work culture was enhanced by a unique set of circumstances. The union backgrounds, union employment, and union membership of office workers at the Trust provided crucial resources for their strike mobilization. Although none of the office workers had participated in a strike before, many of them had experienced previous contact with trade unions that legitimated labor actions. In addition, the Trust women were indirect employees of a labor union, the WEA. Concerned with its image as a labor organization, WEA constrained the Trust from mobilizing its resources for aggressive antiunion initiatives. This decreased the women's vulnerability. The moral encouragement and legal advice from key professional employees of WEA provided an additional, crucial resource. Finally, the office workers were unionized. Although the male professionals dominated the USU, the existence of the union nevertheless provided the Trust women with an opportunity to develop mutually reinforcing ties and networks of solidarity, within both their work culture and their bargaining unit of the USU. It was within this context that the sex-discriminatory working conditions at the Trust, initiated by a group of particularly short-sighted male managers, took on heightened significance and catalyzed resistance.

This case study of the Trust strike suggests that the development of a militant work culture among clerical workers is more likely when:

1. Managerial practices provide working women with a clear target for their grievances;

2. Working women have access to a supportive ideology as well as resources they can control and mobilize;

3. The threat of managerial repression is not prohibitive.

In one sense these conclusions do not differ from those that predict higher rates of collective action for men. When clerical workers are in situations that provide them with a strong reason as well as the capacity to act, they do act.[22]

But in another sense analysis of the Trust strike confirms the centrality of gender in shaping women's work-based activism. Gender relationships conditioned the strike mobilization of the Trust women in several senses. First, the working conditions at this company were defined by both class and gender hierarchies. Not only were the office workers paid low wages for clerical jobs that granted them little autonomy, negligible authority, and minimal promotional opportunities but the managers who set the policies were men. There was little question that many of management's practices at the Trust were shaped by sexist assumptions regarding women's status as "secondary wage-earners." Other policies, such as the work rules imposed by management with the move to the new building are not unusual in workplaces employing mostly male workers. But because these rules were instituted by male managers whose policies and attitudes reflected patriarchal assumptions, the Trust women defined the work rules as sexist.

Second, gender shaped the identification of the Trust women as wage-earners in a sex-segregated occupation and as family members with extensive commitments and responsibilities outside the workplace. It was against the backdrop of this double identification that these office workers developed a female-centered consciousness regarding working conditions at the Trust. At the core of the Trust women's consciousness was the perception that management's policies and attitudes were patronizing, sexist, and disrespectful of their status as working women. Finally, gender also played a key role in the character of the women's work culture at the Trust. The Trust women incorporated traditional examples of women's rituals into their own work culture. Nowhere was this more obvious than in the naming of their newsletter "As the Trust Turns," a play on the title of the soap opera "As the World Turns." More than a reflection of traditional women's values, the newsletter utilized women's commitments—to family for example—to urge its readers to develop a sense of entitlement at work. Once on strike, the female culture forged by the office workers became more radical still. Openly and vocally challenging the right of male managers to assume the power and authority of their gender position, the Trust women transcended conventional expectations of proper female behavior.

But what can this strike tell us about the possibilities as well as the limitations of collective action forged around the rallying cry of working women's rights? On the one hand, the Trust women went beyond the narrow demands of workers for wages and benefits to demand that negotiations between management and union women be dictated by "human rights and principles." For the women at the Trust, this meant respect for their status as working women, equal treatment in regard to work rules, and a heightened sensitivity to the particular responsibilities and problems women bring to and encounter on the job. In the context of working conditions at this company, these were radical demands necessitating radical action.

But as dramatic as this strike was, it would be a mistake to misinterpret the lessons these women took away from their experience. In a certain sense the very factors that catalyzed the development of a radical work-based consciousness also limited the scope of that consciousness. On the basis of their encounters with managerial sexism and harassment, the Trust women developed a particular interpretation of working women's rights—the right to oppose blatantly sex-discriminatory management practices and to demand respectful treatment on the job. Even the demand for strong union input into work rules—a radical demand in any management–labor dispute—was motivated by particular grievances over sex-discriminatory work rules, not by more general grievances over union exclusion from managerial decision making. For many of the women, consciousness of work-based rights did not extend to their right to control other aspects of their working conditions. This limited the clerical workers' ability to respond to the more sophisticated managerial strategies that followed the strike.

The strategies of the Trust women reflected both the extent and the limits of the (working) women's movement. It is partially because feminists have validated women's right to protest disrespectful and discriminatory working conditions that the Trust women were able to mobilize for this strike. But clerical workers need more than equal treatment and respect on the job. Although in certain work contexts the realization of these demands necessitates militant action, as was evidenced at the Trust, management can accommodate such demands without fundamentally altering the authority structure in the office. There is great potential in a movement and an ideology based on "working women's rights." For such a movement to be successful, it must encompass demands for comparable worth, equal representation at all levels of management, and perhaps most important, a real voice in the technological and organizational decisions that determine women's work lives.[23] Unless proposals for working women's rights are linked to broader issues of control at work, the full potential of a working women's agenda will remain unrealized.

NOTES

1. The data for this article were derived from twenty-two oral history interviews and thirty-seven short written interviews with office workers at the Trust, together with six semistructured interviews with Trust managers and an interview with the woman lawyer who provided legal support for the 1979 contract negotiations. The oral history interviews with office workers covered the following topics: work and family history, union background, work and family attitudes, working conditions at the Trust, the strike, and poststrike working conditions. The short written interviews included demographic questions as well as questions on work and family history, union background, and extent of strike participation. The interviews with Trust managers included questions on managerial policies, decisions, and attitudes regarding the organization of work and the strike. Additional materials for the article—union newsletters, grievances, and labor contracts—were provided by the union. Only a small part of the information from the interviews is included in this article. For a more extended discussion, see Cynthia Butler Costello, " 'On the Front': Class, Gender, and Conflict in the Insurance Workplace" (doctoral dissertation, University of Wisconsin—Madison, 1984).

2. See Leslie Woodcock Tentler, *Wage-Earning Women: Industrial Work and Family Life in the United States, 1900–1930* (New York: Oxford University Press, 1979); Margery W. Davies, *Woman's Place Is at the Typewriter: Office Work and Office Workers, 1870–1930* (Philadelphia: Temple University Press, 1982); and Rosabeth Moss Kanter, *Men and Women of the Corporation* (New York: Basic Books, 1977).

3. See Thomas Dublin, *Women at Work: The Transformation of Work and Community in Lowell, Massachusetts, 1820–1860* (New York: Columbia University Press, 1979); Alice Kessler-Harris, *Out to Work: A History of Wage-Earning Women in the United States* (New York: Oxford University Press, 1982); Sarah Eisenstein, *Give Us Bread but Give Us Roses* (London: Routledge & Kegan Paul, 1983); Patricia Ann Cooper, "From Hand Craft to Mass Production: Men, Women, and Work Culture in American Cigar Factories, 1900–1919" (doctoral dissertation, University of Maryland, 1981); Ruth Milkman, "The Reproduction of Job Segregation by Sex: A Study of the Sexual Division of Labor in the Auto and Electrical Manufacturing Industries in the 1940's" (doctoral dissertation, University of California, Berkeley, 1981); Susan Porter Benson, *Counter Cultures: Saleswomen, Managers, and Customers in American Department Stores, 1890–1940* (Urbana: University of Illinois Press, 1987); Barbara Melosh, *"The Physician's Hand": Work Culture and Conflict in American Nursing* (Philadelphia: Temple University Press, 1982); and Costello, " 'On the Front.' "

4. Melosh *"The Physician's Hand,"* 6.

5. Ruth Milkman, Editor's Preface, in Ruth Milkman, ed., *Women, Work, and Protest* (Boston: Routledge & Kegan Paul, 1985.)

6. For an analysis that addresses the contradictory dimensions of women's work culture, see Hannah Creighton, "Tied by Double Apron Strings: Female Work Culture and Organization in a Restaurant," *Insurgent Sociologist* 11, No. 3 (Fall 1982): 59–64.

7. Roslyn L. Feldberg, " 'Union Fever': Organizing Among Clerical Workers, 1900–1930," *Radical America* 14 (May–June 1980): 53–67.

8. Sharon Hartman Strom, "Challenging 'Woman's Place': Feminism, the Left, and Industrial Unionism in the 1930's," *Feminist Studies* 9, No. 2 (Summer 1983): 359–386.

9. See Michael Burawoy, *Manufacturing Consent: Changes in the Labor Process under Monopoly Capitalism* (Chicago: University of Chicago Press, 1979); and Richard Edwards, *Contested Terrain: The Transformation of the Workplace in the Twentieth Century* (New York: Basic Books, 1979).

10. Dair L. Gillespie, Ann Leffler, and Terri Anderson, "Sexism, Sex, and Power: Sexual Harassment in the Workplace" (paper presented at the annual meetings of the American Sociological Association, San Francisco, 1982).

11. Evelyn Nakano Glenn and Roslyn L. Feldberg, "Proletarianizing Clerical Work: Technology and Organizational Control in the Office," in Andrew Zimbalist, ed., *Case Studies in the Labor Process* (New York: Monthly Review Press, 1979): 242–256.

12. Document provided by Judy Neumann, legal adviser to the Trust women for the 1979 contract negotiations and lawyer for the WEA.

13. There is no way to assess objectively what Trust managers actually said. Throughout the interviews, the union women referred to comments and attitudes of the male managers that they found particularly offensive. For the purposes of this article, the determination of the accuracy of managerial statements is less important than the shared understandings of the Trust women about those statements.

14. Two years before the Trust strike, a bitter strike had taken place at the major

Madison newspapers (owned by Madison Newspaper, Inc.). This may partially explain the low level of newspaper coverage for the Trust strike, although the fact that it was a women's strike may also have been a factor.

15. Strike benefits of $100 a week were provided for the first four weeks of the strike. After that time, low-interest loans were available through the union.

16. See Temma Kaplan, "Female Consciousness and Collective Action: The Case of Barcelona, 1910–1918," *Signs* 7, No. 3 (Spring 1982): 545–566.

17. See Edwards, *Contested Terrain,* for a discussion of the use of promotional ladders (internal labor markets) as a managerial strategy of control.

18. See Andrew Herman, "Conceptualizing Control: Domination and Hegemony in the Capitalist Labor Process," *Insurgent Sociologist* 11, No. 3 (Fall 1982): 7–22, for an analysis of human relations strategies in the labor process.

19. C. Wright Mills, *White Collar* (New York: Oxford University Press, 1951), was the first to analyze what we now call the "degradation" of clerical work. Harry Braverman, *Labor and Monopoly Capital* (New York: Monthly Review Press, 1974), followed with a careful analysis of the de-skilling of clerical work. More recent works focusing on the organizational and technological dimensions of de-skilling include Glenn and Feldberg, in Zimbalist, ed., *Case Studies,* 242–256; Anne Machung, "Word Processing: Forward for Business, Backward for Women," in Karen Brodkin Sacks and Dorothy Remy, eds., *My Troubles Are Going to Have Trouble with Me* (New Brunswick, N.J.: Rutgers University Press, 1984), 124–139; Mary C. Murphree, "Brave New Office: The Changing World of the Legal Secretary," in ibid., 140–159; and Judith Gregory, "Technological Change in the Office Workplace and Implications for Organizing," in Donald Kennedy, Charles Craypo, and Mary Lehman, eds., *Labor and Technology: Union Responses to Changing Environments* (Pennsylvania State University Press, 1982), 83–102.

20. For one of the best discussions of work, conflict, and technology, see David Noble, "Social Choice in Machine Design: The Case of Automatically Controlled Machine Tools and the Challenge for Labor," *Politics and Society* 8, Nos. 3–4 (1978): 313–347.

21. See Glenn and Feldberg, "Proletarianizing Clerical Work," 242; and Marteen De Kadt, "Insurance: A Clerical Work Factory?" in Zimbalist, ed., *Case Studies,* 51–72.

22. See Louise A. Tilly, "Paths of Proletarianization: Organization of Production, Sexual Division of Labor, and Women's Collective Action," *Signs* 7, No. 2 (Winter 1981): 400–417.

23. For analysis of comparable worth, see Roslyn L. Feldberg, "Comparable Worth: Toward Theory and Practice in the United States," *Signs* 10 (Winter 1984): 311–328; Donald J. Treiman and Heidi I. Hartmann, eds., *Women, Work, and Wages: Equal Pay for Jobs of Equal Value* (Washington, D.C.: National Academy Press, 1981).

6

The Edison School Struggle:

The Reshaping of Working-Class

Education and Women's

Consciousness

Wendy Luttrell

This article examines the interweavings of gender, class, and race consciousness among white working-class women activists who were involved in a community struggle for quality desegregated education. The Edison School campaign is an example of how one community successfully challenged a city's neglect of working-class education. It also allows us to explore how the texture of working-class women's lives, relationships, and self-awareness shaped their participation and leadership in grassroots organization. Although the events and activities of the Coalition for a New High School can be told in a distinct chronology, the development of these women's consciousness cannot. It is a story of personal change filled with unevenness and inconsistencies.

This article is based on interviews with five white working-class women leaders of the coalition and their shared sensibilities about their political activity. I explore the women's leadership as it is fueled by their current roles and activities as working-class mothers, as well as their past experiences as working-class students. I argue that the women's gender, race, and class consciousness is not fixed or in rigid categories, but changes as they participate in a community struggle.

Then, I argue that there is no single relationship between the dominant social structure and its ideology and working-class consciousness. Instead, the women's perceptions are layered with both compliant and antagonistic responses and adaptations to the dominant culture.

Although the women I interviewed shared certain perceptions about their experiences, they had varied work, family, community, and political backgrounds and attitudes. As a result, it is impossible to characterize one single kind of working-class women's leadership or one working-class attitude toward education, feminism, or race relations. Instead, this article focuses on the full range and complexity of their changing sensibilities in an attempt to counter one-dimensional portrayals of working-class women's lives. It is my hope that the words of women who are themselves in the process of self-reflection, reassessment, resistance, and change, and whose voices have not often been heard will help feminists to sharpen our analysis of working-class women's political consciousness.

MY ROLE

I first became aware of the Coalition for a New High School while I was working in a community-based women's center in Kensington, a Philadelphia neighborhood. My role at the time was adult educator in the Lutheran Settlement House Women's Program, where I was teaching classes and preparing curriculum materials. As part of my responsibilities I was to develop a curriculum guide entitled *Women in the Community,* which was to use the community as a resource for learning as well as illuminating the problems and potential of the lives of women in the neighborhood.[1]

When I first started interviewing students, teachers, and the women's center staff members about what should be included in the curriculum guide, everyone mentioned Edison High School and the efforts of the coalition to get a new coeducational high school facility built in the neighborhood. In fact, my inquiries into people's attitudes toward education became one of the most challenging aspects of my work in the women's center. I learned quickly that discussions about education and its role in people's lives were bound to generate passion and controversy, regardless of whether people had been involved in the coalition or not. The immediate controversy centering around Edison High School was over who was responsible for the poor quality of education in District 5. Was it uninvolved parents who did not take enough interest, was it ineffective teachers who were working only to make a buck, was it apathetic children who just did not work hard enough, or was it the School Board which ignored the needs of students in Kensington? Regardless of different viewpoints on these questions, everyone agreed that a new high school was part of any solution.

I decided to explore these issues and to outline the activities of the coalition. I began by interviewing a number of women about the history of the community's efforts to force local politicians, City Hall, and the Board of Education to make good on a twenty-year-old promise to replace the aging, unsafe Edison High School facility. I arranged in-depth interviews with five of the women organizers in the coalition and attended coalition meetings, twice as a participant and three times as an observer. My relationship to the coalition's activities was complex—I was both an advocate and a researcher. As an educator, I was committed to transforming the educational opportunities available to neighborhood residents. As a feminist, I was anxious to support the efforts of Kensington women. At the same time, as a sociologist, I wanted to document and analyze the coalition's activities.

During the three years that I worked in the women's center, I had the opportunity to get to know people who had been active participants in the coalition and to develop personal relationships with the white women leaders. They shared with me their perceptions about the coalition and their role as women in shaping it. What follows is based on discussions of the history of the coalition, of being women in political organizations, of the quality of education in District 5, of the women's own experiences as working-class students, and of their educational aspirations for themselves and their children.

EDISON HIGH SCHOOL: THE HISTORICAL CONTEXT

In 1903, when Edison High School was built, it was called Northeast High School. At that time the neighborhood was made up of Irish, Polish, and German immigrants, and the student body was predominantly white. Since then the neighborhood has changed significantly. Each decade has seen different ethnic and racial populations move into and out of Kensington. Many white residents who could afford it have moved farther northeast of the city, while Blacks and Hispanics have moved into the areas abandoned by whites. During the early 1960s a new building was constructed to meet the increasing educational needs of the upwardly mobile white families who had moved to the Northeast sections of Philadelphia. The old Northeast High School at 8th Street and Lehigh Avenue was moved out of District 5, taking with it the school's colors, trophies, history, and staff. The remaining building, renamed Edison High School, was an aging, poorly equipped fire hazard. The city promised the parents of both Edison High, a boys' school, and Kensington High, a girls' school (another decaying school in District 5) that a new facility would be built for their children. For nearly twenty years, District 5 parents waited while the city broke promise after promise.

Meanwhile, the quality of education at Edison suffered greatly. Edison High School had a staggering dropout rate, the highest in the city, despite many innovative efforts made throughout the 1970s by the principal and some dedicated teachers.[2] National standardized tests administered at Edison showed students scoring drastically below the national average.[3] In addition, the environment at Edison was not conducive to learning. The actual physical plant was not only unsafe and a fire hazard, but it had no cafeteria or sport or recreational facilities.

In reality, Edison High School mirrored the problems of life in District 5. During the 1960s and 1970s, it had the terrible distinction of having the largest number of students killed in the Vietnam War of any high school in the country. In many classrooms plaques were hung to commemorate the lives of Black and white working-class boys who had been killed. Edison also had a reputation for severe gang trouble—it was a school plagued by racial tensions. When the coalition first started its organizing efforts, the student population at Edison was 80 percent Hispanic and Black. Although officially the student body was 20 percent white, it was estimated that less than half of the white school population attended the school daily.

Edison's poor education had far-reaching effects in District 5, creating a negative self-fulfilling prophecy for the community at large. Though trends signaled in the 1980 Census indicated an increase in high school graduates in Kensington from 20 percent in 1970 to 32 percent in 1980, these figures were misleading when compared to those for the city and country as a whole. Between 1970 and 1980 the percentage of high school graduates in the United States more than doubled from 31.1 percent to 66.3 percent. In Philadelphia the increase was not so high, 39.9 percent to 54.2 percent, with the effect of the city losing ground nationally. But in Kensington only 32 percent of the population had graduated from high school in 1980, reflecting the growing disparity in educational attainment for this working-class community.[4]

For the most part, students at Edison did not see a bright future for themselves. They knew that the education they recieved could not assure them a job in a community where plant closings have eroded the economic base of the neighborhood and unemployment exceeds 16 percent.

THE DEVELOPMENT OF A MULTIRACIAL COALITION

For twenty years, groups of Black and Hispanic parents had repeatedly tried to organize for a new high school facility. Though each of these efforts had its own unique history and reasons for failure, these efforts had one thing in common: they did not engage white parents in their struggle.

This is not surprising, given the violent history of race relations in District 5. In one neighborhood, the first Hispanic family to move into a white section was firebombed, bringing citywide attention to the growing hostility among residents of this neighborhood in flux. To this day, the women's center, located in a predominantly white neighborhood, has trouble attracting Black and Hispanic women to its programs, in part because of their lingering fear of racial violence.

Despite growing racial tensions in the 1970s, many white parents in District 5 could afford to ignore the problem. For years, a small percentage of students could opt to attend Frankford High School, which is 85 percent white. Other parents could bargain for favors from local politicians or use the addresses of relatives living in the Northeast sections of the city to get their children into Frankford High School. Still others could send their children to Catholic schools. Nevertheless, all of these options were temporary and could not continue to meet the needs of all Kensington students. By September 1979, things had begun to change. The School Board had closed all fourteen "optional" areas in the city (schools that had openings for students outside their districts), forcing 120 white former students of Frankford High School to attend Edison. At the same time, fewer political favors were being given, and rising tuition costs in parochial schools were forcing increasing numbers of white students into the public schools.

It was within this changing context that the Kensington Joint Action Committee (KJAC) entered the Edison School controversy. KJAC, like many anti-poverty groups of the 1970s, grew out of a community-run social service agency. As a publicly funded organization that could not be partisan, it hired an experienced white male community organizer to bring together a separate local action group. This group, though originally spearheaded by a man, found its success through the effective participation and leadership of women who defined the community issues. For example, KJAC won its first victory and gained community confidence when it successfully organized Black and white residents to close a local flophouse that attracted drug traffic and crime. KJAC mobilized women residents to picket the flophouse after a fire in the building threatened the safety and lives of neighborhood children.

Then in 1979 KJAC was instrumental in coordinating the Coalition for a New High School. The coalition included twenty local churches and community organizations as well as many interested but unaffiliated parents in School District 5. Again the issue focused on children, safety, and the future of the community. The initial task was to find a location for the new school that could draw easily upon Black, white, and Hispanic neighborhoods. This was difficult because of segregated housing patterns and strong neighborhood loyalties, but finally a site was chosen. The next step was a districtwide petition drive that collected eight thousand names of supporters of the new school. In their door-to-door campaign, coalition participants came into contact with people who had never been reached by earlier efforts—especially white people who had been too afraid or unwilling to be associated with a multiracial organization.

The coalition's most difficult task was to challenge dominant racist attitudes and organizational efforts for segregated education. When local white politicians informed their constituents that the new Edison High School would bring racial trouble and deteriorating property values, the coalition organized repeated meetings with community groups to counter the rumors. While local politicians were claiming that the new school would be mostly for Blacks and Hispanics and that a small number of white students would be forced to attend the school for desegregation purposes, the coalition organized local committees within the parent–teacher organization to discuss quality education and desegregation as issues to be dealt with hand-in-hand. One coalition leader described what she thought was a turning point in the coalition's effectiveness in countering prevailing racist attitudes.

> It all came to a head when the School Board closed the Frankford option. When white parents found that they would have to go to Edison, forty parents sat-in at Frankford High to protest. Even though the School Board closed fourteen other optional areas

throughout the city, nobody organized against the policy, except the Frankford parents. Then we found out that the local representative had organized and led the sit-in action *himself*. They treated those parents like gold. We were never treated so good when we made demands or did actions. But anyway, we decided to go directly and talk to the Frankford parents involved in the sit-in. And do you know what we found—they didn't even know the coalition was organizing for a new Edison High School to be built for white, Hispanic, and Black students equally. The local politicians had purposely fostered misunderstanding and fear within the Frankford parents and when they heard about our plan they were behind it 100 percent.

Perhaps the most important role of the coalition was that it provided people with oppositional ideas and the organizational support to counter dominant racist attitudes. Since most traditional, local white organizations were opposed to the concept of an integrated Edison, this was crucial. At one rally a white woman from a local Catholic church that had been organizing community meetings against the new Edison site stood up to speak. She explained her disagreement with her church's community council and its efforts to stop construction of the new school.[5] She expressed her fears about speaking up in public but said she felt the coalition gave her the opportunity to support quality desegregated education for her children. An event such as this was a key factor in confirming the coalition's suspicion that there were other white residents in the community who had not been heard from. Consequently the coalition consolidated its efforts to maintain the visibility and accessibility of the organization to white, Black, and Hispanic parents.

Throughout the entire campaign, the coalition was faced with attempts by politicians and the School Board to divide the multiracial organization. One example came in the form of a proposal by the school superintendent to create a special "alternative" high school at the proposed Edison site for the 120 white Frankford students who had refused to attend Edison or Kensington High School. The coalition got wind of the plan and confronted the superintendent at a Board of Education meeting with signs that read, No FAVORITES. As one woman organizer explained, "If he [the superintendent] can open up the site for 120 kids, he can open it for every kid in this neighborhood." The coalition organized a letter campaign for District 5 parents to register their opinions with local legislators and School Board members opposing the alternative school proposal.

Attempts at racial division continued even after the coalition had won support from the new mayor[6] and had worked out the details for the new facility with the Board of Education. A key white woman leader of the coalition described what happened:

We met with the Board of Education representative and a verbal agreement was made that everyone could live with. However, when the actual letter of support came to me, I recognized that the conditions had once again changed. The letter stated that the students with first priority to attend the new Edison would be those students currently enrolled at Edison. The second priority would be those students in the immediate area of District 7. The very people who had fought against sending their kids to Edison would now have priority over other District 5 students. Well, we were furious. I immediately called the superintendent and told him that if the letter was not changed to reflect the verbal agreement we had made, that we would take the issue to the streets again. There was no way we were going to let the Board of Education divide District 5 again as a community. Within a couple of days they had sent us a new letter.

CHANGING RACE CONSCIOUSNESS

While the women's female consciousness—their concern for their children's education—originally fueled their fight against City Hall and the School Board, it was their new experience in a multiracial coalition that actively refocused and reshaped their political analysis of the situation. One woman explained:

> The main reason why whites did not take up the struggle for the new school was because of racism. During the height of the struggle in the early 1970s, the mayor and his cronies were fanning the flames of racism to the point where the white community was blinded to the fact that our children were also being hurt by the situation. We weren't really getting a piece of the pie. Our children weren't going to school, never learned to read or write, and could not find work. Even though I was aware of the situation, because my kids were dropping out and getting in trouble, I didn't know what to do. I just never had had anything to do with Black and Puerto Rican people before.

In addition to their growing political awareness of how racism was used to divide the community, some women also described changes in their own consciousness about racism. One white woman explained an insight she had gained about her fears of working with Black and Hispanic parents:

> But what was most important about the coalition was that when Black, Hispanic, and white parents got together, we found out that we all wanted the same things for our children—especially when it came to quality education. Once we were all in the same room, we found out that we all wanted our kids to go to schools where they would be safe, where they wouldn't be chased home after school by other kids and hurt, and where they would get the best quality education. As a white mother, because of my own prejudice, I had thought

that Black and Hispanic parents would settle for something a little less for their kids, that if I joined with them I might have to compromise something for my kids. I learned I was wrong.

When describing the close relationship that developed among some of the women organizers, a Black woman who had been one of the original parents involved in the Edison struggle twelve years earlier explained changes in her understanding about racism as well:

> Working with the coalition really made me challenge my own prejudices about white people and made me realize that we all want the same things for our kids. My mother used to say to me, "Never be proud of your color, be proud of your heritage and who you are." I never quite understood what she meant but I think this is an important thing to remember because I have really learned that poverty knows no color. We do share the same problems.

Through both the influence of KJAC's community organizer and the proximity of women working together, the women developed new insights into the race relations that dominated their community. But one woman poignantly described the isolation and discomfort she felt as a result of her new attitudes:

> I still get uptight when people in the coalition start talking about racism. I just don't feel comfortable talking with people in my neighborhood about how racism hurts them. They just don't see it and they don't want to hear about it—even if it means that their kids lose out. We've talked about this in KJAC in meeting after meeting and I know that white people have to understand how their own racism is keeping them—keeping us—back. As much as I agree with it all and understand it all, it is hard for me to go out in the community and isolate myself from all my neighbors, friends, and family. But I can't go back to thinking the way I used to—it is like once you work day in and day out like I have with Sheila and you watch her think all the same things, treat her kids the same way, and want the same things as you do—my life just isn't the same.

Despite the success of these women in bringing together the issues of quality education and desegregation, the issue of racism, particularly its effect on white residents, was still potent. The women's consciousness about racism was unresolved and was tangled with threads of awareness that rejected an old way of life but had not yet been replaced with new models and new patterns.[7] In fact, their emerging consciousness about racism cannot be described apart from their experiences as women. For one, as they became increasingly conscious of their own subjugation as women, they became aware of the parallels for minorities. Second, as mothers, they began to see a common ground with Black and Hispanic women—protecting the safety and well-being of their children.

FEMALE CONSCIOUSNESS AND WOMEN'S LEADERSHIP

In late 1979, one year after the coalition's initial petition drive, a thousand people gathered in the Edison auditorium for a "Break Ground in '80" rally. Coalition activists spoke about the victory but also reminded parents that their continued active participation was crucial for Edison's future. A planning and curriculum committee was formed to ensure that community members maintained their participation in all levels of the process. The intense activities of the coalition had subsided for the while. But vivid in the minds of the people I interviewed about the coalition and its success was the leadership role that women had played.

The fact that women were active participants in the coalition was no surprise. In community struggles in many other urban working-class neighborhoods, women have often been the backbone of organizations—attending demonstrations, writing letters, posting publicity, and going to meetings. In District 5 there is a rich tradition of women activists in churches, workplaces, neighborhoods, and schools.[8] White, Black, and, more recently, Hispanic women in District 5 can all find examples of women in their communities who have been politically active. Black women in District 5 have perhaps been most visible in their efforts in welfare rights organizing; white women have been more active in local parishes or home-association groups. Hispanic women, newer to the city and to District 5, have their own women's center located in a local social service agency serving Blacks and Hispanics.

Despite this rich heritage, what was interesting about the white women's reflections about their involvement was a growing recognition of themselves as women and as leaders. One woman who had been involved in community organizing for years summed up nicely what all the white women leaders described:

> An exciting thing I learned from the Edison fight was that women *were* and *can* be leaders. We weren't just writing letters and going to meetings, we were giving public speeches to hundreds of people. I gained a lot of confidence in my ability to think through problems, and I was proud of myself. For the first time, a lot of us were putting ourselves forward talking to people and not getting scared.

The women often mentioned the thrill of becoming visible—of gaining public recognition for their leadership qualities—especially when it came to dealing with public officials who had the power to make decisions about their lives. One woman explained:

> I began to feel proud and excited about my own knowledge and strength as a woman. The best part was dealing with those men at City Hall and the Board of Education. At each meeting they set you up when you walk in. You can just see them looking you up and down saying to themselves, "What do these dames know; this is going to be a breeze." Then when you start talking, throwing statis-

tics at them, exposing the facts, you can see their attitudes change in minutes. They can't believe that these chicks who just walked in the room are strong, individual, and intelligent women. What really surprises these men is that we women can stand just as firmly on our positions as they can. It means that they have to think of us as leaders. I think it scares them too.

Two of the most active white women involved in the coalition reflected on the differences between these male officials and themselves as women:

One of the most striking things that I really learned from those actions was that women *do* all the things that these men get paid to do. We have to organize budgets, organize our time between jobs, school, the coalition, our kids and organize what we need to get done and what we need to say. While we are dealing directly with our kids and their education, they are just dealing with each other. . . . Yeah, that's right, and men don't have to change roles—those men at the Board of Education are just lawyers, administrators and all—that is their job, and they see it as their only role. But women have to change roles all the time. At one instant we are dealing with our children and keeping them together; then we switch to meetings, talking on the level of administrators. Afterwards we can go right into the community and explain what happened in language everybody understands. Then, at night, we go home and explain it to our kids. I think this makes us even stronger leaders.[9]

Throughout the interviews the women reflected on their unique qualities as women organizers—their ability to listen to parents' concerns; their willingness to compromise creatively both within the organization and with School Board officials; and their unshakable commitment to the issue because it involved their children. They also persistently pointed out that the very conditions that foster women's oppression—their multiple responsibilities as workers, wives, and mothers—were also conditions that enabled them to be more effective as leaders. Their ability to change roles and to negotiate between the worlds of politics, community, and family grew directly from those multiple responsibilities. While some feminist theories have focused primarily on the constraints involved in women's "double-burden," these women explained the positive effects.[10] Once they saw themselves as capable of participating in the public, political arena, the skills they had developed in the private realm of family and community, such as interpersonal communication and organization, translated nicely into leadership abilities.

On one level it could be argued that the women I interviewed had a woman-centered analysis, one in which they saw women as being virtuous as a result of their subordination.[11] These women often discussed women's capacities to nurture, to affiliate with others, and to work collectively as crucial characteristics for all organizers and leaders. In many ways the coalition could be analyzed as the development of a woman's culture, where women came together through their connection as women, mothers, and community members.[12] This is suggested by the ways the core women organizers talked about their experiences in working together—how their experience in the Edison struggle entered into their daily family lives and how their lives changed as a result of it all. For example, one woman described the benefit of her involvement for her kids.

> One of the best parts of the campaign was how much it became part of our lives—our kids began to hang out together while we did leaflets, we all ate dinners together—it felt like a big family. My kids became part of something bigger, and I think it will make them stronger and better people because of it.

This same daily involvement is what underscored the changes in the women's consciousness about racism and its effect on their lives.

But on another level, the interweaving of the women's daily family lives with their success in organizing the community was discussed by the women I interviewed as "given." It was seen as part of the natural terrain of community organizing, as "something that just happens when women organize things." They weren't claiming it as uniquely virtuous, but simply as what works. In fact, these women's understanding of what works in community organizing reflects a challenge to a woman-centered analysis that locates the source of women's oppression in the structural separation of "public" and "private"—where men dominate the public sphere and women attempt to exert control within the family. These women did not separate their roles as public leaders from their roles as private mothers, but saw both roles as intimately related. Rather than dichotomizing the separate spheres in their lives, these women found success and power by merging their public and private roles.[13]

At the same time, it is important to emphasize that in these women's growing confidence as leaders, they still doubted their own capabilities, intelligence, and effectiveness *as women*. One woman explained:

> I think women don't do things because we fear failure. But in the Edison struggle we found that we could make mistakes and that we could learn and grow from them. We became better leaders and organizers as a result.

Another woman added:

> But we often got treated like a bunch of hysterical women who were being too emotional about our kids. I used to try real hard to speak calmly, to get all my information out about the issue without getting excited. They wouldn't have listened to us if we hadn't been able to act like *men*. (my emphasis)

In fact, their conviction that the success of Edison was built on women's participation and leadership was full of mixed messages of pride, anger, and self-doubt. For it was their experiences as women in the coalition trying to make changes that brought them face-to-face with constraining notions of womanhood. And these notions came from both external and internal sources. Their consciousness as women was a tangled knot woven with threads of both acceptance and rejection of dominant ideologies about women. On the one hand, they had internalized a sense of fear, lack of confidence, and guilt for which they had come to blame themselves. At the same time, they were aware of their external oppression as women—being treated like hysterical women by members of the School Board; not getting the support they often needed from family or friends because what they were doing was not deemed appropriate for women; or being ignored and minimized by local politicians or the press.

What was most significant about the way these white working-class women discussed their experiences and perceptions about being women activists and leaders was its complexity. In fact, the development of their consciousness as women within the coalition is extremely difficult to chart. It was not a linear process that in retrospect the women can identify with ease. Instead, it is a multilayered process that includes many different factors, and changes over time, and involves unique life circumstances. For example, divorce had catapulted two of the women into new lifestyles filled with new economic and psychological hardships. As they dealt with these changes and sought help from local agencies, they came across or were referred to the women's center. In fact, the women's center was a critical factor in the development of the coalition and in the growth of its women leaders. The most active white participants in the coalition were also part of the women's center. One woman, a displaced homemaker, started at the women's center as a student and then became part of the staff for the hotline for abused women. Another woman, also a displaced homemaker, came to the women's center for job training and became one of the KJAC paid organizers. These two women had attended college classes at the women's center that were designed to incorporate women's studies into the college curriculum. They described what they thought the effect of the center and its educational program had been on their political work and in their lives as women leaders:

> It's funny, I can't say that taking college courses has affected my community work except that I got into community work through the course, I think.
>
> Yeah, that's true. But I don't think it was taking the college courses themselves, but really the whole consciousness-raising part of the women's center as a whole. The experience of being aware of things that are going on, that things happen to you because you are a woman. The college courses have taught me how to think about some things—how to get information that I don't have and how not to be afraid to ask for information I don't have. But I don't think you need a college education to be an effective leader.
>
> What college courses really helped me with was relating to politicians on their same level. I mean with those college courses you can

really understand their language and make your points stronger with them. I guess you could say that college helped me to deal with people outside the community better, but not so much for the members in my own neighborhood.

Here the message is complicated—the women are filled with an awareness of themselves both as women and as members of the working class. It is hard to separate out the factors that have given them confidence as women leaders. Is it increased education that has strengthened their confidence as working-class people to deal with middle-class people, professionals or politicians—"people outside the community"—or is it the community of women in the women's center that has consolidated their growth? In fact the "consciousness-raising" process they refer to is interwoven. It has grown out of their participation in the women's center, their increased education, and their political activity in the coalition. Though participating in the women's center may have contributed to these women's increased awareness of how "things happen to you because you are a woman," it was their involvement in the coalition that provided them with a vehicle for discovering their "knowledge and strength as women."

WORKING-CLASS EDUCATION: AN ARENA OF CONFLICT

The experience of schooling—both past and present—in shaping these women's political activity cannot be underestimated. From their past schooling experiences, these women had come to accept images of themselves that reflected the dominant message of school: They were working-class kids, and they were not expected to achieve or excel. Instead, they were expected to be obedient and subservient.[14] Most often schooling was described as an uncomfortable experience that working-class people share: Schools were a place where they felt judged and where they had come to view themselves as deficient, regardless of their educational attainment. But at the same time, they had images of themselves and their schooling that reflected their working-class heritage and community. They saw themselves as willing and able to make responsible choices and to be agents in their own destinies.[15] Despite the constraints of working-class schooling, these women had survived in the middle-class institution of education by balancing the dominant culture and their own class values, traditions, and experiences. These efforts to survive shaped their reaction to the issue of quality education in District 5 and, for some women, were a powerful catalyst to their political activity.

For example, when the women described their adaptation to school, they emphasized alternative criteria for "success" that were an integral part of their culture—criteria like being responsible, independent, and adultlike. One woman made this point clear when she responded to my question:

When you say you weren't encouraged in your education, do you mean by the nuns or by whom?

My mother worked as a waitress for sixty-five cents an hour and raised three children without any assistance. She just really didn't have any time to encourage us much. But I also worked since I was fifteen—I was very independent, and I didn't expect to get any encouragement. I had to be very responsible—not like a child at school. When my mother died my sister was only fifteen and I had to take care of her. I'm very proud that she made it through school and graduated. That was my big goal, and I worked to put her through.

Another alternative criterion for success in school that was an integral part of the women's working-class culture was "speaking up when things were unfair" and establishing a personal integrity in the face of authorities. Some women talked about the antagonism and rebelliousness that developed as a result of their attempts to gain dignity with teachers. One woman described how her leadership abilities first developed in school in reaction to excessive discipline:

I always had a mouth—mostly in school. It was just with authorities I had this trouble. With friends I was kind of a leader, you know how kids are in school, always working on a dare. I remember we were all kind of rebellious against the strict rules. We even revolted once and took over the lunch room—I was a leader in that one too. I guess we had so much freedom at home but were so restricted at school that it was ridiculous. We *had* to stand up for ourselves.

Another woman explained:

I could only take so much with my teachers like Mr. Graff—the sergeant—and then I had to say something. I could never watch anything unfair without speaking up. I guess I didn't have enough self-control to make it in school.

And though she is simultaneously self-blaming but proud of her reaction and adaptation to school, this same woman expresses dual notions about compliance and resistance for her child:

My son is the same way I was. I can't blame him much when he tells me about his teacher and how he had to speak his mind. But I know what is ahead of him if he doesn't make it in school.

These women's perceptions about the role of education in their lives were also complex.[16] Despite their own experiences and their understanding of how the School Board had actively thwarted the possibility of quality education in District 5 by offering inferior educational facilities and opportunities, these women still believed in education as a ticket to upward mobility. Along with their concern for their children, it was their belief in the prevailing ideology of American education that fueled their energies to fight for a new high school in the first place. They embraced the myth that if you successfully pursue educational opportunities you will be rewarded with a better job and a better life. But at the same time, they were painfully aware of both the structural inequities in schools and their own discomfort as working-class students. Even though they knew at some level that the promise of equality in education and success through education was hollow, they had also accepted part of the blame for not fulfilling this promise. A key organizer explained:

> The important point is that the system is not working. People's mobility is very limited. People really need education in order to get out of their ruts. The system keeps people in their place, in their class. You need intelligence to get out of your place.

And when I responded, "I know a lot of intelligent people living here in Kensington," she replied:

> Yeah, but if they were more ambitious, like me, then at least they'd have half a chance of getting out of their ruts.

Despite their organizing efforts in the coalition the women lacked a clear idea of who or what was the primary culprit behind the problems of working-class education in District 5. Their consciousness about working-class schooling shifted back and forth between what they knew about external or structural class inequities and what they had come to believe about their own deficiencies and faults as members of the working class. Just as their experiences as women had simultaneously facilitated and inhibited their political awareness and activity in the coalition, so had their experiences as working-class students been a source of compliance and resistance.

FEMALE VS. FEMINIST CONSCIOUSNESS

It is important to point out here that these women defy the stereotypical image of white working-class women. At best, white working-class women are described as strong survivors, despite many hardships and limited resources,[17] and at worst they are described (mostly by men) as conservative, traditional, dependent on men, uneducated, anti-intellectual, bigoted, and generally uninteresting.[18] In fact, the perceptions of the women I interviewed stand in bold relief to the literature—their self-portraits depict neither romantic survivors nor passive victims but are instead rich, textured tapestries woven with complexities and conflicts.

Similarly, these women defy the literature about white working-class women and their views of feminism. Though the women I interviewed are not antifeminists, they span a continuum in terms of their identification with the women's movement and with key women's issues. They never discussed the issue around which they were organizing as a "woman's issue" or saw the efforts of the city and School Board as being sexist. They did not see the women's movement as shaping their activity in the Edison struggle, nor did they look to the women's movement to provide them with models of women leaders. As one woman remarked when I asked her about her views on the women's movement:

> I just knew you were going to ask me about that eventually. And I'm just not the right person to talk to. I don't believe in abortion under any circumstances. I don't like what I see in the news from women libbers and I don't think that women should be in the army or in the Presidency.

Even when asked about the women's center and its impact on their work, the women I interviewed still described the women's movement as something removed from their lives and specifically apart from their class identification—a "middle-class" movement. Yet these women's perceptions are not to be seen as a rejection of feminism. Rather they reflect concrete class conditions and pressures that shape women's consciousness.[19]

What is important about the Edison School struggle is that it encompassed more than a demand for quality education; it also included the kernels of women's empowerment. In the waging of a struggle against middle-class and male-dominated institutions, a new women's self-concept emerged that challenged gender, race, and class relations. The new self-concept, built on a female consciousness, which values affiliation and nurturance, became a vehicle for change. These women came together as women and challenged racial distinctions. As an outgrowth of their female relationships and activities, and their imbeddedness in working-class community life, they realized their power and developed distinctive leadership styles.

At the same time, leadership that is born from women's role as primary caretakers of family and community life is necessarily different from leadership born from women's quest for self-realization. The feminist notion of being able to fight for women's self-interests is shaped by certain objective and subjective realities that may not be part of working-class women's culture. Economic necessities, educational and employment opportunities, cultural and religious expectations of women and women's specific roles and experiences within working-class culture—all mold self-concepts that do not necessarily embrace ideas about individual female autonomy or male/female equality. For example, in their roles as mothers, these women were able to advocate for their children in ways that they could not advocate for themselves. This duality can be seen in the following quotes:

> But I guess some people would say I am a woman's libber just because I speak my mind and won't sit back and watch what is going on in my neighborhood. If that means I am a woman's libber then okay—but I don't consider myself one. And I tell all my girls the same thing—don't ever let anybody else tell you what is best for you. It's your life and you need to stand up for yourself.

> When I grew up there were four choices—you could be a mother, nurse, teacher, or a nun. I want my daughter to know there are plenty more choices than that.

Indeed, these are women in transition who value women's independence and self-sufficiency and are seeking ways to ensure new options for their daughters. These women's perceptions reflect the kernels of both female and feminist consciousness, not as polarities but as parallels. Perhaps feminist analysis needs to understand gender consciousness better, not as a linear continuum moving from female to feminist values and perspectives, but as a more fluid set of concerns which, at times, may overlap and, at other times, conflict.

In the end we are left with more questions than answers about the relationship between female and feminist consciousness. But from these women's experiences we can identify guidelines for examining working-class women's political activity, leadership, and consciousness.

THE SHAPERS OF CONSCIOUSNESS

First and foremost, women's political efforts should be examined according to the specific histories and political–economic conditions that surround each struggle. For example, political activities of different groups of women vary in relation to the nature of the issues being struggled for; the characteristics of the organization in which the women take part; each cultural group's expectations about women's political involvement; and the different structural as well as psychological factors influencing participation. This article is based on the reflections of the white women; it should not be generalized to the experiences of the Black and Hispanic women leaders. However, because the article focuses on the *dynamics* of these women's political experiences and the interwoven relationship between gender, race, and class consciousness, it may be theoretically, if not specifically, applicable to varied groups of women.

Second, rather than seeing gender, race, and class as separate, distinct, or fixed variables that impact upon women's political activity, it is more helpful to see the intersections between gender, race, and class as the *context* for women's lives and political activity. For example, just as each woman's political involvement stemmed from her concerns as a mother, each woman's working-class educational history also helped shape her participation in the coalition. Just as these women's leadership qualities were formed by their earlier experiences as working-class students, their success in organizing the community also derived from their particular responsibilities and skills as women. Similarly, just as their political awareness was shaped by their connection to KJAC, their race consciousness was also crystallized by their daily activity and interaction with Black women and their families. *All* these realities made up the context of their political activity and leadership; they cannot be separated out, with one being regarded as more significant or important than another.[20]

In other words, these gender, race, and class relations continually altered and re-altered how the women made sense out of their lives. As R. W. Connel et al. argue in *Making the Difference: Families and Social Division,* it is not enough to see these relations as separate systems that interact. Instead, they write about gender and class as "structuring processes" that constantly organize and reorganize social life:

> What is most important about them is their dynamics, the ways in which they exert pressures, produce reactions, intensify contradictions and generate change. . . . Thinking about intersection; however, is not enough. Class and gender don't just occur jointly in a situation. They abrade, inflame, amplify, twist, negate, dampen and complicate each other.[21]

Gender, race, and class amplifications and complications are the core of the Edison School struggle, which is why its women leaders and their consciousness defy simplification or dichotomization.

IMPLICATIONS FOR THE FUTURE

Over the past twenty years, feminist scholarship has tried to incorporate the lessons learned from women—their biographies, histories, and changing culture—into new understandings about society, politics, and social change. But simply placing women at the center of study has not automatically reshaped our understanding. We are just beginning to apply our new knowledge about women and to redefine such male-dominant concepts as success, power, autonomy, and personal freedom. As Ackelsberg suggests in her article in this volume (*Chapter 13*), women's political experiences have been built upon liberal bourgeois traditions of individual "rights." However, because of women's particular oppression in a male-dominated society, their demands have expanded the parameters of what "rights" within society should mean.

This expansive redefinition of "rights" has its roots in the complexities of women's lives and consciousness. On one level, women's lack of access to public "rights" has constrained their selfhood—not just in terms of their resources but also in terms of their self-concepts, dreams, and aspirations in the world. So when women have organized for their "rights," they have broadened the concept of "rights" that secure additional resources to encompass "rights" that also include new personal choices and options. At the same time, because women's political activity comes directly out of their embeddedness in the community—their roles within families as wives, mothers, daughters, and sisters—the notion of "rights" that women have developed is also more relational than men's. Since women must juggle conflicting needs and interests within families and communities, their concept of "rights" must somehow accommodate conflicts and facilitate affiliation and connection between people.

This is why it is so important to emphasize the multidimensional and complex nature of women's lives and consciousness that emerges in the Edison School story. In the end the Edison School struggle is a story about the changing texture of a working-class community and the changing of working-class consciousness. But it is also a story that challenges one-dimensional and narrow conceptions of working-class political demands. The demands of the Coalition for a New High School for quality, desegregated education cannot be understood only as a demand for equal educational opportunities and "rights" for white, Black, and Hispanic children. The struggle for a new Edison High School was also more than a fight for a safer, better-equipped facility. The women I interviewed did not see themselves as simply fighting for what their children would *get* but what their children and they themselves would be allowed to *become*.

Throughout the interviews the women emphasized the importance of their children's seeing themselves as having options, being able to have the broadest possible choices about who they would become in the world. As one coalition leader explained, this requires involvement and change:

> Actually, my whole attitude about college has changed since I first started at the women's program and got involved in the Coalition. At first I wanted to go back to school and go to college to do better for my family and get a better job—so I could be better off financially. I'm just trying to use my education now to make it a little better for a whole lot of us here in Kensington.

The desire for increased options that these women attribute to better quality education cannot simply be seen as their acceptance of the prevailing ideology of American education as a ticket to upward mobility. It must also be seen as an attempt to redefine personal opportunities, rights, and achievements. As the parents and students of District 5 face new options at the new Edison, they will have to reshape the constraints of working-class education to fit their own working-class heritage, values, and concerns. As one coalition leader concluded:

> My daughter keeps asking me "Mom, why are you working so hard when we are not even in high school yet?" I have to explain to her, "Someday, when you get to be somebody, when you grow up and are your own proud person it will be because a lot of mothers got together and made some changes."

NOTES

1. Much of the history of the Coalition for a New High School first appeared as a curriculum piece: Wendy Luttrell, "The Edison School Story," in *Women in the Community: A Curriculum Guide for Students and Teachers* (Harrisburg: Pennsylvania Department of Education, 1981). Inquiries about this manual for adult basic education classes, which includes units on parenting, education, and unemployment, can be made to the Lutheran Settlement House Women's Program, 1340 Frankford Avenue, Philadelphia, PA 19125.

2. Official statistics collected by the Board of Education in 1978, which underestimated the problem, indicated that 22 percent of District 5 high school students dropped out, almost double the rate for the city as a whole. Daily attendance rates in District 5 were particularly appalling: on any one day, attendance at Edison was 60 percent; at Kensington it was only 54 percent.

3. In 1977, 97 percent of District 5 high school students scored below the 49th percentile on the California Achievement Test as compared to the national norm of 64 percent. Edith S. Kemp, "Survey of Philadelphia High School Dropouts," Office of Research and Evaluation, School District of Philadelphia, 1978–1979.

4. David Segal, "Economic and Social Indicators for Philadelphia Census Tracts—1980," Philadelphia City Planning Commission (November 1982).

5. For a different instance of white working-class women's activism, see Kathleen McCourt, *Working-Class Women and Grass-Roots Politics* (Bloomington: Indiana University Press, 1977), 30–53. These women fought desegregation.

6. Some of the success of the coalition's efforts can be linked to political upheavals within Philadelphia's Democratic party, including a broad-based, citywide, Black–white coalition that had been instrumental in replacing Mayor Frank Rizzo (a white conservative) with Mayor William Green, (a white corporate liberal).

7. See David Wellman, *Portraits of White Racism* (London, New York, Melbourne: Cambridge University Press, 1977) for a compelling description of the complexities of white racism—its sources and dynamics.

8. "The Invisible Sex: Women, Wages, Work, and Worries: A View from History, 1600–1920" (Community Women's Education Project, 1978). This article, researched and written by members of the Women's History Class, traces the lives and accomplishments of working-class women in Kensington. It was published as a series in the *Penn Treaty Gazette*. The article can be obtained through Community Women's Education Project, Frankford Avenue and Somerset Street, Philadelphia, PA 19134.

9. Like the women Kathleen McCourt interviewed in her book *Working-Class Women and Grass-Roots Politics* (*see note 5*), the women in the coalition shared a sense of importance and the conviction that if the Edison struggle was to be successful it would be they, the women, who would make it happen. But whereas McCourt claimed that the women she interviewed took the responsibility of organizing around community problems because they had more time than men (p. 35), the women I interviewed seemed to think they were in fact better prepared than men to do the task.

10. Mariarosa dalla Costa, "Women and the Subversion of the Community," in *The Power of Women and the Subversion of the Community* (Bristol, England: Falling Wall Press, 1972); Juliet Mitchell, *Women's Estate* (New York: Pantheon, 1971); Sheila Rowbotham, *Woman's Consciousness, Man's World* (Baltimore: Penguin, 1973), and Ann Oakley, *Woman's Work* (New York: Pantheon, 1974) all refer to the constraints of women's double-burden.

11. Gerda Lerner, *The Female Experience: An American Documentary* (Indianapolis: Bobbs-Merrill, 1977) and *The Majority Finds Its Past: Placing Women in History* (New York: Oxford University Press, 1979); Adrienne Rich, *Of Women Born: Motherhood As Experience and Institution* (New York: Norton, 1976), and "Compulsory Heterosexuality and Lesbian Existence," *Signs* 5, No. 4 (Summer 1980): 631–660; and Susan Griffin, *Woman and Nature: The Roaring Inside Her* (New York: Harper & Row, 1978); and *Rape: The Power of Consciousness* (San Francisco: Harper & Row, 1979) are perhaps best known for referring to the concept of a woman-centered analysis—the view

that female experiences should be applied to the development of dominant values for the culture as a whole. See also Hester Eisenstein and Alice Jardine, *The Future of Difference* (Boston: G. K. Hall, 1980), for an elaboration of the basic tenets of a woman-centered analysis.

12. See Temma Kaplan, "Female Consciousness and Collective Action: The Case of Barcelona, 1910–1918," *Signs* 7, No. 3 (Spring 1982): 545–566, for her discussion of how women's physical proximity and shared routines—in short, women's culture—has contributed to female collective action.

13. Joan Kelly-Gadol in her article, "The Double Vision of Feminist Theory," *Feminist Studies* 5, No. 1 (Spring 1979): 216–227, argues against feminist dichotomies between the public and private spheres.

14. Samuel Bowles and Herbert Gintis, *Schooling in Capitalist America* (New York: Basic Books, 1976), 125–148, provide an excellent discussion of capitalist social relations through educational institutions.

15. See Wendy Luttrell, "The Getting of Knowledge: A Study of Working-Class Women and Education" (doctoral dissertation, University of California, Santa Cruz, 1984), for a more thorough discussion of how these women, as well as other local white women, described the complexities of their past educational experiences and perceptions, which defy characterizations of working-class people as blank slates ready to be molded by the middle-class institution of education. Instead, working-class education is analyzed as an arena of struggle—where teachers, students, parents, and administrators all battle over conflicting values such as achievement, success, and merit.

16. Lillian Rubin, *Worlds of Pain: Life in the Working-Class Family* (New York: Basic Books, 1976); Richard Sennett and Jonathan Cobb, *The Hidden Injuries of Class* (New York: Vintage, 1973); and John Ogbu, *The Next Generation: An Ethnography of Education in an Urban Neighborhood* (New York: Academic Press, 1974) attempt to counter prevailing stereotypical images of working-class people as less interested in education than middle-class people. Instead, these authors describe working-class ambivalence between believing in the ideologies of the dominant culture and believing in the reality of their own circumstances and experiences. But the best accounts of working-class experiences and perceptions of the role of education which analyze the schooling process as an interplay of class, gender, and race relations are R. W. Connell, D. J. Ashenden, S. Kessler, and G. W. Dowsett, *Making the Difference: Schools, Families, and Social Division* (London: George Allen & Unwin, 1982), and Paul Willis, *Learning to Labour: How Working-Class Kids Get Working-Class Jobs* (Westmead, England: Teakfield, 1977).

17. See, for example, Rubin, *Worlds of Pain,* or Nancy Seifer, *Nobody Speaks for Me* (New York: Simon & Schuster, 1976).

18. This is especially true for the women described in Peter Binzen, *Whitetown USA* (New York: Random House, 1970) about the neighborhood where the women's center is located. Local women explicitly mentioned that they found this characterization insulting.

19. Wendy Luttrell, "Beyond the Politics of Victimization, *Socialist Review,* No. 73 (Vol. 14, No. 1) (Jan.–Feb. 1984): 42–47, discusses these and other local women's complicated relationship to the women's movement.

20. Linda Gordon, *Women's Body, Women's Right: A Social History of Birth Control in America* (New York: Grossman, 1976), is an excellent recounting of the interweavings of gender, class, and race within a political movement.

21. R. W. Connell et al., *Making the Difference,* 180, 182.

REVERBERATIONS AMONG THE

SPHERES: FAMILY, WORKPLACE,

AND COMMUNITY NETWORKS

7

Unionization in an Electronics Factory: The Interplay of Gender, Ethnicity, and Class

Ann Bookman

This article is based on a two-year field study of union organizing at Digitex (a pseudonym), an electronics factory in the Boston, Massachusetts, area. Of the four hundred union-eligible production workers, slightly over half were women and one-third were first-generation Portuguese immigrants. Thus a majority of the work force was composed of groups that mainstream social scientists, and some labor leaders, have argued are resistant to unionization. However, the story of union organizing at Digitex reveals that a majority of women and immigrant workers did join the union and that the factors that have been held responsible for the resistance of these groups to unionization—namely gender-related roles and strong ethnic identification—were the very factors that aided the unionzation of Digitex.

This case poses many interesting questions about how women and immigrant workers actually become politically active in a workplace context. For example, what are the most important factors determining whether workers join a union? What is the interplay between such factors as gender, ethnicity, and class in shaping workers' response to unionization? This study allows a close examination of the changes that unionization produces in the social relationships and ideology found in an industrial workplace. It further shows how the process of social change that unionization sets in motion varies for different groups of workers.

There are several schools of thought, or bodies of literature, that address these questions. First of all, there are a number of studies that were conducted in the 1950s and early 1960s by mainstream social scientists. These are replete with the stereotypes of that era and basically argue that women and immigrants are unorganizable. For example, Karsh et al. argue that "women are the group most resistant to labor organization." This is based on their view "that women are 'secondary wage earners' who enter the labor market for extra money and can leave it at any time, that they tend to be more dependent on and loyal to the company than men, and that internecine warfare constantly rages among them."[1] The essence of this and similar studies is that women do not take their jobs as seriously as they do their families and their interpersonal relationships, and therefore are unlikely to join unions. In a study of Italian immigrant workers and unions, Edwin Fenton states, "They were village minded, fatalistic and self-reliant, three qualities which made them poor union members."[2] Fenton concludes that as long as Italian immigrants maintained their ethnic identity they would not choose to participate in or be effective members of trade unions. There appears to be a similar model underlying these studies of women workers' and immigrant workers' trade union activity. The family, in the case of women, and the community of origin, in the case of immigrants, are assumed to play a negative role vis-à-vis the receptivity of these groups to unionization.[3]

Second, there are studies influenced by the classical Marxist tradition that see all workers as organizable, with no distinctions among them in their responses to unionization, depending on their ability to develop class consciousness.[4] In this tradition, "class" is defined as a relationship embodied in groups of people and determined by their role in the production of goods or services. The development of "class consciousness," so the argument continues, occurs when people experience and articulate their relationship to production as something that they hold in common with others like themselves, and as distinct from or opposed to others with a different relationship to production.

Though the development of "class consciousness" is certainly a part of the process of social change that occurred at Digitex during the union drive, this study shows that there are other factors or central experiences that shape class consciousness beyond what happens at the point of production. In particular, I explore the intersection of gender and ethnicity as they affect the ability of women and immigrant workers to organize in their own class interests. Drawing on the work of historians like Alan Dawley, this study shows how "the labor movement in the city was a community affair."[5] This was true both because jobs at Digitex were vital to the economic survival of the ethnic communities surrounding the factory and because family members of both sexes worked in the plant.

Third, there is a body of recent women's history and labor history that explores union organizing in a more complex and balanced manner than either of the aforementioned traditions. This scholarship, however, also has weaknesses. For example, some of the "new" labor history does not use gender as an important analytic category and has continued to obscure the multifaceted relationship of women to unionism. In the new women's history, some scholars have tended toward cataloguing and description, while others have painted a false and romanticized picture of women as supermilitants.[6] Ruth Milkman addresses these problems in her introduction to the anthology *Women, Work and Protest,* which makes a major break with both of these limiting tendencies.

The old myths of women's lack of interest or involvement with labor struggle were effectively supplanted with new myths which were equally one-sided, and indeed the mirror-image of the old. In the new feminist orthodoxy, each discovery of female militancy was taken as evidence of a virtually limitless potential for women's labor activism in the labor movement.[7]

Milkman and a number of other feminist historians have called for an examination of the "conditions which have encouraged women's labor militancy, and those which have impeded it," as well as the need to analyze the "organizational forms and techniques . . . rooted in women's own distinctive culture and life experience."[8] The study of union organizing at Digitex affords such an opportunity.

The macroeconomic and political conditions that contextualized the union drive were significant in both the inception and in the ultimate fate of unionism at Digitex. The dramatic growth of a largely nonunion electronics industry in and around the Boston area[9] provided a healthy economic climate and made wage and benefit improvements for Digitex workers seem possible. The upsurge of various progressive mass movements throughout the 1960s and early 1970s brought the United Electrical, Radio and Machine Workers of America (UE) and a group of feminist trade unionists[10] together at the gates of Digitex in the fall of 1973. Their joint efforts began a process of unionization. However, it was the lives of Digitex women workers—inside and outside of the shop—that shaped the direction and outcome of the union organizing campaign. Women's roles in their families, their communities, and their workplace each had a particular and important bearing on their relationship to unionism. Women's ability to resist and change conditions they found undesirable and oppressive at work often involved transformations in their relationships to kith, kin, and community, as well as to their jobs.

METHODOLOGY

Before presenting the data from my fieldwork, I would like to make a few methodological points that differentiate this study from most studies of unionization. During the fieldwork period, I worked as a "light assembler" in the Coil Department of the Digitex Electronics Company and was a founding and active member of a union organizing committee affiliated with the UE. The standard method for conducting anthropological research is "participant observation," in which observation is the primary aspect and participation is secondary, being confined to those events and routines the anthropologist chooses to investigate. The method I utilized could better be termed "observation through participant activism," in which the primary aspect of my work was being an agent of social change within the factory as a union organizer and the secondary aspect was being an anthropological observer with the same hours, pay, working conditions, and relationship to management as the other workers in the shop.

For many people the pursuits of social science and social reform are incompatible. Some social scientists argue that as a union activist one cannot possibly produce an objective or scientifically sound study of blue-collar women. Some union organizers argue similarly that social science research is simply a lot of complicated phrases and theories that have nothing to do with the day-to-day reality of workers' lives and problems and serve only to obscure the need for action. My own view is that these pursuits are not only compatible but mutually necessary. I think that if social science is to have any social value, it must proceed from an engaged perspective on and position in social life. And if social reformers are to create real change, they must proceed on the basis of a systematic study of the social conditions they are seeking to transform.

My dual roles as activist and researcher are the basis for both the strengths and limitations of this study. The limitations stem from my assignment to a sex-segregated production area, which limited my access to male workers; my position as a worker, which limited my contact with management; and my role as a union organizer, which estranged me over time from some antiunion workers. However, for each door that was closed, a particular view of factory life was opened, vividly revealing the impact of unionization on the structure and content of social relationships at Digitex.

INDUSTRIAL ETHNOGRAPHY: THE DIGITEX FACTORY AND THE WORK FORCE

The process of unionization, and the extent of social and political change that occurred during the union drive can best be understood with some background on the conditions that existed before the drive began. There are two sets of questions on which I would like to focus in this brief industrial ethnography. First, what were the sources of management's control before the union drive and what, if any, were the sources of workers' control and potential resistance? Second, what were the sources of division and conflict among the workers and what were the sources of cohesion?

The Digitex Electronics Company was originally a family-owned-and-controlled firm that manufactured products in the electronic components sector of the electrical industry. (Digitex has since been taken over by a large multinational corporation.) The company employed between four hundred fifty and five hundred people of whom about four hundred were union-eligible production workers. Of the production workers, about 55 percent were women and 33 percent were first-generation Portuguese immigrants. These two groups overlapped substantially; 75 percent of all Portuguese workers were women and 40 percent of all women workers were Portuguese. The factory had a highly multinational character as there were also a fair number of Afro-American and Hispanic workers, Italian and Polish workers, and a small number of Greek, Haitian, and Asian workers.

The ethnic and national differences among workers were accentuated by the fact that many did not speak the same language. Degrading racial and ethnic stereotypes abounded in this atmosphere and centered on the Portuguese workers, most of whom had immigrated very recently and lived in two towns adjacent to the factory. They tended to be neighbors, to have friendship and kin ties which operated inside and outside of work, and to see each other in stores, social clubs, and churches on the weekends. For all their cohesiveness as a group, there were also divisions among Portuguese workers. Those from urban areas did not socialize with those from rural areas. The mainland Portuguese and the Azorean Portuguese were two distinct groups, and the Azoreans were further divided by their island of origin.

There were also divisions among women workers. Among non-Portuguese women, the divisions were generational, centering on dress and family values, and especially on family size and the appropriateness of divorce. Among the Portuguese women, there were tensions because some women were more traditional, wearing long hair, long skirts, and black clothes when in mourning, while the others were more "Americanized" in their dress, hair styles, and mourning customs.

The most obvious source of management's control came from the particular conditions of work and pay that were set up in the shop. The factory conformed in every respect to the commonly held stereotype of a sweatshop. The production departments were housed in a long, one-story structure built during World War II when the company was founded. This building was dark, dirty, and very poorly ventilated, hot in summer and cold and drafty in winter. The majority of the workers were paid close to the minimum wage, which in 1973 meant a starting wage of $1.95 to $2.10 an hour. Management's control was also derived from the way in which production was organized. The most significant aspect of this organization was the social division of labor, as seen in the sexual and ethnic segregation of the work force. The workers in most production departments were either all men or all women, and the women's departments were predominantly Portuguese.

The women's departments were characterized by intricate assembly operations requiring "manual dexterity" and "good eyesight." Most women worked with fairly simple machinery or none at all, doing routinized tasks that repeated themselves tens or hundreds of times an hour. The women were paid for the most part on the piecework system. The company could easily enforce speedup by raising the base rates, and the constant struggle to "make the rate" produced an atmosphere of competitiveness among the pieceworkers. The men, on the other hand, worked with more complex machinery, such as drill presses, punch presses, lathes, and screw machines, and were paid on an hourly basis at an average of two-and-a-half times what the women were making. These so-called skill and wage divisions were reinforced by the fact that the majority of supervisors in the women's production areas were non-Portuguese men.

Other aspects of production further extended management's control over the work force. The workers' degree of mobility during production hours varied tremendously. Male hourly workers often left their machines to get parts outside their department areas, whereas pieceworkers, who were mainly women, stood little chance of exceeding the base rate if they left their benches for even a few minutes. The extent of discipline and supervision in each production area also varied. The time-study man and the foreman of each piecework department were constantly watching and timing the pieceworkers, but the men in the machine shop and screw machine department worked on their own at their own pace. The degree of technical division of labor—that is, how isolated or interdependent workers were in the production of the electronics parts they made—also varied. In sum, the day-to-day life of male and female workers was strikingly different. Women were less mobile, more directly supervised, and more interdependent in the production process than their male counterparts.

The ideology of paternalism created further divisions among workers already divided by the structure and organization of production. The company insisted that Digitex was just like "one, big, happy family" in which every member was treated with care. But it was a classical patriarchal family in which the company owner "knew best" and treated all the workers like children who had no rights or bases on which to make decisions. Everything was done on a case-by-case basis, and there were no written policies that governed wage rates, benefits, hiring, or firing. This created a climate in which paternalism flourished, as each individual worker had to cultivate a good relationship with his or her supervisor to get a raise, a promotion, or even to keep the job.

While there were many aspects of factory life that created divisions among the workers and ensured management's control, there were other factors that created cohesion among workers, or at least, in the words of economist Richard Edwards, were "contested terrains" and therefore threatened management's control.[11] One of the clearest examples of a contested terrain was nonproduction time during working hours. On the one hand, the sexual and ethnic segregation found in production areas was often reproduced in the composition of social groups during coffee breaks and lunch periods. The tables in the cafeteria, one of the few places where workers could intermingle, were more often than not composed of workers from the same production department. And ethnic divisions were fairly rigidly maintained in break groups within the production departments.

Yet the social life of the production departments also contained some examples of cross-cultural exchange and unity. For example, within the Coil Department, there were "life crisis" parties held when someone was getting married or having a baby, complete with Portuguese sweet bread, Polish kielbasa, Italian meatballs, black-eyed peas, and other ethnic specialties. There were also "life crisis" collections taken up when someone was seriously ill or had died. Ethnic divisions were also bridged through the constant showing and sharing of photographs. Young Portuguese women showed pictures of their boyfriends fighting in Angola or of their grandparents and friends still living in Portugal. Non-Portuguese workers brought in wedding albums or pictures of family vacations. It was workers' relationships with their families, as well as with friends, church, and community organizations that provided the basis for contact and limited cohesion, especially between women of different ethnic and national backgrounds.

Another important contested terrain lay within the production process itself. In production areas where there was a high technical division of labor and workers were very interdependent in the production process, there was a strong feeling of solidarity and cooperation among the workers involved. This was most evident on "the Belt," a primitive assemblyline in the largest women's production department, and could also be seen in the Coil Department, where women workers sat closely packed together at long benches doing the same routinized piece of the production process hour after hour, day after day. Laughing and pointing at the time-study man while he did his time-and-motion studies was often more powerful than the fact that the workers could not speak the same language. Furthermore, the ethnic and sexual segregation of the production areas had a dual effect, for though it kept men and women workers divided, it ultimately aided the organization of women workers as a group into the ranks of the union. The pattern of organization building that emerged during the drive was one in which women often organized first as women within their departments and then joined the factorywide cross-sex, multiethnic organizing committee. In a sense, each of the women's production departments had its own departmental organizing committee.

THE UNION ORGANIZING DRIVE AT DIGITEX

The unionization of Digitex may be viewed as a drama unfolding on three interrelated levels: the factory as a whole, the shop floor in particular production departments, and the experiences of individual workers. For the purposes of this article, I shall discuss all three levels simultaneously, focusing on the Coil Department and the experiences of women workers, both Portuguese and non-Portuguese.

The union drive that began at Digitex in 1973 was not the first unionization effort the shop had seen. There had been five other union drives that failed through the company's two-pronged strategy for dealing with prounion workers—fire them or promote them to management. The company's success in containing and repressing unionization had resulted in a strong climate of fear and antiunionism in the shop. As one woman worker put it:

> My first day at Digitex I was told, "Do not mention union. Never mention union. If you do you'll be fired." Matter of fact, I know of an instance—a girl came to get a job, she had union affiliations prior to coming to Digitex, and they wouldn't hire her.

It is also significant that trade unions were illegal in Portugal at the time that the union drive began, and many Portuguese workers and other immigrant workers in the shop were uninformed that their right to unionize was protected by American labor law.

The UE did not initiate this drive on its own. The union was approached by a woman who had taken a job in the shop with the specific intention of investigating whether or not it could be organized. Deciding it could be, she recruited a number of other people, including myself, to get jobs at Digitex. These "worker/organizers" were white, mostly middle-class, and all veterans of the antiwar, student, and women's movements of the late 1960s and early 1970s. On the part of the UE, the decision to organize Digitex was part of a comeback the union was experiencing locally and nationally as a result of the progressive mass movements of that period.

The union drive can be roughly divided into three periods, which correspond to important shifts in the balance of forces inside the shop, and the primary task of the organizers. Period One was in essence a period of "laying the foundation," Period Two was a stage of "base building," and Period Three was characterized by "consolidation and conflict."

During Period One both the union and the company operated in secret. The worker/organizers were responsible for identifying prounion workers in the shop and then passing their names on to the union staff, who approached them individually outside of work by paying them "home visits."[12] For example, in the Coil Department several women were identified as prounion and visited at home. Three of these women were, in fact, very sympathetic. One of them was Maureen Agnati, an Italian American pieceworker who had worked at Digitex on and off since dropping out of high school in her junior year. Although she admitted during her home visit that she hated the company and the piecework system, she was cautious about making a commitment to be active in the union. She was a mother with two small children and a difficult, and at times abusive husband. She said it was hard for her to get out of the house to see her girl friends, much less to attend a union meeting. Although neither Maureen nor the other women visited at home signed union cards, they did begin "talking union" in their respective sections of the Coil Department.

It was also during this period that Rose O'Brien, an Irish-American hourly worker in the "Special Coils" section of the department ("special" because all the workers were paid on an hourly, not piecework basis and performed a number of steps in the production process themselves), began talking against the union. She had worked at Digitex since 1959, was very friendly with many people in management, and was often the center of attention at the company Christmas party and in the company bowling league. She had no use for unions as a result of her negative experience in a union shop before coming to Digitex, and she used her influence to discredit the union among many long-service workers when the drive was just a rumor on the company grapevine. The views and activities of Maureen and Rose were consistent with those of short-service women pieceworkers and long-service women hourly workers throughout the plant. By the end of the first period, the majority of workers were still unaware of the drive, but there was a core of approximately twenty-five workers who had signed cards and begun to meet with the UE.

While the union drive was going on sub rosa, the company pretended to conduct "business as usual." However, they were busy trying to gather information on the union's activities. After the first open union meeting—at which the company must have had a spy—two young men who attended were fired. The union immediately filed charges against the company with the National Labor Relations Board (NLRB), knowing that it must be demonstrated that workers would have job protection if they joined the union.

The major turning point during the drive occurred in Period Two with a favorable NLRB ruling on the firings case. Both men were rehired and given back pay. The union took a picture of the two workers holding their back-pay checks. Union supporters posted copies of it all around the shop and took great pride in watching the faces of various supervisors as the photos turned up on every departmental bulletin board. Even antiunion workers were impressed that the company had had to back down on a firing. The union used the NLRB decision to stop the company's tactics of repression, and this in turn created the conditions for a change in the balance of forces inside the shop.

After the drive became public, the company was still on the offensive, sending workers a letter about the generosity of the "Digitex family" and the callousness of the UE, whose only interest was in collecting dues money. While the union staff prepared and distributed leaflets, making contact with workers at the plant gates, the workers/organizers began to do open union organizing inside the shop and make home visits. Most important, they began the production and distribution of a rank-and-file newsletter. The first appearance of "Union News," passed out by Digitex workers during coffee and lunch breaks, was a very dramatic moment in the drive. There was great curiosity about who had written the newsletter and open enthusiasm about its contents.

The inception of "Union News" spurred a number of prounion workers to attend organizing committee meetings outside work. Through these meetings they met with workers from other departments and began to learn what they had in common with workers who had different kinds of jobs or were of a different sex or ethnic group. Male workers began to see that their assumptions about "broads" and "Portagees" were not true, and that there were ways in which women pieceworkers from "the Belt" and men hourly workers from the stockroom had more in common than either had with the company.

As women learned how male workers were paid and treated, they began to see two things: one, that their mistreatment was related to their gender; and, second, that they did have problems in common with men workers—particularly the company's paternalism, which deprived all workers of a plantwide wage scale and seniority system and prohibited any formal procedure for dealing with grievances.

It was also during this time that there was a coup in Portugal. The repressive Caetano regime was toppled by the Armed Forces Movement, which named General Antonio de Spinola as head of state and called for an end to Portuguese colonialism in Africa. The reaction of almost all the Portuguese workers in the shop was positive. Hatred of Caetano seemed universal, and events in Portugal had an observable and positive effect in countering the fears of Portuguese workers who wanted to support the union. The number of workers who became union members increased dramatically in this period. The union was able to sign up in a little over a month as many workers as had taken seven months to sign up previously.

Developments in the shop as a whole were again mirrored in the Coil Department, where twenty-four workers had signed cards by the end of Period Two (twenty of these were pieceworkers and half were Portuguese). These changes were evident in the composition of the break-time groups in the department as groups began to form on the basis of people's position on the union and not according to ethnic- or production-related divisions. It was also during this period that several women pieceworkers emerged as departmental union leaders and organizers. Maureen and a Black pieceworker named Bella Caldwell were the first workers from Coils to attend an organizing committee meeting. It was there that they met Lucia Perriera, a Portuguese pieceworker from "the Belt." Lucia was one of the first Portuguese people to have found employment at Digitex. As she was bilingual, she often translated for other Portuguese workers when they were called to the Personnel Office, and in the Portuguese community she often accompanied people to the Social Security office and various public agencies. When Lucia spoke up at a union meeting about the situation in her own department, Maureen and Bella were moved by her indictment of the piecework system. They agreed with her about how unfair the rates were and were angered to learn that Lucia had never received a promotion in her eight years of service with the company. They were also impressed with how rapidly she had been able to sign up women in her department and asked her for help in talking to workers in Coils. This was the beginning of the kind of cross-departmental, cross-ethnic cooperation that was crucial to building the union. These ties laid the basis for a form of social organization (the union) that was significantly different from the social organization that had characterized the factory before the drive.

There were several other factors that positively affected the participation of Portuguese women in the Coil Department. The first was a union meeting held at a social club in the Portuguese community, and the second was the coup in Portugal. Immediately, after the coup, a young Portuguese woman, Isabel Sousa, became very active in the Coil Department. She confided that her uncle, with whose family she had just immigrated to the United States, had been exiled for illegal trade union activity. "Now that we have Spinola I can tell you this," she said. "Now that we have Spinola, I can help you." She and Maureen both worked on "Union News." Maureen, with help from the worker/organizers, wrote an article about the Coils Department that Lucia translated. And Isabel and Maureen distributed each issue in the department. Other workers in Coils were impressed by the bilingual newsletter and commented on articles which showed the similarity between their own complaints about the company and those of workers in other departments whom they did not even know.

It was also during Period Two that Rose attended her first union meeting "out of curiosity," she said, never one to be far from where the action was. Immediately following the meeting she was given a promotion to the prestigious Inspection Department. This was not only a step up in the company but also removed her from the increasing flurry of prounion activity in Coils. She was the first to say that the company was just trying to "buy her vote" and that she had deserved the promotion long before the UE had ever come along. By the end of Period Two she was truly "on the fence."

During the third and final period the atmosphere inside the shop became highly politicized as all—be they production workers, office workers, or managers—had to decide which side they were on. Was the company president "Boss Snidley" or "Mr. Snidley"? Were those who worked in the company "workers" or "employees"? These were not just questions of semantics but questions about the basic power relationships in the factory, and the terms you used told people which analysis you believed—the company's or the union's.

While the company had conducted its early antiunion campaign through selective repression, or polite letters from top levels of management, its tactics changed as the union gained in strength. First company tacticians tried red-baiting after a particularly well-attended organizing committee meeting in April. When that did not work, they took their message to the shop floor. They enlisted technicians, office workers, foremen, and, most important, Digitex workers. They encouraged homemade antiunion leaflets, buttons, and signs, and condoned verbal intimidation of prounion workers during production hours. They even hired a fancy downtown Boston firm that specialized in union-busting campaigns. The firm sent letters to workers' homes and set up display cases inside the shop with various goods, like canned food and children's clothes, worth $6.85—the amount of the union dues that would be taken out of workers' checks should the union win.

In the final weeks before the election, the UE staff concentrated on card signing, while the worker/organizers focused on political education, trying to deepen workers' understanding of the meaning of unionism and the nature of class relations in the factory. They tried to prepare people for the fact that the election was just one step in a long process and that further struggle would be required to win a first contract. The final issue of "Union News," containing appeals to vote for the UE in seven different languages, impressively demonstrated that the union represented a broad cross section of workers who had resisted the company's efforts to divide them. As one article said in Italian, *"Siamo venuti in America trovare una modo di migliore. Miglioramci la vita!"* ("We came to America to make a better life for ourselves. Let's make a better life for ourselves!")

In the Coil Department, though only one more worker signed a union card during Period Three, many workers deepened their commitment to the union. This was demonstrated by a further realignment of the break groups reflecting workers' position on the union and by varying kinds of activism, especially inside the shop. For example, Isabel took on Beatrice Arruda, who was the lead woman in Coils and one of the most vocal antiunion Portuguese workers. Both Portuguese and non-Portuguese pieceworkers watched their verbal jousting matches with delight, especially when Beatrice threw up her hands and retreated to the foreman's desk. Maureen wrote more articles for "Union News," without any assistance, and her growing self-confidence was reflected in her announcement during one lunch break that she had enrolled in a General Education Diploma (GED) course and was preparing to take exams for her high school equivalency diploma.

Both Maureen and Isabel faced tremendous odds against becoming and continuing as union activists. Isabel's boyfriend (who also worked at Digitex) refused to allow her to be seen without him in public and would not accompany her to union meetings, despite the fact that he supported the union and had signed a card. Maureen's husband refused to take care of their children for even a few hours on the weekend so that she could attend organizing committee meetings. He was verbally abusive about her participation in the drive and often threatened her with physical abuse if she continue to be involved. But both women were able to define and develop a role inside the shop during working hours that more than compensated for the meeting they could not attend. Their commitment to the union was being constantly challenged, not only by their foreman and the time-study man, but by the men with whom they were personally involved. Their ability to remain involved went through constant ups and downs, but the value that their coworkers placed on their leadership served to build their self-esteem and renew their commitment to the union cause.

It was also during Period Three that Lucia started actually coming into the Coil area during coffee and lunch breaks to talk to other pieceworkers. Such interdepartmental socializing was unheard of before the drive. Her purpose was not so much to sign up more workers as to allay the fears of those who had already signed cards and encourage their activism. Lucia's efforts in her community reinforced her in-shop organizing. She obtained letters from two Portuguese community organizations and the priest of the largest Catholic Church in the Portuguese community in support of the union. This visibly bolstered the morale of Portuguese union supporters and infuriated Beatrice and other Portuguese antiunion workers.

The greatest change during Period Three occurred among long-service, non-Portuguese hourly workers like Rose. At this time she had a confrontation with the company vice-president, who had acted against her advice on some inspection-related matters. Rose had already been turned off by the company's packaged antiunion campaign, and this blatant disregard for her job-related experience and opinions crystallized her estrangement from management. She signed a union card about a month before the NLRB election and became a vocal and influential member of the organizing committee in its final days.

Though the core of workers who attended meetings remained small, many women fought against management's antiunion campaign on the shop floor. Whether it meant wearing a UE button on their blouse, taking ten minutes in the ladies' room (a *long* time for a pieceworker) to talk to someone who was frightened, or talking back to the foreman, all of the activities reflected a level of class-conscious behavior that would have seemed impossible in the shop only a year earlier.

When the ballots were counted on election day, the vote was 204 for the UE and 165 for the company. The majority of workers wanted union representation, and they had constructed a new type of social organization in the factory. Many factors that had formerly been the basis for division among the workers were now the basis for diversity in an all-worker organization. On the night of the election, I asked Isabel if she could come to the union victory party, a special one-time occasion. She answered, "My boyfriend is working second shift now. If you'll pick me up and bring me home by eleven, he will never know." When I arrived to pick her up, she led me into her room and with a big grin pointed above her bed to a large poster of General Spinola, on whom she'd pinned a UE button!

FINDINGS AND ANALYSIS

By summarizing data collected after the union drive was over, the process of social change that occurred at Digitex can be further illuminated. Using both quantitative and qualitative data, two of the questions posed at the outset can be answered: (1) What were the significant factors determining whether or not workers became union members? (2) What was the process of social change that occurred during the course of unionization, and, particularly, what accounted for changes in the political activism and consciousness of women and immigrant workers?

In order to answer the first question, being a union member will be viewed as synonymous with signing a union card. Although signing a union card is an act associated with different levels of commitment to the union and different levels of participation in its activities, it does represent a conscious decision to join an organization of workers dedicated to confronting the company collectively on a range of job-related matters. Card signing is also an index for which there are data on all the workers in the factory.

It was found that women at Digitex, rather than resisting unionization, joined the union in equal proportion to men (65 percent of all women, 64.6 percent of all men). It was also found that first-generation Portuguese immigrants, rather than resisting unionization, joined the union in even greater proportions than indigenous workers (73.5 percent of Portuguese, 61.4 percent of non-Portuguese). Having established that these social characteristics of workers were not an impediment to unionization, it is possible to explore whether these factors or other, job-related factors were more positively correlated with workers' union membership. Using data on the whole factory ($N = 379$), the factors that were most significant in determining union membership were related to workers' relationship to production. Union membership was correlated with data on method/amount of pay (piecework or hourly work/average rate of pay), and seniority, which determines the extent of benefits. Union membership was also correlated with data on the social relationships surrounding production (degree of technical division of labor, degree of mobility, degree of supervision). The data show in this case that workers with low pay and low seniority who were paid on a piecework basis were most likely to join the union, while workers with high pay and high seniority who were paid on an hourly basis were least likely to join the union. The data further show that workers whose jobs involved a high degree of technical division of labor (and were therefore highly interdependent on other workers in the actual manufacture of products) were more likely to join the union than workers who completed a number of phases of the production process by themselves, had high mobility during working hours, and experienced little supervision over their work.[13] The need for other studies to corroborate or further test these findings as a general proposition in a variety of industrial workplaces is suggested by the Digitex case.

Although the primacy of production-related factors was established in determining the receptivity to unionization of workers as an aggregate group, this was most true (that is, statistically significant) for non-Portuguese women, also true for non-Portuguese and Portuguese men, but not true for Portuguese women. In the case of Portuguese women, their ethnicity[14] was more important in determining whether or not they joined the union than their role in production. Although it has been established that a high proportion of Portuguese women were low-paid pieceworkers with low seniority, their social ties to people in their community seem to have been an even more positive force in creating the conditions for their joining the union than their role in production.

These findings raise serious questions about many of the mainstream social science studies summarized earlier. Much of that research assumed that women relate to work through the demands and pressures of their family roles. However, this study suggests that there is a greater disjunction, or at least a different relationship, between women's sexual/domestic roles and their experiences outside the home than has been supposed. The data suggest that for non-Portuguese women at Digitex, their job-related experiences were key in their deciding to join the union, whereas for Portuguese women at Digitex their relationship to ethnically defined groups and activities, both inside and outside the workplace, was key to their deciding to join the union.

Although this type of analysis may be useful for understanding which factors were most significant in determining whether women workers joined the union, it is much too simplistic and one-sided to explain the process of decision making and activity that preceded and followed card signing. In assessing the political experience of women workers during the organizing drive, many of the most important and interesting changes that occurred defy quantification. In fact, the only way to understand the process fully is to examine further quantitative data on the experiences of the four rank-and-file women—Lucia, Isabel, Maureen, and Rose—described above.

In the cases of Lucia, Isabel, and Maureen, their prounionism was immediate. There was little if any discrepancy between their view of worker–management relations and the view put forward by the union. But the reason for this was different in each case. Isabel came from a prounion family in Portugal, so she had grown up with a heritage of involvement in trade union activity. Lucia was indignant about the way the company treated Portuguese workers, taking advantage of their lack of familiarity with English and placing them in the lowest-paying, least-skilled jobs no matter what their level of education or previously acquired skills. Maureen's views stemmed mainly from her on-the-job experiences in the shop as a pieceworker who could never make much above minimum wage no matter how hard she worked.

The inclination of these three women to act on their views also differed. Lucia was immediately ready to act and organize. She was used to fighting the company in the sense that she often complained to the general foreman or the Personnel Office on behalf of her Portuguese coworkers. Maureen, on the other hand, was held back from activity by a combination of factors including hostility, abuse, lack of help from her husband with child care, and very low self-esteem. Isabel, on the other hand, believed that what was illegal in Portugal was also illegal in the United States and it was not until Spinola came to power that she felt free to organize inside the shop. But having surmounted that obstacle, she found that her domestic duties to her uncle's family, and her boyfriend's possessiveness and male chauvinism limited her prounion activities to things she could do in the workplace.

In Rose's case, the view of the company presented by the union was at odds with her own view. Her initial loyalty was to management, not to the workers. Despite some complaints, she had received certain privileges from and had social ties to management. It was management's refusal to continue to treat her as a "special" worker that changed her views.

The changes these workers experienced as they began to resist management's policies and control were also different and demonstrate that the process of becoming class conscious is complex and variable even among women who belong to the same class. The major change in Lucia's case was in her ability to work with others in fighting the company. She began to talk and strategize with workers in other departments and to fight for both Portuguese and non-Portuguese workers. Her role in her community was also transformed. Previously she had been a "go-between" facilitating communication. During the union drive she became an advocate, mobilizing important institutions in her own community against the company in support of the union.

In Rose's case, when she no longer identified with management she could relate to the grievances of unskilled, low-paid pieceworkers. She began to talk to workers with whom she had had no previous contact. Her social ties with management were replaced by social ties with an ethnically diverse group of workers from a range of departments, including Portuguese workers. She was able to transcend her own negative experience with one union in one shop and see what the UE might accomplish for workers at Digitex.

With Maureen and Isabel, their ability to begin to question the confining, patriarchal relationship with husband or boyfriend was closely linked with their ability to develop a role in the union drive. For Maureen, support from other women in the department about her child-care problems was critical to her involvement, along with her growing sense of her own intelligence and ability through her success in organizing her coworkers and her writing efforts for "Union News." For Isabel, the political activity of Portuguese people back in her homeland was pivotal, along with the support she received from her Portuguese coworkers when she took on anti-union harassment from the Portuguese lead woman in the Coil Department. Neither of these women could escape housework, child care, or other traditional female duties, but these traditional jobs did not prevent them from being activists during working hours or from beginning to define some limited autonomy outside the home.

There are two interesting points to be underscored here. First, without change and motion in the personal lives of rank-and-file women workers at Digitex, the union drive would not have succeeded or had the vitality it possessed. Second, the strength and contribution of many women union members lay in their in-shop organizing efforts, not in their participation in meetings held after working hours outside the factory. Though this characteristic of women's political participation crossed ethnic lines, there were differences related to women's stage in the life cycle. This was more true for women like Maureen with young children, and less true for women like Rose and Lucia, who had grown children or no children.

One of the common threads in the lives of these four women and in the experience of other Digitex workers like them was the movement from an individual to a collective view of what it meant to be a worker at Digitex. In part, this was a view based on seeing that all workers, regardless of sex, ethnic group, or role in production shared a similar (if not the same) relationship to the company, which implied that their interests and those of management were in conflict. Equally important, it was a view based on seeing that particular subgroups of workers, such as women and Portuguese workers, had an additional set of problems with the company. Class consciousness therefore not only includes an ability to extend ideas about one's own job into an analysis of relations between the company and the workers, but also an ability to understand the relationship between the company and workers of different genders and different nationalities. When class consciousness is related to an appreciation of difference within the working class, it can transform both social relationships among workers and between workers and management. This transformation was apparent in the success of union organizing at Digitex.

To return to the work of those who insist that women in general and immigrant women in particular are resistant to unionization, their error lies in part, I think, in looking at the effects of patriarchy and sexual subordination only in the family context, where women are for the most part isolated from each other. In the workplace context, because of the sex-segregation of production departments, women work collectively with other women from diverse cultural backgrounds and have opportunities for social contact with other women. Simply to assume that women's sexual subordination in the family will negatively determine their ideas and activity in every sphere is wrong on two counts. First, this assumption adopts a narrow "gender model" for analyzing the totality of women's experience. Second, it fails to acknowledge that women can mount a successful campaign of resistance both in the family and in the workplace, and that their resistance in one area strengthens their ability to resist in another.

Having demonstrated that a woman's role in her family does not necessarily impede her becoming politically active in her workplace, how in the case of the women at Digitex did these two roles combine? The majority of non-Portuguese activists had no children or had high-school-age or grown children. It is interesting that the two women at Digitex, Lucia and Rose, who eventually assumed positions as shopwide leaders, were both women without children who were close to the end of their childbearing years. One might assume this to be a particularity of this case, but a similar finding has been made by Carol Turbin in her study of women's industrial labor militancy in the late nineteenth century.[15] Looking at the data more closely, we find that the age of their children did not seem to limit the activities of the majority of Portuguese women workers in quite the same way as it did the non-Portuguese women. The Portuguese workers with small children had a larger and more reliable network of female kin and friends on whom they could rely for help with their children. However, their husbands and boyfriends were often less willing to let them leave their homes and housework to attend union meetings or other union functions. The variability of child-care and housework strategies among women of different ethnic groups, and their composite effect on women's political activism, certainly bear further investigation in our attempt to understand the relationship between work and family in women's lives.

Finally, how can a woman's ethnic group membership and her role in her community be integrated into a model that incorporates both family and workplace? In the case of women Portuguese workers at Digitex, their common language, kin ties, neighborhoods, and other bonds gave them a cohesiveness as a group that most workers lacked. Their common culture provided them with common standards by which to judge the changes they experienced upon becoming industrial workers in the United States. Many Portuguese workers, especially women, had not worked before, either in industry or in any other paid context. The unfavorable comparison between life at Digitex and their life in Portugal or the Azores proved an incentive for joining the union. Their common culture was both a source of resistance to the inhuman aspects of factory life and a source of continuity with more humane social forms. This was true for Lucia, who was clearly a leader in both the community and the workplace before the union drive began, and also for women who were not leaders in either sphere.

For the majority of Portuguese women, their positive response to the union is clearly related to three community-related factors: some organizing committee meetings were held at clubs in the Portuguese community where these women felt comfortable and where their spouses felt comfortable; both the Catholic Church and Portuguese community organizations gave their sanction to the UE and encouraged voting for the union; and the Portuguese language was used and respected in union literature, including both UE leaflets and "Union News," and at union meetings held outside the Portuguese community. It is hard to describe the impact that this had on the Portuguese work force. The fact that the company had never made any attempt to have its rules, regulations, benefit plans, or any kind of employee notices translated into Portuguese, and that the union had everything translated presented a dramatic contrast and favorably impressed even the "antiunion" Portuguese workers.

Thus, contrary to the findings of Fenton and others, ethnicity was a positive and significant factor in determining the receptivity of Portuguese workers, and particularly Portuguese women workers, to unionization. Rather than acting to obscure class relations, the maintenance of strong ethnic groups became the social and cultural vehicle for interpreting common class experiences. This study also suggests that political movements linked to immigrant communities, such as the Armed Forces movement in Portugal, can have a significant and positive impact on the receptivity of workers to unionization and the extent and particular nature of their class consciousness.[16]

CONCLUSION

A holistic approach to working women's empowerment and political activism is not just a question of remembering to look at two or three factors rather than one. It is fundamentally based in the way we conceptualize those factors and their interrelationships. To understand the impact of class, one must look beyond women's relationship to the production process as it occurs in the workplace. Class also affects the nature and scope of woman's subordination in the family and often the possibilities and limitations placed on her participation in her community. Gender likewise must not be narrowly viewed as restricted to woman's role in the family and how her domestic duties and obligations delimit her role outside the home. Sexual subordination in the workplace, including both the sexual segregation of production *and* the particular culture of production departments in which the work force is predominantly female, are important components for understanding gender oppression and gender identity. Similarly, ethnic and cultural differences must not be narrowly viewed as customs and traditions that comprise people's lives in their communities. National and cultural differences also affect the way people relate to their jobs and their ability to mobilize ethnically specific institutions to aid their activities in the workplace.

I want to conclude with two main points that are specific to the case of Digitex but that I believe have implications for a large number of industrial workplaces. First, unionization *is* a form of empowerment in which women and immigrant workers have and can play an important and leading role. In this study, women and immigrant workers not only joined the union but built social groups in the workplace based on the sharing of important kin- and community-based experiences. Their ability to mobilize ethnically specific institutions in support of the union and to resist male chauvinism and antiunionism in their families significantly aided the unionization of Digitex.

Second, there is great variability in the pattern of empowerment for different groups of workers. For some women, their resistance began on the job; sharing their individual grievances against the company with female coworkers enabled them to participate in a collective fight against the company. This collective political experience, in turn, enabled them to transform their relationships with—and gain some autonomy from—men and their families. For other women, their resistance began in the community and in their identification with a resistance movement in their homeland. This, in turn, enabled them to become active in a workplace-based movement. There is, in sum, no single model that can explain the complex interplay of family, community, and workplace in shaping the political consciousness and activity of women workers. But we can make a commitment to a method of analysis that recognizes women's multiple roles and the importance of cultural and racial difference, as our methods will greatly affect what we learn from the struggle of Digitex workers and in other workplaces across the United States.

ACKNOWLEDGMENTS
This study was funded in part by a National Institute of Mental Health Predoctoral Research Grant. I would like to thank my mentors and advisers, Beatrice and John Whiting, for their support of this project in the dissertation phase. I would also like to thank my colleagues in the Harvard Anthropology Department, Andrea Cousins, Sandy Davis, and Steve Fjellman, who listened and thoughtfully responded so many times during the conception and execution of my thesis.

The comments on and criticisms of my completed dissertation were very helpful in paving the way for this article, particularly those of Meredith Tax, Hal Benenson, and other members of the Sarah Eisenstein Series Editorial Board. I would also like to thank Paula Rayman and Roz Feldberg for their substantive comments on an early draft. Sandra Morgen, Martha A. Ackelsberg, and other contributors to this volume provided additional response and encouragement.

NOTES
1. Bernard Karsh, Joel Seidman, and Daisy Lilienthal, "The Union Organizer and His Tactics," in Jack Barbash, ed., *Unions and Union Leadership* (New York: Harper & Bros., 1959), 98.

2. Edwin Fenton, "Immigrants and Unions, A Case Study: Italians and American Labor, 1870–1920" (doctoral dissertation, Harvard University, 1957), 30.

3. Although it is certainly true that working-class women have been socialized traditionally to view their family roles and duties as primary, it does not follow that their experience at work and their receptivity to unionization are completely and adversely

determined by the sexual and domestic roles they play within their family units. It is interesting that in studies of working-class men, it is usually assumed and argued that work outside the home determines how they function in other spheres. The opposing assumptions underlying these studies of working-class men and women have led some critics of traditional social science, such as Feldberg and Glenn, to argue that sociology and other disciplines are "sex-segregated" and that there are two models of work and workplace behavior being used, one for men (a "job model") and one for women (a "gender model"). Roslyn Feldberg and Evelyn Glenn, "Male and Female: Job versus Gender Models in the Sociology of Work," in *Social Problems* 26, No. 5 (June 1979): 524–538.

4. For a fuller discussion of such studies, see J. A. Banks, *Marxist Sociology in Action: A Sociological Critique of the Marxist Approach to Industrial Relations* (Harrisburg, Penna.: Stackpole, 1970), esp. chaps. 4, 6, 7, 8.

5. Alan Dawley, *Class and Community: The Industrial Revolution in Lynn* (Cambridge: Harvard University Press, 1976), 228.

6. There are of course exceptions to this generalization, for example, the excellent book by Sarah Eisenstein, *Give Us Bread but Give Us Roses* (London: Routledge & Kegan Paul, 1983).

7. Ruth Milkman, ed., *Women, Work and Protest: A Century of U.S. Women's Labor History* (Boston and London: Routledge & Kegan Paul, 1985), xii.

8. Ibid., xiii.

9. For a fuller discussion of the history of the electrical industry and a history of electrical workers' trade unions, see Ann Bookman, "The Process of Political Socialization Among Women and Immigrant Workers: A Case Study of Unionization in the Electronics Industry" (doctoral dissertation, Harvard University, 1977), chap. 3; and Ron Schatz, "The End of Corporate Liberalism: Class Struggle in the Electrical Manufacturing Industry, 1933–1950," *Radical America* 9 (1975): 4–5.

10. There is a long, rich history of alliances and organizing between middle-class feminists and working-class women, and among the feminist, labor, and socialist movements. How this relationship functioned at Digitex, how it paralleled or diverged from its historical antecedents, is a fascinating topic beyond the scope of this article. For an excellent historical discussion of the issues involved, see Meredith Tax, *The Rising of the Women: Feminist Solidarity and Class Conflict, 1880–1917* (New York: Monthly Review Press, 1980).

11. Richard Edwards, *Contested Terrain: The Transformation of the Workplace in the Twentieth Century* (New York: Basic Books, 1979).

12. "Home visits" were a very important component of the methodology utilized in this study. It was the opportunity to make home visits to a broad spectrum of Digitex workers, male and female, that facilitated data collection on their domestic roles, responsibilities, and relationships.

13. For a fuller explanation of the statistical methods and results, see Bookman, "The Process of Political Socialization," esp. chaps. 8 and 9.

14. "Ethnicity" was measured by a set of interrelated variables including location of residence, membership in particular social clubs, churches, neighborhood associations, and the like.

15. Carol Turbin, "Women's Life Cycles and Nineteenth Century Labor Militancy" (paper presented at the Sixth Berkshire Conference on the History of Women, Smith College, June 1984).

16. My own findings bear striking similarity to those of Lynn Goldfarb in her work on the unionization of service workers in Washington, D.C. She found that the unionization of Afro-American workers in that city was bolstered not only by the use of existing networks of social and religious support in the Black community but also by the linkages that were built between the civil rights movement and the labor movement. See "Women Organizing in Commercial Service Work, 1940–1980" (paper presented at the Sixth Berkshire Conference on the History of Women, Smith College, June 1984).

8

Urban Politics in the Higher

Education of Black Women:

A Case Study

Andrée Nicola-McLaughlin

Zala Chandler

All too often the potential for full intellectual development and goal realization on the part of minorities and women is suppressed by denying these groups the appropriate job training and educational opportunity necessary to assume a role which white males consider to be their domain.
—Shirley Chisholm, first Black woman member of Congress[1]

The history of Black women's struggle for education in America can be characterized as one of resistance to social policies of containment and to racist and sexist oppression and violence.[2] Second to the abolition of slavery, the education of Black people has symbolized the cutting edge of the African–American quest for freedom. In this pursuit of formal learning against forces desirous of ensuring a docile slave population and a pool of cheap, unskilled Black labor, successively, Black women have been on the frontlines of the battlegrounds for both the education of Black women and that of Black people as a whole.

In the decade after the demise of American slavery, the onset of the post-Reconstruction campaign of white terror brought new socioeconomic proscriptions by the broader society. Nevertheless, countless Black women continued to teach and to establish schools to assist in the African–American struggle for first-class citizenship over the next century. Proponents of African–American and women's rights, such as nineteenth-century Black feminist Anna Julia Cooper, advocated the higher education of Black females as a route to both the advancement of Black women and the promotion of Black community development.

The plight of Black women was most substantively challenged by the political movements for civil rights and Black power and the new feminist movement that emerged in the 1950s and 1960s. Yet even as civil rights legislation outlawing discrimination and segregation was enacted in the mid-1960s, a new attack on Black women surfaced, alleging their participation in education and paid employment were causal factors in Black male unemployment and Black family instability.[3] Still, the civil rights legislation enabled an unprecedented number of Black women to seek advancement at American colleges and universities. During this period, when the locus of the Black struggle had shifted from the South to urban centers where African–Americans were concentrated, Black demands for empowerment resulted in greater access and educational opportunity for Black women. The reforms in higher education by the late 1960s included the establishment of compensatory programs, Black studies, open admission, and increased recruitment of Black faculty and administrators.

Since the mid-1970s the African–American feminist movement has tried to eliminate additional barriers to higher education for Black women. This has translated into political action for child care, Black women's studies, women's centers, and Black women faculty and administrators. This activism is historically situated in a period of eroding social commitment to mass education represented in diminished student support services, limitations on federal financial assistance, and skyrocketing tuition costs.

The struggle of women at Medgar Evers College of the City University of New York (CUNY) in 1982 offers a poignant and historic instance of Black women's resistance to racist and sexist policies and practices that threatened their quest for higher education. This example of militant organizing in defense of the *right* to quality education exemplifies how Black women students brought diverse groups together to make institutional change in one community. At the college, their actions resulted in the revision of the curriculum to include Black and women's studies, the provision of child-care facilities, the establishment of a women's center, the appointment of a predominantly Black female college administration, the construction of a new campus, and state legislation proposing the reinstatement of senior (four-year) status for the college. The political activism of Black women at Medgar Evers College had far-reaching ramifications; it fostered a revitalized push for child care within the City University of New York, the naming of the first Black woman trustee to the University's board of trustees, and the appointment of the first Black woman president at another college within the City University.

The focus of this case study is a six-month period (March–August 1982) within a sixteen-year struggle to develop a college in Brooklyn, New York, that would be responsive to the educational needs of the Black community there. The authors played significant roles in the campaign as activist educators committed to high-quality education for all Black people. The detail provided in this account of the struggle at Medgar Evers College presents a story of Black women's empowerment in very concrete and practical ways as Black women students, faculty, and community residents took the lead in mobilizing a community, developing strategy and tactics, and organizing and taking decisive political action to facilitate a people's movement for change.

BACKGROUND AND EARLY YEARS OF THE COLLEGE

The creation of Medgar Evers College was the City University of New York's response to the militant demands of the Black power movement during the mid to late 1960s for equal educational opportunity. In its own statement of mission, Medgar Evers College defines itself as a "college for developing people," aiming to address the particular needs and issues of the community in order to revitalize and develop that community. Appropriately, the college took its name, "Medgar Evers," from the Mississippi leader of the National Association for the Advancement of Colored People (NAACP), who died in the struggle for Black human rights in the state of Mississippi in 1963.

Medgar Evers College is one of the twenty institutions in the City University of New York and is located in the Crown Heights section of Central Brooklyn. Part of the institution's uniqueness rests in its location in one of the largest Black communities in the Western hemisphere (Brooklyn), in its service of a predominantly adult population (average age twenty-six), in the composition of its faculty, 83 percent of whom are people of color, and in the fact that it employs and serves the largest concentration of Black females in the CUNY system.

The approximately three-thousand-member student population of Medgar Evers College is 95 percent Black, with nearly half of the student body having origins in the Caribbean, Latin America, or Africa, representing more than seventy nationalities of origin. The student population as a whole reflects the cultural characteristics that distinguish the African diaspora, including strong religious, work, and achievement orientations; strong kinship bonds; and adaptability of family roles.[4] It is not unusual to have three generations of a given family in attendance at the college in any given semester, but the overwhelming majority of the student body consists of first-generation college students.

Three-fourths of the student population are female, and 69 percent are mothers, with more than half of them single heads of household. The student body reflects the demographic features of the Black Brooklyn community, where nearly 50 percent of all households are headed by females and 70 percent of those households live below the poverty level. Common problems confronting the female population of the college and its community are insufficient child-care facilities, a shortage of decent affordable housing, haggling with the bureaucracies of public assistance and the public school system, inadequate financial resources, domestic violence, and depression.

Of the college's teaching and administrative staff, 65 percent are women, the majority of them Black, and more than 80 percent of the clerical staff are

Black females, constituting the highest percentages of Black women workers in any part of the CUNY system.

Medgar Evers College was chartered in 1969 and opened its doors to students in 1971. From the outset there were crises and unrest, beginning when the CUNY trustees disbanded the original, community-based planning committee for the college upon its recommendation that an educational leader and advocate of "community control" be named the founding president. In 1971, the predominantly white male CUNY board of trustees installed Richard Trent as the college president.

Within one year the college community attempted to oust President Trent. A growing perception of his ineptitude came to a head when he fired nearly a dozen faculty members who had criticized his lack of leadership. Although the CUNY trustees retained Trent, a new crisis erupted two years later. Militant student demands were issued for a day-care center, Black studies, a bookstore, and the retention of activist faculty; additionally, there were formal student allegations of alcoholism, sexual abuse of students, and fiscal impropriety on the part of Trent and his team of administrators. The CUNY board of trustees and the university chancellor again came to the rescue of the college president.

To the college community, the events from 1971 to 1974 were evidence that the seventeen-member CUNY board of trustees, comprised of predominantly white male mayoral and gubernatorial appointees, did not have the interests of the college at heart and wanted this educational experiment to fail. This suspicion was further fueled by the events of the New York City fiscal crisis in 1975–76. By early 1976 the university's trustees were proposing the closure of several CUNY colleges, including Medgar Evers College. The Student–Faculty Coalition to Save Medgar Evers College was founded to take militant action to focus public attention on the plight of the college after petitions of appeal, letter-writing and telephone campaigns, and lobbying of elected officials failed to ensure the college's future.

In the aftermath of a brief takeover of a facility of the CUNY central administration by the coalition, violent clashes with the police, and several arrests, university officials negotiated a compromise of "community college status" with the college president. In September of 1976 Medgar Evers College was stripped of its four-year status and designated a community college for alleged "budgetary" reasons. This compromise resulted in reduced funding for educational programs and services, a reduction in library resources, the reduction of the college's physical plant from nine buildings to two, and an increased workload for faculty and staff. In light of the ground swell of community support for retention of the college's original mission, the college community felt betrayed by President Trent; it viewed the conversion to community college status as a racist measure to undermine the development of the college and its community. This view was reinforced when the trustees granted approval of four-year status to two former community colleges that were based in white communities (in 1976 and 1980). Finally, the concerns of the college were compounded when also in 1976, the banking community successfully pressured the city and state governments to end the 129-year tradition of free tuition at the city colleges. By 1982, the force of the Medgar Evers College community's actions for redress would match the erosion of its hope for equal education.

THE HISTORY OF THE STRIKE AND SIT-IN

Beginning in March 1982, the college president was confronted for the fourth time by students and faculty. Ten demands were issued, and a two-week strike was called. A leaflet was widely distributed:

THIS IS A SERIOUS MATTER!

STUDENTS HAVE RIGHTS!

The Student Government Association, on behalf of the student body has issued the following list of demands for which President Trent is being held accountable. Satisfactory resolution of these issues include President Trent's immediate attention to these matters and concrete plans within a negotiable time frame for rectification of the issues as stated:

1. We demand that President Trent meet with the student population and present an explanation of his faltering commitment to the student body. We believe that the credibility of the Chief Administrative Officer of this institution has diminished and therefore, the credibility of the college is in jeopardy.

2. We demand an explanation of President Trent's statement that he, ". . . does not believe in Black Studies," (as printed in the Village Voice) in view of the fact that the majority of students in the college have expressed a desire to pursue this line of studies. In addition, we are seeking an explanation of the administration's failure to update the academic curriculum.

3. We demand immediate rectification of the deteriorating status of the Business Division, including the appointment of a qualified and stable Division Chairperson.

4. We demand the allocation of funds for the implementation of an academic excellence recognition and incentive program, in addition to the Community Council Scholarships (i.e. honor society, tuition waivers, book scholarships, certificates of merit, etc.).

5. We demand faculty course loads be kept at a minimum and that faculty members not be required to teach in areas outside their field of expertise. In addition, students should be advised, prior to registration, of instructors' course assignments thereby enabling students to select courses accordingly and to be exposed to various teaching techniques.

6. We demand that the administration investigate and correct the deteriorating physical conditions of the college which inhibit motivation, participation, and the general health and well-being of the faculty, staff and student populations (i.e. ventilation, broken windows, cold/overheated classrooms, leaking ceilings, falling paint and plaster).

7. We demand improved security measures in order for the student body, faculty and staff to move freely and safely within and between the college's buildings. (On Friday, March 12, 1982, a female student was attacked by a male student in the lobby of the Prep Building while the Security Guards looked on. We were informed that they do not have the authority to interfere in student disputes.)

8. We demand the improvement of the coordination of services and communication between the administrative offices (i.e. Financial Aid, Registrar, Bursar) in order that the day and evening students can be serviced more efficiently.

9. In view of the female student population percentage, we demand that arrangements for child care during day and evening class attendance be made a priority on the administration's agenda for the college's services.

10. We demand the improvement of plans and strategies for student recruitment (i.e. greater community interaction, wider distribution of printed material, improved utilization of media sources, utilization of on-campus student organizations as recruitment sources).

We, the students of Medgar Evers College, believe that the implementation of certain programs and services are necessary if we are to acquire the quality level of education guaranteed by CUNY By-Laws and Medgar Evers College recruitment literature.

The event that precipitated the student strike was the president's refusal to meet with students at the regular biannual assembly of the Student Government Association when the president traditionally addresses and answers questions from the student body.

Most of the demands made by the students were not new; they had been issued in the previous confrontations with the president. As early as 1974 a blue-ribbon commission of distinguished, nationally renowned educators had evaluated the college and concluded that the provision of day care was necessary if the college was to fulfill its mission. In addition to the hardship caused by absence of child care, women students, faculty, and staff encountered intimidation and sexual harassment. The clerical staff was used as a reserve labor pool, members being intermittently terminated and rehired. Even at the highest levels, sex discrimination was apparent; in an eleven-year period, only three women received deanship appointments (out of twenty), and each was ultimately demoted, forced to resign, or fired. An additional issue for women in particular was the inadequate security, which resulted in numerous muggings and assaults on female members of the general college community. All of these issues had serious consequences for women on campus, including students who were forced to leave the college because of unmet child-care needs. In 1982, the major charge against President Trent was his refusal to allow Black women equal educational opportunity through his failure to establish child care for the predominantly female student body.

Spurred by student action, the faculty conferred with Trent. After further deliberations, eighty-eight members of the faculty voted "yes," twenty-six voted "no," and seventeen abstained on a motion calling for Trent's resignation. Two days later the results of a student poll revealed that an overwhelming majority of the student body, 69 percent of day students and 83 percent of evening students, also desired the president's resignation.

Representatives of faculty and student bodies met, and a decision was made to end the strike and form a Student–Faculty Coalition. Its goals were "to remove Dr. Richard D. Trent, the College president, who has been an albatross around the College's neck; and to rebuild Medgar Evers College in the image of Medgar Evers, the man."

Publicity about events at the College led to broad-based support for the coalition in the larger community of Central Brooklyn. At an April 7 meeting, educators, clergy, elected officials, local shopkeepers, community organizers, and relatives and friends of the college's student and faculty met with members of the coalition and endorsed the campaign. The coalition was broadened to include concerned individuals and groups from the Central Brooklyn community, becoming the Student–Faculty–Community Coalition to Save Medgar Evers College. In an editorial a week later, the largest Black newspaper in New York State, the *Amsterdam News,* called for the college president's resignation.

Day and evening rallies at the college, letters of appeal to the CUNY trustees, a telephone campaign directed at city and state officials, and demonstrations in the streets adjacent to the College became part of the daily routine of the Student–Faculty–Community Coalition. On April 19, CUNY officials reluctantly met with coalition faculty representatives while the coalition held its own community hearing on the president's alleged dereliction of duties. At the hearing, students—including student members of a two-year-old student and faculty study group—agitated for more decisive action by the coalition. The militant mood of the hearing intensified upon receipt of news that CUNY officials had said that they would "look into" the crisis.

The next day more than two hundred students marched to the college president's office. He fled through a side entrance. As a result, students began a peaceful sit-in in his office, demanding his ouster, quality education (as represented in the ten student demands), and an end to the racist and sexist policies of the CUNY board of trustees.

Meanwhile, additional community support for the students' militant action came from members of Black women's organizations, and from Black veterans' and other community groups who lent their physical presence to the students when the police threatened violence to terminate the sit-in. The Black media surged onto campus and reported the occupying students' rationale for the escalation of events—over the air, live. Students' parents, local shopkeepers, and other members of the community supplied the students with food, eating utensils, bedding, and towels. The coalition's steering committee (which comprised students, faculty, and community representatives) held successive meetings with progressive and mainstream individuals and bodies of influence to enlist their support.

Unprepared for the coalition's act of civil disobedience, the CUNY headquarters and the New York City mayor's office sent their legal counsel and secret service representatives to the college to conduct emergency negotiations with the coalition. The discussions broke down on the second day when it was learned that the CUNY officials had received a temporary restraining order to enjoin the student-led sit-in. With tensions increasing and the prospect of violence everpresent, several members of the faculty, the community, and the Black media joined the sit-in. That night, when white male municipal authorities, accompanied by a college administrator, CUNY legal counsel, and local police, entered the college to serve the court order, they were blocked by hundreds of student supporters—Blacks, Hispanics, Asians, and whites; women and men; students and workers; some from the college and some from the broader community—who filled the college corridors to ensure the security of the students occupying the president's office. The authorities tossed the order into the midst of the supporters in a final, frustrated attempt to serve it.

The first response of the coalition was to ignore the notice of injunction. However, legal advice led to a decision to present the concerns of the college community in court. The faculty responded with the unanimous passage of a resolution supporting the students' actions and abhorring "any police violence to remove students or criminal prosecution to resolve [the] crisis." Preceding and throughout the court hearing, which began by April's end, community support persisted and expanded to include more college students, the Black media, the women's movement, Black community organizations, the Black church, and elected officials.

NETWORKS AND ALLIES: AN EXPANDING COALITION

Students from various colleges joined with Medgar Evers students in support of their demands. Pre-existing student networks, reflecting the extended consciousness of the civil rights and antiwar movements of the 1960s (such as the CUNY chapter of the national Progressive Student Network and the CUNY- and SUNY-based Black Students Communication Organizing Network), were able to mobilize their constituencies readily. Through news coverage in their campus newspapers and on their radio stations, by their presence at the CUNY trustees' regularly scheduled public meetings, and in meetings with local church, civic, labor, and special-interest groups, these student organizations and numerous student unions presented the crisis at Evers as part of a larger struggle of poor and working people for quality public higher education and as part of the long tradition of Black struggle for justice. The sole (Black male) student representative on the CUNY board of trustees (also president of the University Student Senate) was equally vigilant in voicing the will of the Medgar Evers College student body in every possible forum. The students also joined in the ongoing picketing in front of the college president's home. Letters of support for the president's ouster and the ten student demands poured in from student unions around the nation, putting the college's crisis in the eyes of academic communities and media from coast to coast.

As the college president and the CUNY trustees refused to act, the Black media joined the effort. They focused on the students' demands, especially the absence of Black studies at a predominantly Black institution.[5] The student demand for Black studies and the faculty vote for Trent's resignation formed the bases for the Black media's calls for the college president's resignation in the early weeks of the crisis. It was the reporters and broadcasters of expressly progressive media, including Black women journalists, station managers, and program hosts, who kept the events at the college in the public eye after editorials in the established Black media had earlier called for the president's ouster.[6]

The involvement of the women's community of Greater New York City in the crisis was an outcome of the active membership of many of the college's women in local women's organizations. For example, in 1981 some women faculty and student members of the college had joined other women in New York City to organize a Mother's Day march to express concern about the insufficient social and governmental responses to the murders of Black children in Atlanta, Georgia. This was the first time in recent history that a citywide coalition of progressive Black women had existed in Greater New York City. Out of this undertaking emerged the Coalition of Concerned Black Women, some members of which already belonged to the Brooklyn-based Sisterhood of Black Single Mothers. The women in this coalition were activist women who worked in various organizations and in health, education, media, labor, and private industry throughout the city's five boroughs. Having roots in the civil rights, welfare rights, Black, and women's movements as well as the political left, they possessed a theoretical and practical understanding of the concerns of the college's predominantly Black female population. This loose network of women had the capacity to respond quickly and substantively to the issues of the general and women's communities of Medgar Evers College.

Members of the Coalition of Concerned Black Women and the Sisterhood of Black Single Mothers were instrumental in bringing together progressive women from around the city to assist with security and to use their resources and networks to publicize both the crisis and the mobilization for direct mass actions. As coalition members, they were able to articulate the interconnectedness of race, economic class, and gender to the larger coalition membership, to the media, and to community organizations. The linking of the Black liberation movement to the antisexist struggle of the women's movement was the result. It was this linkage that lent the struggle at Medgar Evers College a distinctly female character.

The united antiracist antisexist voice that emerged was especially noteworthy in contrast to events beyond the college: the failure of the Equal Rights Amendment, the dismantling of social programs, increasing unemployment, and severe setbacks in regard to civil and reproductive rights. The coalition linked the alteration of financial aid guidelines to federal economic policies restricting support for equal opportunities, a feature of "Reaganomics." It linked the CUNY trustees' neglect of the institution to the racism of the federal administration's endeavors to dismantle the Civil Rights Commission and to the massive budget cuts in programs for people of color and the poor. It attributed the absence of attention to the needs of the college's female population to the neoconservative climate of the era, which aimed to discourage women's participation, advancement, and equality in various social arenas. The politicization of practical gender issues influenced the coalition's strategies and tactics as the predominantly female student body and the Student Government Association, including one Hispanic and three Black female officers, took more strident positions to address their triple oppression as women of color and members of the working poor. In the days to come, the students would call for women's studies, a women's center, a dean of women, and, most challenging of all, a Black female college president.

From the onset of the student sit-in, state and local Black elected officials threw the weight of their offices behind what had come to be the struggle of the Central Brooklyn community and a struggle for Black self-determination in Greater New York City. The Black clergy, media, and educators joined with student, women's, labor, and community groups to issue a joint written statement to the CUNY trustees that requested the reassignment of the college president and the appointment of an interim administrator. Elected officials made appearances at evening community rallies held at the college and linked the struggle to other crises in housing, education, and employment; lack of political representation on key municipal bodies; police brutality; and racism. Community organizers lauded the college students for their continuation of the tradition of Black resistance and advocated student participation in the struggles of the broader community. By April's end, the first Black congresswoman, Shirley Chisholm, pledged her support for the students' demands; this coincided with the first days of the hearing held in the Brooklyn Supreme Court.

That hearing lasted five days. A team of well-known civil rights lawyers and the CUNY student legal counsel defended the students occupying the president's office (who were not present at the hearing). In their stead, hundreds of students, faculty members, and community residents filled the courtroom daily to hear the cases of the plaintiff and the college community. The defense counsel's cross-examination of CUNY witnesses revealed the employment of false statements by the college and CUNY administrations, including allegations of violence and destruction of college property that they admitted were made to secure the temporary restraining order. Also exposed were other endeavors to intimidate the college community in an apparent effort to neutralize, discredit, and dissipate the push for change. The case for the college heard testimony from student government officers, "Ms. Medgar Evers College" (the female student ambassador), college faculty and administrators, and community residents, exposing the college president's eleven-year history of "intimidation, mismanagement, mediocrity, and anti-community sentiment."

On the date of concluding court testimony, May 3, the Medgar Evers College Alumni Association took strong action, voting to remove from office two alumni who were untenured members of the faculty and supporters of the college administration. The Alumni Association also voted to support the students' sit-in action. This expression of solidarity expanded the constituency of the coalition; the coalition was now the Student–Faculty–Community–Alumni Coalition to Save Medgar Evers College.

Fearful of losing their case, the CUNY legal counsel requested an indefinite postponement of the judge's decision on its request for an injunction. With the ruling postponed until May 7, the coalition declared "Solidarity Day" on May 6 to determine community solidarity for the continuation of the action of civil disobedience in the event that the court ruled for CUNY. The outcome was a student boycott of all classes and a sit-in in other administrative offices of the college. The message was clear: The community wanted the sit-in to continue until the college president resigned. On May 7 student, faculty, community, and alumni demonstrators marched through the streets of Brooklyn from the college to the Supreme Court, with banners and placards, to hear the court decision. It was an historic occasion; the Irish–American judge who heard the case rendered a precedent-setting decision in the coalition's favor, upholding the students' right under the First Amendment to protest peacefully until the crisis was resolved. The victory in the courtroom was followed by a press conference, a rally at the college, and a march in the streets of Crown Heights informing the surrounding community of the court decision and pledging resolve to continue the effort to force Trent to resign.

After the victorious court ruling, Trent and the CUNY trustees refused to negotiate with the coalition. They threatened to cancel commencement and the summer session, and exerted pressure on faculty and staff of the college. The seemingly intransigent racism and sexism of university officials were met with the coalition's announcement to the news media of the formation of a search committee for a new president. Predictably, this action by the coalition caused the university to break its silence. The college president was ordered to meet with the press and return to campus to exercise his authority. The events that followed, more than anything else, foreshadowed the imminent change.

On May 13, 1982, Trent returned to campus to chair a meeting of the college's legislative body, the College Council, after issuing an inflammatory statement to the press charging students with criminality and threatening to suspend students and fire untenured faculty. Coalition students and faculty openly challenged his chairing of this meeting, and within moments of its inception Trent fled the meeting and the institution, flanked by college security officers. Local police were called in by the college administration to escort the president's vehicle from the parking lot; it had been surrounded by hundreds of angry students chanting, "Fired up! Can't take no more!"

In the days to come, the college president then attempted to run the institution from his home through a few loyal faculty members and administrators. His efforts to block funds for all graduation-related expenses, to cancel the rental contract for the original, student-selected site for graduation and to change to a new site were widely reported by the media. The community was further outraged. Student members of the church that Trent had arbitrarily chosen to be the new site for the graduation then met with the minister who in turn refused him the use of the church. The Student Government Association announced its own plan to conduct commencement exercises for graduating students. Several weeks later, five thousand community residents attended the student-held graduation exercises with the lone Black student trustee representing the CUNY board.

Within a week after the graduation ceremony, the CUNY board of trustees agreed to conduct hearings on Richard Trent's leadership and management of the college. Students, faculty members, community residents, alumni, and elected officials testified. On July 6, 1982 the college president resigned, and the CUNY board of trustees transferred him to another college of CUNY. The students, however, continued the sit-in, appealing to the trustees for the appointment of a Black woman acting president.

When the CUNY board of trustees appointed a white male, who had been a dean in the ex-president's administration, to head the predominantly Black female college, coalition protest prompted them to reverse themselves and appoint a Black male. It was clear to the students involved in the sit-in that the struggle for quality education and community control of the college was to be a protracted one. On August 25, 1982, the students, in a formal ceremony, announced the planned conversion of the ex-president's office into a child-care center, naming it after the (now late) civil rights leader and inspiration of the Student Nonviolent Coordinating Committee (SNCC) Ella Baker, and a late Medgar Evers College professor of chemistry and adovcate of quality education, Dr. Charles Romain. On the 110th day of the sit-in, August 7, 1982, the students ended the sit-in and opened the Baker/Romain Child Development Center, thereby launching the struggle for the coalition's second objective, "to rebuild the College in the image of Medgar Evers." In 1987, that struggle remains in process.

"WOMEN FINDING THEIR VOICES"

The six-month campaign gave many Medgar Evers College students (and faculty, community, and alumni members) the opportunity to learn a great many concrete skills and political lessons. In particular, the women students (and faculty, community, and alumni) became empowered. They were not only a majority of the people participating in the campaign to save Medgar Evers College; they also predominated the leadership of the struggle.

The process of women "finding their voices" and becoming empowered at the college was not automatic despite their numerical majority there. Women were forced by the circumstances of history at the college and their lives outside the college to learn through doing, to raise issues of sexism (including food preparation, child care, and security while they were engaged in the sit-in in the president's office), and to become leaders in their own rights. It was a woman student, for example, who was given the tremendous responsibility of representing the college in the University Student Senate as a senator charged with convincing the entire Senate (and thus other colleges throughout the university) to support the coalition's struggle for parity and justice. Included in her responsibilities were several trips to Albany, New York, in order to lobby with various state politicians in behalf of the institution. This woman has since moved to Albany in pursuit of a law degree.

Many of the women involved in the struggle at Medgar Evers later went on to lead community tenant associations, parent–teacher associations, women's organizations, food co-ops, coalitions for political prisoners, and welfare rights groups, and to organize significant cultural programs, community demonstrations against injustice, forums, film series, and conferences. Such leadership evidenced that the skills and the lessons they learned were tools of empowerment that could be applied to the day-to-day life struggles of the Black community.

As the previous section suggests, many students were involved in a wide variety of activities during the campaign. Picket lines, rallies, and demonstrations complemented a 110-day sit-in. For each of these events, students were required to develop pamphlets, press releases, chants, and placards. In the occupied room itself, student activity ranged from the study of the history of African-Americans and their literary works to drills on how to handle a confrontation with the police. Their leadership responsibilities required that they learn how to strategize, to agitate, and to organize for change. In most instances, the "how" was learned through trial and error, through doing.

The Student Government Association, consisting of four women and one man, worked along with other student leaders to provide the leadership necessary to steer the mounting anger and frustration on the part of the student body into concrete action. Each day rallies were held to keep the student body up-to-date on events and to elicit suggestions regarding actions that should be taken in response to the actions of the president. Many students developed speaking skills and the courage to stand before large audiences. The "speak-out" atmosphere allowed many students, most of whom were women who had never spoken in public before, to "find their voices." As Jennifer Weeks, a secretarial science student, put it:

> I was scared to death the first time that I got up in front of all those people in the auditorium. My knees were shaking! But I got it together because I believed in what we were doing. After that first time, it became a whole lot easier for me to talk in front of all those people.

The formation of the coalition steering committee helped further develop the leadership skills of the students, thus contributing to the empowerment of women. This committee met daily, and in this forum students learned to chair meetings, develop short- and long-term plans, and negotiate with university officials, university lawyers, and representatives from the mayor's office and the police. They learned practical skills, including the maintenance of minutes and accurate records, and social skills, such as how to work in an egalitarian manner.

In making written and verbal appeals to various community, religious, and labor organizations, as well as to elected officials, the student leadership learned how to convey the conflict lucidly and succinctly for public comprehension. They learned how to file and catalogue news clippings, photographs, and correspondence as well as to chronicle events for resource materials. The coalition adopted a method of criticism and self-criticism to sum up and evaluate all activities, including rallies and daily meetings, and the division of labor. With nearly forty people occupying the office and a cadre of approximately one hundred persons in the corridor to the office at any given time (including children), there had to be fine-tuned organization and coordination. The president's office was a suite furnished with a kitchenette, refrigerator, bar, shower, dimming lights, plush carpet, and couches as well as a conference table, desks, and office machines. Committees for cooking, cleaning, shopping for food, and taking care of the children as well as such matters as scheduling showers and sleeping shifts constituted a model of what one writer calls the "techniques of transformation, adaptation and survival" true to the Black experience.[7] When there were lapses, the coalition used a "unity-criticisms-unity method" to address the problems (that is, assessment of successes with credit to those responsible, analysis of weaknesses in execution of tasks with criticism of the appropriate group or individuals, and solidarity to achieve objectives).

Toward the end of bolstering the college community's confidence in ultimate victory and by using language and symbols that were culturally significant, the coalition employed what it referred to as the "culture of struggle." Upon entering the institution one would be met by the Black Liberation flag; banners calling for educational justice; posters displaying political cartoons that depicted the latest events and revelations in the struggle; photographs of people engaged in different activities in the struggle; a bust of Medgar Evers; pictures of Malcolm X and Harriet Tubman; and the music of Sweet Honey in the Rock or Eddy Grant's "Living on the Frontline," the theme song for the college community's struggle. Student creativity was challenged as students in the Christian Club modified the lyrics of gospel songs to speak to the issues of the crisis and other students wrote poems lauding the student vanguard and the struggle itself.

Finally, the students exercised constructive programming to address many of their own demands—for example, developing a child-care center, convening college committees, holding graduation. They gained a working knowledge of the bureaucracy of the college and its vehicles for policymaking and governance as well as those of the CUNY system and the City of New York. This process enabled the students to appreciate better the role and significance of research and knowledge of power structures and their governing processes in a movement that was working to effect change; a consciousness that could prove vital to any future campaigns for change at the college or in the community.

Ultimately, the greatest lesson the students learned was the history of the African–American struggle and their role in it. During the course of the struggle at Medgar Evers College, many students had risked their education, forfeited employment, lost relationships when spouses failed to understand their commitment to the college, suffered ill health, and lost financial assistance from social services as a result of having to miss scheduled meetings with welfare workers. But the result was their collective empowerment. These sacrifices should not be taken lightly, nor should their significance be underestimated. There were moments of great suffering. And victory would not have been certain without them.

A representative picture of the types of development and involvement that the women at Medgar Evers College experienced can best be given through a brief synopsis of the specific roles played by three women in the campaign. (All names are pseudonyms.)

Carol Smith is a thirty-eight-year-old divorced mother and former church deaconess with five children. After suffering in a violent marriage, she came to college with the goal of becoming an accountant. Her main role during the campaign was as a security person. During the sit-in, she maintained coverage for twenty-two hours a day of the door to the president's office—joining in discussion groups with people in the corridor, helping write leaflets, and giving instructions to her children over the phone. When CUNY attempted to get a court order served to evict the students, there was her face-to-face standoff with police. She decided to become a lawyer after her courtroom experiences and her conversations with other students and progressive lawyers involved in the case. Exhibiting a growing appreciation of the importance of self-pride and self-determination for herself and her children, she began to "dread" her hair and changed her clothing to reflect a greater African influence. Smith was one of the most vocal leaders in the decision to convert the president's office to a child-care center, and she personally led the fight for and, after graduation, became a staff person in the Center for Women's Development at the College. She says of her experiences:

> More than anything, I learned that I am a powerful person! You see,
> it's important to realize that no matter what your age or what you've

been through, each person can make a contribution to changing the
conditions of our people. . . . It's never too late, and you're never
too old. At age thirty-eight, I learned how to chair meetings, write
leaflets, speak to the press, organize meetings and various events,
and how to address all of the "big wigs." More, I learned to take
each day to be the beginning of the rest of my life. And the struggle
at Medgar Evers has made me determined that each new day will be
built upon a meaningful "yesterday." Now, no one can tell me that
I'm too old to pursue a law career, or stand in a demonstration, or go
to jail for a just cause, for that matter! From South Africa to Medgar
Evers (and all the other places in-between where Black people are
oppressed), people of African descent, old and young, have got to
start standing up and fighting for change.

In 1986, Smith enrolled in graduate school at a prestigious university in New
York. She continues to work at the women's center on a part-time basis and still
has plans to become a lawyer.

Ingrid Taylor is a twenty-three-year-old Trinidadian who came to New
York in search of a more rewarding life for herself and her young daughter,
whom she had left in the care of her parents back home. A Dean's List student,
Taylor planned to attend graduate school and eventually to become a college
administrator. One of her models was a woman dean at the college whom President Trent removed, according to him, at his "discretion." Taylor's anger at the
dean's removal added to her outrage at the lack of services at the college—from
the dismal, small, and unsafe physical space to the crowded classes, the lack of
an honors program, and the absence of Black studies.

Taylor turned her anger into action through her participation in the strike
and the sit-in, and through her leadership in the writing and dissemination of
leaflets, newspaper articles, press releases, and the daily "updates" to the college community. She did not confine herself to writing, however. When Trent
returned to campus and the students surrounded his car, Taylor stepped forward
and began to rock the car and shout, "We're fired up, can't take no more. . . ."
She says of her experience,

I learned so much—more than I could ever learn in the classroom! I
learned that there's a whole lot more than getting a degree and getting ahead financially. You must do so with principle and dignity.
You can't just sit back and watch all the atrocious things continue to
happen, take your little class notes, read your books, and do nothing
to change conditions. I was basically a shy and reserved person prior
to the struggle at Medgar, but I found my voice—and I used it! Now,
I will never lose my voice again! I will speak out and act out wherever or whenever I see myself being treated as something less than a
first-class human being with rights and a chance to be the absolute

best that I can be. And yes—I learned that as the African proverb goes: "When spider webs unite, they can tie up the lion!"

After graduation Taylor took time off to spend with her daughter and new son. She is an active member of the church and still plans to become a college administrator.

Winifred Johnson had always been what she calls a "stand-up-for-your-rights" person. As a single parent she had come to college to make a better life for herself and her daughter. She joined the sit-in, and her family took care of her child until the tensions on campus eased somewhat. After that, her daughter often joined her after school, sometimes staying the night with the sit-in group. Johnson was part of a collective that made decisions, shared in cooking and cleaning and child care, and endured the threats of ouster by the police. She had to take her turn chairing meetings, and though she was very hesitant at first, she soon became comfortable and competent at the task. Her secondary school education had been woefully inadequate, and she found the experience of the sit-in academically useful when willing tutors emerged from the ranks of students and faculty. Her writing had to improve because she had writing assignments for the collective. The experience empowered her as she learned through practice and with help to be a better writer and critical thinker. She says of the campaign:

> Can't *nobody* talk no stuff to me anymore I'm talking about NO-BODY—whether it be a teacher in a classroom, a boss on a job, a preacher on a pulpit, a politician on a microphone, or a man in my personal life—can't nobody talk no stuff to me. Hey—sometimes I feel like Martin Luther King must have felt—I've been to the mountain top. I can't get no more scared than I was when we heard that the New York City SWAT team was coming in that room. And I can't feel no more good than I felt when I heard that Trent had resigned. Hey, we danced and cried all over that place! Like Eddy Grant says, "Living on the frontline gets you ready for everything!"

Winifred Johnson will graduate from Medgar Evers College in 1987. Her plans are to enter divinity school and become a minister.

COALITION POLITICS

One of the strengths of the struggle at Medgar Evers College was the breadth of the coalition that was built. This particular coalition was initiated and built primarily by *students,* the majority of them women, who were able to use the issue of "quality education" to mobilize and organize broad sectors of the college and community. Different groups and individuals became a part of the coalition as students articulated how each particular constituency would benefit from a quality Black institution of higher learning in Central Brooklyn. Specifically, the students needed their various demands met to effect changes in their learning environments. The faculty wanted academic freedom and treatment and resources comparable to those of other CUNY faculty. Staff persons believed they deserved to be treated with decency and respect and to have a positive working environment. The alumni wanted a reputation for the college that would render their degrees competitive in the labor market; and the community wanted access to the college's facilities and the provision of specific academic programs and services that would benefit the community. Coalition politics at Medgar Evers was built around a program for concrete changes from which each component of the coalition could benefit and thereby support.

The protracted struggle necessitated the combining of resources and networks of all the organizations and people involved in the coalition. To maintain unity within this coalition each sector had to retain some degree of autonomy—ideologically, politically, and organizationally. The combination of interdependence and autonomy fostered democratic interaction that increased the potential for success even in the eventuality of particular groups deciding to pull out.

Like most coalitions, the Coalition to Save Medgar Evers College was not devoid of intense struggle within the ranks. The group with the most to win *and* lose was the students, and they tended to be the most militant, the most vigilant, and the most committed to long-term goals like rebuilding the college. Among the students, the women proved to remain the most committed to the development of a women's center and a day-care center—issues of particular concern to them.

The faculty, on the other hand, often played a moderate to conservative role in the campaign. *Initially,* its members frequently opposed student actions, arguing against the strike, the sit-in, a demonstration at the board, demonstrations at the president's house, the decision to run the president off the campus, and the conversion of the presidential office space into a day-care facility. (Later, they would oppose the establishment of the Center for Women's Development and the call for a woman to be the next president of Medgar Evers College.) The faculty tended to support such strategies as letter-writing, petition drives, and phone calls. However, when the system was unresponsive to these legal strategies, the faculty subsequently became supportive of various student actions. One lesson of the politics of coalition is that because people and organizations within the coalition run the spectrum of political orientations, it is often the group with the greatest interests at stake, the greatest level of organization and base, and the greatest willingness and readiness to take action that defines the direction of the struggle in a crisis situation.

The real test of coalition politics invariably comes at the end of a crisis, when short-term goals have been accomplished and longer-range goals remain to be attained. Once Trent was removed, the base of coalition began to erode. Only a core group—consisting of a small number of students, a considerably smaller number of faculty members, several community organizers, and a few alumni—pursued the hard and protracted work of "rebuilding the College in the image of Medgar Evers, the freedom fighter." The erosion took place because some faculty were silenced by rewards of appointments in the administration of the acting president and other members of the college wanted to have a return to "normalcy" and to give the acting president a chance to exhibit strong leadership. Politicians directed their energies to more newsworthy events, and the broader community returned to its routines. A new group, the Medgar Evers College Support Committee, emerged at this time. This was a group of mostly white women who were committed to the issues of day care, women's advocacy servicing, women's studies, and the selection of a woman president. But other than this new group, it was the student newspaper *Adafi* that carried the bulk of the weight for keeping the issues alive during this period.

THE AFTERMATH

Neither the appointment of an acting president nor the final selection of a second male as permanent president over an equally qualified female, Dr. Gloria Joseph, has quelled the ongoing struggle to save Medgar Evers College from a gradual, systematic demise. Coalition members continue to believe that the treatment of Medgar Evers College is a reflection of the "marrow of tradition" within this society. Without continued struggle, the college will never be a vehicle for the empowerment of Black people in general and Black women in particular because it exists within a political–economic system that seeks to make Black people and women subservient to white males at all levels of the economy and social institutions.

Once the interim administration settled into its "new" presidential office on the second floor of the college, it began systematically to harass militant student and faculty leadership in the coalition. Within four months of its tenure the interim administration threatened the non-reappointment of four faculty activists; they were retained only after another student campaign in their behalf. The acting president questioned and then delayed the student government president's earned designation as the class valedictorian; attempted to challenge the editorship of the student newspaper for alleged academic reasons; temporarily blocked the awarding of a scholarship to the homecoming queen; provided inadequate funding for staffing the Child Development Center, the Tutorial Program, and the Center for Women's Development; and attempted to dismiss—without warning or hearings—a large number of students for alleged academic reasons.

It was during this same period that the women students, aided by some of the progressive women faculty, established and demanded funding for both the Center for Women's Development and the Ella Baker/Charles Romain Child Development Center. It was the resolve of these women that ensured, at the very least, the institutionalization of a minimum program at the college to address some of the concerns pertinent to the survival of working-class Black women in higher education. The continued involvement of these student women, even after graduation, as advocates/activists in the women's center and teachers/activists in the Child Development Center has kept both centers open and providing quality services. Further, the women's example forced the chancellor of the City University to form a special committee to address the issues concerning women throughout the university, including day care. The fact remains, however, that each year of the existence of the two centers has been marred by inadequate (often insulting) funding and rumors of possible closing. This fact speaks to the reality that sexism, like racism, has remained alive and well in spite of coalition efforts to stem it.

Time has proven that without fundamental changes in the City University of New York's system, of which Medgar Evers College is a part, the college will experience very little progress, as this applies to the improvement of conditions or equal treatment. Neither the appointment of one or two more people of color to a politically appointed board of trustees nor the appointment of a "well-intentioned" Black male as president will significantly challenge, much less totally erase, the institutionalized traditions of racism and sexism that exist within the university.

The CUNY board of trustees has been able to diminish the momentum of this Black women–led movement by upholding prevailing forms of gender subordination and dividing sectors of the coalition by class interests. In the first place, there was no firm consensus that Black women in a predominantly Black women's institution should direct their own destinies. Many Black males and a few women in the college actively opposed the coalition students' nomination of an acting Black woman presidential candidate and acceded to the trustees' choice of a Black male nominee. Moreover, agents of racist and sexist institutions and governments have historically been prone to encourage the token advancement of a few as a means of ignoring social justice for the many. The CUNY board of trustees was no exception; students got lip service while more than a few members of the faculty scrambled for administrative posts and some middle-class Blacks attempted to make inroads into the white power structure through white policymakers. The students, women, and poor Black community members were not in status positions to negotiate their collective interests after the sit-in ended. Clearly, mass protest and direct action were the only way in which they were heard in the past and are the only ways they can be heard in the future.

Nevertheless, the strength and the qualified success of the struggle at Medgar Evers College of the City University of New York were based upon the practical unity of the Black community. Key to effecting this quality unity for mass, nonviolent, direct action leading to a precedent-setting court decision, solidarity at the national level, and the eventual removal of a college president—a "first" in the nation's history—was the responsiveness of the progressive local community. This community included mass-based community organizations, independent political parties, radical and liberal Black and white media, women's action groups, student networks, and Black elected officials. Having roots in the movements for civil rights, Black power, or women's rights, these individuals and groups' leadership and support were essential to the mass mobilization of the community to confront the CUNY board of trustees and to the shaping and creation of public opinion in favor of the struggle's objectives. These sectors of the Black community found common cause—across ethnic, religious, gender, class, and age differences—in their opposition to the retrenchment of social gains for Black people in education, and in their insistence on high-quality leadership and education as "rights" essential to the integrity of the social tenet of equality of educational opportunity.

Nor do the limitations of the concrete victory diminish the fact that practical gender interests of Black women at the college were politicized by the crisis. Equality of educational opportunity for women was translated into the perceived "right" to have child care. Quality leadership meant the "right" to have leadership sensitive to the needs of the predominantly Black female college community.[8] Quality education came to encompass the "right" to have curricula regarding Black people and women's history and culture as well as decent facilities and program resources on a par with those of whites.

Members of the coalition have repeatedly voiced the opinion that although they did not achieve every goal conceived, their efforts to effect concrete change did not go unrewarded. They cite as worth the sacrifices the development of the students' political awareness, organizational skills, and belief in the possibility of a unified stand against injustice. There are now graduates of Medgar Evers College who have been armed with *both* academic skills to develop their communities *and* the skills necessary for organizing their communities for improved social, political, and economic conditions. These are the most important fruits of the Medgar Evers College struggle.

NOTES

1. Shirley Chisholm, "The Politics of Coalition," *The Black Scholar* 4, No. 1 (September 1972): 31.

2. This is evidenced by centuries of sanctions against quality education for African–Americans that have met with vigilant individual and mass efforts at defiance: antebellum legislation that made the instruction of African–Americans unlawful; Jim Crow laws that legalized separate and unequal education for America's Black population; and neoconservative federal policies of the present era that have eliminated the protection of racial quotas or proposed major cutbacks in education (that is, the U.S. Supreme Court ruling for Alan Bakke and the Gramm–Rudman Act, respectively). In the struggle for Black women's education, the historical record also abounds with instances of racist and sexist violence. For example, in 1833, arson attacks and vandalism directed at the Canterbury, Connecticut, Female Boarding School for Black girls served to effect the school's demise where ostracism and state law had failed. (See Sylvia G. L. Dannett, *Profiles of Negro Womanhood: Volume I, 1619–1900* (Yonkers, N.Y.: Educational Heritage, 1964), 75–76. Also see Philip Sheldon Foner et al., *Three Who Dared: Prudence Crandall, Margaret Douglass and Myrtilla Miner—Champions of Antebellum Black Education* (Westport, Conn.: Greenwood Press, 1984).

In 1957, the random physical assaults on Black women, the bombing of civil rights activist Daisy Bates's home, the stoning of Black children, and the deployment of the state militia against Blacks marked efforts to integrate Central High School in Little Rock, Arkansas, requiring the presence of federal troops to enforce compliance with a U.S. Supreme Court decision and a federal court order.

3. See Daniel P. Moynihan, *The Negro Family: The Case for National Action* (Washington, D.C.: U.S. Department of Labor, 1965). Reprinted in Lee Rainwater and William L. Yancey, *The Moynihan Report and the Politics of Controversy* (Cambridge: MIT Press, 1967).

4. Robert B. Hill, *The Strengths of Black Families* (New York: National Urban League, 1971), 4.

5. An article in the January 13, 1982, issue of the *Village Voice* (New York City) by Black journalist Ken Thorbourne originally carried Trent's comments about Black studies, including his statement, "I don't believe in it [Black studies]." See also "Academic Freedom and Human Rights," *Adafi* 9, No. 6 (May 31, 1982): 1. A reprinted statement of the Student–Faculty–Community–Alumni Coalition to Save Medgar Evers College, it includes the following statement about Black studies: "In a Black institution, the only one in the City University system, there is no Black Studies program. This is a primary example of the denial of academic freedom through the restriction of the character and the content of the academic activities of both faculty and students. This is a real issue which has led to two conflicts over the resignation of the college president and between the Board of Trustees and the faculty and students of the College. African Americans have the right to study their own culture and their own history as do all peoples, and the critical role of the university scholar in the elimination of American racism has been noted since the earliest days following the passage of the Thirteenth Amendment ending chattel slavery."

6. The focus on Black Studies eventually gave way to the focus on Black women, with Black journalist Freddy Washington reporting on the crisis in a series of articles under the heading "Unfinished Business of the Sixties," which were carried in *The Cuny Voice*, the official communications organ of the University Student Senate.

7. Robert Hemenway, Introduction, to Zora Neale Hurston, *Mules and Men* (Philadelphia: Lippincott, 1978).

8. In April 1987, the Medgar Evers College Faculty Organization voted no confidence in the male president it had overwhelmingly supported to succeed Trent, citing intimidation and harassment of female faculty and administrators and abuse of power. Three months later, in July 1987, the Board of Trustees asked the president to resign. When he did so, the board appointed another man as interim president.

9

The Politics of Race and Gender:

Organizing Chicana Cannery Workers

in Northern California

Patricia Zavella

Scholarship on women workers and labor history is beginning to show the complex issues involved in gender and labor organizing. Much of the literature focuses on the structural characteristics of the labor market or on the gender ideology affecting women union members.[1] This body of research clarifies the importance of gender in organizing women workers. But, as feminist scholars are aware, to understand fully the situations of women of color a multilayered analysis is needed. Women of color experience gender, class, and racial statuses concurrently, and a feminist analysis of labor organizing should focus on the totality of women's experience.[2]

This article discusses the multiple issues involved as Chicanas or Mexican-American women[3] developed a critical consciousness and became participants in rank-and-file cannery labor organizing within the Teamsters union during 1977–78.[4] The study aims to bring out the complexity of gender, race, and class and their theoretical importance, as well as to aid activists in organizing Chicana workers in other industries. The issues involved in this research stem from the various approaches to organizing Chicana workers.

One possible approach is to organize Chicanas on the basis of their gender. Here organizers would have to contend with the presumption that women workers are more difficult to organize than male workers because women have domestic obligations and men do not. Thus organizers must recognize the division of labor within families, guided by the ideology that women should take responsibility for housework and child care and that women's "place" should be in the home and does not involve the movement.[5] This popular ideology takes on a particular meaning when applied to Chicanas because of the commonly held notion that Chicano cultural values—deference to machismo and extreme familistic dedication to home and family—prevent Chicanas from fully participating in labor organizing. This point of view ignores the history of Chicanas' participation in labor organizing.[6] Nevertheless, other problems of organizing Chicanas on the basis of gender remain.

Another approach would be to organize Chicanas on the basis of their ethnicity, making an appeal to Chicanas along with their Chicano cohorts and suggesting that the interests of women can be included within a Chicano ethnic perspective.

In 1977–78, two rank-and-file committees in the Teamsters cannery union—one in "Bay City" and the other in "Sun Valley," California—attempted to organize Chicana cannery workers by using these two radically different approaches.[7] As the following discussion emphasizes, the outcomes generated by the two perspectives were quite different.

One committee emphasized a women's separatist, although not explicitly feminist, strategy. This perspective assumes that female separatist organizing—the formation of women's culture and organizations—is an important organizing strategy for winning women's equality. Estelle Freedman's observation could be applied to the women's committee: "Any female-dominated activity that places a positive value on women's social contributions, provides personal support, and is not controlled by antifeminist leadership has feminist political potential."[8]

The second committee set about organizing Chicana cannery workers primarily on the basis of ethnicity. Chicano nationalism was closely related to union politics in the canning industry. There had been a long-standing union jurisdictional conflict between the International Brotherhood of Teamsters, which represented cannery workers in northern California, and the United Farm Workers Union (UFW). Some Chicano cannery workers identified with the nationalist Chicano movement of the United Farm Workers, and affiliating with the UFW formed the core of their original organizing strategy.[9] Once the Teamsters and United Farm Workers unions signed a jurisdictional pact, Chicano Teamsters were forced to develop a new organizing strategy.[10]

The above-mentioned committees show how cannery activists had "contending ideologies" or approaches to women's participation in labor organizing. Sarah Eisenstein suggests that working women's attitudes and experiences as labor organizers grow out of the women's "active response both to new conditions of work and working-class life, and to the ideas that were available to them".[11] This study suggests that the ideas and ideologies of the feminist movement and the Chicano movement were salient to Chicana cannery workers and to cannery worker organizers. Yet these two ideologies were not used exclusively, and there was an overlap when the "women's committee" and the "Chicano committee" formed an alliance with other cannery workers' committees and launched a successful suit against canning management and the Teamsters union on the basis of race *and* sex discrimination.

Making things more complicated still was the ultimate significance of grassroots organizing efforts aimed at race and sex discrimination. By the late

1970s, economic changes created a new context for organizing workers. Within an increasingly global economy, in which market and other constraints led to the demise of the canning industry in the Santa Clara Valley, the efforts at restructuring the internal labor market through a discrimination suit were ultimately of limited significance. This organizational dilemma reflected the convergence of several historical processes: the decline of the canning industry in which women (Mexican–Americans in particular) had become the predominant labor force, and the structure of the canning labor market in which women and men occupied very different structural positions.

Considering these issues, it becomes evident that women cannery workers' resistance needed to address two problems—women's daily struggles as working women and the transformation of the world economy as experienced in the local labor market. This framework illustrates the strengths and limitations of two perspectives on organizing women that are exclusively gender- or ethnically oriented. Theorists and organizers alike should pay simultaneous attention to Chicanas' experiences as well as to the structural and ideological context within which organizing takes place.

THE CONTEXT OF ORGANIZING

The cannery labor force has long been segregated by race and sex, and more recently even by age. The perishable nature of the raw produce and the need for human judgment in handling it have imposed constraints on organizing production within canneries. These constraints have created a divided cannery labor market: mechanization of certain processes occurred in the late nineteenth century, while other processes continued to be performed by manual labor until quite recently. Further, most canning production is seasonal. Besides mechanization, management and union policies (after unionization by the Teamsters) as well as informal practices contributed to the development of a bifurcated labor force. Men usually held the skilled jobs within canneries; women could get only unskilled, seasonal jobs, usually during summer months.

Mexican-Americans began settling in the Santa Clara Valley after World War II, when finding employment in the canning industry was relatively easy. Cannery employment in the Santa Clara Valley began declining in the late 1950s, however, so that only workers with high seniority could survive the layoffs. The result was that by the late 1960s the cannery labor force was extremely segregated by race and gender. Middle-aged women, especially Chicanas, formed a significant portion of the seasonal labor force.[12] Chicano labor organizers sought to end what they perceived as institutional discrimination against Mexican-American women and men, who found barriers to job mobility.

There were several changes beginning in the late 1960s that influenced labor organizing by cannery workers. One of the most important was the repeal of lifting restrictions on certain cannery jobs. A 1971 court ruling (*Rosenberg v. So. Pacific*, 1971) struck down prior legislation restricting women from holding jobs that required lifting more than twenty-five pounds. The removal of this barrier meant that women could apply for what had been "men's jobs." Further-more, the Equal Employment Opportunity Act (1972), which amended the 1964 Civil Rights Act, provided a legal basis for challenging race and sex discrimina-tion in employment.

Other changes that influenced cannery organizing stemmed from the ide-ologies and resources of prior labor and social movements. In particular, the United Farm Workers Union, led by César Chavez, and the Teamsters union had a long-standing jurisdiction dispute over the representation of agricultural, pack-ing-shed, and cannery workers. Chavez delegated one of the UFW lawyers to begin organizing cannery workers. Many Chicano cannery workers identified with the Chicano nationalist elements of the United Farm Workers movement.[13] Many of them had been farm workers themselves or still had relatives and friends who were farm workers. Beginning in the early 1970s, there were decertification elections in some locals to remove the Teamsters and to include "Teamsters for Chavez" in the UFW.[14]

Organizing efforts within the canning industry were also affected by dissi-dent Teamsters. Teamsters for a Democratic Union (TDU) began organizing caucuses within many Teamsters locals, and their newspaper, *The Fifth Wheel*, provided sympathetic coverage of Teamster struggles in different industries. The women's movement, with its aim of challenging sex discrimination and advocat-ing women's rights to equal treatment at work, was another important influence. The example of feminist legal action was particularly important to the suit filed by cannery organizers.

THE BAY CITY CANNERY WORKERS COMMITTEE

The Bay City Cannery Workers Committee was founded in the late 1960s and was organized primarily by women. However, the women organizers did not envision an explicitly feminist separatist women's group. Rather, they went through a gradual process of establishing close relationships with female cowork-ers and later became politicized. After years of working together in the "wom-en's department," Connie García, one of the founders of the committee, and her friends had established a close "work-based network"—a network which in-cluded friends, acquaintances, and even relatives from work whose members socialized at breaks and lunchtime. There was a variety of these networks, but some of the friendships that women established with coworkers became "work-related networks." That is, coworkers became close friends or even fictive kin of one another, and they socialized together apart from the job. Work-related friends also provided important emotional or social support to one another.[15]

The women who participated in these work-related networks slowly be-came aware of the discrimination against them. Connie García recalled how she became aware of it:

> I never noticed it [discrimination] too much. I wasn't very aware of
> discrimination per se. I had always known it was there; I had felt it

all my life. But it was never clearly defined as discrimination. It wasn't until I got a little older and started looking around and wondering why all we Chicanas, Blacks used to work on the lines all the time [while] the little Anglo girls got work in the lab. They got to work in the bottle lines where it was cleaner, and it wasn't so hard work, and you didn't have to be getting all dirty and wet and everything. And we started wondering why.

It is interesting that García (and apparently her coworkers) did not separate gender from race but saw a similarity of experience between Chicana and Black women. Yet at the same time it was clear that white women workers were receiving better treatment. To García, the discrimination she and her coworkers experienced was based on race and gender: "We felt that not only were we being discriminated against because we were women, but because we were minority women. You know, there are Anglo women who work in the canning industry that have really good jobs, and they got the advancement where we didn't."

These Chicanas began developing a critical consciousness about their experiences through the discussions they had with one another. García said: "Then myself and several other women would talk about it, and we'd say, 'Gee, how come those new [white] kids would go out and work the bottle line, and you know, it's nice and clean over there and its not dirty like here.' So we started asking why we couldn't go over there." The women raised these questions with management, who did not respond to their concerns. García remembered being rebuffed by her supervisor when she inquired about the possibility of being moved to better jobs: "He said, 'Oh no, no, no. You girls are awful good here.' You know, and 'It's the same pay, so why even go to a new job that you won't know?' And crap like that!" Another woman recalled her initial intimidation when she dared to apply for a promotion: "I did, a lot of times, put in bids, applications for better jobs, and never got them. Then you kind of just heard [things], and you just ignored it because you didn't want to really make a hassle about it. But I'm sure it wasn't because I wasn't qualified."

These problems inevitably came up when the women met to eat lunch or when they socialized together during the off-season. After much discussion, García and her friends decided to seek promotions to the better jobs that had usually been held by men:

Well, in about 1972 with the weight restriction lifted, we started pushing for "men's" jobs. And we were told asinine reasons [by supervisors]: "No you can't do that because you have to crawl underneath things, you wouldn't want to get all dirty," and "It's too dangerous" or "This crank is too hard for you to turn," but they never gave us a chance to do it. They assumed that we could not. So when we first started, you know, we used to talk to each other and everything. We kind of got motivated to do something about it.

The women approached their union officials with complaints about how they were being discouraged from applying for better jobs, and they found little support. García said:

> They'd [the union officials] give you some dumb excuse, like "I don't know what you want me to do about it," or "Hey, I'll look into it, I'll see what I can do," and you never heard from them again. So you never bothered calling them anymore. You realize that the union isn't going to do anything for you, so why bother?

After receiving no response from the union, the women decided to try one more season of putting in bids for promotions. When they were not successful, they began organizing women workers:

> That is why we got started, because we needed each other, because we had nobody else. And two heads are better than one. With a little bit of knowledge here and there, we were able to accumulate a greater knowledge of how to fight the company, how to fight the union, how to fight the smear of discrimination in the industry.

The original strategy was to serve as unofficial union officials, a process that continued for a long time: "To this day, I'm an unpaid shop stewardess, because people have confidence in me and because I am bilingual," García said. Elena Gomez, another founder of the committee, said:

> What I have been doing, and the rest of the girls in our group have been doing: It became common knowledge that we were just a bunch of "big-mouthed women", and we were hassling. There's a lot of women who called me up and asked me, "What can I do? I want this job and they won't give it to me." And I'd say, "Well, what are your qualifications?" They'd tell me and I'd say, "Well I don't see why you can't have it. First call the union. Make the grievance to the union. I know what they are going to tell you. But the minute they tell you they are going to look into it, call me, and I'll go to the company and hassle it for you." A lot of the girls got better jobs, jobs they had wanted for a long time.

The women in the group spent several years "hassling," which often included a frenzy of meetings. García recalled:

> It [organizing] was a hell of a lot of work [laughs]! . . . There were days I'd come home just long enough to change clothes, and take off to some other town organizing, or go to a meeting. My phone would ring until eleven at night, people would call and say, "Hey, we're having this problem," and I'd go down and meet with them. . . . A lot of it was just relating to other cannery workers and trying to put this motivation into them, so that they wouldn't be so passive any-

208 Reverberations Among the Spheres

more, so that they would want to fight for their rights. . . . And that's all it was for the first two or three years.

Eventually the women organized a committee of Chicana cannery workers to address the discrimination against them.

Despite their success in organizing Chicanas, the leaders encountered several problems that they had not anticipated in organizing women, problems that stemmed from women's responsibilities in their families. García believed that an obstacle to organizing women was the possible intimidation that arises when women have been socialized to defer to men:

> Women have never been very political, nor had they ever been allowed to speak their mind. We've always been mothers, housekeepers, nurses, maids, and that was our job. . . . We accepted it because that's the way we were taught, that we should accept it. And then they [women] were afraid because they just don't like to make waves, because the ones who have the power in the industry are men: Supervisors are all men fore*men*, lead*men*, and they're [women] afraid that if they caused any commotions, any problems, that they'd [men] make it harder on them. And they did! Hey, you'd better believe they did. But that doesn't mean that you can't fight them back on their own grounds.

García found that husbands' and women's own beliefs that they should take primary responsibility for household tasks were also a barrier to organizing women:

> I had a big problem when I first started doing this kind of work [organizing women]. Their husbands won't let them do it. I never neglected my family, I came home and saw to them first, I saw that they were fed and clothed before I split. But my ex-husband is very fond of saying that if I had never joined the committee we'd still be married. Now our marriage was falling apart ten years ago, but he doesn't see that. And a lot of husbands use the same thing to intimidate their women.

During the canning season, workers often put in a lot of overtime hours and sometimes worked six or seven days a week. Many women had additional obligations to perform household duties at home,[16] so their time was particularly limited during the work season. The organizers learned that they had to take women's home responsibilities into account:

> If I was going to have a meeting here I had to schedule it so that husbands wouldn't be upset because their wives weren't home. . . . So I used to schedule the meeting early so the wives could get home and cook dinner and make sure their husband and the kids were fed before they could come to the meetings.

The demands or desires of husbands also provided excuses for women, excuses that wives did not provide for men: "I don't know how many times girls would agree to go with me [to meetings]," García said, "and then in the morning they'd call and say, 'I can't go 'cause my husband wants to do this, my husband wants that.' Yet the men in the committee never had that problem. . . . It's real difficult to organize the women." García found herself turning her frustration on the women: "I just get so mad for them! I wish that they could feel the same anger that I feel! And when they don't feel it I get angry at them."

These problems came to a head in a later organizing effort when the women's committee decided to have one of the women run for president. Although the candidate was narrowly defeated, rumors suggested that it was her gender that had defeated her: "A girl friend called me up before the election and she said, 'I was talking with [some men], and they're so stupid, they said they weren't going to vote for you because you're a woman.' I said, 'God love them if that's the worst thing God did for me [laughs].'"

Despite these difficulties, García, Gomez, and their cohorts perservered. The members of the committee then extended an invitation to a group of Black women who had organized their own committee, and the two groups occasionally had joint meetings. Elena Gomez believed that the feminist movement provided inspiration for organizing women cannery workers: "I think a lot of it has to do with the women's movement—it's so strong now. Women see all these other lawsuits going on and they realize [that] they have rights." This committee did not exclude men, though one member estimated that about 90 percent of the members were women. But García acknowledged that the Bay City committee was different: "The Cannery Workers' committees are run primarily by men; the members are men. Our chapter was unique because it was essentially all women."

Although they were not explicitly feminist in ideology or identification, these women were concerned with discrimination against minority women, and they took inspiration from the feminist movement. These women of color implicitly used a women's separatist strategy that included female leadership, women members supporting one another, and an overall concern with women's issues. By using this strategy, the organizers implicitly placed a priority on gender as the basis of their organizing. They encountered frustrating problems by using this model—the lack of support by male family members and women's family obligations—that could indicate problems in their approach. The success of their organizing efforts hinged on the support the women provided to one another and the instances when women overcame resistance by their husbands. It was difficult, however, to sustain a women's organization beyond the core group of dedicated organizers.

THE SUN VALLEY CANNERY WORKERS COMMITTEE
At the same time that women were organizing in Bay City, a group of cannery workers were forming the Mexican-American Workers Educational Committee in Sun Valley. The original membership was small and included primarily Chicano

or *Mexicano* men. Like the initial meetings of the women, a Sun Valley member recalled, their early meetings were filled with discussion of their problems: "We would have general meetings at the church. There would be about twenty, twenty-five workers there, and we would have a bitch session." By learning about others' problems, members begin to realize that they needed to change the union. Their goals were to educate cannery workers regarding their contractual rights and to advocate representation of Mexican-American workers within the Teamsters cannery union. Daniel Rodriguez, one of the founders of the Sun Valley Committee, recalled: "We formed the committee to pressure the union to defend the rights of workers, so they [management] would give more weight to the union." Since so many cannery workers spoke Spanish and could not understand the contract, which was written in English, the committee also sought bilingual meetings and the translation of union contracts into Spanish.

The Mexican-American Workers Education Committee soon changed its name to the Comité de Trabajadores de Canería, or Cannery Workers Committee (Comité or CWC). The members elected a president, vice-president, secretary, and treasurer, but the organization operated in an informal manner, with decisions arrived at through consensus. The Comité originally had no funding, and had to rely on donations and fund-raising to support its activities. It was strikingly heterogenous in political ideology and in the organizing skills and experience of its members.

At one end of the political spectrum was Daniel Rodriguez, who had had a lot of experience in labor organizing. His father had been a socialist union official in Mexico, and Rodriguez had participated in union activities himself. He saw many similarities between the situation of corrupt union leaders in Mexico and Teamster officials in Sun Valley. When he was a young man, some corrupt union officials had tried to buy his loyalty, and Rodriguez angrily denounced them: "And my fighting spirit wouldn't let me participate in what for me were dirty activities. Because union leaders are like politicians. They are corrupt because they always gain benefit for themselves, not the worker." (This interview was conducted in Spanish.) Rodriguez believed that unions in the United States should be stronger: "Like in Mexico, unions are very strong and, besides being strong, are political. With the help of a union, one can make disputes locally or at the federal level and, with a lawyer or representative of the government, get support for the workers." Rodriguez recalled that his former union had its own building in Mexico that had served as a center for cultural activities: "There we would have meetings, afternoon get-togethers; [we would] celebrate birthdays, baptisms, dances, and holidays." He went on to explain how work was organized differently in the United States:

> Having a building where they could have meetings and social events, that was very different from the unions here in the United States. Here work and family life are very separated, but in Mexico it is not. There one's family can participate in the union; it was a more general thing.

> For example, on the sixteenth of September [Mexico's Independence Day] the whole family could come to the celebration. It was free, the employers donated money for drinks and food, the union paid for the orchestra. And everyone danced, they ate, they had a good time.

Rodriguez hoped that his activities in the committee would make the Teamsters union stronger, but for the benefit of the workers. He saw his former union in Mexico as a good model for the United States and hoped that the Comité could work toward a more family-oriented union where wives and children could participate in union social activities.

Another participant saw the struggle of the Cannery Workers Committee as part of a larger workers' movement for union democracy:

> We are part of a broad historical process nationally, where union locals, caucuses, or committees are challenging entrenched union leaders, corruption, policies, lack of responsiveness to workers' needs, and lack of meeting the needs of special populations such as Chicanos or Chicanas as women. It is a general rank-and-file movement.

A third member believed that the purpose of the Comité was to build a citywide coalition so as to influence city council elections and otherwise participate in city politics. A younger member, who had received some college education, characterized the group: "The focus ranges from communist world revolution, to leaving the Teamsters, to democratizing the Teamsters, to taking over this local, to getting a little relief for themselves." He believed that the lack of ideological unity was actually a strength of the group: "But that's good, there *should* be a range of ideologies."

The group's tolerance of divergent views also allowed outside organizers to join the Comité relatively easily. Some of these "outside" members often had extensive training and superior organizational skills, and they were able to influence the ideological direction of the Comité. More important, although Marxists were only a small part of the Comité's membership, Marxist literature was used to red-bait the whole group. Despite the ideological differences, nationalism was a core feature, as one member explained:

> Folks experience national oppression and respond to it better than the question of women. For example, Antonio is a shop steward, electrician who works year 'round, and is a seasonal foreman in the pear season. He studied to be an electrician in Mexico City but came here to work in the cannery because it pays more. He understands that he has reached his limit in the cannery; he has experienced racism in his daily life at work. Nationalism is an interest, it has always been the strongest appeal of the Comité.

In this case, nationalism meant the analysis of discrimination against Chicanos and *Mexicanos* on the basis of their racial status and the advocacy for their rights and needs as Chicano workers. Daniel Rodriguez had a different meaning of nationalism:

> The Mexicans from here [United States] and the Mexicans from Mexico; to me they come from the same root, they are the same [people]. I don't understand why the Mexicans from here can't get along as they should with the Mexicans from Mexico. To me, they are both Mexicans. And I care for the Mexicans from here in the United States as much as the Mexicans from Mexico. But today, in reality the Mexican youth from Mexico are better prepared, they understand more, they have more consciousness that we are the same people, that we come from the same root, and that we should be united.

Yet the racial homogeneity of the Comité's membership, and its nationalist platform made it difficult to attract other cannery workers to support them in the local elections.

These problems became apparent during the election of 1975. The Comité ran a slate of four members, only one of whom actually qualified to run for union office.[17] The Comité leadership realized that their candidates would not win, but they used the election as an educational campaign. There was some success. Normally elections were held during the off-season, and union officials could expect about four hundred members to vote. After being threatened with an injunction on the election, the Teamsters International president agreed to hold peak-season elections in the future. The CWC was able to get about a thousand workers to vote. Yet the Comité was very much a marginal organization, and the membership decided to change strategies for the 1978 elections.

One of the major problems in the Sun Valley Cannery Workers Committee was the lack of participation by women. Of the original membership, only a few were women, and most of them left because of pressure from their husbands. After these women left, the remaining women were mostly the wives of the organizers. Further, the original ideology did not include a focus on women's issues per se. Rather, the perspective was one of racial discrimination—Chicano and *Mexicano* cannery workers were victims of discrimination by canning managers and the Teamsters union. This meant that women's issues were subsumed under ethnic interests. For example, when asked what issues were important to women, one male member replied that the Comité did not know; their orientation was toward *la raza* [Latino people]. In other words, there was an assumption that the interests of Chicanas and Chicanos were the same and that an "orientation" toward the interests of all Chicanos would include women's interests.

There were several reasons for the lack of participation by women in the Sun Valley Comité. Most of the male members were workers who had worked for many years in the industry and had high seniority. Their problems were very different from the problems of seasonal women workers. One member realized that a major weakness of the CWC was the inability to recruit female members:

The leadership is centered in men. They have dealt with women's issues but haven't been able to accept women [leaders]. The CWC leadership is year 'round, relatively privileged men—Bracket I, IA, mechanics and foremen—who have a consciousness that that is as far as they are going to go because they are Mexican. It is a privileged section of Chicanos and *Mexicanos*.

Another man with many years of experience as an organizer was disturbed that there was not "significant participation" by women in union or Comité activities:

I tried to figure out how to organize women, and I can't. I think that to incorporate women into the union, first you have to organize separately as women, and then incorporate them into other activities. Women should be organized in the kitchens, in the homes, at *tardeadas, lo que sea* [afternoon get-togethers, or wherever], not in union meetings. They don't attend meetings, they don't have the time to attend, to waste while people talk and start meetings late. The men can all get together, ride together, pick up a six-pack and go to the meeting. Women can't. Women also have children and need some place to leave them; child care at the meetings is not provided. Women also need to organize themselves. Any attempt by men to organize hasn't worked.

This man was inadvertently describing the women's separatist model used by women in the Bay City Committee. He was also willing to acknowledge that the Sun Valley Comité's stance on women's issues may have actually discouraged women's participation in the group: "The men in the CWC felt threatened by domineering women." Another male participant characterized the Cannery Workers Committee: "The Comité has a definite Mexican orientation, with males in control." The few women who had participated in the Sun Valley Comité were mostly middle-aged, without young children, and bilingual. These women were better able to communicate with union leaders and managers, as well as with women workers, and had fewer responsibilities at home than women with young children. One man explained:

It's hard to get women to participate, due to pressure from their husbands, pressure from [having to work] two shifts, doing all the home work. The CWC never responded well to that. The CWC recognizes that they need women on the committee, but in terms of practical tasks such as having child care, there is no need because there are no women in the CWC. But they recognize the contradictions.

It seemed that the solution would be to have women organizers who could recruit women members for the Comité. Yet the group was not able to attract a woman who would organize and remain a part of the Comité. Thus the committee implicitly focused its efforts on educating and advocating primarily for the rights of Chicano and Mexican men, even though it claimed to represent Chicanas as well.

THE REGIONAL NETWORK
Rank-and-file committees were established at cannery locals in six cities in northern California, and representatives from these committees formed a regional network that met periodically between about 1970 and 1977. Connie García described how the women from the Bay City Committee were invited to join the regional network:

> We were approached by a group from [another city], the Cannery Workers Committee. And we decide that these people are having the same kinds of problems that we are, we should all work together and maybe we can learn from each other. Because none of us were really professional organizers. We didn't know how to fight the companies. So we just got together, we rapped, and pretty soon we just kind of organized our own chapters and went from there.

The purpose of the regional meetings was to inform one another of the individual committee activities and to plan strategies so as to coordinate their actions.

Several workers from the regional committees filed complaints with the State Fair Employment Practices Commission. After hearings in Sacramento, their complaints were certified as evidence of discrimination on the basis of race and sex. The workers then filed suit (*Maria Alaniz et al. v. California Processors, Inc.*) in 1973, alleging race and sex discrimination on the part of California Processors, Inc., and the Teamsters California State Council of Cannery and Food Processing Unions.

After the suit was filed, one of the first activities of the regional network was to educate the members about the content of the collective bargaining agreement between the international Brotherhood of Teamsters, the Cannery Workers Council, and California Processors, Inc. The workers invited lawyers to translate and explain the contract in lay terms. One worker recalled, "We went through that contract and we examined it; we memorized it so that they couldn't say, 'Hey you don't know what the hell you're talking about.' This is something that cannery workers had never done before."

While they were waiting for the results of the suit, members of the regional network continued their organizing efforts by producing a newsletter. *The Cannery Worker* was distributed free between 1973 and 1976. Most of the articles were written by workers from all of the regions. The newsletter was a fairly sophisticated product, with well-written articles based on research among workers and a professional layout. Some of the problems discussed included the inadequate pension plan, health and safety problems in the plants, and special assessments by the union.[18] *The Cannery Worker* served a critical function in educating cannery workers about the limitations of their contractual rights with the Teamsters union, and it openly criticized Teamster policies and leaders.

The regional network meetings became the place where the disparate concern with women's issues by the two committees was confronted. Connie García recalled that the women's "biggest problem" in participating in the regional network was "getting the men to take us seriously."

> Sometimes the men freeze you out. I had to hassle in the Comité [about] this problem, in our own group I had to hassle it! Many time, we'd talk about things that we wanted to do to improve the industry, and it was all very male-oriented. I'd say, "Hey I'm here, I'm here for a reason, 'cause I want to make it better for the women. How about a little input for the women?"

The regional meetings often became a forum in which women confronted the male members about the inattention to women's issues and lack of women's leadership in the other committees. Gomez said:

> Well, I'd hassle with them, because you know I don't give up. I'd say, "Women have specific problems." And we'd have some really screaming arguments, let me tell you, until they accepted me. Until they realized that I was not there to give them a bad time, I was there because I was very concerned. Then whenever I brought up something they'd say, "You're right, Elena, yeah we were forgetting that," you know?

These and other struggles were going on[19] at the time that the discrimination suit reached settlement. In 1976, the San Francisco Federal District Court ordered the implementation of an affirmative action program that would provide access to promotions and better wages for women and minorities. The major change was the establishment of plant seniority—based on date of hiring whether in a seasonal or regular job—and the elimination of a rule that had allowed a worker "dibs" on his or her job the following season. The program also established preferential hiring, training programs, and monetary incentives so that women and minorities could qualify for and secure promotions. Affirmative action "parity"—the goal for hiring victims of discrimination—was defined as women making up 30 percent of the high-paying jobs, and "parity" for minorities was to equal their proportion of the county population. For Chicanos, this was 17.5 percent.[20]

The Teamsters union was ordered not to intentionally engage in any discriminatory practice; to provide Spanish translations of all bylaws and collective bargaining agreements, as well as to make an annual determination of which minority groups constituted a significant percentage of its active membership; and to provide translations of bylaws and contracts in the appropriate language if necessary. The union locals were also ordered to record the number of grievances filed by women and minorities and to report them to the State Council of Cannery and Food Processing Unions. Further, the Teamsters State Council was ordered to hire minority and female employees in union staff positions in the same proportion as their representation in the work force.[21]

The affirmative action program provided the possibility of promotions for members of minority groups much faster than for women. By defining parity for minorities as their proportion of the county population—which was relatively low—rather than their proportion of the largely minority cannery labor force, the canners could achieve compliance fairly quickly. Just two years after the settlement in 1978, fifty of sixty-four plants covered by the Conciliation Agreement suit had achieved their goals for hiring minority males in all of the higher-paying jobs, and thirty-six had hired enough minorities as skilled mechanics. Only one plant had achieved the goal for hiring women in high-bracket jobs, and only four plants had hired enough women in the mechanics' jobs. There were no separate parity goals set for minority women.[22] Since these data are for the northern California canning industry as a whole, it is impossible to figure out how many women in Santa Clara Valley canneries were affected by the affirmative action program. I would estimate there were very few.[23] Further, the overwhelming majority of back-pay claims were eventually denied because of insufficient evidence. The result, then, was that the affirmative action program benefitted minority men and, to a lesser extent, white women.

By the late 1970s the canning industry had begun a severe decline in northern California. Chicano women became rivals of Chicano men and white female workers for the few promotions to be had. Not surprisingly, the tension over this competition for jobs was expressed in the regional committee meetings. Connie García said:

> And I had a lot of the guys tell me "Well, women are taking men's jobs, and that means that some of us aren't going to be able to work." In the Comité! At general meetings! I had to explain, "If the woman has more seniority than you, then she has the right to take that job."

The women organizers then, were forced into a situation where they had to "hassle" with their own allies. García found that confronting union officials was hard enough, but having to confront her fellow organizers was discouraging:

> Sometimes I'd tell Elena, "Sometimes I wonder if its really worth it. These people are so damn ignorant that they can't see beyond their noses!" And she'd go, "Aw Con, you know, that's the way things are," and pretty soon she'd get me out of my bad mood, you know [chuckles]? Everybody needs someone like that to calm them down.

Meanwhile, the Teamsters' and United Farm Workers' jurisdictional conflict escalated as both unions sought to represent farm workers. After violent incidents in the fields, in which one farm worker was killed, the two unions negotiated a truce in 1977. They agreed that for the next five years cannery workers would remain under the jurisdiction of the Teamsters, and farm workers would be organized exclusively by the United Farm Workers. Many Chicano cannery workers felt betrayed by this agreement, for it left them in a union that they believed did not meet their needs as workers.

The nationalist tone of the cannery workers' movement became problematic at this point, and the ideological perspective of the various committees was called into question. Some committee members wanted to exclude avowed Marxists or socialists and have only Chicanos or *Mexicanos* as committee members. Others were willing to tolerate different ideological perspectives and wanted a multiracial membership that focused on workers' issues. Eventually the regional network disbanded because this disagreement could not be resolved, and the different committees continued organizing at their union locals.

THE SUN VALLEY UNION ELECTION CAMPAIGN

The Sun Valley Cannery Workers Committee began a strategy of infiltrating the Teamsters local from within and in the process altered its campaign ideology to appeal to all disgruntled cannery workers, especially women.

In the 1978 local union elections, the Cannery Workers Committee ran a slate of candidates for union office. This was notable because the slate was multiethnic—including an Italian-American man who ran for president and a Japanese-American woman who ran for trustee. The slate had the simple slogan: "Vote for a Change." The incumbent secretary-treasurer (the position with the real power) was college educated, and this added to the perception by members of the committee that he could not understand their problems as workers. The Comité sought to replace him with a Chicano worker who would provide leadership regarding the needs of all workers.

The overall message of the Cannery Workers Committee campaign included basic union issues: an end to "special assessments," better health and safety at the plants, worker input into contract negotiation, vigorous contract enforcement. The Comité called for an end to discrimination and the education of cannery workers regarding their contractual rights and grievance procedures. The Comité issued a series of leaflets suggesting that the incumbents had neglected the concerns of workers and that the CWC slate should include candidates who would be sensitive to the needs of cannery workers, including Spanish-speakers. The Comité also demanded Spanish translations of the union contract and bilingual union meetings. The campaign slogan was bilingual—*"Justicia y Igualdad*/Justice and Equality"—as was all of the campaign material.

This was a local election in which the Teamsters were forced to campaign actively for the votes of the largely Mexican and Chicano labor force. The majority of the candidates on the Teamsters slate of sixteen were Spanish-surnamed. Both Teamsters and the Comité purchased spots on the local Spanish radio stations, with Mexican music and announcers exhorting cannery workers to vote, and ran advertisements in local community newspapers to get out their election message—"Experience and Leadership."

The election was a watershed for many reasons. This was the first time that many cannery workers would be present for peak-season union elections. The Cannery Workers Committee provided basic education on how to vote, including procedures and locations and the hours the polls would be open. This kind of education was crucial because many cannery workers could not read or write English and had difficulty in understanding spoken English. The eventual turnout reflected the value of teaching workers how to vote: more than five thousand workers voted, some for the first time. The Comité won six out of the ten positions it sought, a victory that symbolized its potential strength to change the Teamsters union from within.

When asked what were the important issues of this campaign, Tony Divencenzo, who had run for president on the Comité slate, said: "The past regime was consistantly lax—they weren't taking care of issues people were bringing up." He described the meaning of the election results: "It was a breakthrough for the people: People finally realized that they [union officials] weren't doing the job. Finally they [the people] can beat a machine that has been there a long time; [so] any type of machine can be broken. . . ."

By September 1978, with funds from the Catholic Church's Campaign for Human Development, these efforts at union democracy were given institutional support with the opening of the Cannery Workers Service Center (CWSC) in Sun Valley. The center held bilingual classes offering shop steward training, produced a newsletter, and provided legal counseling and referrals to social services. This service center in many ways was modeled on the United Farm Workers' service center. Several members of the Cannery Workers Committee served as board members for the CWSC. With support from its legal consultants, the service center was able to get the union to provide contracts in Spanish after a two-year effort.

Despite the victories in the race and sex discrimination suit, and in the Sun Valley local election campaign, workers from several committees realized the limitations of their organizing activities. They were quite literally outside agitators in the sense that they were not allowed to participate in union activities except in the capacity of union officials. For example, even though Comité members could influence other workers to file grievances, neither they nor workers' lawyers were allowed to attend the arbitration hearings. One Comité member found this to be a problem: "Once you join the union, you give up the right to challenge, other than through the union procedure. You give up the right to self-representation." Thus, they realized that the Comité had a limited role in the highly bureaucratized arbitration procedure and other union activities: "All the Comité can do is agitate, raise workers' consciousness, raise issues." Connie García from the Bay City Committee had similar views about organizing women: "Our main job is education. If somebody comes to us [with a problem], we try to solve it for them. [But] we make them do it [file a grievance] themselves, because we cannot really go and hassle for them because we get locked out of personnel offices, we get thrown out of union halls. We have to push this person."

Soon after the 1978 elections, the decline of canning in the Santa Clara Valley began in earnest. By 1984, eight canneries had closed and almost nine thousand cannery workers had lost their jobs.[24] At the time, several people experienced this period as a "calm before the storm," although most did not realize what was in store for the industry. Connie García said:

I have a feeling that what's happening now is they think we're running scared: "The X plant closed, this one might not be there too much longer, now we can push the people around. We'll stop using the seniority list for advancement, we'll go back to the old slave tactics that we used before." I see it coming. . . . I get very upset! Because I can see the whole thing starting all over again, 'cause for a while there the company was going primarily by seniority and qualifications. Now they're going back to qualifications [only] . . . that we had them throw out in court.

The members of the regional network created a "parallel central labor union"[25] that duplicated the union structure but operated informally, and pushed aggressively for the needs of the rank-and-file membership. The Cannery Workers Service Center functioned as a "shadow" union hall[26] for the alternative labor union, providing the services and advocacy that the CWC membership believed the Teamsters union should have provided. Yet, as outsiders, they had little recourse to internal resources. When the industry eventually began relocating to California's Central Valley, the "outside" labor union was left behind.

CONCLUSION

In reflecting about the two approaches to organizing Chicana cannery workers, it is apparent that both models were successful in some senses but needed to modify and expand their approach in others. Both committees built their organizational membership on relationships that had been firmly established, either in the workplace or in the community or in both. The "women's committee" in particular was formed by women who had intense work-related networks that were continued and deepened in the off-season outside work. For the most part the women had not been prior organizers. They politicized one another in the course of social activities and informal discussions and "motivated" each other to begin more formal organizing. The "men's committee" also was formed by men who had worked, socialized, and "bitched" together. Yet it appears that some of the male members had had a history of participation in labor organizing in other situations.

With the benefit of hindsight, we can criticize the Chicano committee with its ethnic, nationalist approach that did not appeal fully to Chicana workers. Some members of that group were well aware of the need for a gender approach in their organizing efforts, especially in attracting women organizers and somehow modifying what seemed like male dominance within the group. Others assumed that women's interests should be included in an "orientation" based on race. Though this group eventually abandoned its focus on race and sought to recruit all dissatisfied Teamsters, especially women, it had established a tradition of male leadership. The group was successful in securing institutional support in the form of the Cannery Workers Service Center and gained important union elected positions—all of which benefitted women cannery workers. Nevertheless, this committee did not create a significant appeal to women workers or develop women's leadership.

The women's committee, on the other hand, developed out of women's critical consciousness about their experiences on the job. The focus of their political activity was job discrimination. Women's family responsibilities were seen as barriers to their full participation in organizing and were the sources of great frustration. It would have been more helpful to focus on organizing support mechanisms—particularly child care—rather than on frustration. Additionally, the women might have found ways to include husbands in their activities to convince reluctant spouses of the value of the committee's work. Although the women's committee took inspiration from the feminist movement and aimed at changing the institution that supported discrimination on the basis of race and sex, the concerns of women's daily lives were not addressed.

Both of these committees, then, can be seen as products of their context of origin—the Chicano movement and the women's movement—which had an exclusionary appeal. It is only recently that feminists are beginning to articulate a public discourse that goes beyond the critique of women's oppression within families and recognizes how women's work and family roles are related. Chicano activists, on the other hand, have begun forming coalitions with other community and workers' organizations and criticizing the fact that Chicanas' interests are not fully included within a Chicano perspective. As we examine the limitations of these movements, it becomes apparent that a separatist politics, whether based on race or on gender, is problematic when organizing women of color.

Further, the experience of these two rank-and-file workers' committees suggests the importance of the changing structure of the labor market for organizing workers. The U.S. economy has become a global system in which the competitive pressures of production costs and other factors have "de-industrialized" several manufacturing locations, as occurred with canning in northern California. Labor organizers, then, will have to pay close attention to the ways in which capital constantly adapts and restructures to accommodate the changing conditions of production in order to develop appropriate strategies for organizing women workers.

ACKNOWLEDGMENTS

I would like to thank the workers and labor organizers who educated me about the cannery workers' movement, and I regret that they must remain anonymous. Felipe Gonzales made many useful comments on successive drafts of this article. Bill Friedland, Lupe Friaz, and Jaime Gallardo also made helpful comments on this chapter. Ann Bookman and Sandra Morgen deserve special acknowledgments for their patience and enthusiastic support, as well as their helpful suggestions for revisions.

NOTES

1. See Ruth Milkman, ed., *Women, Work and Protest: A Century of U.S. Women's Labor History* (Boston: Routledge & Kegan Paul, 1985); Karen Brodkin Sacks and Dorothy Remy, eds., *My Troubles Are Going to Have Trouble with Me: Everyday Trials and Triumphs of Women Workers* (New Brunswick, N.J.: Rutgers University Press, 1984); Alice Kessler-Harris, *Out to Work, A History of Wage-Earning Women in the United States* (Oxford: Oxford University Press, 1982).

2. For literature that discusses the simultaneous experience of class, race, and gender for women of color in theoretical terms, see Angela Davis, *Women, Race and Class* (New York: Random House, 1981); Amy Swerdlow and Hanna Lessinger, eds., *Class, Race, and Sex: The Dynamics of Control* (Boston: G. K. Hall, 1983); Evelyn Nakano Glenn, "Racial Ethnic Women's Labor: The Intersection of Race, Gender and Class Oppression," *Review of Radical Political Economics* 17 (1985): 86–108; Gloria Joseph, "The Incomplete Menage à Trois: Marxism, Feminism, and Racism," in Lydia Sargent, ed., *Women and Revolution, A Discussion of the Unhappy Marriage of Marxism and Feminism* (Boston: South End Press, 1981), 109–143; and bell hooks, *Feminist Theory: From Margin to Center* (Boston: South End Press, 1983).

3. "Chicana/o" refers here to persons of Mexican heritage who were born or reared in the United States; "Mexicans" or "*Mexicanos*" refers to those who migrated as adults to the United States from Mexico. The terms that my informants used to identify themselves varied, depending on the context, and sometimes different terms were used interchangeably. For a discussion of the context and complexity of Mexican–American ethnic identification, see J. García, "*Yo Soy Mexicano . . .* : Self-Identity and Sociodemographic Correlates," *Social Science Quarterly* 62, No. 1 (1981): 88–98; J. E. Limon, "The Folk Performance of Chicano and the Cultural Limits of Political Ideology," in Richard Bauman and Roger D. Abrahams, eds., "*And Other Neighborly Names*": *Social Process and Cultural Image in Texas Folklore* (Austin: University of Texas Press, 1981), 197–225; P. Gonzales, "Spanish Heritage and Ethnic Protest in New Mexico: The Anti-Fraternity Bill of 1933," *New Mexico Historical Review* 61, No. 4 (October 1986): 281–299; M. Miller, "Mexican Americans, Chicanos, and Others: Ethnic Self-Identification and Selected Social Attributes of Rural Texas Youth," *Rural Sociology* 4, No. 2 (1976): 234–247.

4. Cannery workers were represented by the California State Council of Cannery and Food Processing Unions, International Brotherhood of Teamsters, Chauffeurs, Warehousemen, and Helpers.

5. Rayna Rapp analyzes the facets and pervasiveness of family ideology in American culture. See "Family and Class in Contemporary America: Notes Toward an Under-

standing of Ideology," *Science and Society* 42 (1978): 278–300. Also see Jane Collier, Michelle Z. Rosaldo, and Sylvia Yanagisako, "Is There a Family? New Anthropological Views," in Barrie Thorne and Marilyn Yalom, eds., *Rethinking the Family, Some Feminist Questions* (New York: Longman, 1982), 25–39; and Ruth Milkman, "Women's Work and the Economic Crisis: Some Lessons Learned from the Great Depression," *The Review of Radical Political Economics* 8 (1976): 73–97.

For a critique of how culture determinism has been used to explain Chicanas' labor force participation rates see Vicki L. Ruiz "Working for Wages: Mexican Women in the Southwest, 1930–1980" (Working Paper No. 19, University of Arizona, Southwest Institute for Research on Women, Tucson, 1984); Denise Segura, "Labor Market Stratification: The Chicana Experience," *Berkeley Journal of Sociology* 29 (1984): 57–91; and Patricia Zavella, "The Impact of 'Sun Belt Industrialization' on Chicanas," *Frontiers* 8 (Fall 1984): 21–27.

6. Laurie Coyle and her colleagues and Clementina Duron address the stereotypes of Chicana traditionalism directly, showing the ways Chicanas have established alliances with other labor activists and how Chicanas had to challenge traditional notions within their own communities. See Laurie Coyle, Gail Hershatter, and Emily Honig, "Women at Farah: An Unfinished Story," in Magdalena Mora and Adelaida del Castillo, eds., *Mexican Women in the United States* (Los Angeles: University of California, Chicano Research Center Publications, 1980), 117–144; Clementina Duron, "Mexican Women and Labor Conflict in Los Angeles: The ILGWU Dressmakers' Strike of 1933," *Aztlan* 15 (1984): 145–161. Other works on Chicanas' participation in labor organizing include Tomas Almaguer and Albert Camarillo, "Urban Chicano Workers in Historical Perspective: A Review of the Literature," in Armando Valdez, Albert Camarillo, and Tomas Almaguer, eds., *The State of Chicano Research on Family, Labor and Migration* (Stanford: Stanford Center for Chicano Research, 1983), 3–32; Ellen Cantarow, with Susan Gushee O'Malley and Sharon Hartman Strom, "Jessie Lopez de La Cruz, The Battle for Farmworkers' Rights," in "Moving the Mountain: Women Working for Social Change (Old Westbury, N.Y.: Feminist Press, 1980), 94–151; Mario T. García, "The Chicana in American History: The Mexican Women of El Paso, 1880–1920—A Case Study," *Pacific Historical Review* 49 (1980): 315–337; Alfredo Mirande and Evangelina Enriquez, *La Chicana* (Chicago: University of Chicago Press, 1979); Magdalena Mora, "The Role of Mexican Women in the Richmond Tolteca Strike," in Antonio Rios-Bustamante, ed., *Mexican Immigrant Workers in the U.S.* (Los Angeles: University of California, Chicano Studies Research Center Publications, 1981), 111–118; and Michael Wilson and Deborah Silverton Rosenfelt, *Salt of the Earth* (Old Westbury, N.Y.: Feminist Press, 1978).

7. There were thirteen Teamster cannery union areas in northern California, stretching from Salinas in the South to Watsonville near the Central Coast, Vacaville in the North, and Modesto in the west Central Valley, and there were several within the Santa Clara Valley itself. "Bay City and "Sun Valley" are pseudonyms.

8. See Estelle Freedman, "Separatism as Strategy: Female Institution Building and American Feminism, 1870–1930," *Feminist Studies*, 5 (Fall 1979): 512–529, esp. 527.

9. For discussions of the struggle for unionization by farm workers in California, see William H. Friedland and Robert J. Thomas, "Paradoxes of Agricultural Unionism in California," *Society* 11 (1974): 54–62; Ernesto Galarza, *Merchants of Labor* (Santa Barbara: McNally & Loftin, 1964); Ernesto Galarza, *Farm Workers and Agri-business in California, 1947–1960* (Notre Dame: University of Notre Dame Press, 1977); Sam Kushner, *Long Road to Delano* (New York: International Publications, 1975); Jacques

Levy, *César Chavez: Autobiography of La Causa* (New York: Farrar, Straus & Giroux, 1975); Eugene Nelson, *Huelga, the Frst Hundred Days of the Great Delano Grape Strike* (Delano, Calif.: Farm Worker Press, 1966); Peter Matthiessen, *Sal Sí Puedes, César Chavez and the New American Revolution* (New York: Random House, 1969); Ronald B. Taylor, *Chavez and the Farm Workers* (Boston: Beacon Press, 1975); and Robert J. Thomas and William J. Friedland, "The United Farm Workers Union: From Mobilization to Mechanization?" (Working Paper No. 269, Center for Research on Social Organization, University of Michigan, Ann Arbor, 1982).

10. I did participant–observation with this group in 1977–78, including helping to coordinate a union election campaign. I made my status as anthropologist clear to the organizers, and the members developed organizational ideology and strategies. All of the informants cited here have fictional names.

11. Sarah Eisenstein, *Give Us Bread but Give Us Roses* (London: Routledge & Kegan Paul, 1983), esp. 5.

12. See P. Zavella, *Women's Work and Chicano Families: Cannery Workers of the Santa Clara Valley* (Ithaca: Cornell University Press, 1987), esp. chap. 2, for a discussion of the history of occupational segregation in the canning industry.

13. The United Farm Workers organizing drive, which began in 1965, was an important impetus for the Chicano Movement—or *La Causa Chicana*—which was a political and cultural florescence seeking change in higher education and education generally (for example, the Los Angeles student walkouts), an end to the Vietnam War, and the creation of new cultural expressions in the theater (with the expansion of Chicano *Teátros*), the arts, and literature. See Rodolfo Acuna, *Occupied America, A History of Chicanos* (New York: Harper & Row, 1981); F. Chris Garcia, ed., *La Causa Politica, a Chicano Politics Reader* (Notre Dame: University of Notre Dame Press, 1974); Renato Rosaldo, Gustav L. Seligmann, and Robert A. Calvert, *Chicano: The Beginnings of Bronze Power* (New York: Morrow, 1974).

14. M. Brown, "A Historical Economic Analysis of the Wage Structure of the California Fruit and Vegetable Canning Industry" (doctoral dissertation, University of California, Berkeley, 1981), 246.

15. P. Zavella, " 'Abnormal Intimacy': The Varying Work Networks of Chicana Cannery Workers," *Feminist Studies* 11, No. 3 (Fall 1985): 541–558. I argue that work-based and work-related networks are important expressions of women's cannery work culture. Also see Zavella, *Women's Work*, esp. chap. 4; Susan Porter Benson, " 'The Clerking Sisterhood,' Rationalization and the Work Culture of Saleswomen in American Department Stores, 1890–1960," *Radical America* 12 (1978): 41–55; " 'The Customers Ain't God': The Work Culture of Department Store Saleswomen, 1890–1940," in Michael H. Frisch and Daniel J. Walkowitz, eds., *Working Class America, Essays on Labor, Community and American Society* (Urbana: University of Illinois Press, 1983), 185–211; Cynthia B. Costello, " 'WEA're Worth It!" Work Culture and Conflict at the Wisconsin Education Association Insurance Trust," *Feminist Studies* 11, No. 3 (Fall 1985): 497–518; Louise Lamphere, "Bringing the Family to Work: Women's Culture on the Shop Floor," *Feminist Studies* 11, No. 3 (Fall 1985): 519–540; Barbara Melosh, *"The Physician's Hand": Work Culture and Conflict in American Nursing* (Philadelphia: Temple University Press, 1982).

16. See Zavella, *Women's Work*, esp. chap. 5, for a discussion of women's household responsibilities. I argue that the segregation of women into seasonal jobs, with unemployment during the off-season, influenced many women to remain homemakers. These

women saw themselves as housewives who happened to work seasonally and took responsibility for the majority of household tasks during the work season.

17. To qualify to run for union office, one had to be a union member in good standing, which meant one had to have attended all meetings except two within the previous two-year period. This provision of the bylaws excluded the participation of seasonal workers, who often did not attend union meetings during the off-season. See Zavella, *Women's Work*, chap. 2.

18. *The Cannery Worker*, all issues, 1973–1976.

19. The whole question of participation by "outsiders" (noncannery workers), especially those affiliated with political organizations, was hotly debated. Also, a group of workers intervened in the suit because they found the initial Conciliation Agreement inadequate.

20. This figure was for the "Spanish-origin" population in Santa Clara County—a category that includes greater numbers of people than does the "Mexican-origin" category. So although the cannery labor force was made up of mainly Mexican-American workers, the broader Spanish-origin category was used to represent the class of discriminated-against workers.

21. The intervening workers had been dissatisfied because the goal of 30 percent of new promotions for women did not equal the proportion of women (approximately 50 percent) in the cannery labor force. The true extent of discrimination against Mexican-American women as distinct from Mexican-American men was denied; there was inadequate compensation for the discrimination suffered by minority men; and there were no fines levied on the Teamsters union. The intervenors' motions for reversal were denied. See Zavella, *Women's Work*, esp. chap. 2.

22. Unpublished Status Report, Cannery Industry Affirmative Action Trust, Walnut Creek, September 21, 1979, 2.

23. A Department of Labor study estimated that to gain proportional representation for women, more than half of all promotions would have to be given to females. When the Maria Alaniz suit was filed (in 1973), a pilot training program had been established to provide the necessary training to women and minorities. An evaluation of the three-year program showed that only 35 percent of promotions had gone to women. See U.S. Department of Labor, *Layoff Time Training: A Key to Upgrading Workforce Utilization and EEOC Affirmative Action, A Case Study in the Northern California Canning Industry* (Washington, D.C.: R & D Monograph No. 61, U.S. Government Printing Office, 1978).

24. Zavella, *Women's Work*, esp. chap. 6.

25. See S. Lynd, "Where is the Teamster Rebellion Going?" *Radical America* (1979): 67–74.

26. Brown, "A Historical Economic Analysis," 247.

CONDITIONS, CATALYSTS, AND

CONSTRAINTS: POLITICAL ECONOMY

AND GRASSROOTS ACTIVISM

10

Women, Unions, and "Participative Management": Organizing in the Sunbelt

Louise Lamphere

Guillermo J. Grenier

As more and more working mothers enter the labor force, the structure of industries that employ women is changing. Not only are apparel and electronics firms establishing "runaway shops" in Mexico, the Caribbean, and Southeast Asia, but corporations with branch plants remaining in the United States are "modernizing" their management policies. With the increasing popularity of "quality circles" (adapted from Japanese models), firms have enthusiastically embraced various forms of "participative management"—policies that purport to give workers a measure of control over their work environment. Yet beneath the ethic of participation is often a clear antiunion stance. Women who work in these firms are facing a new workplace where modern plant equipment is often combined with management policies that limit women's ability to organize.

In this article we examine the use of participative management policies during a union drive at a new plant in the Southwest. Since the plant work force was dominantly female and included a large proportion of Hispanic women workers, many of whom were mothers, the case helps us to understand the complex interrelationship between labor activism, gender, and ethnicity. We argue that no one factor accounts for the union's loss by a two-to-one vote. Participative management techniques, the firm's use of legal and illegal antiunion tactics, and the economic vulnerability of young women workers all played a role. In addition, the union's failure to campaign for community support may have been a factor. More important, our interpretation emphasizes the process of the union drive itself and the factors at work in building workers' consciousness of the need for a union, as well as the timing of later management countertactics. A promising start was turned around by a stepped-up, highly orchestrated antiunion campaign.

On the one hand, it could be argued that Hispanic or Chicana women are difficult to unionize because of their lack of commitment to the labor force, language and customs different from mainstream workers, and deference to authority. On the other hand, recent research on Mexican-American women workers in California and Texas has indicated that they have been active participants in early apparel, food processing, and cannery strikes; in farm worker struggles; and in the Farah Strike in the early 1970s.[1] Those who have studied Chicano families have recently attacked the "traditionalism argument," suggesting that women's lack of commitment to the workplace is more an outcome of the lack of opportunity in particular local economies than of adherence to values that keep women at home.[2] Finally, there is evidence that women are no less likely to vote for unions than are men, other conditions being equal.[3]

Certainly, Hispanic women in Sunbelt City[4] do not fit the stereotype of peripheral women workers. Census data indicate that Hispanic women in Sunbelt City entered the labor force in greater numbers between 1960 and 1970, and by 1980 49.8 percent of Hispanic women were working outside the home.[5] In this urban area, few Hispanics are recent immigrants. Many families trace their roots in the state back to early Spanish settlement, most identify themselves as "Spanish" and not as Mexican or Mexican-American, and the majority of those under thirty years of age use English at home and at work. The women we interviewed at HealthTech and other industrial plants are examples of what might be termed the Southwest's "new women workers"—that is, young Hispanic women who are not taking time out to rear their children before returning to the labor force, but who are committed to retaining jobs that are necessary to support their families, even though they have preschool children.

In the case we will discuss, many Hispanic women (along with a number of Anglo and Black women) were able to "see through" the "high-involvement" structure and perceive the need for a union to represent them in gaining higher wages and a real voice in policies. However, union supporters were not able to gain a majority of the needed votes for a union in the face of management's strategies. The reasons lie, we argue, partly in a powerful combination of participative management policies and legal and illegal tactics, and partly in the economic vulnerability of these new women workers.

R. B. Freeman and J. L. Medoff have argued that managers of U.S. firms in recent years have increased their opposition to unions through the use of three strategies: (1) positive labor relations such as wage increases and improvements in fringe benefits; (2) tough legal campaigns to convince workers that they should vote against a union; and (3) illegal actions, such as the firing of union activists.[6] Their review of the literature suggests that the use of legal tactics, particularly leaflets and other communications with workers, the delay of a union election, and the use of consultants to fight unionization all tend to influence the results of an election in the direction of defeating the union.[7] More important, Freeman and Medoff argue that illegal tactics, such as firing workers, have an even more chilling impact on union campaigns. They estimate that unfair labor practices account for from one-fourth to one-half of the *decline* in the number of National Labor Relations Board (NLRB) elections won by unions over the past thirty years.[8]

Freeman and Medoff give little attention in their book to "positive labor relations" and their impact on union drives, partly because these are harder to measure than the use of antiunion communication and consultants (as examples of legal campaign practices used by management) and the number and type of NLRB charges filed by a union (as a measure of "illegal" practices). We believe that the new stress on participative management, particularly if it organizes informal social relations in the plant and puts them more under the control of management has the potential of making loyal company supporters out of employees. Participative-management policies are thus a new form of "positive labor relations," one that is possibly as important as fringe-benefit packages, profit sharing, or wage increases in warding off prounion sentiment.

THE ROLE OF THE RESEARCHER

This article has emerged from material collected during two different research projects. In 1982–83, Louise Lamphere was co-principal investigator on a National Sciences Foundation (NSF)–funded project to study the impact of female employment on families where the mother worked full-time in a production-level job in the apparel and electronics industries. Dual-worker couples and single mothers—all with children under school age—were interviewed about their jobs, their work histories, and how they arranged household and child-care tasks in order to cope with the woman's full-time employment.[9] Women workers at HealthTech were included in the study since it was a new plant whose work process was very similar to that of apparel plants.

Permission to interview workers was given after an interview with the plant manager by Peter Evans, a co-principal investigator. The manager then referred project members to the plant's social psychologist. In initial discussions with the psychologist, Lamphere was told that there was a union drive but was asked specifically not to discuss unions with workers. In initial interviews, therefore, Lamphere and her coworkers maintained the role of "detached researchers." Since we had pledged confidentiality to both the plant manager and the employees, we felt we could not turn over names, phone numbers, or interview material to the union organizers, although, as the drive progressed through the last few months of 1982, we became more and more sympathetic with the union cause. Lamphere was not in Sunbelt City during the last months of the campaign but was able to interview several additional workers whose names she got through the union organizer. These later interviews give a better sense of the role of the campaign in the lives of two of the ten women interviewed by those working on the NSF project.

Guillermo J. Grenier's role began as a researcher and was transformed into that of a prounion spokesperson at a crucial juncture in the campaign, although his research interests remained throughout. During the fall of 1982, Grenier began conducting research on participative-management structures—particularly the "teams" being used at HealthTech—for his doctoral degree in sociology. With the help of the plant social psychologist he was able to observe team meetings and talk with supervisors during the course of the union campaign. In the early months he acted as an unpaid research assistant to the social psychologist, taking up his suggestion to investigate the role that the teams played in the firm's antiunion campaign. When the firm's lawyer became concerned that Grenier's notes might be subpoenaed for an NLRB hearing, Grenier submitted a proposal to the company requesting permission to research "Small Group Dynamics in an Industrial Setting." He informally agreed with the psychologist that he would keep the firm's antiunion strategy as a secondary focus of his research.

As Grenier gathered more information, particularly about the manipulative techniques used in team meetings and the company's firing strategy, he became convinced that there was nothing inherently "proworker" about the new design environment. After a great deal of soul-searching, he spoke out against the activities of the company at a public forum organized by the union in April 1983. His comments resulted in the firing of the social psychologist and were important in eventually gaining a positive judgment from the NLRB concerning a number of worker grievances.

After his public statement, Grenier was barred from the plant, but he was able to conduct interviews with a number of union activists, both male and female. Thus, his data include rich details on management tactics during the campaign as well as postelection analysis by a number of those who sided with the union. Our two roles emerged out of very different circumstances. Lamphere and her coworkers were interviewing workers in their homes, and the structure of their project, plus Lamphere's promise to avoid the topic of unionism, pushed her to collect data only on work and family. Grenier's association with the plant psychologist led him in just the opposite direction and gave him access to information that in turn could be useful for the union. In this article we see these two sets of data as complementary. By focusing on women's work and family lives on the one hand and the team structure and union drive on the other, we are able to analyze the interaction between management and women workers as it was shaped during the course of the union campaign.

THE SETTING
The union drive we analyze took place in 1982 and 1983 in a new branch plant of HealthTech located in Sunbelt City. The city's economy is based primarily on military and government jobs and the city's position as a commercial center. Within the past ten years the city has begun to attract branch plants of large corporations, primarily in apparel and electronics. Recently, several plants have been built with modern equipment, richly carpeted offices, and the latest in com-

puter technology. In addition, a number of plants have introduced aspects of participative management, making Sunbelt City somewhat a "laboratory" for the management of the future.

Thus when HealthTech opened its doors in 1981, it was one of the most innovative plants in the city, operating on what management terms a "high-involvement" philosophy and also hiring a work force that was 90 percent female and 65 percent Hispanic.

The "high-involvement" philosophy at HealthTech had several ingredients. As in two or three other plants in the area, benefits for production and nonproduction employees were equal, there were no time clocks, and the plant had something like "flex-time" in that workers could be late and make up the time at the end of the day. Also, the plant manager maintained an "open-door" policy by which any worker could talk with him about issues of concern. However, HealthTech had gone beyond these forms of participation to completely restructure the labor process around small groups called "teams," which in principle were involved in hiring, training, evaluating, and firing fellow workers.

Workers at the HealthTech plant were involved in making surgical sutures. Trainees learned to attach surgical thread on curved steel needles (a process called "swaging") through the use of "learning curves." Each week the trainee was given a production goal of completing so many dozen swaged needles each day; the number increased until the employee reached "100 percent efficiency." The learning curves used at HealthTech are very similar to production curves used in apparel plants across the country. Although not paid on a piecerate as garment workers are, HealthTech workers were, in effect, pushing against a clock and trying to "make their numbers," increasing their production on a daily basis.

Each department was divided into "production teams" of twelve to fourteen workers. The plant operated on two shifts. Six or seven members of each team worked from 7 A.M. to 3 P.M.; the rest worked evenings from 3 to 11 P.M. The team decided on a rotation schedule, which normally meant that individuals worked two weeks on days and two weeks on nights. Teammates often took breaks or lunch together, and the team met weekly to discuss issues of concern. Building production around small groups meant that management rather than workers created the "informal work" group long ago discovered by the human relations school of management psychology.[10]

In addition, implementation of the "team concept" meant a massive restructuring of the cultural categories through which work and management–worker relations were interpreted. Each team had a "facilitator," not a "supervisor." The "facilitator" was thus not a "boss" but someone who helped improve the interpersonal relationships on the team and aided individuals with their productivity. The team itself was supposed to have an important role in decision making. Two team members interviewed prospective employees (after they had been interviewed by a personnel administrator and the facilitator), and if the evaluation they brought back to the team meeting was negative, the person was not hired.

Weekly team meetings between the facilitators and workers were held at the time of the shift change (between 2:30 and 3:30 P.M.). A good deal of time was spent in these meetings discussing the production quotas of individual team members and the team as a whole. Whereas in a more traditional plant the supervisor or trainer would be responsible for exhorting the worker to do better, discussion of "numbers" in the team meetings involved the use of negative comments by coworkers, and thus public embarrassment, as methods of motivating a worker to perform better. In addition, as part of the "team support evaluation," team members rated one another on whether they "work hard to reach production."

After a two-month probationary period, and for each six-month period thereafter, team members participated in the evaluation of a new teammate. Evaluations were based on "quality," "quantity," "attendance," and "team support." Each team member filled out a form on the worker being evaluated and checked, among other things, whether that worker showed "a positive attitude toward the job," took an "active part in team evaluations," and understood "the team concept/open communication philosophy." In other words, team members were asked to evaluate their peers on social behavior and attitudes unrelated to the production process itself. These evaluations were discussed in the team meeting, and a poor evaluation sometimes resulted in a raise refusal or a termination (especially at the point of the first evaluation after sixty days of employment).

This redefinition of the work environment—turning bosses into facilitators and workers into "team members" who are peers and who control their work lives—mystifies the hierarchical relations that in fact remain. As our data show, during a union drive workers were carefully screened by management before team members talked to them, firings were initiated by managers and were often carried out without the consent of workers, and the interaction in team meetings was orchestrated by the "facilitator."

WOMEN WORKERS AT HEALTHTECH

During the course of the NSF Sunbelt Industrialization study, we interviewed ten female HealthTech workers. Four were single parents and six were married. Like the other forty-seven women interviewed as part of the project, all had children under school age and all worked full-time in a production job. Economically, the HealthTech workers did not differ significantly from women who worked at apparel and electronics plants in Sunbelt City. All had a history of labor-force participation before obtaining the HealthTech job. Most had worked at low-paying service-sector jobs, and the HealthTech position was the highest-paying and most stable job they had had. Like our other production workers, these women had typically been employed since high school in fast-food restaurants, in children's clothing and shoe stores, in day-care centers, or in jobs such as dental assistant or motel maid. Several had some industrial experience as well as a history of jobs in the service sector. They had been employed as sewing machine operator, material sorter, or packer at one of the apparel plants in Sunbelt City. One single mother had been employed for several years at a HealthTech plant in another state and had requested transfer to the new Sunbelt City plant.

The ten HealthTech workers we interviewed were all earning between $5.00 and $5.80 per hour, depending on seniority and shift. The four single parents' salaries (of $10,000–$11,600 a year) were the major support for themselves and their children; all had only one child. However, their pay was not high enough for them to live on their own. One woman lived with her sister and the sister's boyfriend, another with a cousin, a third with her mother, and a fourth with both parents. In the case of the six married workers, the woman's salary contributed almost half or, in two cases, more than half of the couple's income. In three couples the husband had faced several months of unemployment during 1982, so that in these three families the wife's employment at HealthTech was a particularly critical stabilizing factor. Family incomes ranged from $12,500 to $23,600 per year; three of the couples were classified in our larger study as being in a "precariously stable" economic position and three as being in a "stable" position. Median income for the thirty-eight couples (twenty-three Hispanic and fifteen Anglo) in our larger study was $22,300. In other words, the Health-Tech women tended to be in families with incomes in the lower half of our sample and in situations where the husbands' jobs were less stable and the wives' hourly pay not as high as the pay in some of the electronics and electrical equipment plants. For both single parents and couples, female employment was an absolutely crucial aspect of the family's economic situation.

Of the ten women interviewed, five supported the union and five did not. Since the final union vote was 141 against the union and 71 for the union, our sample is biased in the direction of union supporters. However, since we were not focusing on the union issue, we did not realize until writing this article that our sample included proportionately more union supporters than found in the work force. The ten women, however, represent the range of participation in the drive—including a very vocal antiunionist, two members of the union organizing committee, and several women who were quiescent during the campaign.

Among the ten women we spoke with, our interviews show that there were few significant differences in their attitudes toward being a working mother. Instead, feelings about their jobs had been deeply influenced by their own work experiences and by the union campaign. In other words, the interview data suggest that women bring to work quite similar views about how work and family fit or do not fit together, but that attitudes toward the job are shaped in the workplace. These women were committed to both their roles as workers and their roles as mothers, which created some ambivalence when the two roles came into conflict. For example, all ten agreed or strongly agreed that "women need to work to help their families keep up with the high cost of living." Most agreed (but not strongly) that "working is an important part of my life that would be hard for me to give up." In addition, most felt (though not strongly) that "even if I didn't need the money, I would continue to work." All agreed or strongly agreed that "I feel that anybody who works in my line of work ought to feel good about herself." All these items indicated the importance of working outside the home.

Other items, however, showed that being a mother often conflicted with being a worker. For example, all felt that "working mothers miss the best years of their children's lives." They also felt the pressures of the "double day." All but one interviewee agreed (or strongly agreed) that "I have sometimes felt it was unfair that I have to work and also spend so much time taking care of my home and my children." They also agreed that "I sometimes think I cannot do enough for my family when I work." On the other hand, all but two felt that "family responsibilities have *not* interfered with my getting ahead at work." In other words, both union and nonunion supporters in our sample were committed to jobs outside the home but felt the pressures of combining two roles, feeling the double-burden of housework and child care and regretting not being able to spend more time with their children.

Union and nonunion supporters differed more in how they felt about their HealthTech jobs. The views of union supporters had in several cases been influenced by the campaign itself and some of the issues that had been raised about wages and conditions during its course. For one supporter of the union, her treatment by management during the campaign led her to quit her job after the union lost the election.

Union supporters and nonunion supporters valued the same aspects of work. For example, nine of the ten listed job security among the top three important aspects of any job. Good pay and ease of getting to and from work were the next most important attributes, whereas "good supervisors," "opportunities for promotion," "challenging work," and "no conflicts with family responsibilities" were each mentioned only twice.

In contrast, union supporters had a much more negative view of their HealthTech jobs, feeling that their jobs were less secure (perhaps because of their union support) and that they were not well paid. Nonunion supporters were overwhelmingly positive about their jobs, all five feeling that their positions had job security ("very true") and high pay ("very true" or "true"). They also felt that they had good supervisors and opportunities for promotion. They were slightly more positive about their jobs in terms of how little they conflicted with family responsibilities and how challenging the work was. Three union supporters felt strongly that schedules that demanded working on alternating shifts conflicted with their family responsibilities, and one felt that she was unable to work at her own pace because of the pressure to meet production goals ("pressure in meeting numbers"). Three union supporters felt it was "not true" or "not true at all" that they had a good supervisor.

ACTIVISM FOR AND AGAINST THE UNION:
LUCILLE, BONNIE, AND ANNETTE

The similarity in our interviewees' economic situation and attitudes toward combining work and motherhood, and their differences in on-the-job experience suggest that attention should be focused on the workplace and management's strategies during the campaign. The interaction between the work process, the team structure, and the facilitators' tactics to curb union support reveal a great deal about the forces that shaped the range of support and nonsupport for a union that was evidenced in our small sample. This range of opinion and activism can best be illustrated by contrasting Lucille, an antiunion interviewee, with Bonnie and Annette, both strong union supporters.

Both Lucille and Bonnie were among the first workers hired when the HealthTech firm moved to Sunbelt City during 1981. Lucille, an Hispanic, and Bonnie, an Anglo, were both mothers of three children. Neither husband had a good-paying job and both women's HealthTech incomes were a major source of support for the family. Both Lucille and Bonnie were chosen from more than nine hundred initial applicants and were on the first teams formed. Lucille was assigned to Drill Swaging (Team A) and Bonnie to Channel Swaging (Team A).[11]

Lucille learned the drill-swaging technique quickly and was asked to train new employees in the drill department in March. She continued training until December 1981 and then began a period of thirteen weeks' "demonstration" (that is, swaging and winding the newly attached needles and thread at 100 percent efficiency for a period of thirteen weeks). Lucille was the first person in the plant to "demonstrate," and she found the pressure severe. She felt that people on her team were not supportive and that she was not given credit or praise for finishing her demonstration (and getting a raise). This did not dampen her overall enthusiasm for her job, however; she gave her work top ratings on all aspects from pay to supervisor to job security.

Lucille described what she liked about the job:

> What do I like about it? . . . Feeling important as far as what we are making and how it associates with other people. . . . I like everything about that job. The management people, they are so nice, they are just so down-to-earth people. They are not really your bosses as much as your friends. They have never taken that superior attitude over us. Never. They don't have any more benefits than we do. Their benefits are equal to ours . . . . They have an open-door policy. Any time we want to, we can go up and talk to them.

Not only did Lucille do well on her job and feel positively about the management, but she also had a positive assessment of the team structure. She had no difficulty rotating shifts (working both days and evenings, usually two weeks at each); she enjoyed the team meetings and felt positively about her role in hiring decisions: "I really enjoy them . . . Because you get to communicate real good with the people on your own team, plus with your facilitator, and you get input with everything that goes on. There is really nothing that you can't talk about in your team meeting."

Lucille also responded positively to her role in interviewing prospective workers: "I interviewed most of the first people that got hired. . . . It was fun. I'd never done it before and it was really interesting and I really enjoyed it. I highly recommend it."

With these opinions about the company, the participative management policies, and the team system, it is not surprising that Lucille took an active role against the union when it became an issue. She described how the union issue emerged in her team:

> Well, there was quite a bit of conflict, because there was a couple on our team that wanted the union. And the rest didn't want the union, and there was some that didn't care one way or the other or didn't know enough about it to care. . . . We changed the minds of the ones that wanted the union . . . about six or seven weeks ago. . . . The union stopped being pushy. They are being really quiet. I don't know what they are planning, but they are being really quiet. What we did was, several of us from different departments got together and started an antiunion committee. And we had our own meetings and passed our own flyers.

Bonnie's experiences were quite different. At first she was quite nervous about doing well in her job.

> I was really scared at first. Because it's very tedious, you know. Right down into the machine. It really took me a month or so to get into it. I really thought I was going to lose it. . . . All that producing. You only had so many days to produce that much. And if you don't make it . . . well, "goodbye." So I was really kind of panicked, but I picked up on it. . . . There was so much to learn that it was really quite scary.

However, Bonnie did well enough to become a trainer of new employees. She was only one of two of the original twelve team members who was still employed by the spring of 1983. Since the Channel Swaging job was harder than Drill Swaging, taking eighteen months to master, and since Bonnie spent a good deal of time training others, she had not gone through her demonstration period by the time her third child was born in April 1983 (two years after she was hired).

Bonnie initially responded favorably to team philosophy. As Bonnie said, "I thought it was kind of nice. It might be kind of fun. It was all new to me: to have somebody . . . if you had a problem in your team you could have somebody to help you out." However, Bonnie became disillusioned by the team process. The facilitator for the Channel Department Teams A and B (who was later fired) often tried to provoke conflict among workers. In addition, Bonnie felt it was embarrassing for the workers to have to justify their low production numbers or explain their troubles with the machines during a public meeting. Bonnie described the meetings of Team A.

> And he was always on us about numbers. It was always his job if our numbers didn't come up. And why did we do so poorly that week. And we'd have to go around the table. And I really hated that. If your numbers were 80 percent for the week and the week before, and that week you did only 67 percent, you know, "Why did you do 67 percent? You are supposed to be at 80." At the time our machines seemed to be breaking down constantly. Down time [would count against us]. But yes, well, that got to be kind of an "old excuse."

Participating in a firing was also a difficult process for Bonnie. She described her feelings about firing one male team member who had been unable to meet his production quotas.

> Well, it's terrible. That person is sitting right there. . . . It was for his numbers. He really was a good worker and a good person . . . to get along with and everything. But his numbers weren't there. He'd had some trouble with his machine, and I guess it had just gotten down to the wire and they had to fire him. I guess we all agreed that if this was what we are supposed to do, we've got to do it. If you don't make your numbers, you've got to go. Either [the facilitator's] going to fire him or the team was going to fire him, and that was one of our things, . . . knowing that we would have to hire and fire . . . hoping that we would never have to fire. . . . It was awful.

On the whole, Bonnie liked her job, but she often felt that there were some unfair aspects of the production system, such as having difficulties with the machine and "lost time" count against her in meeting her production quotas.

> I enjoyed the job. Because it was kind of a challenge. I always . . . like I say, I always watch the clock. If I could do something in 25 minutes or less, I felt real good about it. . . . I did not like when my machine broke down. Or if I had to do re-work. I did not like that counted against me. I didn't think that it was my fault that the machine broke down and I had to work on it . . . but I enjoyed the people there.

By the summer of 1982, several members of Channel A and B were having doubts similar to Bonnie's about the participatory nature of the team structure. Their expectations that the team concept would create a positive kind of work environment were not fulfilled. They found that workers' advice concerning improvements was not heeded, and many came to feel that the team philosophy was a "charade," especially when they were given lines to rehearse in preparation for a plant tour by visiting executives.

Late in June 1982, six workers from Teams A and B formed an organizing committee with the goal of unionization. By July 27, a group of fifteen workers had written to the plant manager that they favored a union and asked for a debate to take place on the issue of unionization. These workers included Bonnie and three of her female teammates from Channel Team A, three workers from Channel Team B, four from the Devices Department, and one from the Vault Department. Three members of the Drill Department, including two of Lucille's teammates, signed the letter. Since most were from the earliest group of employees hired and almost half were from the Channel Department (the most difficult job with the most demanding production numbers and the most production problems), these workers had begun to develop a critique of how production was administered in the plant. In addition, a number had begun to "see through" the team structure. Possibly because of the way in which the facilitator of Channel Teams A and B administered his teams, workers felt that their participation was only on the surface and actually under the control of management.

Through the next few months, support for the union grew. A union organizer from the national office began to contact workers, emphasizing the high wages at other unionized company plants even though there were few differences in the cost of living. The organizing committee began to pass out leaflets, and by October 25, when a signed leaflet was handed out, the committee's membership had expanded to include twenty-one workers. Sixteen were women, including ten Hispanic women, four Anglos, one Black, and one Asian woman. All five men were Hispanic. Again, about half of the committee members (eleven) were from Channels A and B; several more had been added from Drill (two on Team C and one on Team F), but support in the Devices Department had dropped, and the committee had lost the male worker in the Vault Department. The teams in Channel were becoming strongholds, and there was now additional scattered support in other departments.

Annette was one of the new members of Team B who signed the October 25 leaflet, the day after it was handed out. She was an Hispanic single parent, who was living with her sister and her sister's boyfriend, and whose $5.62-an-hour job was supporting her and her four-year-old son. She and one other team member worked permanently on the evening shift, which allowed her team members more weeks on days in the overall rotation schedule. At the time of our interview, she had been having machine problems and her numbers were low. "When gut first came in to Channel Swaging, I was the first one to work with it. I had to learn. The facilitator had me trying different dyes to find out which dyes the needles worked best with and stuff like that. So my numbers dropped then, too." Along with several other union supporters, Annette had a well-developed critique of the production quota system and the learning curves. She would have preferred a straight incentive system and bonus pay, but she also felt that the numbers were too high. "They are always comparing us to the other plant. . . . But their swagers have been there an average of fifteen to twenty years, and we've only been swaging a year or a year and a half."

She had been hired in September 1981, six months after Bonnie had started on Team A. Her feelings about the team meetings were similar to Bonnie's: "It would be just like one big 'tattle-tale session.' That's the way our other facilitator . . . the one before José. He had the meetings being conducted like that. It got to where everybody was fighting with each other and everything." Annette's complaints, like Bonnie's, were based both on her perception that difficulties with production were unfairly treated and her sense that the team concept was really not "participation."

At the time of our interview, Annette had just been warned that if her numbers did not improve she would be suspended for three days. She felt that this reprimand was related to her union support, "Because they are getting kind of nervous because the union wants to get in. So they are doing anything to get rid of the people that are for. . . . Like, I'm on the union committee . . . so . . . I'm not going to give a reason to get rid of me." Annette's suspicion was correct. As union activity increased, the company's antiunion strategies went into high gear.

MANAGEMENT'S ANTIUNION STRATEGIES

Management presented its high-involvement structure and philosophy as incompatible with a union. One company document stated, "We give everyone a chance to represent themselves without a 'third party' such as a union." Through formal and informal communications, management emphasized that a union would interfere with the effort to get everyone to participate, and the company would therefore "lose flexibility" in implementing the high-involvement design. In management's decision to come to Sunbelt City, the lack of a "strong union environment" had been a factor. Although other branch plants in both the East and the Southwest are unionized, the company would not have located the new plant in an area with a union environment. In addition, the larger corporation of which HealthTech is a part had located plants in Singapore and Taiwan in order both to avoid unions and to pay cheaper wages.

Most important, the company calculated that if it could keep the union out for three years it would save $5 million in wages, benefits, manpower, and administration. And when it reached its employee limit of five hundred, it would save over $10 million every three years.

Freeman and Medoff's framework for analyzing antiunion strategies, as described earlier, provides a useful starting point for our analysis. They focus on three types of strategies: positive employee relations, a tough legal campaign, and illegal tactics. However, the notion of "positive labor relations" needs to be expanded to include ways the company used the team structure to push a procompany and antiunion position. This was called by the plant psychologist the "proactive" approach—an approach in which the facilitator orchestrates and initiates the discussion of the union at team meetings and in that way gets across certain ideas about the union to employees.

In addition, however, this "proactive" or positive labor relations approach was supplemented with informal "negative" relations as well, activities that were not illegal and were not focused on disseminating antiunion information. Called the "individual conflict approach" by the plant psychologist, this was an approach in which management attempted to isolate individuals already known to be prounion at the team and individual levels. Prounion workers were to be isolated from other team members and confronted individually concerning their own attitudes.

In Freeman and Medoff's scheme, the tough legal campaign involves giving workers information not necessarily solicited by them but nevertheless important in informing them about the antiunion stance of the company. At HealthTech this included a barrage of leaflets, bulletins read in team meetings, team discussions to bring out antiunion views, an antiunion contest, and movies that stressed strikes, as well as conflict that was purportedly created by union activity.

There were two sets of illegal tactics that had a profound impact on the election's outcome, as we shall see. First, the firing of prounion employees created a climate of fear among workers. Second, the questioning of new applicants in order to screen out those with prounion attitudes virtually assured the procompany stance of the substantial number of workers hired during the final months of the union's campaign.

The team system became the organizational foundation for developing and implementing these three strategies. The informal relations between facilitator and team members and the more formal team meetings became the context in which management implemented both its proactive and its legal information-disseminating activities. The use of the team as part of management's antiunion strategies can best be illustrated by what happened to Drill Teams A, B, and C, where one supervisor, Dennis, used his team meetings to persuade workers to adopt the company point of view.

In Drill Team A, as we have already reported, Lucille was active in the forming of the procompany organization. She also played an important role as an antiunion spokesperson during team meetings. For example, Andres, one of the two prounion members of the team, reported that at a team meeting in September 1982, Lucille had asked, "How far would the union go to get into the plant?" In response, Dennis pulled out a piece of paper and said something like, "Oh, by the way, I've got something to read you about the union." Dennis read that a union in New York had gotten its members a twenty-five-cent raise. "Is this the kind of union you want representing you?" he asked. Andres retorted, "Why don't you stick to the facts of what the union has done at other HealthTech plants and what it can do here, and not some other union at another place?"

Elena, another antiunionist, responded, "If you're not happy with the company, why don't you resign?" She continued her attack, almost yelling at Andres. Dennis did not speak up. "He allowed the wolf pack to attack me," Andres commented. Such acrimonious conflict meant that workers became reluctant to speak out, afraid of being ridiculed or even fired.

In Drill Team B, prounion support seemed stronger and was quietly developing among the group that worked consistently on the day shift (all women, including two Hispanic mothers we interviewed). At a team meeting on September 17, 1982, Dennis, the facilitator, took action to bring out any antiunion views which might be expressed publicly by team members. He mentioned a television show of the previous evening: "Speaking of TV, did anyone see the piece on Coors on '60 Minutes' last night?" A couple of workers responded that they had, as did a female personnel administrator who had been invited to come to the meeting. She was encouraged to give her views.

> It showed how the union keeps trying to get in at the Coors plant in Colorado, even when the workers don't want anything to do with it. It was real funny because they showed how they got all the employees in a great big room asking them what they thought of the company, and every single one of them said how much they liked working for the company, how much the company was trying to help them and all that stuff. . . . They showed all the stuff the company was doing for the workers—the gym they had set up, the benefits and all that. . . . And it was a really good show."

The administrator's speech was sufficient to bring out antiunion sentiments from three other workers.

After the union leaflet of October 25 and the union's letter to the company naming the organizing committee, the company moved more quickly to use the team meetings as a context for fighting prounion sentiment and to isolate prounion people. As the social psychologist said on October 27,

> But today . . . we have lifted the "hold" we have had on facilitators. Instead of having to depend on employees to bring things up about the union, to try to keep the union out, we are letting facilitators go. They can do what they want on the union issue.

Dennis, for example, stepped up his "proactive strategy," which was also combined with the "individual conflict approach" to isolate prounion workers. The first target was Rosa, a member of Drill Team C who was one of two prounion employees on the Compensation Committee, which dealt with the wage and evaluation system. During a team meeting, Dennis "tore the leaflet apart" and then asked for comments. As Rosa reported:

> Tracy spoke up. She said, "I don't feel Rosa should be on the Compensation Committee because I don't feel she is trustworthy enough now to express what we feel or want." She said my name had been on the union leaflet with other people she thought were not trustwor-

thy enough because we were not for the HealthTech philosophy, compensation plan or team concept. . . . When she got through I said that I'd voluntarily step down from the committee. I didn't want to be on it if people felt that way about it. Plus, I suspected that I was being set up. Tracy had always been my friend. People said we were like sisters, that we even looked like sisters.

Dennis refused to let Rosa step down and said that the other teams should have a chance to decide this issue. The next day at a meeting of about seventy-five members of the whole Drill Department (Teams A–F), Dennis raised the issue of Rosa's resignation and asked for comments. Tracy again stood up and accused Rosa, "almost yelling." Several other antiunion employees hollered agreement and then Rosa was asked to stand up and be identified. Finally, Anne, a teammate, defended Rosa's performance on the committee, and Rosa was asked her opinion. "I feel I'm being harassed for my political opinion," she said, "and that is discrimination." Tracy later said, "You know they forced me to do that, don't you," and asked Rosa, "Do you forgive me?" Rosa replied that she would never forgive her.

Anne, in fact, felt that Dennis had subtly used the team as a way of "getting at" the union supporters.

I think he tried to create conflict. There really were some hard-core [antiunion] people in our team. This is only a guess. But I think he got those people aside and said, "This is what I want you to do— bring up such and such an issue. When I'm talking about something, cut in." . . . These people *had* to be put up. I think that Tracy was put up to do what she did to Rosa. She was supposed to be her best friend. And for her to turn around and do that. Somebody had to put her up to that.

With these tactics, Dennis was able to keep union support in his three teams limited to two workers in Drill Team A (Lucille's team), a small group of three or four in Team B, and a small group in Team C (including Rosa, Anne, and three others). In contrast, the Channel A and B teams, during the fall of 1982, continued to give their new facilitator, José, a difficult time. Prounion women either brought up criticisms of the company directly or, if this tactic did not result in any change or dialogue, refused to participate. Team B was perhaps the most successful in this tactic. One team member, Dee, said, "He said that Team B was too loud or something. Every time we tried to say something, he would shut us up. Then if we weren't going to say something, he'd tell us, 'Why don't you talk?' So, he said, 'You guys just don't function as a team.' "

Annette, the single parent mentioned earlier, explained how the team had developed its own informal support network, "We've gotten closer and we look out for each other, like we are supposed to be doing . . . like what they are saying. You know, disciplining each other and stuff like that. But [José's] getting upset, because he doesn't really know what's going on."

Thus Team B was very successful in becoming united around the issue of the union and in confronting their facilitator. Channel A and B had been the center of union sentiment from the beginning, and José, the new facilitator, had come from a union plant, so perhaps was not as committed as others to fighting the union in team meetings.

A measure of the union's support in early December 1982 was the fact that ninety-three workers (both women and men) signed a petition asking the company to investigate a bad smell that was pervading the production area of the plant. Workers were fearful that ETO, the dangerous chemical that was used to sterilize the sutures, might have seeped into the air filter system in the "clean room" in which the workers worked. The petition stated:

> We, the undersigned, want to know the names of the chemicals causing the bad smell in the plant. We are upset over the complaints of headaches, teary eyes, and nausea resulting from the odor, and we are very concerned about the effects of these chemicals on pregnant women and their unborn children. We have a right to know what chemicals we are being exposed to.

Phrased as a women's issue and backed by union supporters, this petition was signed by fifty-four Hispanic women and twenty-two Anglo and Black women.[12] Not all of the Hispanic and Anglo women who eventually voted for the union signed the petition. Thirty-seven Hispanic women and seven non-Hispanic women did sign it but later did not vote for the union. The company responded to the petition by arguing that ETO is not a compound with a smell and that, although they were looking into the cause of the odor, it was not hazardous to workers' health. A statement to this effect was read in all the team meetings. With this strong response on the part of the company, the issue eventually faded into the background. However, the petition represents a high point in terms of support for an issue that the union brought to the fore. By this time about 49 percent of the workers had signed union cards. The union decided to wait for card signing to increase beyond the 50 percent mark, a point that never came. Both the petition and the card signing may have represented more antimanagement feeling than actual willingness to support the union. In any case, from this period on, the company began to be more successful in eroding the growing union sentiment.

Despite the strong support on the ETO issue and the signing of union cards, most facilitators remained in control of their teams. The tactics that Dennis used with Drill Teams A, B, and C were beginning to have an effect and to keep workers who had been in the plant for a year or more from defecting to the union. Facilitators were using the rhetoric surrounding the "high-involvement" philosophy to isolate union supporters. Prounion workers had "bad attitudes," were not really "team members," or did not believe in the "Team concept" and thus were not trustworthy. To be prounion was to be against the company and against the high-involvement philosophy. The attempt to redefine union supporters as being against the team concept and thus "losers" was another way of strengthening the informal basis of support for the company. More important, however, was the company's major illegal strategy: firing prounion workers.

The evidence presented by Freeman and Medoff suggests that illegal tactics such as firing prounion workers have the most devastating impact on union campaigns. Other tactics that would have a negative impact would be surveillance of union supporters during work hours and discrimination against prounion applicants for jobs. Firings in themselves might result in a negative reaction to the company, a galvanizing of sympathy for the union, and stronger support. We must ask, therefore, why firings would result in fear and compliance rather than resistance on the part of women workers. The effect of firings and other illegal tactics, we argue, is more damaging to a union drive when the company had already laid the basis for support for its antiunion position in the interpersonal relationships between workers and management. Channel Teams A and B may have been strongholds of union support, but the tactics of Dennis and other facilitators had laid the groundwork for antiunion sentiment in other teams, something that could be built on if strong union supporters could be fired. The team system at HealthTech and its use by management to support antiunion workers and isolate union supporters set the context in which firings would have a particularly negative impact on the union drive.

As early as November 5, 1982, the plant psychologist talked to Guillermo J. Grenier about the possibility of firing some of the prounion workers. He said that because the company was restricted legally in how much it could do to stop the union, it would have to act surreptitiously. He referred to one employee whom the company was getting ready to fire as a "fat slob" in the Drill Department. They were toying with ideas about firing her and hoped to put the union in a "no win" situation by doing it. In fact, the company succeeded in firing this woman because the doctor's excuse that she used to account for an absence did not cover the correct time period. A male union supporter was also fired but was later reinstated because of inconsistencies in the policies for making up absences that had been used to justify his termination.

Sometime in November management met with corporate lawyers who recommended using firing as an antiunion strategy. The first two firings had been "trial balloons" to see what the union would do when its supporters were fired for objective reasons. Additional firings were planned, probably to take place after Christmas, since the company "did not want to come across like Scrooge," firing people right before the holidays.

However, on December 16, two women on the Channel B team who were union supporters were fired for "falsifying company records." A worker named Maria had phoned to tell her friend Linda to log her in on the computer, that she would be five minutes late; however, she arrived at work at 8:00 rather than 7:05

A.M. At the end of the day, Maria's facilitator called her into the back room and confronted her with the situation.

I went back there and I talked to him, and he said somebody had seen me clocked in. And I said I'd go look on my time sheet. "But Linda clocked you in early," he said. "Ya, I told her to clock me in, because I'm going to be five minutes late at the most." And he goes, "You're not supposed to do that." There wasn't no rules. Everybody clocks each other in. They knew about it too.

The next day Maria was dismissed, despite the fact that her time sheet (as opposed to the computer) recorded her 8:00 A.M. entry into the plant. Maria suspected that her firing was the result of her name being on the October 25 leaflet. And according to the social psychologist, the plant manager had decided to fire these women because it would be a good symbolic gesture, a good way to scare other prounion employees.

Thus by Christmastime four of the twenty-one employees who had signed the October 25 leaflet had been fired and another had been forced to resign from the Compensation Committee following a large meeting in which she had been publicly embarrassed and had been left visibly shaken.

WORKER RESISTANCE

Women workers who were prounion, and their male peers, did not knuckle under to the company's antiunion strategies. A number of "unfair labor practice" charges were filed with the NLRB on October 27 alleging that workers were being interrogated, threatened with loss of benefits if a union was formed, and threatened with firing. Additional charges were filed after the November 6 firings and after the firings of Maria and Linda on December 19.

Nevertheless, the union was working in a climate of fear. It was clear that supporting the union could mean being threatened with a suspension if one's numbers were down (as in Annette's case) or being fired through the strict application of company policy that had been more leniently applied to non–union supporters (as in the case of Maria and Linda). The first months of the union campaign (between July and October) had resulted in a concentration of supporters in the Channel A and B teams, with some support among some of the Drill teams and in Devices. Between October and December the company stepped up its tactics, adding illegal activities to the full range of other strategies, including the manipulation of attitudes in team meetings and the more straightforward dissemination of information through leaflets and the bulletin board. The union was thus faced with the need to persuade more workers to join the union in a threatening atmosphere. In addition, the company was continuing to expand its work force and was carefully screening new employees to make sure they would be antiunion when they entered the plant. The union committee continued to meet in

January and February, and at the end of February an open meeting was held at a local hotel.

In the meantime, a mechanic who had not previously been associated with the union drive was fired for talking back to his supervisor. This mechanic and a coworker had written to the plant manager in mid-February expressing support for the union. The firing enlisted a great deal of sympathy from workers. The union's filing of an "unfair labor practice" charge on the mechanic's behalf gained his support and that of several other workers in early March. In addition, the union had advertised in the local newspapers seeking information on applicants who had been interrogated about their union views during interviews or training. Clearly, the union was continuing to take an aggressive legal stand in trying to protect workers who had been discriminated against for their views or support of the union drive.

The union also conducted a trip for five production workers (two antiunion, two undecided, and one scared to take a side) to the company's unionized plant in the eastern United States. Although they were not able to see the inside of the plant, the workers met with one hundred union employees and made a videotape of the meeting that was later shown to the Sunbelt City workers at a union-sponsored meeting. All five workers who made the trip were persuaded to take the union's side.

As Rosa's friend Anne said,

> What really opened my eyes was going to [the East] and seeing what they had over there. It's not an individual team over there. It's one big team over there. It opened my eyes, and that was towards the end of the campaign. . . . We need somebody to represent us—to back us up—that's what we need. . . . You go up and talk to them. And after you have that talk, he still has the final say. You have nobody— no other recourse to talk to. You have no other alternative. Who's going to fight for you . . . against the company. And that's basically why I got involved with the union.

Lorraine, a single parent who worked in Devices, had worked at another HealthTech plant for five years and had been a union member. She was the only worker who had transferred from a union plant in another city to the new Sunbelt City plant. In order to do so she had had to drop out of the union, and she had found it necessary to mention her difficulty in resigning from the union in order to become hired. She was advised not to talk about the union, but by February 1983 she was becoming involved with the union campaign. She explained the reasons for the trip and its impact on the drive.

> 'Cause the company had bad-mouthed the union really bad, so bad that everybody was afraid of the union. So they sent five of us and we went to [another company plant]. And when we came back, we told them. And a lot of people turned for us and for the union. [But]

there was a lot of people that wouldn't . . . that's where the tension developed.

In March, sensing that it was not gaining much additional support, the union filed with the NLRB for an election. Between that date and the date of the election, May 18, the company continued to pursue its tactics of isolating prounion employees but also moved in several ways to step up its public antiunion campaign.

THE UNION DRIVE REACHES CONCLUSION

Since late fall of 1982 the plant psychologist had been making a concerted effort to identify union supporters and then to isolate them. In December, he reported to Guillermo Grenier that facilitators were watching prounion workers, and when they saw them talking to antiunion or neutral people, they would go up and interrupt the conversation. The point, he explained, was to control the influence and interactions of the prounion people.

During this period the company began to rate all the employees on their stance on the union. "Plus one" and "plus two" were the procompany employees and "minus one" and "minus two" were the prounion employees. Undecided employees or those the company could not figure out were listed as zeros. The company was continuing to increase the pressure on prounion employees and, in the words of the plant psychologist, was "withdrawing status from them using a strong psychological approach." The company was trying to separate the "winners," or antiunion people, from the "losers," the prounion people.

Women workers reacted in different ways to this strategy of isolating the union supporters. Anne said,

> Some people react different to scare tactics. Me—I stand up and fight. That's the way I am. If someone threatens me, I . . . especially if I am boxed in a corner . . . I come out and fight. Some people don't. They give into the threat. And I think that's what a majority of the people did do. They were afraid. Afraid of losing their jobs. Afraid of the . . . humiliation you were put through . . . and you were humiliated. All these things added up and they just didn't want to go through with it. So they went to the side they thought would win.

Others took rejection by management more personally. Lorraine, the single parent in Devices, was in a large department where the facilitator had come from another plant, bringing many employees with him. Their loyalty to him partially accounted for the low proportion of union supporters (eight out of twenty-six). Lorraine herself felt that she was particularly ostracized by management when they realized that she had become prounion.

They ignored me. Before the campaign started, they were always inviting me to go here and there. Then afterwards . . . not even a "Hi." . . . They'd come onto the production floor and they'd stand like [in groups of] two or three and make faces and stand like they were talking about me. And that would bother me. Because they had never done it before.

As the election approached, the company engaged in a more open expression of antiunion sentiment. Some of the activities had all the earmarks of the "tough legal campaign." In April the company initiated a Union Strike Contest, asking employees to guess how many strikes the union had engaged in between 1975 and 1983. Memos from the plant manager were frequently circulated to employees and plantwide meetings were held. At one meeting in May a film on union violence was shown. The motto of the campaign became "Be a Winner! Vote No."

Lorraine felt strongly about how the company handled this part of the campaign and the image of the union that it presented.

I wouldn't have portrayed the image that these people would. This is a free country. Everybody could do what they want. Sure there's rules . . . but they don't have to go around treating us like that. . . . You couldn't say certain things. You couldn't bring in certain papers. I would have let people bring in their papers; you know equal—both sides. But it wasn't equal. Only one side. And that wasn't right. That wasn't a fair way.

The union's one important strategy during this period was to hold a public meeting on April 12 organized by a group of lawyers and community leaders concerned over the course of the union campaign. As mentioned earlier, Guillermo Grenier read a statement at this meeting arguing that the teams were being used as part of the company's "union-busting" strategy. Shortly afterward the plant social psychologist and the personnel director were dismissed, and Grenier's statement was used by the union in pressing its NLRB charges.

Despite the public exposure of the company's strategies, on election day, May 18, 1982, the union lost, getting only 71 votes; 141 employees voted against the union, and 11 votes were contested.

WHY DID THE UNION LOSE?

In order to understand why the union, in the end, was not able to gain the support of the majority of the company's production workers, it is important to assess the company's heavy-handed strategies in relation to the composition of the labor force. Of the 220 employees in the bargaining unit, 65 percent were Hispanics and 35 percent non-Hispanics (including Anglos, Blacks, Native Americans, and Asians). Seventy-nine percent of the work force (174 out of 220) were female, including 114 Hispanic women and 55 non-Hispanic women (68.4 percent and 31.6 percent of the female production work force). Of the 174 female workers, 46 percent of the women had children (N = 80), 27 percent had no children (N = 47), and we had no data on whether the remaining 27 percent had children or were childless (N = 47). In other words, this was a work force dominantly composed of working mothers, mostly of Hispanic descent.

In the end proportionately more non-Hispanic women (Anglos, Blacks, and Native Americans) and more men (Hispanic and Anglo) voted for the union than did Hispanic women. The proportion of Hispanic women who voted for the union was lower than that in the overall bargaining unit. Thus, while the female labor force was 68.4 percent Hispanic ($^{119}/_{174}$), only 28 Hispanic women or 23.5 percent voted for the union ($^{28}/_{119}$) (*see Table 10.1 and Table 10.2*).

If we look at the mothers (both married and single) in the bargaining unit, the picture is more striking. Of the 80 women whom we knew were mothers, only 30 (or 37.5 percent) voted for the union. And of the 60 Hispanic mothers, only 17 (or 28.3 percent) voted for the union (*see Table 10.3*).

If we take the ETO petition mentioned earlier as an indication of the support the union had gained by early December, before the firings became a successful management strategy, we can see that the union lost 37 Hispanic women (including 18 mothers) and 7 non-Hispanic women (including 5 mothers) who had been willing to sign the petition but did not vote for the union five months later. Clearly the union had been able to raise an important woman's issue and galvanize women's support. However, the company in response was able to diffuse the issue during a period in which it fired 2 Hispanic women. The message conveyed during the period between December and February was that support for the union could mean losing a job. Hispanic women, including a significant number of mothers, dropped from the potentially prounion ranks. Had these 37 Hispanic and 7 Anglo, Black, and Asian women voted for the union, the union would have garnered 115 votes, enough to win the election.

Table 10.1
VOTING PATTERNS AMONG FEMALE WORKERS

Vote	Hispanic		Non-Hispanic		Total	
	No.	Percentage	No.	Percentage	No.	Percentage
Prounion	28	23.5%	22	40%	50	28.7%
Antiunion	91	76.5%	33	60%	124	71.3%
Total	119	100.0%	55	100%	174	100.0%

Note: These figures are estimates. We had a list of 221 eligible to vote and were able to identify 65 of 71 probable voters from petitions signed by workers who favored union policies and from the information given us by the union organizer.

Table 10.2
VOTING PATTERNS AMONG MALE WORKERS

	Hispanic		Non-Hispanic		Total	
Vote	No.	Percentage	No.	Percentage	No.	Percentage
Prounion	12	52.2%	10	45.5%	22	48.8%
Antiunion	11	47.8%	12	54.5%	23	51.2%
Total	23	100.0%	22	100.0%	45	100.0%

Note: These figures are estimates. We had a list of 221 eligible to vote and were able to identify 65 of 71 probable voters from petitions signed by workers who favored union policies and from the information given us by the union organizer.

Table 10.3
VOTING PATTERNS AMONG MOTHERS (N = 80)

	Hispanic		Non-Hispanic		Total	
Vote	No.	Percentage	No.	Percentage	No.	Percentage
Prounion	17	28.3%	13	65%	30	37.5%
Antiunion	43	71.7%	7	35%	50	62.5%
Total	60	100.0%	20	100%	80	100.0%

Note: These figures include both single parents and married mothers, so we cannot assume that these mothers were the sole support of their children, but on the basis of the NSF interviews we can assume that their incomes were vital in supporting their families.

The union was able to attract the support of some Hispanic women, but others were either interested only initially or failed to support the union at all. Although the NSF interviews were not designed to explicate the issue of union support, they do offer some clues to these varying reactions. For some, workplace difficulties provided a context for galvanizing support especially within teams formed early in HeathTech's history. For example, we interviewed Valerie and Delores in Drill Team B. On this team, antiunion sentiment was strongest among the six members who worked on the evening shift. Unlike in other teams whose members rotated on a one- or two-week basis, enough Drill Team B members were willing to work evenings that the six who preferred to work days could do so without rotating. Both Valerie and Delores felt that shift rotation was the biggest disadvantage of the job, and both became union supporters because they felt the union would be able to abolish the rotation system. As Valerie said:

> When we do have to go nights, it's a real big problem. One of the biggest problems I have there. . . . It's hard, because baby-sitter

wise, no baby sitter's going to want . . . okay, these two weeks you can take her and then for two hours the next two weeks. I've got to find somebody that can take her at nights. And that's hard on my husband, it's hard on my little girl.

Delores was equally adamant that the rotating shift system interfered with her time with her family and kept her away from her five-year old daughter. Though neither reported difficulties with their job, Valerie rated "pay," "supervisors," and "opportunities for promotion" low (3 on a scale of 4), and Delores felt that the plant was not a safe place to work at night because of the dark, unprotected parking lot. In addition she felt that her job conflicted with her family responsibilities when she had to work nights, and she felt a great deal of pressure in meeting her "numbers." Valerie also felt that the team meetings were "not working," that workers were not getting anything out of them. Despite these relatively negative comments about the job, the crucial issue for both women in supporting the union was shift rotation and its impact on them as mothers. For both these women, the union was able to capitalize on their frustrations and keep their allegiance, despite the climate of fear induced by the firings and other unfair labor practices.

Other Hispanic workers were part of teams more under the control of supervisors, worked in operations not so difficult as Channel or Drill Swaging, or may have been screened for antiunion sentiments when they were hired. Perhaps typical of the kinds of women workers the union did not win over were Regina, Grace, Karen, and Jenny—the four nonunion supporters, in addition to Lucille, who were interviewed for the NSF project. Regina and Grace were Hispanic single parents, while Karen was an Anglo married to an Hispanic and Jenny was part Native American married to an Anglo. Economically they were in situations similar to those of the union supporters we interviewed. Regina and Grace were single parents like Annette and Lorraine. Jenny's husband had periods of unemployment not dissimilar to Bonnie's and Valerie's spouses. Karen herself had had a series of service-sector jobs, and although her husband had a stable position at a mental health center, his pay was low.

However, all had been at HealthTech for a shorter amount of time than the union supporters (with the exception of Lorraine, who had been a union member elsewhere). And all were in departments where there was a low level of union support (Foil/Overwrap, Drill D, and Devices). Several of these women had complaints about their jobs. Grace did not like working on rotating shifts, and Regina also mentioned that working on two shifts was a major disadvantage of the job. Karen was nervous about her evaluations and did not like the way the teams were being used. Despite these disadvantages, each rated her job more highly than union supporters rated theirs. The negative aspects of the job were outweighed by financial need and job security. These were the kinds of women whom the union needed to win over in order to win the election. But it was difficult to do so in the face of the atmosphere successfully created by the company, partially since these women were in team contexts where there were few prounion voices. In the end, we cannot say for sure why these four women did not vote for the union, but we can assess the impact of the firm's strategies on the female work force as a whole.

In Freeman and Medoff's framework, the firings and the delay of the election would account for the union's loss. But in the HealthTech context workers were also part of a team structure in which facilitators were hard at work using a number of tactics to keep workers from turning prounion. The December firings had created a climate of fear. Although there was a show of support when the mechanic was fired in February, only thirty-seven workers signed the petition, all of them strong union supporters. The fact that the NLRB put off hearings on the firings and other unfair labor practices so that none of these workers was reinstated by the time of the election allowed the company to keep the upper hand. Certainly screening of new applicants had an important impact. The union drew only a smattering of support from teams formed late in the campaign—that is, from Drill Teams D, E, F, and G (2 votes) and from Channel C and D (3 votes). The antiunion votes in these 6 teams amounted to 52, more than one-third of the antiunion support.

Given the economic vulnerability of Hispanic women, particularly mothers, we can see how the team structure and management tactics created a climate in which it was risky for those not already committed to the union to vote for it.

SEEKING COMMUNITY SUPPORT

The union did not attempt to counter the company's strategies by seeking support from church and community institutions early in the campaign. The head organizer believed that shop floor issues were the major ones in the drive and that the media might be more sympathetic to the company's position were the campaign taken outside the workplace. However, a few weeks before the election, the union, perhaps because it knew it needed more votes, attempted to mobilize community support through a public meeting and letters from religious and political figures. For example, the Archbishop's office issues a letter that said:

> An important union election is taking place at HealthTech this week. By getting a Union at this plant, wage earners would gain increased bargaining power, would improve their wages and job rights and would be better able to provide for their families. Support for those who are seeking union representation would advance the cause of workers' rights and human dignity here at home and would be consistent with the Church's teachings about the dignity of labor.

In addition, the former lieutenant governor sent letters to workers and held poorly attended meetings hoping to educate workers on the benefits of unions. His last letter was sent to all employees and said in part:

> I strongly believe that a Union at HealthTech would have a positive impact which would benefit not only HealthTech members but also

the entire community. First, union membership would mean higher wages. Higher wages would mean more money into the economy. In addition, a union would help the state establish itself as a state interested in the kind of industry which provides fair wages and good working conditions.

The letter came at a time when workers were being bombarded with material from the company, including handouts about the impact of a strike on wages, a handout charging that the union had a history of filing unfair labor practices, and a paycheck insert stating what union dues would mean in terms of lost pay.

Support from the church and community leaders came too late to change anyone's mind. In an atmosphere in which NLRB charges were not being heard, fired workers had not been reinstated, and the risks of a union were being clearly pushed by the company, workers who had not been won over to the union side undoubtedly saw union support as too risky. These workers included many Hispanic women, mothers as well as single individuals.

CONCLUSIONS

There is a long-standing literature on human relations and small-group behavior in industrial settings, beginning with the famous Hawthorne experiments at Western Electric in the 1930s. Various forms of the human relations perspective, which include a personnel department to fit workers to jobs and various forms of psychological testing and counseling, are part of the structure of most firms. More recently, social scientists have focused on various forms of control exercised by management over workers.[13] The issue of workplace participation has received recent attention, but little has been done to analyze how new participative-management structures can reorganize the labor process as well as the social relations of the work force to create new forms of management control.

In the HealthTech case, rather than relying on an hierarchical authority structure with large departments under a supervisor who reported to area supervisors and a plant manager, management structured production around small teams of twelve to fourteen members under the guidance of a "facilitator" who was to "facilitate" the human relations within the group, urging workers to help each other increase output as well as to participate in the hiring, evaluation, and firing of their peers.

The team structure was an attractive control mechanism because of its apparent humanizing effect on a bureaucratized and hierarchical work environment. The team structure helped to "debureaucratize" work; and rules and regulations were less formal and appeared to be the responsibility of workers. Peer pressure was institutionalized as the major control mechanism. Workers felt they had more responsibility for the performance of others. Yet the facilitator remained in charge, wielding power in an informal but real way. Managing the discussion of union issues and isolating those with prounion views were just two examples of the ways in which facilitators attempted to control worker attitudes.

Furthermore, the team structure fragmented the labor force. This had both positive and negative aspects. As the union drive developed, the close interaction among team members in addition to difficulties workers faced in meeting production quotas helped to build prounion sentiment in some teams. As one manager said, the team under some circumstances can be just like a juvenile gang. On the other hand, since teams were relatively isolated from each other, the team structure could hinder the spread of prounion sentiment. In some teams, facilitators were able to neutralize prounion activists and keep them from converting other workers. The few activists became isolated and silenced in teams dominated by procompany workers. The company continued to hire new workers, carefully screening them for any union support. As one facilitator said, "We hire antiunion people by screening for them, and it's my job to see to it that they stay that way."

Thus it is important to emphasize the process of the campaign as it interacted with workers' experience of the labor process, the team structure, and the economic vulnerability of a female, predominantly Hispanic work force. In the early months of the campaign, the company probably made some mistakes. Facilitators were new at their jobs, some had had experience in traditional plants or lacked strong antiunion views. Difficulties with the production process plus some obvious evidence that workers were not so powerful as they had been led to believe allowed a number of the first workers hired to "see through" the team philosophy. As the drive progressed to a second stage, management turned to more traditional tactics to keep the union out: (1) legal tactics, particularly bulletins and discussions to persuade workers that their company did not need a union, and (2) illegal actions, including the screening of new workers for prounion views and the firing of union activists. These were implemented within the team structure that had the potentiality of isolating the prounion teams from teams more directly under the control of supervisors and filled with new, carefully screened recruits.

With the beginning of this second stage (starting with the pre-Christmas firings), it became apparent that supporting the union would mean, at the least, being branded as having a bad attitude or being against the "team concept" and, at the most, losing one's job. The plant psychologist and facilitators attempted to control the interactions of prounion activists by interrupting their conversations with other workers. They rated workers on a scale of "procompany" to "anticompany" to keep track of their own support. The careful screening of new employees and the use of team meetings by facilitators made it possible to win over many employees to the company's view. Here, taking key words and phrases from the notions surrounding "team support" and the "team concept" and using them to judge prounion workers as "anticompany" and as "losers" was probably effective. However, the economic threat of job loss was more critical to showing neutral employees what was at stake.

During the last two months, under a barrage of leaflets, meetings, and movies (the more traditional techniques of the tough union campaign), the dangers of losing one's job became more salient. From the company's point of view, spending $1 million on the campaign was well worth it. For most women in the plant, this job was the best job they had ever had. They could put up with team meetings, keep their "numbers" up, and deal with the more strictly enforced absentee policy if it meant remaining in what was basically a high-paying job in a clean, new plant with good benefits and job security.

The defeat of the union cannot be blamed on the passivity of women workers, traditional Hispanic values, or the lack of women's commitment to their jobs. Instead, many women (including Hispanic women) forged strategies of resistance in attempting to fight for union representation. That an initially promising campaign turned to defeat is the result of a number of factors: the team structure in combination with the heavy-handed legal and illegal tactics of management in the context of an economically vulnerable work force. That the union did not succeed is a measure both of the company's power and of the importance that women placed on retaining their jobs in an atmosphere of considerable conflict and threat.

NOTES

1. C. Duron, "Mexican Women and Labor Conflict in Los Angeles: The ILGWU Dressmakers' Strike of 1933," *Aztlan* 15, No. 1 (1984): 145–161; Vicki L. Ruiz, *"Obreras y Madres:* Labor Activism among Mexican Women and Its Impact on the Family," in Ignacio García and Raquel Rubio Goldsmith, eds., *La Mexicana/Chicana,* Renato Rosaldo Lecture Series Monograph, Vol. 1 (Tucson: University of Arizona, 1985); Vicki L. Ruiz, "Working for Wages: Mexican Women in the Southwest, 1930–80," Working Paper No. 19 (Tucson: Southwest Institute for Research on Women, University of Arizona, 1986); L. Coyle, G. Hershatter, E. Honig, "Women at Farah: An Unfinished Story," in Magdalena Mora and Adelaida R. Del Castillo, eds., *Mexican Women in the United States: Struggles Past and Present,* Occasional Paper No. 2 (Los Angeles: Chicano Studies Research Center Publications, University of California, 1980), 117–143.

2. P. Zavella, "The Impact of 'Sun Belt Industrialization' on Chicanas," *Frontiers* 8, No. 1 (1984): 21–28, esp. 21 and 22.

3. R. B. Freeman and J. L. Medoff, *What Do Unions Do?* (New York: Basic Books, 1984), 227.

4. We have used a pseudonym for both the city and the plant; we have also changed the names of individuals whom we interviewed in order to protect their privacy.

5. In the 1950s and 1960s the labor force participation rate of Hispanic women was lower than that of Anglo women, but by 1970 the rate was 40 percent, only 3 percentage points behind the Anglo rate. In 1980, 42.6 percent of married Hispanic women with children under the age of six were employed, and 54.7 percent of those with children between six and eighteen held jobs.

6. Freeman and Medoff, *What Do Unions Do?,* 231.

7. Ibid., 233–236.

8. Ibid., 238.

9. The project was titled "Women's Work and Family Strategies in the Context of 'Sunbelt' Industrialization," NSF Grant No. BNS 8112726. In addition to Louise

Lamphere's interviews, Patricia Zavella, Jennifer Martinez, and Peter Evans conducted some of the interviews used in this article.

10. Elton Mayo, *The Human Problems of an Industrial Civilization* (New York: Macmillan, 1933); F. J. Roethlisberger and W. Dickson, *Management and the Worker* (Cambridge: Harvard University Press, 1939).

11. Drill and channel swaging are two different methods of attaching a surgical needle to a gut or silk cord. The channel technique took eighteen months to master; the drill technique took twelve.

12. Nine men, including five Hispanic men, also signed the petition. Four of the ninety-three signatures were illegible.

13. Harry Braverman, *Labor and Monopoly Capital* (New York: Monthly Review Press, 1974); Richard Edwards, *Contested Terrain: The Transformation of the Workplace in the Twentieth Century* (New York: Basic Books, 1979).

11

Working-Class Women, Social Protest, and Changing Ideologies

Ida Susser

This article focuses on the community activities in which women were involved in Greenpoint–Williamsburg in Brooklyn, New York, between 1975 and 1978. The instability of employment opportunities for both men and women, and the increasing role of the state in providing life-supporting services for the poor have stimulated a new challenge, a new adversary, and a new set of activities and responsibilities for working-class women. In what follows I first review some of the literature on U.S. working-class women with respect to this type of grass-roots activity. I then trace the community activities of poor women in one particular locality, linking the growing instability of the household economy to the development of particular forms of neighborhood organization.

Since the early nineteenth century, working-class women have played a significant role in the labor force and have been involved in community organizations and protest movements.[1] Despite women's long involvement in labor and community action, sociological research concerned with "blue-collar" women and "working men's wives" (from the 1950s through the 1970s) presents a different picture.[2] It almost entirely fails to note these women's direct relationship to the "neighborhood" or "community" and their clear presence in the public sphere. Thus, although recent works on and biographies of working women do document their involvement in neighborhood organizations and protest,[3] most earlier research contains little hint of such a dimension to their activities.

There are at least two explanations for these omissions. First, the problem may be *methodological*. Studies relying on structured interviews rather than participant observation will not yield data concerning women's involvement in com-

257

munity activities unless the relevant questions are asked and their import recognized by the informant. Such studies certainly catch little of the texture of community life. Second, the research may represent accurate historical descriptions of women's behavior and ideas under different *phases* of a changing national economy.

In many of the earlier studies,[4] working-class women are portrayed as miserable, isolated, and passively accepting of their husbands' decisions. They survive just over the borders of poverty. They cook and clean for their husbands and take care of the children. In these descriptions, working-class women daily fight a desperate battle against loneliness and frustration. They live in fear of the awful descent into poverty should their husbands become ill, lose their jobs, or leave. Working women are seldom described in such research. When they do appear, they seem to be regarded as somewhat "deviant" cases. Epidemiological studies of women tend to reinforce this impression. One classic study[5] finds that women who live in damp, rundown housing and who have many financial problems exhibit a greater tendency toward depression than women who have more money and live in better housing. Major factors in the depression of working-class women were low income and three or more children under fourteen years old at home. However, once again the positive impact of community involvement is not considered, and the psychological resilience of working-class women under changing conditions may be underestimated. Thus, it is possible that because of the limitations of interview techniques we have been presented with a "partial reading" of the actual experiences of working-class women.

Obviously, it is not often that working-class women (or women of any class) rise to high office in business, government, or even academia.[6] The dearth of women in the higher echelons of political parties or union bureaucracies, or other positions of power has been well documented.[7] However, under certain conditions, women have been involved in leadership roles in informal neighborhood organizations the constituencies of which seldom reach beyond the local or city level and rarely "make news."[8] It remains unclear whether these activities were present in the communities described in the studies discussed above and failed to be documented simply for methodological reasons. It is likely, however, that particular historical periods generate different types and levels of community organization, and this is the point that will be developed here.

WOMEN, WORK AND THE STATE

It has often been noted that in industrial societies working-class women have historically served as a low-paid labor force and have also provided unpaid domestic labor.[9] These activities are seen as integrated and facilitated by the shared household of husband, wife, and children.[10] The husband supposedly has a higher-paying job and a better chance to find employment than his wife. The wife, tied down by domestic responsibilities and discriminated against on the job market, has fewer alternatives and earns lower wages, being pulled into the work world in periods of high employment or to fill particular niches.

Certainly, involvement in low-paid labor and unpaid domestic work are salient characteristics of women's work in Greenpoint–Williamsburg. However, differential employment opportunities between men and women are not so clear-cut. Male unemployment is high and unionized manufacturing jobs are disappearing.[11] Under these conditions household structures are more flexible than suggested in the above model, and single-parent, sibling, and multigenerational households are common. A more central and related problem is evident in the above model of gender relations in the economy. Such an analysis neglects the pertinence of remittances people (and more specifically at this time in the United States, women) obtain from the state. It is here that women's collective action in demanding resources from the state—their direct political action—becomes particularly relevant. The political activities carried out by women to secure resources from the state are far more significant than might be predicted from an analysis that sees women only in terms of labor-force participation or domestic responsibilities.

Shifts in the structure of the American economy have created a new situation: a subpopulation made up predominantly of women and children who depend on state financing in some form. This population may see its political interests in terms of affecting state policies and not only in terms of employer–employee relationships or male–female domestic–economic relations.[12]

In documenting women's involvement in community organizing, I shall draw on my fieldwork in Greenpoint–Williamsburg from 1975 to 1978.[13] In order to conduct the research, I lived in this neighborhood from September 1975 until September 1976, and in the following two years I continued to visit people informally, conduct interviews, and participate in neighborhood events. In the course of this research I spent time with a large number of families, accompanied people in search of work, housing, public assistance, and other services, and traced the development of a variety of community organizations. I also observed in detail such political events as the election campaign of candidates for the local school board and the protest over the closing of a firehouse (which is briefly outlined below). Racial and ethnic differences are reflected in significant social and geographic divisions in the area. I attempted to work with people from a variety of backgrounds and to trace divisive and cooperative processes among groups in the community.

Greenpoint–Williamsburg is an old industrial working-class neighborhood that is a casualty of the departure of manufacturing industries from New York City and of shifts in the world economy.[14] It is currently characterized by a diversity of ethnic and racial groups, high unemployment, and low-paying service jobs. Women and men find themselves in unstable jobs, in and out of work, and on and off public assistance. For this reason it is imperative to view those who are at any one time dependent on public assistance as part of the working class, rather than to see them as a separate category such as "underclass" or "lower class."

Many of the women with whom I worked in Brooklyn had extensive financial and personal problems. Whether or not they lived with their husbands, they never had enough money for essentials. They were pursued by bills, electricity turn-offs, and eviction notices. They had to face days without food for themselves or their children, lack of money for health care, and major health problems among themselves and their children. They had to cope with unemployment, alcoholism, and drug addiction, wife-beating and child abuse—a full assortment of personal and social ills.

These problems cannot be ignored, and I would not underestimate their impact. However, in spite of—or even because of—them the lives of women I studied were characterized by much more than passive suffering. Above and beyond the difficulties of their daily lives, the people of Greenpoint–Williamsburg were political actors.

In order to demonstrate the importance of historical changes in the economy and state regulations and the way these can interact with a woman's life cycle to influence her involvement in political activities, I outline the careers of two women from the neighborhood. One was a Black woman in her mid-fifties and the other a white woman in her early forties. Each was a leader in her own area of activity.

The first woman I will call Jackie Williams. Born in 1926, she worked in the cotton fields as a child and came to New York City with two young children in 1955. She left her husband after a series of damaging conflicts. In the South she had worked as a milliner; in the North she worked in a laundry at very low pay. Neighbors cared for her children while she was at work. After many years, she was offered a job in a local voluntary agency. From there she moved to a variety of jobs funded by the Office of Economic Opportunity (OEO) and then to a Comprehensive Employment Training Act (CETA) job. With the CETA cutbacks, she became unemployed.

From 1965 on, when her children were in their teens, Jackie Williams became an articulate and extremely active community spokeswoman. She supervised and cooked practically all the free senior citizen lunches provided daily by her agency, organized a protest against rent raises, and attended numerous meetings protesting budget cutbacks. She was not afraid to speak out in public and rallied supporters who covered the full racial and ethnic spectrum of Greenpoint–Williamsburg.

I will call the second woman Mary Sanchez. Born in Brooklyn in 1938, she married a man from Puerto Rico in 1954, and they had four children. In 1959, her husband left her and the children. After that, she would leave her children with her sister while she went out to work in a dyeing factory. When the factory moved from New York City in 1970, she stopped working and applied for Aid to Families with Dependent Children (AFDC), a federal public assistance program.

Mary Sanchez received AFDC assistance until 1977, when she again returned to work—this time cleaning in factories after hours. From 1975 to 1978 she, her children, and her grandchildren were the main force behind the organization and distribution of summer lunches on Norman Street in Brooklyn. As I will point out, this was an act with greater political implications than is immediately apparent.

Neither of these women lived with men while they were politically active and in both cases their children were over ten years old at the time. Both were dependent in some form or other on state funding while they were involved in collective action. Though these characteristics are in no way universal among the politically active women whom I studied, they are significant in that they led to varying degrees of political involvement. Among women with younger children, day care and the particular form it took became an overriding factor in their political participation. Similarly, among married women, the husband's employment or lack of it was a significant determinant of the wife's involvement. Women whose husbands were unemployed or employed in low-paying, insecure service jobs appeared to be more active in neighborhood organizations than those who were living with apparently stable, well-paid, unionized working men. This may explain the variations in working-class women's activism found in the literature. As we enter a new phase of experience in the American economy, in which many of the former stable working class are insecure, women have become more politically active.

A second point that emerges from the careers of Jackie Williams and Mary Sanchez is that both women were politically active in the late 1960s and through the 1970s, the period when extra funding was available from the OEO. Their public careers must be understood, then, in relation to their own stage in the life cycle and to their employment experiences and forms of financial support, each of which was shaped by the historical period in which they were active.

WOMEN'S GROUPS: RESOURCES FOR POLITICAL ACTION

Most families on Norman Street in Greenpoint–Williamsburg during the period of my research were living on low incomes. Social contacts tended to be restricted to the street and a few surrounding blocks, but these were not the only important connections. People had numerous "institutional contacts" (welfare, the penal system, city services, the military). Even distant relatives played a role in local functions. However, the street was the local meeting place, and it was by spending many hours on the block that I became familiar with the lives and problems of the families there.

In three years of interaction with the residents of Greenpoint–Williamsburg, a mass of data was assembled testifying to the frequent involvement in collective action of working-class women in this urban community. Women participated in block associations and tenants' associations. They mobilized to demand health care, day care, and adequate schools, and to prevent the demolition of local housing. Collective-action strategies ranged from demands for the provision of community service to outright confrontation. However, whatever the nature of the community's action, each action required that people evaluate needs in the community, identify gaps in government services, and work collectively to overcome them. Thus, even the least confrontational community activities led people to perceive problems as issues to be approached collectively rather than individually.

Such cooperative efforts, as we shall see in the case of the lunch program described below, generated their own ideology or cultural interpretations that did not correspond with the "victim-blaming" or individual-centered explanations underlying many service-providing institutions. In addition, the participation of poor women in local associations and activities developed and strengthened links between families, friends, and neighbors that were often the basis for future, more obviously political mobilization (as will be seen in the case of the firehouse, outlined below). From this perspective, community activities such as participation in block associations and tenants' associations or running a play street or lunch program can be seen as political. In many instances, these activities may reflect community resistance to hegemonic values and the redefinition of local problems in collective terms. Such actions seldom proved successful, and successes proved limited and rarely long-lasting. They usually did not "make news." However, persistent efforts to control the environment, with whatever small success, were a significant feature of life.

The basis for women's collective action on the block was to be found in the daily round of domestic responsibilities. Child care, for example, constituted an important way by which women developed social groups that later proved effective in local organizing. It was in these small groups that patterns of cooperation, communication, and analysis were established and that the value of collective effort as opposed to individual competitiveness was experienced. These values were expressed in concern for "the block" or "the neighborhood" and in reminiscences about growing up in the same area. An emphasis on one's responsibilities to kin was extended to responsibilities for the community.

The need for assistance with young children was widespread and crucial to the women of Norman Street. For working women, child care was essential, but there were times when it was important for a mother to have additional help with her children. If a woman appeared overwrought and likely to abuse her children, her sister, mother, or a neighboring relative would offer to take the children. Wives, sisters, and mothers, as well as brothers and uncles all aided the working mother on Norman Street, although brothers and uncles watched children more rarely than sisters or aunts or grandmothers. Women took these responsibilities as a matter of course. The existence of a support group, based largely on neighbors and kin on the mother's side of the family, in which each individual provided small amounts of assistance, was combined with a high degree of flexibility in household structure. Assistance might be limited and the household fraught with conflict, but there was, nevertheless, a firm base of kindred to provide for members in need. Those same kindred, as we shall see, were mobilized for more direct political action. As Rapp has noted, "Kinship networks are part of 'community control' for women."[15]

Neighborhood women watching children spent many hours together. They also kept "an eye out" for every child in the vicinity. The constant hours spent together formed the basis for strong friendships among the women on Norman Street. This was the meeting ground through which other levels of cooperation and reciprocal aid formed and were reinforced in daily interaction.

As they sat on the block, women traded information about money problems, compared bills, and discussed eligibility for, and the methods they used, to obtain Medicaid benefits. They discussed what they were going to cook for supper and the problems they had in managing to feed their husbands and children. They calculated whether they might have enough money to go to bingo, where they might possibly win the "windfall profits" they could find nowhere else and keep alive the vain hope that they might escape from it all. They also kept a general watch on everything that people on the block were doing. And it was here that small but essential loans might be negotiated.

Young mothers on the block received advice from experienced mothers—and were constantly teased about their pregnancies and their—mostly nonexistent—affairs. Men, on the other hand, did not spend time on the street. They visited local bars, or sat in front of television sets with their beers. Social groups for them were not centered in the neighborhood—except as they involved their wives or kindred. Young, unemployed men did congregate on the street corners and were often in trouble with the law. However, though they were reprimanded and criticized by the women on the street, they were seldom enlisted in the women's collective activities. I would suggest that it was, in part, the absence of clearly defined responsibilities (other than employment for money—which was not easy to come by) that led to this adversarial but not clearly directed behavior on the part of the young men.

Long before their involvement in formal neighborhood politics, the women of the neighborhood exercised "local control." For example, they had known the local street gang members from infancy and did not hesitate to confront them. Several times during my stay they intervened in dangerous fights between groups of young men and boys. They kept these conflicts from escalating into neighborhood-wide brawls.

THE SUMMER LUNCH PROGRAM

The organization of a program to distribute bag lunches to children during summer vacation demonstrates the resistance to media and government perceptions of a problem and the emergence of cultural reinterpretations generated by the collective efforts of poor people to improve conditions in their community. It indicates the way in which the provision of community services by local women was itself political and took place within a highly politicized context.

In 1973, New York City established a summer program to provide lunches for children in the neighborhoods of New York. In 1976, Mary Sanchez and six other women, who formed a friendship group, requested the summer lunches for their block and supervised their distribution. They made numerous independent, but collective policy decisions that reflected the needs of the community but not the legal priorities of the state. There were needy persons in the neighborhood who were not children. The program provided them with free lunches, too. The elderly and disabled, in particular, were a target group for the women. Lunches were distributed to children but eaten by household members and kin. Women would collect the lunches and store them for their evening meal. For some, the summer lunch program provided the major part of the household's nutrition.

Throughout New York City, the lunch program became the target of defamatory news reports accusing the poor of scattering food in the streets. The lunch program was vilified daily on local television. Contrary to the image portrayed by the media, the lunch program was valued by the people who received food, and its importance was reflected in the energy they expended in maintaining it. Street cooperation reached a high level in administering the lunch program—and the priorities were established by the women who administered the program.

The women on the block, building on their kin and neighborhood groups, exhibited strong collective control of the program in the face of a variety of threats to report illegal behavior to the city administration and in spite of the many bureaucratic inefficiencies on the part of the agencies hired by the state to deliver the food. The women allocated resources according to their own values and their own evaluation of community needs, in direct contradiction to priorities established by state legislation. In other words, they created their own cultural and political context for the identification of community needs and distributed resources according to collectively negotiated priorities. In so doing, poor women reinforced views of their problems as rooted in social rather than individual shortcomings and constructed local ties based on such common interpretations. It was the development of such cultural reinterpretation and community links in a wide variety of activities that provided the basis for more demanding, long-term, and out-of-the-ordinary events such as the mobilization around the threatened loss of fire protection described below.

THE FIREHOUSE

A more dramatic, and grueling, activity, which also depended in part on preexisting links between women, was the takeover of the firehouse. In 1975 the city, as part of fiscal cutbacks, had announced plans to remove the neighborhood's fire engine. This was a period of an extremely high incidence of arson, and the removal of the truck was a genuinely life-threatening matter.

The response from the neighborhood was rapid. A siren was sounded from the firehouse, and concerned residents, recognizing the signal, telephoned their friends and neighbors to call them to action. Before the fire engine could be removed, a large crowd of neighborhood residents had gathered in front of the firehouse to prevent the truck from driving out. A man of Polish immigrant parentage who had just suffered an injury at work and was unable to return to his job took leadership at this point. He, his wife, and their four children moved into the firehouse, where they stayed, with widespread community support and numerous other visitors, for more than a year. This man's mother also moved in and brought in her wake many of the elderly people who supported the takeover to spend time and play chess in the firehouse. Neighboring women assisted with cooking, laundry, collecting children from school, and generally helping the family in the firehouse to continue under particularly harrowing conditions. Ultimately, the community mobilization proved successful; the firehouse was reopened.

An earlier experience of women involved in defending the firehouse was an important factor in the success of this mobilization. In 1972, when the S&S Corrugated Paper Machinery Company planned to expand, it was given permission by the New York City administration to pull down nineteen houses in Williamsburg, the homes for ninety-four families, to make room for plant buildings. Residents of Williamsburg (specifically residents of the "North Side," where the firehouse was also located) organized to try to prevent the destruction of their homes. In the face of highly visible protests and demonstrations, the company proceeded with the demolition. Angry and despairing residents sat in the streets in front of the bulldozers in a final attempt to prevent the destruction of their homes. Finally, S & S was forced to build fourteen new three-storey houses that were designed as "moderate-income cooperatives" and could be bought by the displaced residents. In spite of the loss of the nineteen houses, this outcome was viewed as a major success in the neighborhood. The strength of community links forged in this previous struggle, the political experience (in public speaking and political negotiation), and the common culture generated in antipathy to the decisions of the New York City administration, combined with the overall sense of the possibility of success, provided important groundwork for the later firehouse demonstrations.

A second significant factor in the case of the firehouse was that that household around which the demonstration was organized was partially supported by state funds. The husband received disability benefits, while his wife was employed as a meat packer. In this case, although it was the man, rather than the woman, who was receiving state funds, once again dependence on the state helped to shape the nature and target of political activism. A third factor was that the wife's women friends and neighbors continued their support and increased their aid in maintaining the household in the firehouse. The patterns of cooperation and the links the women had utilized in their daily lives were activated in the firehouse takeover.

The firehouse demonstration was, however, different in significant ways from the smaller events described earlier. It was orchestrated and perpetuated partly with the help of male community organizers and community spokespeople. This was a stronger and more effective movement than any of the other demonstrations for several reasons. First, the coalition was built between community residents and the firefighter's union, and this link broadened and deepened the constituency of the action. Another factor contributing to the success of this activity was the pressure brought to bear on local politicians to support the neighborhood's demands. This pressure was applied at a pivotal time, just before the pending elections. Thus, it could be more effective, especially as voting participation in the areas around the firehouse and in Greenpoint was higher than in even poorer areas of Williamsburg.[16] In this instance, both men and women residents were active in picketing and demonstrating, in blocking the Brooklyn–Queens Expressway, and in other protest activities.

It seems likely that it was the *coalition* of work and community interests combined with the relationships forged with city and state Democratic politicians that gave the firehouse demonstration both its uniqueness and its strength. It has been suggested that divisions between men and women in United States society are reflected in divisions between work and community.[17] In this instance, the women of Greenpoint–Williamsburg did not take a separatist or particularly feminist approach. However, it was the collective experiences and values among women in the community, combined with the differing experiences of men, specifically with unions in the workplace, that made effective resistance possible.

DISCUSSION

On the basis of this research, let us now reexamine the issues raised in the introduction to this article. I would suggest that the difference between the descriptions of working-class women in the 1950s and 1960s and those presented here can in part be understood in terms of phases of historical development in neighborhood action in relation to the changing experiences of America's working class. This experience is conditioned by the disappearance of stable, male-oriented jobs and a concomitant, growing dependence of families on the state. The working-class political movements of the 1970s and 1980s frequently become bitterly adversarial in relation to the state (as in the case of the movement around the firehouse) with the worsening of conditions and the deepening severity of the "crisis" faced by the national and world economy.

Neighborhood movements in recent decades have incorporated direct action and collective protest into their strategic vocabulary. Such movements show some similarities to the "bread and meat" riots of the early twentieth century.[18] Like the civil protests early in the century, they involve direct action and, frequently, open conflict. However, the movements of the 1970s and 1980s differ from these and earlier voluntary associations in that they presuppose the *welfare state* and the historical changes wrought by the Roosevelt and Johnson eras.

During the presidency of Franklin Delano Roosevelt a variety of measures were introduced to combat mass economic misery and in response to the development of militant unions and populist movements. These included the Social Security Act of 1935, which created retirement pensions and unemployment insurance, income maintenance for specific groups, aid for dependent children and aid to the blind, as well as funds for maternal and child health services. Although aspects of the welfare state (such as workers' compensation) already existed, the 1930s represents a watershed in the provision of social services and the legitimation and expectation of government assistance.

A second major shift occurred during the presidency of Lyndon B. Johnson with the "War on Poverty." The reforms of the 1960s can be seen partly as a response to the burgeoning civil rights movement and the ghetto riots, but they also represent changes that had been taking place since World War II in every advanced industrialized nation. In 1965 the Social Security Act was amended to include Medicare and Medicaid funding. Similarly, the Older Americans Act (Public Law 89–73), also in 1965, established nutrition programs and senior citizen centers for the elderly. All of these programs provided assistance for the care of household members that had previously been regarded as the responsibility of women household members. These acts also established the right to health care, nutrition, and caretaking in old age for all members of American society. Whether or not such care is currently provided, the legislation enacted in the past fifty years has created a fundamental legitimacy for demands that the government provide caretaking services for the needy.

Now, rather than focusing on the distribution of resources or the ownership of production, people demand that the *state* take action to ameliorate bad conditions. Women have begun to mobilize communities to demand action and funding from state agencies. They have been demanding that a broad range of services be funded by the state *as a right*.[19]

In Greenpoint–Williamsburg, women were involved in the formulation and organizing of political demands. They took leadership roles. They became presidents of local block associations; they made speeches, coordinated demonstrations, organized food distribution, and dealt with politicians—both local and national.

These women seldom expressed a coherent political ideology. They certainly regarded it as their duty to cook for their families, do the shopping, and take primary responsibility for the children whether or not they were also employed outside the home. The expectations and ideology surrounding women's domestic work have not changed dramatically as more women have been going to work.[20] Studies from all over the world show that when women work they take on paid employment as an extra job.

However, neighborhood organizations and the demand that the state finance caretaking activities represent in themselves a rejection of the full range of duties assigned to women in this society. The fact that women are central in the organizing of these movements reflects both their concern with their "traditional" duties and the changing nature of their experiences. Although the movements focus on what are now regarded as women's "traditional concerns"—the care of the young and the disabled, for example—they demonstrate women's ability to build on their collective experience for organizing purposes and to demand collective goods and services from the state. Women are demanding that the state take over caretaking activities that are commonly thought to be women's responsibility.

CONCLUSION

Historians have analyzed the changes in the form of political expression corresponding to the emergence of industrial society.[21] Such studies, however, have been largely concerned with men and their political activities. In a sense they may have contributed to the idea that women did not participate in industrialization and that their traditional role has always been that of homemaker. Recent feminist scholars have begun to redress this imbalance.[22]

Women's participation in community organizations has seldom been subjected to historical analysis.[23] Clearly, women's work and unemployment experiences have been very different from men's, and it was to be expected that women's collective action would have emerged at different times and in different ways. However, if one is to understand the ways in which women's protest has differed from men's, one must understand these differences in terms of a changing relationship among corporate power, working-class people, and the state. Within this context, one must be sensitive to the consequences of the changing nature of and demand for labor as well as the changes in the demand for reproduction of the labor force.

In this context, I have shown that neighborhood and community organizations have their own history and have evolved their own forms parallel to, but in no way subsumed by collective action at the workplace. Here, too, women have developed methods for extracting more goods and services from the state and sometimes even from corporations (for example, the S&S Corrugated Paper Machinery Company) in their efforts to raise the value of wages by supplementing them with public financing of the collective needs of the community.

Working-class women have acted on the basis of their common experiences and assigned child-care roles in society to develop effective collective action and to both demand increased financing from the state and protest reductions in the maintenance of community services. Whether or not they have become leaders on a national level, such women are still significant for their reinforcement of collective values, their exercise of local control, their actions in redistributive activities, and their persistent demand for public services. In their participation in conflict within neighborhoods, they contribute to changing definitions of the responsibilities of the state to the growing sector of nonworking or low-paid workers in our economy. In neighborhoods where services are deteriorating and people are suffering a loss of political influence because they have lost their employment, the ability to influence events through recognized channels is also declining.

With the decrease in employment opportunities, the major route by which working-class people were able to maintain some control over the conditions of their lives is lost; union membership and support are also disappearing. It is in this context that we see women's collective organization becoming more focused and the resort to direct action more frequent as women fight to maintain the few remaining services allocated to the working poor. The local protest movements of the last two decades are the result of women's fighting to make up for the departure of industry and the loss of stable, well-paying jobs.

The firehouse movement in Greenpoint–Williamsburg is particularly significant in that it demonstrated the effectiveness of coalitions built between the residents of a working-class community (both men and women) and workers concerned for their continued employment. The important theoretical issues raised by current changes in the United States economy (marked by increasing unemployment and declining industrial work) concern the ways in which the growing unemployed nonworking or low-paid and state-supplemented sectors of the population mobilize to extract resources from the state and negotiate a redefinition of government priorities. I would suggest that the collective activities of working-class women and their changing experiences and expectations are central to this endeavor.

ACKNOWLEDGMENT
Portions of this paper appeared in an earlier version in the *American Ethnologist* 13, No. 1 (1986) under the title "Political Activity among Working Class Women in a U.S. City."

NOTES
1. For examples see Milton Cantor and Bruce Laurie, eds., *Class, Sex and the Woman Worker* (Westport, Conn.: Greenwood Press, 1980); A. Kessler-Harris, *Out to Work* (New York: Oxford University Press, 1982); M. Tax, *The Rising of the Women* (New York: Monthly Review Press, 1983); S. Eisenstein, *Give Us Bread but Give Us Roses* (Boston: Routledge & Kegan Paul, 1983); K. Sacks and D. Remy, *My Troubles Are Going to Have Trouble with Me* (New Brunswick, N.J.: Rutgers University Press, 1984).
2. For examples, see M. Komarovsky, *Blue-Collar Marriage* (New York: Random House, 1964); L. Rainwater, R. Coleman, and G. Handel, *Workingman's Wife* (New York: Oceana, 1959).
3. M. Ackelsberg, "Women's Collaborative Activities and City Life: Politics and Policy," in J. Flammang, ed., *Political Women: Current Roles in State and Local Government* (Beverly Hills, Calif.: Sage, 1984); K. McCourt, *Working Class Women and Grass Roots Politics* (Bloomington: Indiana University Press, 1977); N. Seifer, *Nobody*

Speaks for Me (New York: Simon & Schuster, 1976); T. Kaplan, "Female Consciousness and Collective Action: The Case of Barcelona, 1910–1918," *Signs* 7 (1982): 545–566; M. Castells, *The City and the Grassroots* (Berkeley: University of California Press, 1984);S. Joseph, "Working-Class Women's Networks in a Sectarian State: A Political Paradox," *American Ethnologist* 10, No. 1 (1983); S. Morgen, "Women and Community Organizing: The Intersection of Gender and Class in a Grassroots Health Action Coalition" (paper delivered at symposium, "U.S. Women and Resistance in the Community and the Workplace," American Anthropological Association meetings, Denver, 1984); F. F. Piven, "Women and the State: Ideology, Power and the Welfare State," *Socialist Review* 74 (March–April 1984): 13–23; J. Wolf, "A Rising Vote of Thanks, Afro-American Women, Club Activities and Social Welfare in the 1920's," unpublished ms., 1984; C. Gilkes, "Successfully Rebellious Professionals: The Black Woman's Professional Identity and Community Commitment," *Psychology of Women Quarterly* 6 (1980): 289–311; C. Nelson, "Public and Private Politics: Women in the Middle Eastern World," *American Ethnologist* 1 (August 1974): 551–565.

    4. Specifically those of Lillian Rubin, *Worlds of Pain* (New York: Basic Books, 1976); Komarovsky, *Blue-Collar Marriage;* and Rainwater et al., *Workingman's Wife*.

    5. G. Brown and T. Harris, *Social Origins of Depression* (New York: Free Press, 1978).

    6. M. Githens and J. Prestage, eds., *A Portrait of Marginality* (New York: McKay, 1977).

    7. Center for the American Woman and Politics, "Women in Elective Office, 1975–79" (Fact Sheet issued by the National Information Bank on Women in Politics, Eagleton Institute of Politics, Rutgers University, 1980); M. Stacey and M. Price, *Women, Power and Politics* (London: Tavistock, 1981).

    8. See H. Gutman, *Work, Culture and Society in Industrial America* (New York: Vintage, 1976); Seifer, *Nobody Speaks for Me;* Castells, *The City and the Grass Roots*.

    9. D. Gordon, *Theories of Poverty and Underemployment* (Lexington, Mass.: Lexington Books, 1972); P. Quick, "The Class Nature of Women's Oppression," *Review of Radical Political Economics* 9 (1977): 42–54; M. McIntosh, "The State and the Oppression of Women," in A. Kuhn and A. Wolpe, eds., *Feminism and Materialism* (Boston: Routledge & Kegan Paul, 1978), 254–290; V. Beechey, "Women and Production: A Critical Analysis of Some Sociological Theories of Women's Work," in Kuhn and Wolpe, eds., *Feminism and Materialism,* 155–198.

    10. For examples, see W. Secombe, "The Housewife and Her Labor under Capitalism," *New Left Review* 83 (1974): 3–24; V. Oppenheimer, *The Female Labor Force in the United States* (Berkeley: University of California Press, 1970); M. Barrett, *Women's Oppression Today* (London: Verso Editions, 1980); J. Brenner and M. Ramos, "Rethinking Women's Oppression," *New Left Review* 144 (March–April 1984): 33–72.

    11. G. Sternlieb and J. Hughes, "Metropolitan Decline and Interregional Job Shifts," in R. Alcaly and D. Mermelstein, eds., *The Fiscal Crisis of Cities,* (New York: Random House, 1977), 145–165.

    12. It is not entirely correct to see this population that is reliant on state funding as new. It is more accurate to view it as greatly expanded and more visible. Black women have been in this situation for a much longer period, and the impact of this on community mobilization can also be traced. See also Carol Stack, *All Our Kin* (New York: Harper & Row, 1974); and B. Valentine, *Hustling and Other Hard Work* (New York: Free Press, 1978).

13. For a more complete account of working-class life in Greenpoint–Williamsburg, see I. Susser, *Norman Street: Poverty and Politics in an Urban Neighborhood* (New York: Oxford University Press, 1982).

14. W. Tabb, "The New York City Fiscal Crisis," in W. Tabb and L. Sawers, *Marxism and the Metropolis* (New York: Oxford University Press, 1978); R. Alcaly and D. Mermelstein, eds., *The Fiscal Critics of American Cities: Essays on the Political Economy of Urban America with Special Reference to New York* (New York: Random House, 1977).

15. R. Rapp, "Family and Class in Contemporary America," in B. Thorne, ed., *Rethinking the Family* (London: Longmans, 1982).

16. This issue is discussed in more detail, including its implications for minority representation and access to political power, in Susser, *Norman Street*.

17. See Ackelsberg, *Women's Collaborative Activities*.

18. See Gutman, *Work, Culture and Society*.

19. Piven makes this point and sees it as the explanation for the much-discussed "gender gap" in the voting patterns of men and women of the 1980s, as well as a basis for a mass movement of women.

20. P. Hunt, *Gender and Class Consciousness* (New York: Holmes and Meier, 1980).

21. For examples, see E. P. Thompson, *The Making of the English Working Class* (New York: Vintage, 1966); E. Hobsbawm, *Primitive Rebels* (New York: Norton, 1955); D. Brody, *Steel Workers in America: The Non-Union Era* (Cambridge: Harvard University Press, 1960); J. Scott, *Glassworkers of Carmaux* (Cambridge: Harvard University Press, 1974).

22. Viz., Einstein, Tax, Kessler-Harris, and Sacks and Remy (*see note 1 above*), and R. Milkman, ed., *Women, Work and Protest: A Century of U.S. Women's Labor History* (Boston: Routledge & Kegan Paul, 1985).

23. However, see Kaplan, "Female Consciousness," for one such analysis.

12

Vending on the Streets: City Policy, Gentrification, and Public Patriarchy

Roberta M. Spalter-Roth

In a worldwide movement for economic independence and personal autonomy, women have migrated to cities, gone to work for wages or, when wage jobs were not available, set up small businesses such as the vending or hawking of goods on urban streets. In the process, they have competed with better-capitalized merchants, have broken registration laws, and have invaded male turf. As part of their struggle, women have had to develop a wide variety of strategies to resist exploitation by employers and politically influential merchants, domination by men, and control by the state.

This is a case study of women who earned their livelihood by selling cheap goods on the streets of the capital city of a major First World country—Washington D.C. Their efforts to earn a living have taken place in the face of three processes: capital accumulation by large-scale businesses, sexual harassment by male customers and male vendors, and a strict new city regulatory policy. This regulatory policy was designed to promote upscale, fixed-location retailers, developers, and investors. If successful, the city government hoped to "revitalize" downtown Washington, D.C. Another result of this policy, perhaps unintended by city officials, was to increase male domination of the streets by reducing the number of women vendors using them.

This study recounts the individual, cooperative, and collective strategies (including participation in a newly formed union) that women vendors used to empower themselves in order to earn a living. Finally, it attempts to explain why women vendors' attempts to deal with sexual harassment—a gender-specific issue—never went beyond the level of individual coping strategies while they used more collective efforts to protect their livelihood and dignity.

INTERNATIONAL BACKGROUND

Street vending has often been seen by development specialists and some Third World policymakers as a remnant of a traditional goods distribution system and an impediment to modernization. This study casts doubt on that view. What follows is a brief review of some of the literature on survival strategies used by women vendors in Third World cities in the face of unsympathetic government policies. I note the absence of studies on the effects of government policies on women's right to use the streets free of sexual harassment and women's response to this failure. This case study attempts to fill the gap.

In cities throughout the Third World, women hawk goods on urban streets as a means of earning a livelihood and sometimes as a path to personal autonomy. An increasing number of women are entering this impoverished tertiary sector or informal sector, because, in a situation of permanent underemployment, vending helps poor women and their families survive. It generates household income and distributes cheap goods.[1] Vending or hawking is a source of economic independence for women, and it is one of the few jobs in which women can avoid the close supervision involved in being a domestic, factory, or clerical worker.

Although women report feelings of autonomy while working as vendors, they also report trouble from a variety of sources: customers wanting even cheaper goods, politically influential fixed-location merchants regarding them as unwanted competition, and fellow vendors wanting their spots. City, state, and local government officials and apparatuses try to regulate them out of existence.[2] Third World city governments often attempt to sweep away this small-scale mode of goods distribution in order to "modernize" commerce and get rid of "eyesores" for the sake of tourists.[3]

Some development specialists and some Third World policymakers regard vendors as unemployed parasites; often they are not counted in government censuses.[4] The reemergence of street vendors in First World cities has shown that vending is not just the survival of an earlier mode of redistribution but one that can thrive in the midst of modern retailing. In cities across the United States the numbers of street vendors are growing, causing much consternation among large-scale merchants, who are turning to city officials to restrict them.[5]

Recent feminist scholarship on street vending has noted its place in women's striving for economic independence and in aiding the urban poor. The literature has also described the constant struggle between local governments (who often represent the interests of larger merchants) and vendors.[6] This scholarship shows that women vendors, exploited though they may be, are not the passive victims of government campaigns. Rather, they are social actors who have definite views about which strategies can be applied in order to pursue their goals of economic and personal independence; they use a variety of strategies in their efforts to earn a living at jobs that offer some flexibility and autonomy.[7]

In portraying vendors as political actors, the above-mentioned studies clarify the relation between state-initiated efforts to restrict street vending and the economic independence of women vendors. Quite simply, as noted by Bunster and Chaney, institutional harassment diminishes women's ability to earn a living.[8] If there are institutional threats to their livelihood, women vendors will protest, organize, and engage in acts of resistance. Sometimes they use cooperative or collective strategies to help each other evade fee collectors, alert their neighbors to new policies, and guard their spots and merchandise in the face of government-initiated sweeps.[9] Yet, as Obbo notes in her study of African women, despite the potential of group action, problems are often articulated and strategies developed at an individual level.[10] Obbo attributes this lack of collective action to most African women's reluctance to enter into public discussion of issues affecting them.[11] Despite the growth of street vending in First World cities, no comparable body of literature describes First World women vendors and the strategies that they develop to stay on the streets.

What is absent from almost all the studies on street vending is an exploration of the relationship between male domination and increasing government regulation, on the one hand, and women's ability to earn a living by street vending, on the other. At least in Western industrial cities, the streets are a place where direct sexual harassment, both verbal and physical—to insult, frighten, demean, or put women in their place—is used as a form of social control. As a result, women get the message that they are asking for trouble if they linger in public places without male protection.[12] The right of women to work safely in public spaces and the role of government policy in protecting that right has only recently become a part of research agendas and policy discourse.[13] Despite recent important studies of sexual harassment at outdoor workplaces such as construction sites, additional studies are needed to understand more about how women who work on the streets organize to resist sexual harassment and the scope of their success in these struggles.

METHODOLOGY

This study started as a comparison between women vendors in First World and Third World cities. To facilitate this comparison, I developed with Eileen Zeitz, who worked with me on much of the study, a questionnaire based on one used in studies of Southeast Asian cities. It asked about sources of goods and kinds of goods sold, hours worked, how locations were chosen, method of transportation used, and amounts of income generated.[14] A small grant from the Center for Washington Area Studies of George Washington University made possible the hiring of Mindy Shapiro as an interviewer and coder. All three of us began to interview women vendors in the summer of 1984.

Of the seventy-five women we interviewed formally (in ninety interviews) over the course of the study, the first five spontaneously mentioned their problems with safety and sexual harassment. I revised the questionnaire to reflect these concerns and also made it more open-ended so that we could pick up other unsolicited issues.

We had completed close to forty interviews when a set of stiff new vendor regulations was made public. In response, I designed yet another questionnaire that omitted demographic and merchandise questions and added questions about vendors' reactions to the new regulations. Interviewing continued after the new regulations were put into effect, with further modifications to the questionnaire. We talked with some of the women several times as the struggle against the regulations progressed. As a result of the process of changing the questionnaire as the situation changed, few comparable questions were asked of all seventy-five respondents, though some questions were asked of the same person several times.

While a "random sample" was not used, we did cover all major downtown vending locations during prime selling hours. We did not, however, conduct interviews in all the neighborhoods where vending takes place, especially not those in the almost entirely Black Southeast section of the city. In addition, because we had no Korean or Vietnamese translators, we had difficulty interviewing many of the non–English-speaking Asian women vendors. Thus, the sample may not be representative of all women vendors in the District of Columbia, and may especially underrepresent Black and Asian women vendors. Throughout the text the women we interviewed are referred to by their first names only. These were the only names they gave to us, following a common practice on the streets. We too, were called by our first names. The two members of the vendors' union that we interviewed are referred to by their full names or their last names, because they had become public figures as the result of several newspaper interviews.

In addition to interviewing vendors, we attended hearings, union meetings, and demonstrations, followed the story as it was covered in the local media, searched the archives of the Washingtoniana Collection of the Martin Luther King, Jr., Memorial Library for old newspaper clippings on previous attempts to regulate vending, and examined the District of Columbia Department of Consumer and Regulatory Affairs printouts of licensed vendors. The printouts provided some basic data on licensed vendors (including name and address of each license applicant and payer of the license fee if different from the applicant). Unfortunately, the data of most interest—the gender, race. and ethnicity of license applicants—were not given on the forms. Since gender data were not gathered on license application forms, we were not able to calculate the exact ratio of women to men. But we were able to estimate the ratio on the basis of whether the applicant had a male- or female-sounding given name. This technique could not be applied to all vendors' names, especially non-Western ones, and hence the ratio of one female vendor for every three males is only an estimate.[15]

A major purpose of this study was to see the issue of street vending from the perspective of women vendors rather than from the perspective of policymakers. As a result of interviews, observations, and informal talks, we began to identify with the women vendors and to assume the roles of advocates as well as researchers. The first product of the study was a policy paper in which Zeitz and I tried to convince District Officials that vending provided needed jobs, that the number of women vendors on the streets should be increased instead of decreased, and that women vendors should have a greater say in public policy.[16] Thus, although we were clearly researchers we were, to use Maria Meis's term, "consciously partial" rather than objectively neutral.[17]

WOMEN VENDORS: PERSONAL AND ECONOMIC AUTONOMY

As one walks streets in the District of Columbia, there appear to be far fewer women than men vendors. Before the new regulations were implemented, we estimated that one out of every four vendors was a woman. Thus, in this city, street vending is a "nontraditional" job for women.

In contrast to some Third World cities, there does not appear to be any typical woman vendor in terms of age or marital status in the District. Of the women we interviewed over the course of the study, 40 percent were Black, 40 percent were white, and the remaining 20 percent were Latina or Asian. As can be seen from Table 12.1, which shows the demographic characteristics of the first forty women to be interviewed, Black women were more likely to be young and much more likely to be currently unmarried than white, Latina, or Asian women. In contrast to the latter women, the Black women and the white women in the sample were relatively well educated, with two-thirds of the white women having at least some college education and only 13 percent of the Black women having less than a high school education. Unlike their counterparts in many Third World cities, the majority of women we interviewed were not illiterate, and the lack of formal education was not the reason they became vendors.

There was, however, a notable difference between the Black and white women vendors whom we interviewed. Of the seventy-five women interviewed over the course of the study, a much higher percentage of the total sample of white women (60 percent) owned their own stands than did the total sample of Black women (37 percent). The difference in ownership patterns did not appear to result either in a different consciousness of their situation or in public hostility toward one another. In contrast to studies that show overt conflict between Black and white women in hierarchical workplace positions, the only racial or ethnic comments we heard during the course of the study were expressions of bad feelings toward Asian vendors, especially Koreans.[18] For example, a white woman complained about Korean vendors who hung around her table to see what she was selling, copied her merchandise, and sold it at a lower price.

Prior to the new regulations, the largest number of women vendors sold a variety of mass-produced goods. In winter, they sold hats, scarves, purses, gloves, and legwarmers, along with stockings, belts, and jewelry. In summer, they switched to sunglasses, tee-shirts, Indian cotton dresses, and jewelry. Although most vendors sell a mixture of goods, some specialize in toys, ethnic clothing, oils and incense, art objects, leather goods, jewelry, fruit and flowers.

Table 12.1
CHARACTERISTICS OF A SAMPLE OF WOMEN VENDORS IN WASHINGTON, D.C., 1984

	Black	White	Other
Age in Years			
20–29	11	9	1
30–39	2	5	1
40–49	2	3	3
50–59	0	3	0
Marital Status			
Currently married	0	5	4
Currently unmarried	15	15	1
Education			
Less than high school	2	1	2
High school graduate	7	6	3
More than high school	6	13	0
Previous Job			
Sales and cashier	6	5	0
Clerical	5	4	0
Other (waitress, nurse)	2	8	1
Not previously employed	2	3	4
Daily Earnings			
Less than $75	1	2	2
$75–$99	4	4	2
$100–$124	5	8	1
$125–$149	2	2	0
$150 and more	2	4	0
No information	1	0	0
Ownership			
Self-employed	11	18	7
Works for other	19	12	8

Note: For ownership, N = 75.

Stiff regulations prevent most vendors from selling food, the staple of many Third World women vendors. They vend little that is handcrafted, homemade, or unique. They frequently sell fad merchandise such as Gucci look-alike purses and *faux* Ralph Lauren polo shirts. At Christmas, they sell cheaper versions of the latest toys like Transformers and Cabbage Patch dolls. Frequently the same kinds of goods can be purchased (although usually at a higher cost) fifteen feet away at a fixed-location retail outlet. The manager of a women's apparel shop complained, "They destroyed our accessory business. We gave up selling handbags, sunglasses, and less expensive earrings."[19]

Despite accusations by fixed-location merchants that the street vendors sell inferior goods, women vendors think of themselves as providing consumers with a service that is convenient and with goods that are less expensive than the merchandise available through traditional stores and shops. As Betty Galloway, a Black woman who later became vice president of the vendors' union, said, "Rich people go to Raleigh's [a local specialty store]. My customers are secretaries who can't afford shopping at expensive department stores." Other vendors said that customers buy from them because they like a bargain—and they like to bargain.

Most vendors begin to set up before nine o'clock in the morning, unloading their merchandise from station wagons or small trucks, often with the help of partners or men they hire to help them out. The women who work for someone else usually meet their employer at the site and help unload at the beginning of the day and pack up at the end of the day, often going to and from work by subway. Prime working hours are 11 A.M. to 6 P.M., with the most traffic occurring at lunch hour or from 4:00 to 6:00 P.M., when people are getting out of work. The best times to vend are during the good spring and summer weather, when tourists are at their peak in the nation's capital, or just before the Christmas holidays.

WHY WOMEN VEND

Most of the women we interviewed had been previously employed; about 60 percent had been employed in pink-collar jobs, mainly as sales clerks and cashiers. The balance had been in jobs such as file clerk, bookkeeper, secretary, or waitress. A small minority had been on welfare. They all made it quite clear that they had been happy to leave those jobs. The reasons they gave for leaving their previous jobs were that they disliked close supervision, they resented the lack of decent pay, or they found the inflexibility of work hours very difficult. In contrast, they liked the feeling of autonomy and the decent earnings that vending offered. Almost none of them regarded vending as a transitional occupation.

A woman who worked for someone else and thus was a "disguised wage laborer" was most often employed by a friend who owned and supplied several stands.[20] A few of the women, especially those who sold fruit and flowers, worked for corporations that owned and supplied numerous stands. The owner's role was to obtain the merchandise, to cover its cost, and to bring it to the vending site each morning and collect it each evening.

Whether self-employed or working for someone else, the women we interviewed, like many Third World women, thought of themselves as autonomous workers.[21] Those women who did work for others still claimed a sense of autonomy because of the absence of the close supervision found in many women's workplaces. Selena, a twenty-seven-year-old Black woman who sold toys, socks, scarves, and place mats, had previously worked as a cashier in a super-market and in several restaurants. She had hated the shift work involved in these jobs and said that there was always "dead" time in between shifts that ended up costing her extra transportation money because she had to go home and then return to work. And she had had to buy uniforms for some of the jobs. But mostly she had hated "people always telling you what to do." Lorraine, a twenty-eight-year-old Black woman who had worked as a clerk and as a word pro-cessor, seized the opportunity to vend when a friend made her the offer. She "got sick of offices years ago." Jeanette, a thirty-five-year-old white former book-keeper became a vendor because she "was tired of little numbers and tired of working for other people." Rhea, a former sales woman in a department store, summed it up: "It was warmer inside in the winter and cooler in the summer, but at least now no one is telling me what to do."

Other vendors value the flexibility of working hours without sacrificing pay. According to Maureen, a white woman in her late thirties who was support-ing two children, "The work is relatively easy and I can always take off days if there is some emergency and I can work shorter hours. And *I* can make those decisions." Those Korean and Vietnamese women whom we did interview indi-cated that the job was possible for someone who did not speak English; the only English they needed was the price of an item.

Those women who owned their own stands saw vending as a way to own a small business without having to invest a significant amount of start-up capital. In exchange for ownership, they worked ten to twelve hours a day, and they had total responsibility for the success or failure of their ventures. In addition, they did a fair amount of traveling in order to pick up supplies from wholesale outlets in Pennsylvania, Virginia, and New York. They also reported that during both holiday and tourist seasons they had to get out as early as 5:00 A.M. in order to guard their spots. Yet despite these hardships, none of these women wanted to return to her previous job.

Although personal autonomy, flexibility of hours, and the ability to start one's own business with little capital were all important reasons for working as a vendor, a decent income was the primary reason for doing so. The women we interviewed reported earning between $75 and $100 a day on an average. Those who worked for someone else were paid a flat fee and did not appear to know how much their employer made in profits. Assuming that weather conditions would prevent them from working more than forty weeks per year (this estimate was arrived at after consultation with the National Bureau of Weather Services), we estimated the average annual income of these women in 1984 at approx-imately $12,600 if they worked four days a week and $18,000 if they worked five days a week. Though they are not paid for sick leave or vacation days, their earnings are higher than those of cashiers, waitresses, or sales clerks.[22]

Tawana, a young Black woman who vended African-style sculptures, oils, and incense, had previously supported her two daughters through payments from

Aid to Families with Dependent Children. She had dropped out of high school when she became pregnant. At the time we interviewed her she had been employed as a vendor for seven months and was earning $75 a day. She said she was vending because she was "sick of sitting home and never having any money." Rita, a twenty-five-year-old Latina woman, also a former recipient of AFDC, said that vending made it possible for her to put her son in a decent day-care center rather than having him sit home watching television with her all day. Shirleen, a Black former cashier, summed it up: "I vend because there's money and freedom in it."

PROBLEMS AND STRATEGIES

Although women vendors see very positive aspects to their jobs, part of the struggle to stay in business includes dealing with the difficult experience of being one of the few groups of women who work the streets. Because they are on male turf, they are seen as targets by men on the streets, by shoplifters, by male vendors, and by the police. Questioned about her main on-the-job problems, Verna, a young Black woman, answered, "Cops, guys, and people trying to rip you off." Although they are tough women, virtually every one of them expressed fears that resulted from an encounter she had experienced while working. These fears were in sharp contrast to the feeling of autonomy also expressed by the women.

Like men, women vendors told of being harassed by the police. They complained that the police did not protect them if they were robbed or harassed, but instead operated in the interests of fixed-location businesses. In addition, they reported that the police treated them like criminals and contributed to keeping customers away by constantly scrutinizing their licenses, measuring their tables, and looking for other violations. The women did not think that the police did this to them more often than to male vendors; however, they did feel in greater need of police protection, and they did not think that the police were either sympathetic or present when they needed help.

The issue of sexual harassment was a recurrent theme. Like women working on construction sites, women vendors were faced with hostile and threatening sexual remarks and actions that made the streets a sexually demeaning work environment.[23] The offenders were mostly male customers, men on the streets, and sometimes male vendors. Elaine, a very young white woman, said, "I never wear jeans or tight clothes because men have literally come up behind me and tried to feel my ass . . . and it's not only the creeps but real respectable-looking ones, too." Celeste, another white woman in her early thirties, agreed that it was mainly the customers and other men passing by who made "grabs at women all the time." Jackie, a twenty-five-year-old Black woman said, "Men try to hustle you all the time, both customers and other men—you have to be cool and unfriendly."

In addition to being harassed by customers and men on the streets, women vendors also reported being both physically and verbally harassed by male vendors whose actions let the women know that they should not be working on the streets. Sometimes verbal harassment was used to get the women off the streets. Several women said that they were "pushed around" by male vendors. They claimed that often these men insisted that they had a right to a woman's spot, and they would threaten or intimidate her until she moved. Susan, a white woman of thirty who sold jewelry with a woman partner, told us that male vendors "frequently set up right on top of you and try to crowd you back into the wall. They only do this to women because another man would punch the shit out of them."

Male vendors harassed the women by comparing them to prostitutes, another group of women who work on the streets. Verna reported the following unsolicited opinion from a male vendor: "He said he would never let his woman work on the streets. He wanted her in an office where there is a desk between her and everyone else." Earlene, another young Black woman, said that she felt safe enough if she was on a busy corner and was visible from a lot of directions; but she added, "The men vendors are a pain in the ass; they think they own the streets and can tell you where to go and where to set up." One male vendor actually said to her, "If you're going to sell on the street, why don't you sell something expensive like your pussy and really make some money." Thus, through what they see as disrespectful comparisons, women vendors are notified that they do not belong on the streets.

The women we interviewed also felt that they were easy targets for shoplifters. As a result they were more limited in their choice of vending locations than were men vendors, and some of them were sure that there were certain areas of the city that they had to avoid entirely. This avoidance of whole areas of the city was especially true in the view of the white women, who felt particularly unprotected in Black neighborhoods.

Rhea, the fifty-five-year-old ex-sales clerk, described a situation in which another woman vendor had had merchandise stolen from her stand in full view of other vendors. She said, "Only the women vendors tried to help her—the male vendors claimed not to see a thing." Feeling particularly vulnerable to this kind of attack, few women would work on the streets at night. The fear of being ripped off in the dark becomes a serious problem in the fall and winter, when standard time is in effect, because it gets dark at rush hour—a time when people are coming out of offices and business is good.

Women vendors must learn to use a variety of survival strategies to deal with these daily problems of harassment. According to our interviews, the women engaged mainly in individual strategies but also in some cooperative strategies to protect their economic interests and their personal safety. All of these strategies are political in that they are power struggles over the right to work on public streets unmolested.

Some women told us that they made a concerted effort to appear "cool, distant, and unfriendly." Others learned to be aggressive and give tit for tat. Still others modified their dress so that they never appeared fo be wearing anything that could be described as provocative. Some of the younger women said that they went so far as to try to make themselves look unattractive and kept as much of their bodies covered as possible. Many of these women consciously learned to be as aggressive and abrasive as their attackers. Celeste told us, "You learn very fast to be as quick and as vulgar as they are, because if you do the standard female thing of being coy and shy and try to back off gently, they take it as encouragement and it gets worse." Angela, a young white woman, told the following story:

> He kept on circling the stand and telling me how much he wanted to see me later. . . . I was alone and starting to get scared . . . but I couldn't leave the stand. So, I started yelling, "Get the fuck out of here before I kick your balls in!" That stopped him in his tracks because everyone else anywhere nearby stopped to see what was going on. It's hard to do that kind of thing because women are used to trying to turn people off without hurting their feelings. . . . But if you don't learn you aren't going to make it . . . you have to try to be as aggressive as they are.

Another widely-used strategy was to select a safe vending spot. About half the women we interviewed prior to the new regulations reported choosing their own vending spots. The remainder had their locations chosen for them by the men they worked for. When possible they chose spots with heavy pedestrian traffic. Although the crowding made for more cutthroat competition for customers, it also resulted in feelings of greater safety and less possibility of being harassed or ripped off. As Lorraine told us, "If you aren't in a good location with lots of traffic, it's easy to get robbed." Earlene agreed, "It's better to be in a busy area with other vendors for safety." It is more difficult for the women to engage in cooperative strategies because the workplace is spread out across the city and there is no necessary daily contact among vendors. Some women did try to work in fairly close proximity to one another, and others reported moving to different parts of the city that they thought would be safer and then passing on this information to other women vendors. They also reported warning each other when they saw police officers coming, and most said that they would come to another woman's aid if she were in trouble.

A final strategy for survival is to give up the right to work on the streets unattended and to seek out male protection. Some women have husbands, boyfriends, or hired men watch out for them. Several women told us that they would not consider vending without such protection because the streets were dangerous and they got treated with more respect and less like prostitutes if they had a man with them.

The variety of strategies that women vendors used for daily survival were put to the test when the Washington, D.C. government joined officials in cities such as New York, Philadelphia, and Los Angeles in clamping down on the reemergence of vendors selling their wares on downtown streets. The promulgation of the new regulations in 1984 led to the development of a more collective form of action—a vendors' union—as well as the continuation of individual acts of resistance.

THE NEW REGULATIONS

In the United States, there have always been antagonistic relations between autonomous vendors and the dominant mode of distribution of consumer goods—whether that mode was public markets or mass retail outlets. Local governments have almost always passed laws to restrict vendors. From the mid-nineteenth century onward, with the growth of large-scale chain and department stores, street vending became less necessary for the feeding and clothing of both urban and rural households.[24] Vending no longer flourished, but it persisted—much to the annoyance of fixed-location businesses.

In response to the complaints of large-scale merchants, and in the hope of gaining a share of the wealth the merchants were accumulating, city governments attempted to restrict or ban all peddling from downtown streets.[25] At this same time that city governments were facilitating the accumulation process, they were also facilitating the process of male domination. Prostitutes were removed from city locations as part of an urban reform movement that believed that only "good women"—wives accompanied by husbands and children—would set the necessary high standards of behavior on city streets.[26] As a result of movements to clean up city streets, women who used these streets as a workplace did so at their own risk and were open to sexual bartering by would-be customers and to harassment by police.[27] In contrast, men were generally allowed to dominate the streets and to harass women who lingered there. Thus, state policies reinforced the idea that the streets were male turf.

In the post–World War II era, city officials became concerned with revitalizing these commercial areas by the "leveraging" of private capital with public funds, the creation of urban enterprise zones, and the use of tax abatements and interest-free loans to downtown developers.[28] With the beginning of downtown revitalization, vendors returned to downtown streets because of unemployment, immigration, and the demand for cheap goods. With the vendors' return, the historical conflict among vendors, city officials, and organized business interests moved into a new phase.

In Washington, D.C., the restriction of street vending has periodically been a consuming interest of fixed-location businesses and city officials.[29] The latest round in the conflict began with the complaints of organized business interests. These complaints resulted in the appointment in 1984 of an advisory committee to the District Office of Business and Economic Development to issue policy guidelines, to hold hearings, and to suggest new regulations.

This latest round of the conflict over vending took place in a downtown sector whose small retail shops, five-and-tens, and dowdy department stores with bargain basements catered to the city's largely Black, working-class population. This decaying sector was in the process of being turned into an upscale retail center for a growing high-income professional and managerial class.[30] The beneficiary of what has been called the "malling" of downtown Washington—with its Banana Republics, its atriums, and its futile attempt to attract Bloomingdale's—was a group of developers, investors, and retailers. They belonged to organizations such as the Board of Trade, the Connecticut Avenue Association, the Apartment and Office Building Association, the Restaurant Association, and the Chamber of Commerce.

This interest group had many resources at its disposal and presented a solid front at public hearings and in public pronouncements about the proposed regulations. Members of the group scoffed at charges that they had undue influence with the city government. At public hearings, they argued that vending displaced jobs from legitimate businesses, presented unfair competition, and failed to pay its "fair share" of taxes. They also argued that vendors gave the city a "bazaarlike image" by selling shoddy goods and creating dirt and crowding. They suggested that vending be greatly curtailed if not banished from the rapidly gentrifying downtown streets.

Although the public role of the District government was to mediate among this interest group, the vendors, and the public interest, the government was accused by the vendors of being "in cahoots" with the Board of Trade. Publicly, city officials stated that the city government was not trying to ban vending. But, they said, because vending "had gotten out of hand," they were exercising their responsibility to regulate congestion, dirt, crowding, and the collection of tax revenues in as equitable a manner as possible.[31] This image of fairness was maintained by the appointment of an Advisory Commission composed of representatives from fixed-location businesses, vendors, and the community. In addition, public hearings were held on the new regulations that this commission recommended. In private, however, one official said that street vending was not congruent with the image that the city government wished to project to investors. Vending was seen as unattractive to investors in the newly developing downtown areas, because of its "Indian-bazaar appearance."

The new regulations that were promulgated by the District government, based on the recommendations of the Advisory Commission, did not ban all vendors from the streets as many retail merchants desired. They did contain the following antivendor provisions: a large decrease in the number of vending licenses to be issued and a limitation on the number of vendors allowed to sell in the most desirable downtown locations; a sevenfold increase in the cost of a license to $106, along with the payment of a $500 cash bond; an increase in the space required between vendors and between vendors and fixed location businesses; and a limitation on the kinds of goods that vendors could sell. In addition, the new regulations mandated that vendors must sell their goods from a wooden cart that met a precise set of design criteria and cost at least $700.

VENDORS AND THE STRUGGLE AGAINST THE REGULATIONS

The third group in the conflict were the vendors. In public testimony they contended that the new regulations were the result of an effort by fixed-location businesses to stifle low-cost competition and that the city was working hand in glove with the Board of Trade. At these hearings, however, no collective strategy was apparent, and some vendors appeared willing to ensure their own survival at the expense of other types of vendors. For example, representatives of the roadway vendors argued for restrictions against sidewalk vendors; representatives of District vendors argued that they should be given priority over out-of-state vendors; and both Black and white U.S.–born vendors spoke out against non-native–born vendors.

The lack of collective strategies was evident during the first forty-five days after the enactment of the new regulations, when the Police Department's special vending unit was instructed to issue warning citations rather than levying fines, seizing property or making arrests. During this period many vendors used an individualistic strategy of selective disobedience and resisted some of the regulations with relative impunity. Most did not purchase the specially designed wooden carts. Others sold goods prohibited by the regulations. Still others set up their stands in spots that were illegal under the new regulations.

Believing that individual selective disobedience would not keep them on the streets, a group of 150 to 200 vendors banded together and founded a union. This union was part of Local 82 of the Service Employees International Union. This was the first time (according to AFL–CIO spokesmen) that street vendors had organized in a major city in the United States. Although approximately 20 percent of the members were women, the organizers of the vendor unit were mainly Black Muslim men. They claimed a sense of kinship with the low-paid service workers despite the fact that the vendors were not just wage workers but also small-business owners. "We are business people, but we are also laborers," sad Kwasi Abdul Jahlil, a vendor who became president of the union local. "Vendors lack political and economic clout held by groups like the Board of Trade. Like service workers we're at the bottom." Despite their consciousness of the power of the organized-business interests, the majority of vendors continued to practice individual noncompliance and did not become involved in any collective action.

After the union was formed, it took a unified stand opposing the regulations and was able to exert pressure on the mayor to modify them in what it perceived to be the interests of all vendors. Although most of the union's members were Black men, they made efforts to get other ethnic groups involved in the union, appointing a Korean vendor as a representative of the "Oriental vendor community."

The union's first major action was to file a lawsuit in U.S. District Court challenging the constitutionality of the new regulations. The presiding judge expressed his sympathy for vendors who would lose their livelihood but nonetheless upheld the regulations' constitutionality and legitimated the city government's right to enforce them. The union responded by filing a motion for reconsideration but dropped it in the face of the mayor's offer to suspend enforcement of some of the merchandise limitations and the cart requirement.

At union meetings the leadership attempted to build a feeling of strength and solidarity. After the union lost the first round of the court case, the treasurer told the forty people assembled at a meeting, "We're still going to struggle. We're going to try and build a political movement. We're making history."

But the male leadership's attempt at building solidarity often had a macho style. Dressed in army fatigues and combat boots, members of the political action committee gave long lectures on how they prevented crime on the streets in the neighborhoods where they vended. In contrast, of course, many of the women felt that they themselves were the targets of crime and harassment, even from male vendors. At one meeting, a woman who said that she was having difficulty organizing other vendors in her area was told that the Arabs she was talking to were real revolutionaries who did not want her to waste their time. When she protested that she wasn't talking to Arabs, she was hushed up. The union's treasurer talked about getting tough with those vendors who would not join the union by surrounding their carts. Finally, meeting attendees were warned that anyone who was not willing to be arrested in the struggle should not be a vendor.

In addition to the lawsuit, the union used a variety of other tactics in order to get the regulations modified. Union representatives met with the mayor and with members of the City Council. Union members began displaying signs depicting the mayor as a puppet of bigger business interests. They picketed, demonstrated, held press conferences, and had petitions signed by their customers. The union's president was arrested (the only male who was). These tactics produced some relief for the vendors—the pre-enforcement period was extended, the standardized cart requirement was abandoned, merchandise constraints were narrowed, and the mayor appointed yet another commission to study the problem. The $606 bond and license fee, the spacing requirements, and the curtailment of downtown vending spots, however, became law.

WOMEN'S RESISTANCE TO THE REGULATIONS

The women we talked with during this period were frustrated, worried, and angry. They had difficulty finding out what the new regulations were. They worried about keeping their spots, their inability to afford the new fees, and their inability to afford, manipulate, and store the new carts; and they worried that their jobs would become more dangerous if too many other women vendors left the streets. Once again, they used a variety of strategies to deal with these new threats to their livelihood. But though they worried about the regulations' impact on both their livelihood and their safety, no collective strategies developed around the issue of safety on the streets.

In daily conversations with other vendors, the woman vented their anger at the city government. They complained about the cost of the license fees and the burden of the heavy wooden carts. They said that women vendors were in a different economic position from men, who often owned several stands, and that therefore they were less able to pay the fee. Tawana, who could not afford the $606 license and bond fee, and whose employer would not pay for fees or carts for all the vendors who worked for him, cried, "I was on welfare. Now I support my two kids on my vending income. I will go back on welfare. This city is so stupid. Here they have people working and off welfare, but with these new regulations lots of jobs will be lost." The women we interviewed thought that the regulations would have a more negative impact on them than on the men vendors, who they thought were better able to pay the licensing fees.

Though the licensing and bond fee was considered a burden by many of the women, the regulation requiring the heavy wooden carts that had to be removed from the streets nightly brought forth even more ire from the women we interviewed. As Shirleen, a young Black woman who vended because she had epilepsy and could not hold a steady job, said, "Those carts are a real problem. They have to be taken off the streets at night. Where can I store it? I don't have a car and I can't get it into my apartment building." Even those women who said that they could live with the new license fees claimed that women would have trouble loading and unloading the heavy carts and that this requirement would make them less able to survive on their own.

During this round of interviewing, we asked women if they would try to keep working as vendors even if the new regulations were enforced. Two out of three of the women who owned their own stands said that they would try to keep working as vendors, but one-third said they could not afford the new fees. Among the women who worked for somebody else, more than one out of two thought that they would be forced to quit or were not sure that they would be able to continue vending. Thus, between one-third and one-half of the forty women we interviewed during this period did not expect to be able to continue to earn a livelihood at a job that despite its drawbacks gave them a sense of freedom and economic independence.

The women were equally worried that the new regulations would make the streets more dangerous for them because they would not be able to use some of their usual survival strategies. For example, by requiring that vendor stands be at least 10 feet apart and by decreasing the number of vendors allowed at many locations, the new regulations made it more difficult to use the "safety in numbers" strategy. The women worried about the dwindling numbers of vendors even if, as a result, they did more business. As one of the flower vendors told us,

> If there are a lot fewer vendors no one can help anyone out. On a regular Saturday there are lots of vendors so you can take a break and have someone watch your stuff. With fewer vendors it's harder to work. It's not good to be too busy to watch for shoplifters. It may be less competitive, but I don't like it.

As the warning period for the new regulations went into effect, the women, like the men vendors, were selectively disobedient, choosing the regulations that they would follow and the ones that they would not. Most of the women we interviewed during this period claimed that they would continue this strategy of selective disobedience after the warning period. As Jackie said, "I'll paint my table and put up an umbrella, but I'm not pushing that ton of weight [the cart] around for anyone."

Like the men vendors, the majority of women we interviewed did not join the union even though they had a consciousness of themselves as vendors in opposition to the Board of Trade. Rose, a fifty-five-year-old Black woman, told us that she did not think that it would do any good to unionize because the Board of Trade was too powerful. But if the union did win any battles, she reasoned, the benefits would spill over to her anyway whether she joined or not. Other women told us that they were not interested in paying dues or sitting through meetings, or "paying for the privilege of being ignored" by the men running the union. Their strong sense of individualism and their experience in solving problems by themselves made it difficult for them to want to participate in what some of them perceived as a hierarchical union structure (with men at the top of the hierarchy). Women were also discouraged from joining the union by the men they worked for. As one woman told us, "The man I work for thinks that the union is garbage and just a way to get another trade to pay dues."

Betty Galloway, the union's vice president, suggested to us that more women would have to become owners before they would join the union. Thus the pattern of half-owners and half-paid workers in the District was a drawback to union membership and solidarity. In addition, Galloway suggested that the police discouraged many vendors from joining the union, especially Asian women who barely spoke the language. The lack of daily contact between vendors, who were spread out over the city, made organizing them difficult. And last, many women did not join the union because they did not have the time. Even Galloway dropped out because she said she had to be on the street making money and did not have time to keep going to meetings and demonstrations.

Despite these problems, some of the women did take the step of engaging in collective political action and did join the union. Like men vendors, the women joined because they wanted more political clout to effectively fight the regulations so that they could continue to work on the streets. Those women who did join were active in the local—attending union meetings, producing posters, demonstrating, circulating petitions, encouraging other vendors to join, and lobbying City Council members. Galloway, for example, had often been a spokesperson for the union in interviews with the press, the mayor, and City Council members.

As union women fought the regulations side by side with union men, they kept silent about their experiences with men on the streets and with male vendors. Problems with harassment and safety were not raised as issues in the union campaign. When asked why not, Olivia told us that to raise these issues would not be fruitful at a time when the union was fighting to modify the regulations. "Maybe later," she suggested. Another woman activist told us that she had tried to raise some women's issues, but that they "got washed over." "Maybe later," she suggested, "when there are more women in the union." This was never to come to pass because the union fell apart shortly after the revised regulations went into effect.

There were some obvious reasons women's issues were not raised within the union structure. The first was the perceived need for solidarity among union members as they attempted to fight the regulations. The issue of sexual harassment, especially where men vendors were the perpetrators, would have been divisive. Women members were willing to put their needs on hold for what they saw as the greater good of the union. Second was the women's lack of numerical strength (union officers estimated that only 20 percent of the members were women) and the macho style of union meetings. As Betty Galloway recalled, "It was tough working with those guys. Most of them were Muslims who thought that women should be at home with the kids—they didn't respect women who were out on the streets."

Thus, like women in other nontraditional jobs where the harassers are fellow union members, women vendors did not publicly raise the issue but continued to use individual strategies to cope.[32] Despite the fact that street harassment was as much a bread-and-butter issue for women as the kinds of merchandise they could sell, many women did not perceive sexual harassment as an economic issue but as an expected consequence of working on the streets.

Although they were not successful in bringing up women's issues, and ultimately were not successful in preventing many women from having to leave vending, those women who participated in the union had a sense of empowerment. Some of them, like Galloway, were in visible positions, whether they felt respected or not. As Galloway stated, "I fought them [the Muslim leadership of the union] and I fought the city, and I stood up for myself, and I'm still here!"

CONCLUSIONS

This case study describes how women vendors try to earn a decent living on Washington, D.C. streets, where they are regarded as purveyors of dirt, crowding, and unfair competition by bigger, politically influential businesses. This study reveals that women who vend on the streets are visible targets for harassment for male customers, male vendors, and the police. Because urban streets are still seen as male turf, places where nice women do not linger, many men feel free to act as if the women themselves are objects for sale. In response to a costly, well-organized effort by investors and retailers in the new upscale "malling" of downtown, Washington District officials, like their Third World counterparts, promulgated new regulations designed to curtail severely the number of street vendors.

In response to these strict new regulations, women vendors, like their male coworkers, used a number of strategies to stay in business. The most effective of these strategies was the formation of a union to fight the regulations and counter the influence of the Board of Trade. The union was successful in modifying some of the regulations and getting rid of others. It was successful in gaining some political power. Betty Galloway—the former union vice president—was offered an appointment by the mayor to a new vending Advisory Committee charged with developing activities that could stabilize the economic base for those vendors who remained.[33] Galloway turned the appointment down because she needed to be "out on the streets making money." But she stated, "The struggle over the regulations raised the political awareness of the vendors, and, as a result, the mayor—he had to become more accountable to 'the little guy.' "

The union was not successful in getting rid of the high bond and licensing costs required by the new regulations, and many vendors had to leave the streets. The most recent figures available from the Department of Consumer and Regulatory Affairs indicate that women vendors were right in their fears that they would have to leave the streets if the new regulations were implemented. By June 1986 there were only twelve hundred licensed vendors on the streets of Washington, D.C., down from the fifty-six hundred who were operating when this study began. District officials are calling the results "a success." According to one such official, "Vending had gotten out of control. . . . This year, the streets are less congested. We lost more than four thousand vendors when the bond requirements went in."[34]

Both male and female vendors were affected by the new regulations. The Board of Trade and other politically influential groups of merchants and investors did not appear to single out women vendors for special persecution. The regulations they asked for were gender-neutral in their attempt to get all vendors off the streets. According to the women I interviewed most recently, the regulations have had a negative impact on male vendors, but they have had a worse impact on women. Women vendors were less likely to own several stands and hence were less likely to be able to afford the new licenses. And, in contrast to the men, the women face more street and sexual harassment. Harassment is especially severe when there are fewer women on the streets to help protect one another. Estimates from the 1986 District of Columbia Government printouts of vending license applicants indicate that a greater proportion of women than men have left the streets. One consequence of the regulations, therefore, has been to move a group of women away from economic independence in a city with more than 40 percent of female-headed households living in poverty. With fewer women vendors on the street, those who remain feel more dependent on men and police to protect them.

Although women vendors developed both individual and cooperative survival strategies to cope with harassment, they had difficulty seeing harassment as a political and economic issue. It was also hard for women who needed to see themselves as autonomous, tough, and street-wise to admit publicly that they felt afraid, powerless, and vulnerable on male turf. As a result women vendors did not raise harassment as a public issue but rather dealt with it as an individual problem.

The ideology that sexual harassment is a personal problem is strong, and its strength is reinforced by a government policy that removes women from the streets. City officials did not appear to be interested in discriminating against women vendors. The intended purpose of the new regulations was to curtail the dirt, congestion, and competition created by all vendors. By assuming that the regulations were gender neutral without exploring the alternate possibility, city officials increased women vendors' dependence on men and increased male domination of the streets. By increasing male domination of public and economic life, city policy reinforced public patriarchy.[35]

Despite their intensifying struggle for economic and political autonomy, many women, including most of the vendors we interviewed, accept male domination of city streets as natural. As a result, they frequently fail to organize as a conscious constituency. Women are less likely than men to use streets, parks, and other public places, thus themselves contributing to public patriarchy or male domination of public life.[36] Campaigns for a "hassle-free zone" conducted by the local rape crisis center to raise consciousness about street harassment as a public issue are an important antidote.[37] Likewise the presence of women vendors on the streets is another antidote. As a young flower vendor stated, "The more women become vendors, the more people will accept them, the less people will think it's freaky and try and keep them vulnerable."

ACKNOWLEDGMENTS

I would like to thank George Washington University's Center for Washington Area Studies and especially Professors Howard Gillette and Jeffrey Henig for all their efforts in making this study possible. In addition, I would like to thank Jennie McKnight for her patient and skillful editing; Mindy Shapiro for her assistance in coding and interviewing; Micaela di Leonardaro, Phyllis Palmer, Karen Sacks, Tara Wallace, and John Willoughby for their helpful reading of earlier drafts; and Ann Bookman and Sandra Morgen for their many editorial and content suggestions. Finally, I would like to thank Eileen Zeitz for her work on earlier versions of this study and Hank Leland for his final editing.

NOTES

1. The distinction between vendors in the informal and tertiary sectors depends on whether or not they are counted as workers in government censuses. Informal-sector workers are not counted.

2. For a description of these problems in Lima, Peru, see Ximena Bunster and Elsa M. Chaney, *Sellers and Servants: Working Women in Lima, Peru* (New York: Praeger, 1985).

3. For a description of (and rating system for) a variety of government policies in Southeast Asia on street vending, including antivending policies that discourage vendors

by high license fees, legal punishment, and banishment from all city locations, see T. C. McGee and Y. M. Yeung, *Hawkers in Southeast Asian Cities: Planning for the Bazaar Economy* (Ottawa: International Development Research Center, 1977).

4. For a discussion of this phenomenon in Africa, especially in Uganda, see Christine Obbo, *African Women: Their Struggle for Economic Independence* (London: Zed Press, 1980), esp. 25.

5. For two summary articles on street vending in cities throughout the United States, see John C. Freed, "Surge in Street Vendors Evokes Mixed Reviews," *New York Times*, July 20, 1985, A6, and Constance Mitchell, "Downtown's Overflowing with Vendors," *U.S.A. Today*, August 23, 1983, A1.

6. For some of the important scholarship in this tradition, see Lourdes Arizpe, "Women in the Informal Sector: The Case of Mexico City," *Signs: Journal of Women in Culture and Society* 3 (Autumn 1977): 45–59; Florence Babb, "Women in the Marketplace: Petty Commerce in Peru," *Review of Radical Political Economy* 16 (Spring 1984): 45–59; Victoria Durant-Gonzalez, "Higglering: Rural Women and the Internal Market System in Jamaica," P. I. Gomes, ed., *Rural Development in the Caribbean* (New York: St. Martin's, 1985), 103–122; Karen Transberg Hansen, "The Informal Sector as a Development Issue: Poor Women and Work in Lusaka, Zambia," *Urban Anthropology* 9 (Fall 1980): 199–225; Dorothy Remy, "Underdevelopment and the Experience of Women: A Nigerian Case Study," in Rayna Reiter, ed., *Toward an Anthropology of Women* (New York: Monthly Review Press, 1975), 358–371.

7. The description of these women as actors with definite strategies comes from Obbo, *African Women*, esp. 144.

8. Bunster and Chaney, *Sellers and Servants*, esp. 98–101.

9. Babb, "Women in the Marketplace," 45–59, esp. 55.

10. Obbo, *African Women*, esp. 156.

11. Ibid., esp. 158.

12. For some examples of feminist work on the relationship between street harassment and city policy, see Jos Boys, "Women and Public Space," in Matrix Books, ed., *Making Space: Women and the Man-Made Environment* (London: Pluto Press, 1985), 37–54; Galen Cranz, "Women in Urban Parks," in Catherine R. Stimpson et al., eds., *Women and the American City* (Chicago: University of Chicago Press, 1981), 76–92; and Christene Stansell, "Women, Children and the Use of the Streets: Class and Gender Conflicts in New York City, 1850–1860," *Feminist Studies* 8 (Summer 1982): 309–335.

13. For a discussion of the lack of research on how women are given the message that they are out of place in public spaces, see Gerda R. Wekerle, "Women in the Urban Environment," in Stimpson et al., eds., *Women in the American City*, 185–211. For a brief report on a feminist effort to do research on assaults on women and children in Toronto parks, Gerda R. Wekerle, "Space and Women's Safety," *Urban Resources: Special Issue on Women in the City* 3 (Winter 1986): 28. For a study of sexual harassment at outdoor workplaces such as construction sites, see Suzanne C. Carothers and Peggy Crull, "Contrasting Sexual Harassment in Female- and Male-dominated Occupations," in Karen Brodkin Sacks and Dorothy Remy, eds., *My Troubles Are Going to Have Trouble with Me: Everyday Trials and Triumphs of Women Workers* (New Brunswick, N.J.: Rutgers University Press, 1984), 219–228.

14. See McGee and Yeung, *Hawkers in Southeast Asian Cities.*

15. As noted, the gender distribution of vendors was determined by their given names. We went through a printout of the 4,200 vendors listed in the District of Columbia

Department of Consumer and Regulatory Affairs 1984 license file, categorizing each vendor as "male," "female," or "don't know." If we could not decide, names were put into the "don't know" category, which includes names like "Robin" or "Terry," and Asian, some Middle Eastern, and African names. We thus determined that vendors were 22 percent female, 65 percent male, and 13 percent of unknown gender. Assuming the same ratio for the unknowns, we estimated that one in four vendors was a woman.

16. See, Roberta M. Spalter-Roth and Eileen Zeitz, "Street Vending in Washington, D.C.: Reassessing the Regulation of a Public Nuisance," Occasional Paper No. 3 (Washington, D.C.: George Washington University Center for Washington Area Studies, September 1985).

17. Maria Meis, "Towards a Methodology for Feminist Research," in Gloria Bowles and Renate Duelli Klein, eds., *Theories of Women's Studies* (London: Routledge & Kegan Paul, 1983), 117–139, esp. 122.

18. For a study of racial conflict between white registered nurses and Black ward secretaries that nearly destroyed solidarity during a hospital walkout, see Karen Brodkin Sacks, "Computers, Ward Secretaries, and a Walkout in a Southern Hopsital," in Sacks and Remy, eds., *My Troubles*, 173–190.

19. As quoted in Linda Wheeler, "Street Vendors Scarce as Rules Begin," *The Washington Post*, May 16, 1985, C3.

20. The term "disguised wage laborer" was coined by Babb, "Women in the Marketplace," 45–59.

21. For example, Bunster and Chaney, *Sellers and Servants*, esp. 93, describe these feelings of autonomy and independence.

22. See *Women, Employment and Training: A Status Report on Programs and Needs in the District of Columbia*, compiled by the D.C. Women's Employment and Training Coalition (Washington, D.C.: District of Columbia Commission on the Status of Women, 1985), esp. 46.

23. Carothers and Crull, "Contrasting Sexual Harassment," 219–228, esp. 222.

24. Susan Strasser, *Never Done: A History of American Housework* (New York: Pantheon, 1982), esp. 14–30.

25. *Improving the Management of Downtown Public Spaces: A National Overview of Programs for Private Sector Downtown Organizations* (New York: Project for Public Spaces, 1982).

26. Cranz, "Women in Urban Parks," 76–92.

27. Stansell, "Women, Children and the Uses of the Streets," 309–335.

28. For discussion of these processes, see Todd Swanstrom, *The Crisis of Growth Politics* (Philadelphia: Temple University Press, 1985), or John M. Mollenkopf, *The Contested City* (Princeton: Princeton University Press, 1983).

29. The notion of periods of "consuming interest" in street vending by fixed-location businesses is based on a perusal of newspaper articles, dating from 1910, under the heading "Street Vendors" in the Washingtoniana Division of the Martin Luther King, Jr., Memorial Library of the District Public Libraries.

30. Mark Jenkin, "Malling the Core: Suburban Visions Conquer Downtown," *City Paper*, Washington, D.C., July 25–31, 1986, esp. 8 and 14.

31. For an interview with Benjamin Johnson, an administrator with the Business Regulatory Administration who consistently gave voice to this view, see Paul Thiel, "D.C. Vending Problems Reduced Since New Rules Took Effect," *Washington Post*, July 14, 1986, Washington Business Section, 3.

32. See Corothers and Crull, "Contrasting Sexual Harassment," 219–228, esp. 25.

33. See Mayor's Order 86–84, "Establishment—Mayor's Advisory Committee on Street Vending," *District of Columbia Register,* August 8, 1986, 4843–4849.

34. Benjamin Johnson, as quoted in Thiel, "D.C. Vending Problems Reduced Since New Rules Took Effect," 3.

35. Here I am defining "patriarchy" as a set of power relations, legitimated by state force, that assume the dominance of males in public positions, politics, economic life, and social life. This is based on the definition given in Jean Grossholtz, "Battered Women's Shelters and the Political Economy of Sexual Violence," in Irene Diamond, ed., *Families, Politics and Public Policy* (New York: Longman), 59–69, esp. 60.

36. For a survey of these fears and strategies, see Gordon et al., "Crime, Women and the Quality of Urban Life," in Stimpson et al., *Women and the American City,* 141–157.

37. Unfortunately, campaigns against harassment and public violence directed at women are often ignored by city planners who do not or will not see the relationship between the design of public streets and facilities and the vulnerability of women. According to Wekerle, "Space and Women's Safety," *Urban Resources* 3, sometimes the spatial and planning component of public violence is not well understood by the feminist community or by the media, city officials, and urban investors.

GRASSROOTS ORGANIZING

AND POLITICAL THEORY:

TOWARD A SYNTHESIS

V

GRASSROOTS ORGANIZING

AND POLITICAL THEORY

TOWARD A SYNTHESIS

13

Communities, Resistance, and Women's Activism: Some Implications for a Democratic Polity

Martha A. Ackelsberg

Women have been, and continue to be, centrally involved in resistance movements in many workplaces and neighborhoods. Studies reported in this volume and elsewhere document the active role of women in social movements and challenge the conventional view of women as passive members of the polity who live their lives in a private sphere protected (in the case of middle- or upper-class women) or isolated (in the case of working-class women) from the mainstream of "public" life and politics. Not only have women been active in what have been presumed to be the male preserves of work and political life; a closer look at women's lives belies the notion of distinct public and private spheres altogether. Although an ideological split between "public" and "private," community and workplace may be alive and well in American political ideology—even among feminists—women's activities challenge the existence of the distinction in practice.

In this article I examine the patterns of women's activities and the relationship of activist women to their communities. In the first sections I explore the limits of both American pluralist ideology and of many of the Marxist and neo-Marxist critiques of pluralism. I then examine the implications of women's activism for a more comprehensive conception of democratic politics.

DEMOCRATIC THEORY AND DEMOCRATIC CITIZENSHIP
Democratic theory (particularly in the "pluralist" form dominant in the contemporary United States) rests on certain assumptions about people, their interests, their relationships with others, and their relationship to the larger polity, each of

which must be unraveled before our analysis can proceed. Liberal theories of democracy assume self-interested individuals with clearly felt needs and preferences. Each of these individuals aims to assure the attainment of his or her ends or, in utilitarian terms, the maximization of his or her interests.[1] In theory, a democratic political community treats each of these individuals equally, guaranteeing to all its members the right to pursue their own ends as they see fit, while setting as few constraints as possible on the definition of what those ends might be.[2] Politics—and even community—take on essentially instrumental value: We engage with others primarily for the purpose of achieving our individually chosen ends.

In the above view, interest in politics is not significantly different from interest in any other set of activities: some of us may enjoy softball, others reading, and still others, politics. Those who find fulfillment in attempts to manipulate power engage in what is termed "political life"—voting, lobbying, or even running for elective office. The rest of us (the vast majority) turn our attention to politics only when we feel our interests directly threatened.[3] Apathy or nonparticipation is the normal state. We can assume people's consent to prevailing policies unless they indicate their dissent through action. Since political life is of real interest only to a few, differences in degrees of influence or power within the polity are the result of differences in degrees of participation: the greater influence of some is a direct consequence of their more consistent participation.

A variety of critics of U.S. democracy have argued that this model is fundamentally flawed, that it limits our understanding of politics and the political process, masks significant levels of discontent, and mystifies the actual exercise of power and influence in the United States.[4] First, political interests are not analogous to an interest in football. Since politics involves decision making about public matters, it is, in fact, of concern to all. When we define politics narrowly, as activities in the electoral political arena, for example, we treat politics as a specialized activity of concern only to a few. This move effectively *depoliticizes politics;* it prevents many citizens from recognizing that their concerns could be represented on the larger political agenda and convinces them that "politics" is an activity beyond their ken. The seeming apathy that results from such experiences is less a sign of popular consent to the political process (or to the outcome of voting, for example) than of people's frustration with the options available to them and, ultimately, of resignation to their relative powerlessness.[5]

Second, as many of the case studies in this volume attest, who participates (effectively) in political life is not simply a matter of who happens to be interested in politics. People's perceptions of themselves and their possibilities are very much affected by their position in the social and economic structure of our society, by levels of education, and by a variety of factors that contribute to a sense of "political efficacy"—including, for example, in the case of the electronics workers studied by Louise Lamphere and Guillermo, J. Grenier in Chapter 10—efforts on the part of the authorities to undermine the development of a sense of efficacy.

Finally, citizens do not meet as equals in a free and open political arena. In any structure of relationships (including pluralist democracy), some interests are perceived as more legitimate than others—and those who articulate them are treated with greater respect. Even beyond that, the resources available to people, whether as individuals or as members of groups, vary greatly; as a consequence, representatives of some "interests" (especially those of the status quo) have much readier access to formal structures of political power and influence than others. Even on its own terms, then, the pluralist model is flawed. But, as we shall see, women's experiences of resistance highlight other serious problems with this model.

DEMOCRATIC IDEOLOGY AND THE DEFINITION OF THE POLITICAL

Crucial to the development of either resistance or resignation is the prevailing societal definition of what constitutes the appropriate subject matter of politics.[6] If what matters most to me is considered not to be appropriate to "politics," I will tend not to participate in (electoral) political activity. Furthermore, in the absence of a community to validate my perceptions, I may well come to see my own concerns as "merely" personal and profess little interest in politics. (Articles by Sandra Morgen and Ida Susser in this volume [*Chapter 4 and Chapter 11*] provide evidence of these sorts of perceptions—and of their changing through activism.) If the activities I undertake in the larger political context are ignored, or their political significance denied, my frustration may well end in resignation and the process of the production of consent. Examples of this phenomenon include the early efforts of women in the United States and Britain to gain the suffrage; civil disorders and unrest on the part of Blacks in this country during the 1960s (characterized by Edward Banfield, for example, as "rioting mainly for fun and profit"[7]); and many activities of the contemporary women's movement. As numerous feminist critics have pointed out in recent years, prevailing societal expectations that "woman's place is in the home" have contributed both to many women's perception of themselves as apolitical and to the failure of many political analysts to recognize women's activities *as* political.[8]

What is defined as "political"—that is, as publicly relevant—determines what is available for open discussion, the categories in which people come to understand their experience, and the possibilities they see for resistance. I wish to focus here on two aspects of the structuring of political consciousness in the United States that are particularly problematic when we attempt to understand women's political behavior: the split between public and private, and the relationship between individuals and their community(ies). With respect to both of these formulations, much contemporary democratic theory posits dichotomous separations that misrepresent the experience of many women and, I will argue,

make it difficult for us even to imagine what a truly democratic, participatory
polity might look like.

EXPLORING THE "PUBLIC–PRIVATE SPLIT"

Three arenas of research on the so-called public–private split are of particular
interest to us here. The first, less overtly focused on women, has been the purview of political economists: a concern with the division between economics and
politics in American political ideology and its implications for political resistance. The second, a concern with the supposed separation between the public
and domestic realms, and the relegation of women primarily to the domestic, has
been the focus of many works by feminist social theorists. Finally, urbanologists
have explored the separation of public and private space in the structure of urban
and suburban life. While the foci of these studies are different, these critics point
to the fact that both in ideology and in the physical structures of our lives Americans tend to divide the world into public and private spheres; and, furthermore,
that this division is detrimental both to radical political organizing and to women.

The ideological separation of economics and politics, or workplace and
community, is one manifestation of the public–private split. A number of recent
studies have focused on different aspects of this conceptual division, which treats
economic issues (those related to the workplace or to the distribution of income
and economic power in the society more generally) as private, not properly falling within the purview of public, political control. One effect of this division is
the virtual sanctification of "private property" in American political life. More
generally, the dichotomizing perspective prevents people from seeing the ways
in which their work relationships affect their home and community lives, or the
ways in which political decisions (or nondecisions) affect economic relationships. Most important, that perspective helps to sustain the perception that
there is nothing citizens can do, either as individuals or as members of communities, to affect the broader context of economic and political relationships in
which their daily lives are embedded.[9]

Sexual stereotyping, the designation of separate "public" and "domestic"
realms and the relegation of women to the latter, further compounds the public–
private distinction. In its earliest formulations (with roots in Aristotle's *Politics*),
politics was identified with the public, moral world and limited to men; the
home, the arena of private morality, was assigned to women. In post-Machiavel-
lian times, politics came to be identified with the amoral, male domain of force;
the home became the symbol of purity, morality, and privacy, the domain of
women. In this view, women have no proper place in the public sphere; their
participation is neither encouraged nor welcomed.[10] When women have acted
outside their homes (which, despite this ideology, women have been doing for
centuries, whether as workers or as activists), their activities have often been
ignored or ridiculed, defined as lying outside the domain of politics properly
construed.[11]

The full effect of these ideological separations limits both the agenda of politics and the range of likely participants. On the one hand, the dichotomization weakens the impact of moral issues on politics and excludes what are perceived as private concerns from public discussion. Many women, as a result, have found that the issues of greatest concern to them (safe neighborhoods, decent jobs, day care and education for their children, availability of health care) have been treated as irrelevant, or of secondary significance to politics.

Most recently, feminist urbanologists have explored the confluence of these two dichotomies in the *spatial* separation of workplaces and communities, both in terms of the sources of the division (its roots in patriarchal relationships and in capitalism) and of its *consequences* for women (the overrepresentation of poor women and children in central cities, with inadequate access to jobs and services).[12] They argue that women are particularly disadvantaged by the separation of workplace from residence and the inadequacy of facilities for the care of young children. As a result of the translation of this dichotomous thinking into social policy, many women do not have the freedom (from child-care responsibilities) necessary to take advantage even of those jobs that do exist.

Each of these schools of analysis points to the ways in which prevailing stereotypes and ideologies about the public–private split limit our conceptions of what constitutes the appropriate subject matter of politics and consequently limit the ability of many people (and, in particular, women, workers, or people of color) effectively to introduce their concerns into the political arena. Conversely, when members of such "out" groups *do* take action on their own behalf, its political significance is often ignored or denied, again on the basis of prevailing conceptions of what constitutes "political" action.

INDIVIDUALITY AND COMMUNITY

Although the liberal theory of democracy is rooted in a presumed separation between the public and private realms (designed to protect the individual from the demands or encroachments of others), it also rests on a series of assumptions about the relationship of individuals to their communities more generally. I suggested earlier that liberal democratic theory asserts the priority of the individual, with his or her wants and needs as *given;* and that the purpose of the political community is to provide the least restrictive environment possible in which each may pursue his or her own ends. Freedom, then, means to be let alone; and politics (and community) take on a purely *instrumental* value. Finally, citizens will often find themselves in conflict with others over the realization of their interests. (Political) communities stand both as the arenas in which we fight out these conflicts, and, at times, as protagonists in them.

In this theoretical context, the key problem of politics is to overcome at least some of what is perceived as "natural" self-interest and to create allegiance to a *community,* to something *larger* than the self. Given their tendency to naturalize self-interest, democratic theorists recognized that a considerable imposition of force, a major transformation of the human psyche, or massive "public education" would be necessary to create community.

However, the individualist premises of the liberal paradigm provide little basis for that community other than "interests," which, in the words of Irene Diamond and Nancy Hartsock, "reduce the human community to an instrumental, arbitrary, and deeply unstable alliance."[13] Further, the methodological individualism implicit in the liberal perspective obscures the extent to which the desire for *connection* and *relationship* is a human need, not just a means to achieve individually focused ends.[14] Liberalism denies, that is, that politics is about more than simply meeting individual needs: that it can be, as well, an arena in which people work together with others and find pleasure and fulfillment in mutuality. Finally, in its insistence that all people come to politics equally, as individuals, the liberal paradigm denies people their roots *in* communities (a fact that particularly denies the social reality of many Black and white working-class women's lives); denies the class, race, and ethnic constitution *of* communities; and further masks the impact of economic inequality on political participation. In sum, the liberal paradigm tends to homogenize and isolate people in the name of preserving and protecting individuality.[15]

WOMEN'S ACTIVISM AND DEMOCRATIC POLITICS

Attention to the many forms of women's activism and resistance highlights the limitations of these dichotomous forms of thinking. As Cynthia Cockburn has argued, and Ida Susser has demonstrated in this volume (*Chapter 11*), even women's traditional household roles may lead them into activities that challenge the very assumption of a dichotomy between public and private, community and workplace. Women in industrial societies bear primary responsibility for the nurturance of both children and adult males within their households. But that responsibility means that women must be active in the urban arena considerably beyond the boundaries of the so-called domestic sphere: They are the ones who negotiate with landlords, markets, welfare officers, health-care providers, and the like. They are the ones who must make the adjustment when wages, prices, or rents fluctuate. Far from being isolated in the home, most working- and middle-class women are forced into relationships with a variety of people and institutions in the so-called public sphere. Women dependent on public assistance, in particular, but others as well, soon come to recognize that the state and other public institutions have an immediate impact on their daily lives. Carrying that recognition one step further, women have joined together with their friends and neighbors to meet their needs and, often, to demand of public institutions that they fulfill their obligations to citizens. As Wendy Luttrell summarizes the situation of community women in her article in this volume (*Chapter 6*), "Their ability to change roles and to negotiate between the world of politics, community, and families grew directly from those multiple responsibilities [as workers, wives, and mothers]. . . ."[16]

Making these sorts of connections is not new for women. Scholars have uncovered a long tradition of women's activism that specifically bridges the community–workplace dichotomy. We now know that women have been leaders and activists in "bread riots" and tenant organizations; that they have participated actively in factory-based strikes that engendered, and depended on, local community support; that they have led struggles for new and better schools.[17] In each of these cases, not only have women crossed the boundaries between the so-called public and domestic arenas, they have also drawn on their relationships with other women (and men) to create networks through which they have engaged in public activity.

But the articles in this volume highlight the complexity of this process. On the one hand, gender, racial–ethnic, and class divisions can contribute to the development of feelings of solidarity within homogeneous groups, facilitating radical consciousness and resistance. On the other hand, those same divisions—often exacerbated by dominant social forces and institutions—can serve as barriers to the development of feelings of solidarity across those racial–ethnic or class lines and can impair the growth of resistance.

Despite these complexities, however, attention to women's networks forces us to call into question some of the basic premises of the democratic theory discussed above. For one thing, the existence of these networks suggests that women do not necessarily enter the public arena as "individuals." Networks and community associations develop from women's responses to issues that confront them not as isolated individuals but as members of households, and, more important, as members of the communities in which those households are embedded. The white working-class women Ida Susser studied in Williamsburg–Greenpoint, the Black women community workers Cheryl Townsend Gilkes describes in her articles, including that in this volume (*Chapter 2*), the members of the multiethnic coalitions Wendy Luttrell (*Chapter 6*) Andrée Nicola-McLaughlin and Zola Chandler (*Chapter 8*), and Sandra Morgen (Chapter 4) describe in Philadelphia, New York, and Fleetport, and the ethnic women workers discussed by Ann Bookman (*Chapter 7*), Patricia Zavella (*Chapter 9*) and Louise Lamphere and Guillermo J. Grenier (*Chapter 10*) did not come together as isolates, but as women strongly rooted in their class, ethnic, or cultural communities. For these women, the "problem of politics" is less that of creating an allegiance to something *other* than the self—building community out of isolated individuals—than of finding ways to link the concerns, visions, and perspectives they share with their neighbors and coworkers to the "political system" that stands apart from them and seems to control their lives.[18]

Moreover, women not only see themselves as members of communities (whether in neighborhoods or at the workplace); they work hard at developing and maintaining the networks and relationships that give life to these communities. As the work of both Carol Stack and Cheryl Gilkes makes clear in the case of contemporary urban Black communities, Black women play extremely important roles in sustaining one another and their communities, providing services to young and old, male and female.[19] Without those networks, and women's work in and for their communities, neither isolated individuals, nor even isolated families would long survive. Susser and Luttrell, in this volume, and McCourt elsewhere, have found similar patterns in white working-class and ethnic communities. Others have discussed, more generally, women's roles as "community-builders."[20] This role is hardly a modern invention, nor is it limited to neighborhood-based communities. As articles in this book document, women workers also develop "work cultures" and "work-related networks" that sustain them both in the workplace and outside it.

In addition to providing nurturance and contexts for activism, women's networks can be crucial to the process of consciousness-change. Kathleen McCourt, for example, notes that strong feelings of "community belonging" accompany activism, although it is difficult to determine the direction of causation.[21] Through working with others, confronting institutions, many women have come to a better understanding of the power relations that affect their lives and of their own abilities—together with others—to have some influence on them. The process, of course, is a dynamic one. A number of the articles in this volume show that the development of a changed consciousness is multilayered. On the one hand, participation in campaigns can contribute to refocusing and reshaping women's political analysis, enabling them to forge links between their own experience and that of others (particularly others within their own racial–ethnic class group). On the other hand, racial–ethnic and class divisions can isolate women in homogenous networks and make effective coalition-building very difficult.

As Sandra Morgen's article demonstrates, although many of the women involved in the CAFH health organizing effort began with what might appear to have been a relatively unsophisticated analysis of their local health system, their confrontation with doctors and the hospital helped them to recognize the role that assumptions about gender and class had played in the treatment they received from health professionals. Through their resistance, they developed a new understanding of the relationship among doctors, patients, and the larger socioeconomic context in which both operated—but not before class and racial–ethnic divisions among them threatened to destroy the group (and did, ultimately, lead it to disband after the "Ten Taxpayers" suit).

Similarly, McCourt's study of women in assertive community organizations in Chicago suggests that the more active women "may well be those who are experiencing an expanding realization of the ways in which they . . . are being mistreated" (p. 220)—even when their organizations are not focused on remedying that mistreatment. Zavella, Bookman, and Lamphere and Grenier all demonstrate the ways in which ethnic and class identities can draw women into supportive networks that, in turn, can aid unionization struggles that may involve cross-ethnic organizing. Cheryl Townsend Gilkes's studies of community workers in urban Black communities suggest, even beyond the development of a broader political awareness (which, because of societal racism, is a characteristic shared by Black community members more generally), a developing ability to use the connections they have—especially those crossing the boundaries between Black and white communities—to further "Black interests." In short, community-based activism, itself a product of changed consciousness, can, in turn, generate new knowledge, a renewed commitment to resistance, and new—possibly more effective—strategies of resistance.

To put it another way, for many of the women discussed in these studies, the process of coming to political consciousness seems to be a process of making connections—between their own lives and those of others, between issues that affect them and their families in the neighborhood or community and those that affect them in the workplace, between the so-called differing spheres of their lives—a process of overcoming precisely the "fragmented consciousness" that, in Katznelson's view, constrains political action in the United States. (Katznelson, of course, argued that it is precisely the tendency of workers to *separate* workplace and community concerns that is important to the understanding of "American exceptionalism.") In fact, as Susser demonstrates, much of the power of women's activism derives precisely from making those connections—from their perceiving a relationship among state policy, work possibilities, and the availability of social services, and then using whatever resources are available to them (regardless of the "sphere" in which they are located) to provide for their families and communities.[22]

To return to our discussion of democratic theory and politics: Many urban women seem to have little or no difficulty in acknowledging the connections between their concerns and those of others—at least within their class- or ethnic-based networks. They may feel themselves to be in a competitive relationship with members of other groups—particularly as politicians or employers attempt to use ethnic, class, or gender divisions to isolate them from one another and hinder the development of resistance. At the same time, however, work-related or community-based networks do provide strong sources of solidarity that cross the "community–workplace division." Most of the working-class women studied in these pages were by no means isolated—either from public life and the world of work or from one another. In Cockburn's words,

> Women bring a totality, an all-or-nothing feeling to action. It is something of which trade unions and political parties with their hierarchies and agenda know little, and to which they can give little. This totality is not just of the work day but of the whole day, not just of wages but of feelings, not just of economics but of relationships.[23]

It is in this context that we must undertake a rethinking of the categories of democratic theory. It seems clear from these studies that women's coming to political consciousness (and I suspect that this applies to men as well) may be more a phenomenon of *relationship* and *connection,* than one of recognizing *interests* in the traditional, individualistic sense. It is in and through networks (located in their neighborhoods, at their workplaces, or at the interface of the "public" and "private" realms) that most women engage in collaborative activity and, through that activity, can begin to experience themselves as confident, competent beings, citizens of a democratic polity. This is not to suggest that political life for women is nonconflictual: The studies in this volume certainly belie any such claim. Rather, it is to point out that when these women engaged in political struggles, they did so not as the isolated individuals the pluralist paradigm would lead us to expect but as people rooted in networks and communities.

There is, of course, another aspect to relationships and the feelings of commonality they support. Communities also divide those who experience the commonality from others who do not. Feelings of group identity almost always imply that some are considered in, others, out. Urban and workplace communities, through which we meet (and, often, struggle with) people and groups unlike ourselves, can be highly conflictual settings. Though they heighten solidarity *within* groups, they may also increase conflict *among* groups. As we have seen, resistance movements often suffer from, and sometimes are undermined or destroyed by, the divisions among women that surface (or do not surface!) during these confrontations. Yet, at the same time, we have also seen that those same confrontations can provide contexts for *change,* for the development of cross-ethnic and cross-class coalitions among women, however tentative they may be. Through the diversity they incorporate, cities and many of the workplaces in and near them provide contexts in which the forming of relationships among different groups of people is at least a possibility. It may well be such contexts, then, that facilitate women's and men's seeing themselves as social–political actors in the fullest sense.[24]

In sum, if we take seriously the "relatedness" that seems to characterize the lives of many women, we are forced to see that the vision of isolated individuals that is at the center of much democratic theory is much too starkly drawn. Conversely, the assumption central to the Marxist paradigm that the development of a truly radical consciousness requires the transcendence, or abandonment, of all sources of community feeling other than class (in particular, those feelings based in racial, ethnic, national, or—we might add—sexual identity) is equally flawed. In fact, rather than acting as a "drag" on radical consciousness, communities—and the network of relationships that they nurture and on which they are based—have been, and can be, important contexts for politicization.[25] Political activism—rather than necessarily deriving from and reinforcing antagonistic social relationships among individuals—may more accurately reflect (and reinforce) community and connection.

What are the implications of these findings for the ways in which we think about politics?

To question the reality of dichotomous distinctions in people's activities and relationships is not to deny the power of those dichotomies as political ideology. As all too many of the studies in this volume make clear, although many women ignore these supposed boundaries in their daily lives, the ideology of separate public and private spheres still affects both people's perceptions of their situation and their ability to organize in resistance to it. Belief systems—particularly those that define the boundaries of "the political"—structure both what can be conceptualized as a problem and what solutions to that problem fall within the realm of possibility. Institutions such as schools, families, and the media socialize people to perceive a distinction between public and private, politics and economics, that then predisposes them to accept, for example, the legitimacy of management prerogatives in the workplace.[26]

Lamphere and Grenier's article (*Chapter 10*) provides an example of a way in which ideology may constrain resistance. In that case, a management-articulated ideology of participative management prevented workers from building on a sense of commonality with one another. Management was able to use the ideology of democracy effectively to undermine democratic organization in the plant. Ideology functioned to remove from the "political" agenda of the workplace precisely the issues that most concerned the women workers, leaving those issues to be understood, instead, either as individual psychological problems or as matters beyond the bounds of workers' proper influence.

We can see the inhibiting effects of ideology even in the more successful organizing contexts. The campaign Morgen describes in Fleetport, for example, had to combat doctors' and health officials' claims that the issues were "medical, not political" (an assertion based on the assumption of a public–private split); that the women in the campaign were not proper judges of what constituted quality medical care; and that their grievances ought to be brought through "appropriate channels" (a claim meant to enforce a particular definition of what counts as political action). As members of the organization soon learned, the doctors and hospitals had more than just economic and social power on their side. They also defined the agenda. That power to define what is political, rooted in the dichotomizing of public–private and individual–community, can effectively constrain the development of consciousness and limit the range of resistance.

Nevertheless, despite ideological and economic pressures, women have managed to organize in ways that transcend these dichotomies. Their activities point to the need for a new, more comprehensive conceptualization of what politics is about. One clear message is that networks of relationships, and the activism that they support, can be important sources of empowerment. Communities and workplaces can nurture consciousness-change by contextualizing issues, enabling people to recognize that what they may have perceived as their own particular problems are shared and may even be socially structured. Moreover, participation in resistance often engenders a broader consciousness of both the nature and the dimensions of social inequality and of the power of people united to confront and change it.[27] Since the relationship between the development of consciousness and participation in assertive community or workplace organizations is an interactive one, the most effective organizations seem to be those that flow directly from people's own experiences and concerns. Finally, since those concerns do not necessarily respect a division between public and private, it is important that organizations do not assume such a division in their goals and strategies. What this review suggests, in short, is that democratic theorizing ought to address the ways in which people experience *connections* and the ways in which those connections can be conceptualized as *political*. New theory must enable people to overcome, conceptually, the boundaries they have already crossed in practice.[28]

CONCLUSIONS

The implications of this change of viewpoint for democratic politics are potentially profound. Some years ago, Carole Pateman used a focus on women's experience of rape to explore the limitations of a politics based on liberal-democratic notions of "consent." Sara Evans and Harry Boyte have called for a new paradigm that would move beyond the individual/community dichotomy inherent in that same liberal tradition.[29]

My own sense is that any new paradigm must take account of—in fact must have as a central focus—the politics of *relationship*. Such a politics would move beyond liberalism in a number of respects. First, it would treat people *as they live,* not as isolated individuals but in the complex and multifold contexts of their communities and workplaces. Second, it would recognize that these webs of connection may well entail relationships based in workplace, residential, racial, or ethnic–cultural concerns (or, more likely, a combination of all of them). Rather than assuming these networks to be completely independent of, or necessarily antagonistic to one another, a new paradigm should recognize—and build on—the ways in which they can sustain and nurture their members, allowing people to come to social–political life not as monads, desperate to overcome their isolation, but as beings in relationships, concerned with protecting and improving the households, communities, and workplaces in which they live and work. Finally, such a paradigm would recognize that politics is not a narrow range of behaviors undertaken by a few, meant to influence the formal structures of governmental power. Rather, it is precisely that web of activities in which people engage out of concerns generated by their daily lives. For many of the women whose lives are reflected in this volume, political life *is* community life; politics is attending to the quality of life in households, communities, and workplaces.

This is not to suggest, of course, that all friendship networks necessarily become communities of political resistance, nor that all resistance is empowering. Some communities seem simply to reinforce powerlessness, and failed resistance often leads to increased frustration and even resignation. Nor is it to envision a public life devoid of conflict. But it is to suggest a model of social struggle, rooted in and nourished by ongoing social relationships, to replace the pluralist model of interest-group bargaining, a model that masks both the intensity of the feelings and commitments people bring to political life and the power relationships that structure their interactions.[30]

Unless we begin to change our conceptual framework to incorporate a broader conception of politics, and of who can and does participate in it, much of the radical potential of actions that are already taking place will be lost—even to those who participate in them. Ideologies do not control behavior, but they do set the categories within which we understand it.

In this respect, attending to "communities" in democratic theorizing offers an important new perspective. Along with Marxists, feminist theorists have criticized democratic theory both for its individualism and for its assumption of a public–private split. Marxists have insisted that this individualism must be transcended but have articulated an alternative paradigm requiring that people deny connections to any community other than one based on class. Drawing on the work of Carol Gilligan, many feminist theorists have focused their attention on the "women's values" of relationship, connection, and nurturance, suggesting that these, rather than the "male values" of competition and achievement, ought to be the basis of our political–social communities and theorizing. But that feminist strategy—which tends to define these values as rooted in biologically based sex difference, or, at best, in women's capacity to "mother," rather than in the complex social realities of many working-class women's lives—runs the risk of biologistic reductionism, of reinstituting traditional male–female dichotomies in a new guise.[31]

A focus on communities and networks offers us another language, one not necessarily burdened with gender-based connotations.[32] It can provide a way to speak of transformed interpersonal and social relations that does not link them, specifically, to women's domestic roles but allows us to explore the ways in which, in given societies, women have undertaken a disproportionate share of the work of sustaining communities.

There is no reason to assume, after all, that a need for relationship and connection is felt only by women. The extent to which traditional democratic theorists strove to define bases for the creation of a political community is significant evidence to the contrary. The relative neglect with which human connectedness has been treated in that same theoretical tradition is, I would suggest, a reflection more of the way in which men, and male-defined perceptions of experience, have dominated the construction of *theory* than of any full assessment of the ways in which real human communities operate. Once we integrate women's experiences into those constructions, new possibilities emerge. To do so should allow us to tap more fully into the sources of (women's) political consciousness and to begin to build a democratic polity that is respectful not just of our *interests* but of the fullness of our relationships and of our integrity as people.

NOTES

1. In fact, most theorists seem to assume that the ideal–typical citizen is male. On this point, see T. Brennan and C. Pateman, " 'Mere Auxiliaries to the Commonwealth': Women and the Origins of Liberalism," *Political Studies* 27, No. 2 (1979): 183–200.

2. The most sophisticated contemporary articulation of this perspective is John Rawls, *A Theory of Justice* (Cambridge: Harvard University Press, 1971). Michael Sandel criticizes precisely Rawls's claims of the primacy of "right" over "good" in *Liberalism and the Limits of Justice* (Cambridge: Cambridge University Press, 1982).

3. The clearest explication of this perspective may be found in Robert Dahl, *Who Governs? Democracy and Power in an American City* (New Haven: Yale University Press, 1961), 223–225, 276–281; see also Max Weber, "Politics as a Vocation," in H. H. Gerth and C. W. Mills, eds., *From Max Weber: Essays in Sociology* (New York: Oxford University Press, 1958), 77–128, esp. 78–83.

4. See, for example, Peter Bachrach and Morton Baratz, "Two Faces of Power," *American Political Science Review*, 56 (1962): 947–952; Isaac Balbus, "The Concept of Interest in Pluralist and Marxian Analysis," *Politics and Society* 1, No. 2 (1971): 151–177; William Connolly, "On 'Interests' in Politics," *Politics and Society* 2, No. 4 (1972): 459–477; Lewis Lipsitz, "The Grievances of the Poor," in P. Green and S. Levinson, eds., *Power and Community* (New York: Random House, 1970), 142–172; Michael Parenti, "Power and Pluralism: The View from the Bottom," *Journal of Politics* 32 (1970): 501–530; E. E. Schattschneider, *The Semi-Sovereign People* (New York: Holt, Rinehart, & Winston, 1960); and Michael Walzer, "Town Meetings and Workers Control: A Story for Socialists," *Dissent* 25 (Summer 1978): 325–333.

5. In addition to the works cited above, see Frances Fox Piven and Richard A. Cloward, *Poor People's Movements* (New York: Random House, 1979); Manuel Castells, *The City and the Grassroots: A Cross-Cultural Theory of Urban Social Movements* (Berkeley and Los Angeles: University of California Press, 1983), esp. 329–330; and John Gaventa, *Power and Powerlessness* (Urbana: University of Illinois Press, 1980).

6. The classic works on agenda-setting are Murray Edelman, "Symbols and Political Quiescence," *American Political Science Review* 54 (September 1960): 695–704; Bachrach and Baratz, *Two Faces of Power;* and Schattschneider, *The Semi-Sovereign People*.

7. Edward C. Banfield, *The Unheavenly City Revisited* (Boston: Little Brown, 1974), esp. 211ff.

8. See, for example, Susan C. Bourque and Jean Grossholtz, "Politics as Unnatural Practice: Political Science Looks at Women's Participation," *Politics and Society* 4, No. 2 (1974): 225–266; and Jean Elshtain, "Moral Woman and Immoral Man: A Consideration of the Public–Private Split and Its Ramifications," *Politics and Society* 4, No. 4 (1974): 453–473.

9. See, for example, Sheldon Wolin, "The People's Two Bodies," *democracy* 1, No. 1 (1981): 9–24; Frances Fox Piven and Richard A. Cloward, *The New Class War* (New York: Pantheon, 1982); Ira Katznelson, *City Trenches* (New York: Pantheon, 1981); for a fuller analysis of these works see Martha Ackelsberg, "Women's Collaborative Activities and City Life: Politics and Policy," in Janet Flammang, ed., *Political Women: Current Roles in State and Local Government*, Sage Yearbooks in Women's Policy Studies, Vol. 8 (Beverly Hills, Calif.: Sage, 1984), 242–259, esp. 243–246.

10. See, for example, Bourque and Grossholtz, "Politics"; Elshtain, "Moral Woman"; and Nancy Hartsock, *Money, Sex, and Power: An Essay on Domination and Community* (New York: Longman, 1983).

11. Among the numerous studies exploring this process of devaluation, see Kristen Amundsen, *A New Look at the Silenced Majority* (Englewood Cliffs, N.J.: Prentice-Hall,

1977); and William Chafe, *Women and Equality* (New York: Oxford University Press, 1976), especially for his comparison of the Black and feminist movements in this country.

12. See especially Jo Freeman, "Women and Urban Policy," *Signs* 5, No. 3 (Suppl.; 1980): S4–21; Ann R. Markusen, "City Spatial Structure, Women's Household Work, and National Urban Policy," ibid.: S23–44; Gerda Wekerle, "Women in the Urban Environment: Review Essay," ibid.: S188–214; Dolores Hayden, *The Grand Domestic Revolution: A History of Feminist Designs for American Homes, Neighborhoods, and Cities* (Cambridge: MIT Press, 1981), and *Redesigning the American Dream* (New York: Norton, 1983); and Evan Gamarnikow, "Introduction," "Women and the City" Issue, *International Journal of Urban and Regional Research* 2, No. 3 (October 1978): 390–402.

13. Irene Diamond and Nancy Hartsock, "Beyond Interests in Politics: A Comment on Virginia Sapiro's 'When Are Interests Interesting?' The Problems of Political Representation of Women," *American Political Science Review* 75, No. 3 (September 1981): 717–721, esp. 719. See also Carole Pateman, *The Problem of Political Obligation* (Cambridge: Cambridge University Press, 1980); and Raymond Plant, "Community: Concept, Conception, and Ideology," *Politics and Society* 8, No. 1 (1978): 79–107.

14. The term "methodological individualism" is explicated in Stephen Lukes, *Individualism, Key Concepts in the Social Sciences* (New York: Harper & Row, 1973), esp. chap. 17. On the more general point, see Robert Paul Wolff, *The Poverty of Liberalism* (Boston: Beacon Press, 1968), esp. chap. 5; Michael Taylor, *Community, Anarchy and Liberty* (Cambridge: Cambridge University Press, 1982); Michael Sandel, *Liberalism and the Limits of Justice* (Cambridge: Cambridge University Press, 1982), 59–64, 173–174, and "Conclusion"; Pateman, *The Problem of Political Obligation;* and Castells, *City and the Grassroots,* esp. 292–3 and sources cited there.

15. I have explored this process in "Personal Identities and Collective Visions: Reflections on Being a Jew and a Feminist," manuscript, Smith College, 1983. See also Maria Lugones and Elizabeth V. Spelman, "Have We Got a Theory for You! Feminist Theory, Cultural Imperialism, and the Demand for 'The Woman's Voice,'" *Hypatia,* Special Issue, *Women's Studies International Forum* 6, No. 6 (1983): 573–581; and Castells, *The City and the Grassroots,* 171.

16. See also Sandra Morgen's discussion of the contexts of women's developing consciousness at the end of her article in this volume (*Chapter 4*), as well as Cynthia Cockburn, *The Local State* (London: Pluto Press, 1977); Kathleen McCourt, *Working Class Women and Grass-Roots Politics* (Bloomington: Indiana University Press, 1977); and Ida Susser, *Norman Street: Poverty and Politics in an Urban Neighborhood* (New York: Oxford University Press, 1982), and Chapter 12 of this volume.

17. On "consumer" riots, see Temma Kaplan, "Female Consciousness and Collective Action: The Case of Barcelona, 1910–1918," *Signs* 7, No. 3 (Spring 1982): 545–566; Paula Hyman, "Immigrant Women and Consumer Protest: The New York City Kosher Meat Boycott of 1902," *American Jewish History* 70 (Summer 1980): 91–105; and Ronald Lawson, Stephen E. Barton, and Jenna Weissman Joselit, "From Kitchen to Storefront: Women in the Tenant Movement," in Gerda R. Wekerle, Rebecca Peterson, and David Morley, eds., *New Space for Women* (Boulder, Col.: Westview Press, 1980), 255–271. On factory-based strikes, see Ardis Cameron, "Bread and Roses Revisited: Women's Culture and Working-Class Activism in the Lawrence Strike of 1912," in Ruth Milkman, ed., *Women, Work and Protest: A Century of U.S. Women's Labor History*

(Boston: Routledge & Kegan Paul, 1985); Albert Balcells, *"La mujer obrera en la indus-tria catalana durante el primer cuarto del siglo XX,"* in *Trabajo industrial y organización obrera en la Cataluna contemporánea, 1900–1936* (Barcelona: Editorial Laia, 1974), esp. 45–54. On school struggles, see David Rogers, *110 Livingston Street: Politics and Bureaucracy in the New York City School System* (New York: Random House, 1968); Lillian Rubin, *Busing and Backlash* (Berkeley: University of California Press, 1972); Wendy Luttrell, "The Edison School Struggle: The Reshaping of Working-Class Educa-tion and Women's Consciousness," in this volume (*Chapter 6*); and Andrée Nicola-McLaughlin and Zala Chandler, "Urban Politics in the Higher Education of Black Wom-en: A Case Study," also in this volume (*Chapter 8*).

18. See Ackelsberg, "Women's Collaborative Activities."

19. Carol Stack, *All Our Kin* (New York: Harper & Row, 1976); Cheryl Gilkes, "Holding Back the Ocean with a Broom," in LaFrances Rodgers-Rose, ed., *The Black Woman* (Beverly Hills, Calif.: Sage, 1980), 217–231; "Going Up for the Oppressed: The Career Mobility of Black Women Community Workers," *Journal of Social Issues* 39, No. 3 (1983): 115–139; and Cheryl Townsend Gilkes, "Building in Many Places: Multiple Commitments and Ideologies in Black Women's Community Work," in this volume (*Chapter 2*).

20. Shulamit Reinharz, "Women as Competent Community Builders: The Other Side of the Coin," in Annette U. Rickel, Meg Gerrard, and Ira Iscoe, eds., *Social and Psychological Problems of Women: Prevention and Crisis Intervention* (Washington, D.C.: Hemisphere, 1984), 19–43.

21. McCourt, *Working Class Women,* 220–224, 231–232. This finding is not sur-prising in the light of studies by Verba and Nie, Baxter and Lansing, and others on the relationship between political efficacy and feelings of racial or ethnic community. See, for example, Sidney Verba and Norman Nie, *Participation in America: Political Democracy and Social Equality* (New York: Harper & Row, 1972), chaps. 8, 20, 12; and Sandra Baxter and Marjorie Lansing, *Women and Politics* (Ann Arbor: University of Michigan Press, 1981).

22. See also Sandra Morgen's comments at the end of her article in this volume (*Chapter 4*).

23. Cynthia Cockburn, "When Women Get Involved in Community Action," in Marjorie Mayo, ed., *Women in the Community* (London: Routledge & Kegan Paul, 1977), 61–70, esp. 69–70.

24. See, on this point, Richard Sennett, *The Uses of Disorder* (New York: Vintage, 1970); Iris Marion Young, "The Ideal of Community and the Politics of Difference," unpublished manuscript, Worcester Polytechnic Institute, 1984; and Suad Joseph, "Working-Class Women's Networks in a Sectarian State: A Political Paradox," *American Ethnologist* 10 (1983): 1–22.

25. See Sara Evans and Harry Boyte, "Strategies in Search of America: Cultural Radicalism, Populism, and Democratic Culture," *Socialist Review* No. 75/76, Vol. 14, Nos. 3 and 4 (May–August 1984): esp. 75, 87n; Evans and Boyte, *Free Spaces: The Sources of Democratic Change in America* (New York: Harper & Row, 1986); Martha Ackelsberg, *"Mujeres Libres:* Community and Individuality: Organizing Women in the Spanish Civil War," *Radical America* 18, No. 4: 7–19; and Craig Calhoun, *The Question of Class Struggle: Social Foundations of Popular Radicalism During the Industrial Revo-lution* (Chicago: University of Chicago Press, 1982).

26. Originally, a paper by Nina Shapiro-Perl was to be included in this book. Her study of women jewelry workers showed how schools, families, and the media socialized people to perceive a distinction between public and private. See Nina Shapiro-Perl, "The Impact of Gender on Workers' Resistance and Consent" (paper delivered in organized session on Women and Resistance, annual meeting of the American Anthropological Association, Denver, Colorado, November 1984).

27. Patricia Zavella's and Ann Bookman's articles in this volume (*Chapter 9 and Chapter 7*) are particularly revealing on this point. See also Zavella, " 'Abnormal Intimacy': The Varying Work Networks of Chicana Cannery Workers," *Feminist Studies* 11, No. 3 (Fall 1985): 540–557, esp. 533–539.

28. Carole Pateman makes a similar argument about the "lag" between the day-to-day creativity of feminist and "alternative community" groups in the United States and the recognition of those activities by contemporary political theorists—even theorists of "participatory democracy"—in "Feminism and Participatory Democracy: Some Reflections on Sexual Difference and Citizenship," manuscript, 1986.

29. Pateman, "Women and Consent," *Political Theory* 8, No. 2 (1980): 149–168; and Evans and Boyte, "Strategies in Search of America," 98, and *Free Spaces*.

30. Castells makes a similar argument about the need to abandon pluralist models. See *The City and the Grassroots*, 169–172, 299–305.

31. Sandra Morgen and Ann Bookman make a related argument in their Introduction to this volume.

32. Ongoing dialogue with Irene Diamond has been crucial to the development of my thinking in this area.

14

"Carry It On": Continuing the

Discussion and the Struggle

Ann Bookman

Sandra Morgen

Working-class women today confront most of the same issues and problems as the women portrayed in this book. However, the political and economic landscape has changed in significant ways, posing great challenges to women who struggle for social change. The last few years have witnessed the defeat of the Equal Rights Amendment and the resurgence of racism, highlighted by increasing attacks on people of color—from the schools and college campuses of the Northeast to the small towns of the South. There has been dramatic backsliding at both the legislative and judicial levels of support for affirmative action, school desegregation, voting rights, and civil rights for lesbians and gays. Budget cuts have sliced into programs to provide day care, job training, human services, and financial support to low-income women and men. The prolife movement, with political support from the White House, continues to try to reverse women's hard-won rights to control their reproductive lives. The Reagan administration has made no secret of its intention to dismantle the programs and government infrastructure that fostered political equality and economic opportunity for women, people of color, and the poor. The hard work of social reform has been replaced with a facile political discourse that promises a return to traditional values, lower taxes, a "sanctified" family, and a "strong America."

Meanwhile women see images of "their" success paraded across magazine headlines and television screens—supposedly evidence that the old days of discrimination are over. In fact, the gains of the "New Woman" are disproportionally reaped by white professional and managerial women. In the workplace, most women face occupational segregation and gender-based wage differentials, as well as higher rates of unemployment and underemployment than men. In the home the "double day" continues, as women in the paid labor force struggle to construct adequate support systems to make their work and family lives viable. The United States remains the only industrial nation in the world (with the exception of South Africa) to have no national policy guaranteeing parents job-protected leave to care for newborn or newly adopted children. Many working families also lack affordable housing, day care, and health care. The rudiments of a national family policy remain on the books as defeated bills or proposed legislation, but not yet as law. The number of elected officials who are advocates for women's rights and working families remain a small minority of women and men in our national Congress and state houses.

In this political and economic context, it is clear that working-class women, indeed all women, still face an uphill battle for change. What can we learn from the cases in this book that might help guide the struggles of the present period? Briefly, we will draw out a few of the lessons these cases, taken together, suggest for organizing. We hope others will find in these pages questions, examples, and strategies that, considered in light of their own experiences, will stimulate political discussion and action.

First of all, in the face of the dramatic political swings of the past two decades, it is instructive to remember that politics is more than the sum of advances and losses of contending groups. This book reaffirms what we all too often forget in the flush of victory or the demoralization following defeat; the impact of political mobilization cannot simply be measured by election results or how many demands were won in a particular campaign. The historian Ferdinand Braudel has spoken eloquently to this point:

> Victorious events come about as the result of many possibilities among which life has made its choices. For one possibility which is actually realized, innumerable others have been drowned. These are the ones that leave little trace for the historian. And yet it is necessary to give them their place because the losing movements are the forces which have at every moment affected the final outcome.[1]

Braudel underscores the importance of analyzing both successful and unsuccessful organizing efforts, as we have in this book. An analysis of victories may lead to building new levels of political organization; an understanding of failure may help to win small gains where none seemed possible. But no matter what the outcome, political engagement creates change. For the women in this book, we see changes in their political consciousness, their relationships with other women, and their relationship to the structures of economic and political power. These changes transcend the categories of winning and losing and place women unquestionably at a critical juncture in contemporary politics.

Second, the cases shed light on questions about the efficacy of autonomous organization based on gender, an issue widely debated in the women's movement, in the left, and in mainstream political parties. We believe that a number of the campaigns described demonstrate the value of autonomous political organization for women. In several of the workplace campaigns, for example, the sexual segregation of production areas had a positive aspect in that it facilitated the ability of women to organize support for a union drive, a strike, or other activities among themselves. These all-women teams, caucuses, or organizations were often part of, or later joined, larger organizations that included men, but the initial mobilization and politicization came through single-sex networks and women's day-to-day activities. Similarly, it was often women coming together through ties of friendship or kinship around common concerns that spurred the formation of community-based campaigns or organizations.

The ability of women to articulate their individual problems to each other and to learn that other women have similar problems moves them to see the world differently. In this context, they develop leadership skills and organize themselves in ways that emerge from, or are consistent with, their responsibilities, interests. and relationships as women. The example of the street vendors shows the muting of women's particular concerns and participation because their union did not provide any "space" for women as women. This exemplifies how women's gains can be diminished in organizations that do not attend to their interests beyond those of "fellow" worker. On the other hand, the example of the Chicana cannery workers' committee demonstrates the critical difference between *separatism* as ideology or organizational principle and the value of autonomous organizational forms in particular moments or facets of a struggle.

It is important that the value of autonomous organization for women not be interpreted in a mechanical or formulaic way. There is no single path to political activity for women nor one sequence of steps that will guarantee collective political action. In fact, the building blocks of a cross-sex or multinational organization may vary widely. For example, women of color may organize with other women of color before joining with white women, or they may ally with men of color before joining with others of either sex. It is essential that organizers support the principle and the practice of separate organizations for women, for women of color, and for people of color, as these forms may often provide the only viable basis for unity among groups with different histories and interests.

It is commonplace to hear organizers, especially in the labor movement, talk about the difficulties of organizing working-class women. The cases in this book challenge the assumptions underlying these "difficulties." First, the conditions of women's lives necessitate a reconsideration and reformulation of conventional organizing strategies. For example, a number of the cases described here show women playing important roles *within* workplaces *during work hours,* but unable to attend meetings outside of work due to their family responsibilities. The traditional model of union organizing, which relies on convening key shop leaders at a local tavern for a beer and strategy session, may promote male workers' activism, but not that of women. This points not only to the importance of providing child care for political meetings outside work, but also to the need to develop new strategies that are based on the realities of women's multiple roles and responsibilities. To the extent that women's family lives are taken seriously by both community and workplace organizations, women's active involvement in creating social change can be fostered.

The point is not merely that presumed "obstacles" to women's activism can be removed by innovative organizing methods, but that some of these obstacles can become powerful resources for political movements. Some of the most successful campaigns described in this book used networks and relationships that bridged family, community, and workplace in the development of political organizations. Women's work cultures often use events associated with family and community life, such as weddings and baby showers or holiday parties, as the basis for bringing women of different racial and ethnic groups together, thus overcoming management's "divide and conquer" strategies. Far too often these kinds of activities are discounted by political activists who bemoan women's embeddedness in family or "apolitical" community organizations, seeing these as competitors for women's limited time and energy. For example, some (especially white) organizers see the regular Wednesday evening church activities of southern Black women as one less evening a week to schedule political meetings. But these activities may provide a catalyst and a base of support for the political activities of church members. The multiplicity of women's responsibilities—among and within spheres—can provide women with both insights about the interrelatedness of workplace and community issues *and* the resources they need to wage effective political action.

One of the most important uses of women's diverse and often extensive networks is for the development of strong coalitions. The Medgar Evers College case shows how powerful a formal coalition of professional and nonprofessional workers, students, community organizations and elected officials can be. Other cases, such as the union drive at Digitex or union reform in the Teamsters, document how the mobilization of ethnic, religious, and other community organizations can be essential to victories within workplaces. To the extent that organizers can frame the demands of political movements in ways that tie together the different arenas of people's lives—as workers, family members, and community residents—strong alliances can be built based on the realities of people's everyday lives.

Building coalitions also depends on representing the different interests and needs of groups within the coalition. Sometimes this takes the form of respecting different languages and utilizing different cultural and political symbols in a campaign. It also means confronting racism and sexism within coalitions. The case material shows the fruits of these difficult processes, as in the struggle for a new integrated high school in Philadelphia. These accounts also serve as warnings that in the absence of concerted attempts to deal with racism or sexism, political groups are weakened. For example, the street vendors union did not garner the kind of commitment from women street vendors that it might have if the issue of sexual harassment had been an organizational concern.

Some of the case studies suggest how multiracial unity can be fostered in organizing. Gilkes points out that community workers frequently have to identify and confront individuals with evidence of their own racism. Although direct confrontation is often called for, this should not always mean (as in Gilkes' study) that the responsibility for such actions falls on women (or men) of color. In other cases—for example, the Edison school struggle—multiracial unity emerged less from direct confrontation than from the gradual process of white women's recognition that they shared interests with women of color (because of gender and class) that their racism had previously blinded them to.

Successful coalition building depends on two sometimes conflicting approaches. The basis of unity must be broad enough to foster alliances among a wide spectrum of organizations or groups. At the same time, the political agendas or demands of the coalition must recognize different needs of coalition constituents. Working-class women often come into coalitions with needs, networks, and life skills that can form the basis for broad coalitions. Precisely because their structural position in society cuts across the boundaries of home, work, and public space, they may be able to articulate political agendas that go beyond those which have characterized workplace or community organizing in the past. Many working women, especially if they are heads of households, need quality, affordable child care and parental leave to meet their dual responsibilities as mothers and breadwinners. Several articles in this book, such as Dill's on domestic workers and Morgen's analysis of health care struggles in Fleetport, show working-class women facing issues and making demands that reflect the interconnections of family, work, and community and defy assumptions about separate public and private spheres.

Another important lesson the studies suggest is the need to develop organizing strategies that link local struggles with large-scale political and economic processes. Without these linkages, most local struggles are doomed to ultimate failure. For example, the dramatic structural changes in the canning industry in California ultimately undermined the successful rank-and-file organizing among cannery workers. Similarly, the purchase of Digitex by a huge multinational corporation and the transfer of production to the United States–Mexico border was one factor among others that led to the final dissolution of the union in that workplace. The dynamics of the national political economy are also reflected in local struggles for education, housing, and health care. While social service cutbacks and other forms of retrenchment are experienced at the local level, the source of these cutbacks are usually changes in public policy and budget priorities at the federal level.

Grassroots organizations must try to understand how forces external to workplaces or communities may profoundly limit what it is possible to achieve in a local campaign. Once that is clear, it may be necessary to combine a variety of political strategies in order to achieve both long- and short-term goals. Plant closing legislation, for example, might be an essential prong of a union organizing campaign, or a campaign around urban fiscal policy might be necessary to advance the cause of affordable housing within a community.

In calling attention to the range of women's involvement in local grassroots activism, we do not mean to replace one definition of the important political terrain—electoral—with another—the grassroots. Rather, movements for social change must harness different forms of political activity in order to achieve their goals. Although there is relatively little information in this book about how to combine electoral and grassroots strategies, the fact is that without some degree of institutionalized political power, the victories of workplace and community organizations are all too easily eroded. In both the instances of Medgar Evers College and the neighborhood organizations in Greenpoint–Williamsburg, the struggles to retain access to public services required ongoing, militant, grassroots organizations to keep the heat on elected officials to be accountable to their constituents.

Over the last twenty years, a number of state and national coalitions made up of local grassroots organizations have served as vehicles for combining electoral and direct action strategies. A classic example from the 1960s is the National Welfare Rights Organization. This organization provided local grassroots groups with direction and resources, and lobbied Congress for large-scale welfare reform. In the 1970s the Coalition of Labor Union Women (CLUW) served to link individual trade union women and union locals with the AFL–CIO power structure to lobby for working women's rights. Today, in our own state of Massachusetts, there are a number of statewide women's organizations based on local grassroots organizations. The Coalition for Basic Human Needs and Women for Economic Justice both provide a state forum, resources, and lobbying for the many local antipoverty and welfare rights organizations.

The real issue is whether grassroots and electoral strategies, if combined, can respond effectively to the rapid transformations in the political economy of the United States today. It is interesting that, while the changes in the national and international economy seem to make many companies almost untouchable by even the most organized workers, the state is growing more and more important as the force affecting the quality of everyday life. As the traditional sectors of working-class employment become less reliable, working-class families are forced to maintain themselves by looking to the state for a broad range of support. Because it often fails to provide these essential goods and services, or provides them in an inequitable manner (especially by race and gender), the state has become an increasingly important focus of working-class women's political demands.

There is no question that much of what has been accomplished in the past twenty years in legislation and programs to foster gender equality has been done *through* the state—for example, affirmative action, pay equity, the legalization of abortion, and changes in housing, welfare, and family policies. Each of these, it must be remembered, ultimately resulted from the continuing work of women's national and local grassroots organizations. Much of women's neighborhood and community organization is essentially concerned with a struggle with the state, and increasingly women workers turn to the state to seek protection from discrimination in workplaces.

In the last decade there has been a renewed effort by feminist and Marxist scholars to understand the nature of the state in advanced capitalism. Although none of the papers in this collection elaborates a theory of the state, a number of them do demonstrate the way women's collective action is affecting "statemaking," a concept that "involves not only state initiatives and the reactions of social groups to them, but also social mobilizations that target the state and trigger responses by its governors."[2] In the context of recent regressive changes in state policy, it is crucial to understand how women have been able to force the state to respond to their own needs and those of their families. Whether the social-change strategy is electoral or grassroots, women are organizing in ways that challenge both prevailing conceptions of state responsibility and the traditional, male preserves that have excluded women from the political process. It is significant that while some of the issues and priorities of working-class women and feminists may still diverge, increasingly they are both targeting the state in their campaigns for social justice.

Some people have asked us if this is a book about working-class women and feminism. The answer is both "yes" and "no." Most of the articles describe campaigns comprised and led primarily by working-class women who did not identify their struggles as feminist. Feminist organizations and individuals, however, sometimes provided leadership and often lent support to these struggles, including many of the scholars represented in this book. But the nature of that leadership and support still needs to be analyzed to understand whether it actually fostered a closer connection between feminist and working-class activists. Closer connections will certainly require change. Feminists will need to broaden their definitions of the women's movement's priorities to include the kinds of struggles described in this book. It will also mean two other, related things: that the problems and issues of cross-class organizing will have to become central concerns of feminists *and* that the struggle around issues of racism and multicultural unity must move to the forefront in predominantly white feminist organizations.

There are signs that the women's movement has grown and matured. In the twenty years since the first national conference of the National Organization for Women in 1967, more women have come to understand that feminists must directly address the issues of women of color, poor women, working women, and lesbians. One of the encouraging signs that the movement is growing and broadening is the development of a women's wing in the labor movement, both in the form of the Coalition of Labor Union Women and the spawning of women's committees in union locals, in all regions of the country. Moreover, there are significant organizations of working women outside the labor movement, such as Nine to Five, which are attempting to go beyond traditional union issues of wages and benefits to take up the more subtle, yet crucial dimensions of sexism in the workplace, such as sexual harassment. Another positive sign is the development of some multiracial organizations of women and the attempts of predominantly white organizations to sponsor forums and conferences on racism within the women's movement, to seek out multiracial formations, and to fight racism in the larger society and in South Africa. Additionally, increasing numbers of women have become involved in the formation of public policy and have run for public office, especially at the state and local level.

While these are signs that a broader women's movement is possible, they should not provoke too much optimism about the way ahead. The challenges of the current period are formidable—with the agenda of the New Right institutionalized by Reagan's policies, his Supreme Court and judicial appointments, and his increased militarization of our economy and society. The work of creating and sustaining real multiracial and cross-class alliances among women remains great. There is evidence in this book to confirm the extraordinary power of corporations and of the state to limit the gains of women's activism. But there is also plenty of evidence of creative, diligent organizing, successful mobilization, and a changing political consciousness among women. If this book inspires the hope of a progressive movement that truly combines the major concerns of women, people of color, and the working class, or if it aids activists and feminist theorists as they consider the political experience of working-class women, it will have more than served its purpose.

ACKNOWLEDGMENT

We want to acknowledge the title and spirit of the song, "Carry It On," written by Gil Turner (Melody Trails, BMI) and sung by Joan Baez and Judy Collins. It conveys our sense of a tradition to be continued and of the need for persistence despite the odds in women's quest for political empowerment.

NOTES

1. Fernand Braudel, quoted in Herbert G. Gutman, *Work Culture and Society in Industrializing America* (New York: Knopf, 1976), 67.
2. Charles Bright and Susan Harding, "Processes of Statemaking and Popular Protest: An Introduction," in their *Statemaking and Social Movement: Essays in History and Theory* (Ann Arbor: University of Michigan Press, 1984), 10.

The Contributors

MARTHA A. ACKELSBERG is Professor of Government at Smith College. Her articles on the politics of community life, women's political activism, and the Spanish anarchist movement have appeared in *Feminist Studies, Radical America, Tikkun,* and other publications. She has long been active in Jewish feminist activities, in both the Jewish and the secular feminist communities, and is a member of the board of Equity Institute. Ackelsberg is currently at work on *Strong Is What We Make Each Other,* a book about Mujeres Libres, a Spanish anarchist women's organization.

ANN BOOKMAN is an anthropologist and Assistant Director of the Mary Ingraham Bunting Institute of Radcliffe College. Her research has focused on the interface between women's work and family lives in her study of Luo women in Kenya and of blue-collar women workers in the United States. A longtime activist in the women's movement and the labor movement, Bookman has worked on reproductive rights issues and on increasing women's role in their unions. Her current research, initiated while she was a Research Associate at the Stone Center of Wellesley College, is on parental leave as a key public policy issue for working mothers and fathers.

ZALA CHANDLER is Associate Professor of Education at Medgar Evers College, City University of New York. She has published articles on the Black liberation struggle in the United States and in South Africa, and on the role of Black women in those movements. Chandler is a founding member of SISA (Sisters in Support of Sisters in South Africa) and a member of the International Resource Network of Women of African Descent. She also serves on the Board of MADRE, an organization which promotes woman-to-woman exchange between the peoples of the United States, Central America, and the Caribbean.

CYNTHIA B. COSTELLO is Director for the Program in Employment and Volunteerism Opportunities for Older Workers at the Villers Foundation in Washington, D.C. She was

322

formerly Study Director of the Committee on Women's Employment and Related Social Issues at the National Academy of Sciences and was a Fellow at the Russell Sage Foundation. Costello has published articles on clerical work, home-based work, and feminist disarmament politics in several scholarly journals including *Feminist Studies, Signs,* and *Frontiers.* She is presently completing a book *"On The Front": Women's Work and Activism in the Insurance Industry.*

BONNIE THORNTON DILL is Associate Professor of Sociology and Director of the Center for Research on Women at Memphis State University. She has published numerous articles on the intersection of gender, race, and class and the issue of racism in the women's movement in journals such as *Signs* and *Feminist Studies.* Dill recently completed a study on race and pay equity for the National Committee on Pay Equity based in Washington, D.C. and is now working on a volume of readings about women of color.

CHERYL TOWNSEND GILKES, formerly a member of the faculty at Boston University, is the John D. and Catherine T. MacArthur Assistant Professor of Black Studies and Sociology at Colby College. She is studying the importance of the Sanctified Church as an institution of Afro-American life and culture and has published articles in *Signs, Journal of Religious Thought, Journal of Feminist Studies in Religion,* and *Journal of Social Issues.* Gilkes is an Associate Minister at the Union Baptist Church in Cambridge, Massachusetts, and an Assistant Dean of the Congress of Christian Education of the United Baptist Convention of Massachusetts, Rhode Island, and New Hampshire.

GUILLERMO J. GRENIER is Director of the Center for Labor Research and Studies and Assistant Professor in the Department of Sociology/Anthropology at Florida International University. He is the author of *Inhuman Relations: Quality Circles and Anti-Unionism in American Industry* (Temple University Press, 1987) and of recent articles in *Labor Research Review* and other labor relations publications. Born in Havana, Grenier is currently working on projects dealing with the privatization of the public sector and the history of union busting in the United States.

LOUISE LAMPHERE is Professor of Anthropology at the University of New Mexico and taught for many years in the Anthropology Department at Brown University. She has done research on urban working-class women in the Sunbelt and the Frostbelt, as well as on Navaho women and family life. She is the author of *From Working Daughters to Working Mothers: Immigrant Women in a New England Industrial Community* (Cornell University Press, 1987) and the co-editor, with Michelle Zimbalist Rosaldo, of the now-classic reader in anthropology and women's studies, *Women, Culture and Society* (Stanford University Press, 1974).

WENDY LUTTRELL is a Visiting Lecturer and Research Associate in the Department of Sociology at Duke University. A major focus of her work, both as a scholar and an activist, has been the role of education in social change, particularly for working-class women. Luttrell has written participatory curriculum manuals for use in varied settings, including a community-based women's center and a workplace-based literacy program. She is currently preparing a report on the politics of economic decline in the South for the Highlander Education and Research Center.

ANDRÉE NICOLA-MCLAUGHLIN is Professor of Humanities and Planning Coordinator of Women's Studies, Research and Development at Medgar Evers College of the City

324   The Contributors

University of New York (CUNY). She was the first woman Dean of Administration in the CUNY system (1979–1982), and an Honorary Visiting Scholar at the University of London Institute of Education. A poet and social theorist, Nicola-McLaughlin's scholarship, creative writing, and speeches appear in such publications as *Black Scholar Journal*, *Women of Power Magazine*, and *Kenya Woman's Digest*. She is currently co-editing a book on Black women writers, *Wild Women in the Whirlwind: Culture and Politics of the Renaissance in Afro-American Writings*, to be published by Rutgers University Press in 1988.

SANDRA MORGEN is Assistant Professor of Women's Studies at the University of Massachusetts–Amherst. She also directs the Gender and the Curriculum Project for the American Anthropological Association and is an Associate Editor of *Signs*. Morgen's long-term involvement in community organizing has focused on women's health and reproductive rights issues and on antiracist struggles. She has published articles in *Women's Studies* and *Social Science and Medicine* on the women's health movement and the relationship between women's political consciousness and the state, subjects which form the core of a book she is currently writing.

KAREN BRODKIN SACKS is an anthropologist and long-time activist in the women's movement. Author of *Sisters and Wives* (Greenwood Press, 1979) and co-editor of *My Troubles Are Going to Have Trouble With Me* (Rutgers University Press, 1984), her most recent book, *Caring By The Hour* (University of Illinois Press, 1987), focuses on health care and health-care workers in the United States. Sacks is Associate Professor of Anthropology and Director of Women's Studies at the University of California, Los Angeles.

ROBERTA M. SPALTER-ROTH is a sociologist in the Women's Studies Program at George Washington University. She teaches and directs an applied policy research project called "Training Women to Make Public Policy in Women's Interests." Spalter-Roth is also active as a member of the Women's Employment and Training Coalition and the local Private Industry Council working to broaden services, increase benefits, and training programs. She is currently writing about ideology and methodology in the measurement of living standards as well as feminist issues and organizations in the policy process.

IDA SUSSER is Associate Professor at the School of Health Sciences of Hunter College and at the Doctoral Program in Anthropology of the City University of New York. Her book, *Norman Street: Poverty and Politics in an Urban Neighborhood* (Oxford University Press, 1982), examines the lives of working-class women and their participation in community-based political action. Susser has published articles on women and social movements in both the United States and Puerto Rico, and she is currently working on a book about the emergence of an environmental movement in Puerto Rico.

PATRICIA ZAVELLA is Assistant Professor of Community Studies at the University of California in Santa Cruz. She has published widely on her research on Chicano workers, including articles in *Frontiers* and *Feminist Studies*, and a book-length study, *Women's Work and Chicano Families: Cannery Workers of the Santa Clara Valley* (Cornell University Press, 1987). Zavella was a member of the National Research Council's Panel on the Impact of Technology on Women's Employment and has worked to build academic programs on Chicano life and culture through her membership in the National Association for Chicano Studies and Mujeres Activas en Letras y Cambio Social (Activist Women in Letters and Social Change).